THE FOREST TRILOGY

Winifred Foley was born in Gloucestershire and has lived there most of her life; her present home is just 10 miles from that of her childhood. She did not become a professional writer until the age of 60, since when *A Child in the Forest* has sold over half a million copies.

The Forest Trilogy

WINIFRED FOLEY

Oxford   New York

OXFORD UNIVERSITY PRESS

1992

Oxford University Press, Walton Street, Oxford OX2 6DP

Oxford New York Toronto
Delhi Bombay Calcutta Madras Karachi
Petaling Jaya Singapore Hong Kong Tokyo
Nairobi Dar es Salaam Cape Town
Melbourne Auckland

and associated companies in
Berlin Ibadan

Oxford is a trade mark of Oxford University Press

A Child in the Forest *first published 1974*
No Pipe Dreams for Father *first published 1977*
Back to the Forest *first published 1981*

First issued as an Oxford University Press paperback
in a single volume 1992

British Library Cataloguing in Publication Data

Data available
ISBN 0–19–283076–7

Library of Congress Cataloging in Publication Data
Foley, Winifred, 1914–
The forest trilogy / Winifred Foley.
p. cm.
Includes bibliographical references.
1. Dean, Forest of (England)—Social life and customs. 2. Foley,
Winifred, 1914– —Homes and haunts—English—Dean, Forest of.
3. Country life—England—Dean, Forest of—History—20th century.
4. Dean, Forest of (England)—Biography. I. Title.
942.4'13—dc20 DA670.D25F65 1992 92–8313
ISBN 0–19–283076–7

Typeset by Best-set Typesetter Ltd., Hong Kong
Printed in Great Britain by
Biddles Ltd.
Guildford and King's Lynn

Contents

A Child in the Forest

Dedication

To my parents, husband, four children, their
spouses, and the grandchildren, for all the
rewards I have garnered as daughter, wife,
mother, mother-in-law and granny.

PART I

Our Village

At home I was 'our Poll' to my little sister and brother; 'my little wench' to Dad; 'a reglar little 'oman' sometimes, but often 'a slummocky little hussy' to my sorely tried Mam; to the ribald boys, 'Polish it behind the door', and to my best friend Gladys—just 'Poll'. Gladys was an only child, always clean and tidy, but she never turned up her nose at playing with me, even when the school nurse found lice in my hair, and my neck was covered in flea bites.

I was born in 1914, the fourth child of Charlie and Margaret Mason, but an elder brother and sister had died in infancy. Bess, called after Great-Aunt Lizzie, and four years older than I, was the eldest. When I came into the world, Dad was away in Wales because work was short in the Forest mines. A letter home to Mam included his 'love to my little fat Poll'. So Poll stuck, and though I was baptised Winifred in the village chapel, Poll I remained throughout my childhood.

When I was a child, the Forest of Dean was remote and self-contained. We were cut off from the world—from the rest of Gloucestershire by the Severn estuary, from Monmouthshire by the River Wye; and where our northernmost hills stopped, we stopped. A *Royal* Forest, it had been. Ten by twenty miles of secluded, hilly country; ancient woods of oak and fern; and among them small coal mines, small market towns, villages and farms. We were content to be a race apart, made up mostly of families who had lived in the Forest for generations, sharing the same handful of surnames, and speaking a dialect quite distinct from any other.

Few people visited the Forest of Dean. They thought us primitive, and looked down on us. I remember one visitor expressing pity for an elderly crippled man in our village, who'd never been outside the Forest. Looking slowly round, the old man said, 'Doosn't thee fret for I, me booy; I bain't tired o' round 'ere yet.' The Forest was that sort of place. As my father once said, 'Nobody wants to come 'ere if they can 'elp it; but once they do settle down, you'd atter shoot 'em to get 'em to muv.'

We children didn't think about whether we were isolated, of

course, or about what the Forest was, or what its history had been. With our heads uncomplicated by lessons in botany or geology we took it for granted that hundreds of massive oak trees bordered our village, that the woods were full of ferns, that our fathers worked in coal mines. What was it to us that such a luxuriance of ferns was peculiar to oak forests? They were just there, to play and hide in. Some of us did know that the primeval forebears of the oaks we played under had formed the layers of coal far beneath us, where our dads crawled on their bellies to pick-axe it out; but we were too far away to feel the vibrations when a tunnel pit collapsed and somebody's dad or uncle, brother or grancher, wouldn't see the sunlight again.

Birds of a feather flock together, and in our village at that time the few feckless, filthy and friendly tended to live at one end; the prim, prudish and prosperous at the other. Between these two extremes lived a group of middling families, and this was where we fitted in. Here, in the centre of the village, lived a dozen or so families, not yet well off enough to move from their ancestral poverty, nor yet driven into complete squalor. The cottages—two up, two down, with a back-kitchen-cum-coal-house, had large gardens wrenched from the Forest under harsh 'Crown Rights' by industrious forefathers. Here were many children, but efforts were made to keep them clothed and fed, and even educated. Here gardens were cultivated and flower beds maintained. Pigs were kept and fowls. Most of the men were colliers, who showed a strong solidarity and fraternity. We were never anything but poor, but while we may not have been able to hold our noses in the air, we did try to keep our heads above water. We didn't carry pocket handkerchiefs or know what a dinner napkin was, but we were taught to show extra respect to the old and the handicapped. The dirt brought home from the pit, and on our boots, fought a constant battle with Mam's determination not to have her house 'turned into a turnpike road'.

Coal was no problem, except for the miners too old or too ill to work, for every working miner had an allowance of twelve hundredweight a month. The wonders of gas and electricity we only knew of second-hand from girls on holiday from service. Candles and paraffin lamps lit us up.

Often our home couldn't afford paraffin—or even, on occasion, a candle. Many's the time I've been sent around trying to borrow 'a stump o' candle'. Come to that, I was often sent for 'a pinch o' tay', 'a lick o' marge', 'a screw o' surgar', 'a sliver o' soap', or 'a snowl o' bread'. No one was ever optimistic enough to try to borrow money.

Each cottage garden was fenced with a dry-stone wall to keep out the sheep and pigs. Old iron bedsteads mostly served as garden gates. Any cottager who could afford it kept a pig; some were spare-time sheep-badgers, taking advantage of an ancient right to graze their sheep in certain areas of the surrounding forest. We children loved watching the dipping, shearing, and marking rituals, but only a hardy few could bear to watch the slaughter of a pig.

Pigs were regarded practically as neighbours. They had their own little stone dwellings alongside the cottages, and were christened with pretty names like Rosie, Sukey, or Ginny. Knots of men leaned over the pigs' gates to drool over the plump, succulent charmers in the pens. A weary, coal-grimed man would stop for a slap and a tickle with the pig before going indoors from work, answering her welcoming squeals and grunts with his own brand of piggy endearments. Shopkeepers would often refuse credit for family groceries, yet supply bran on tick for the pig; then they could claim half the pig at killing.

When the time came, poor Rosie's legs were tied and she was carried, squealing with terror, to the bench outside for the plunge of the butcher's knife. Mrs Protheroe was at the ready, with her great china washstand jug, to catch the gushing blood for her black puddings. Little girls stuck their fingers in their ears to deaden the pig's cries, and huddled together like wailing mourners. Boys war-danced round the blazing straw piled over the dead pig to burn off the bristles, and they waited to see who would catch the pig's bladder. When inflated, the bladder could be kicked around like a football.

Even when the grocer had had his half, the rest of Rosie still went a long way. The near neighbours all got a small share of the meat. The fat was rendered for lard (so tasty on bread with a sprinkle of salt). The big side-flitch was carefully salted on the slab in the back-kitchen. Later, when ready, it was hung on the living-room wall for the smoke to help keep it, as it was cut for use during the winter.

A flitch of bacon was considered the nicest decoration to have hanging on the wall, but the women were very fond, too, of religious texts to hang among the pictures. One new young wife artlessly hung two on the wall behind the double iron bedstead. One read 'I need Thee every hour', and the other 'Lord, give me strength'. It was years before she lived it down.

When I think of the 'slums' at the feckless end, the colour that comes to mind is grey. The children's skins were grimed grey with dirt; often a toddler's wash was from Mother's spittle on a corner of a filthy pinny rubbed around his protesting face. The interiors of the cottages were mostly grey, like the outsides. The ashdust from the grates settled in layers on the flagstone floors, on the home-made rag hearth-rugs and, mixing with the greasy cooking steam, finished curtains, walls and windows with a matching patina of drabness.

The feckless women 'dabbed out a bit o' washin'' when they felt like it, if they had the water; but all our water, apart from the rainwater, caught from the roofs in tubs, came from a well a quarter of a mile away, and one summer, when there was a drought, it dried to a trickle.

Hardly surprising that whatever colour curtains or clothes were to start with, they all ended on the clothes-line a uniform grey—at any rate, at the feckless end of the village.

Our mams, who never so much as had a dab of face powder to put on their noses in their lives, lugged the water from the well every day, but the washing was still done regularly every week.

When they got the water home, it was heated by a fire under the wash-copper, then poured over the dirty washing into a wooden tub; and the clothes and our mams were brought to a lather by the use of the unwieldy heavy wooden 'dolly'.

Clothes that today cannot be got rid of at a penny a bundle at the tail end of a jumble sale would have been thankfully washed and hung out with pride in those days.

Washing wasn't out on the line long; if the weather was wet, it must somehow be dried round the fire. Few had more than one change of clothing. In long wet spells, you might hear a woman call across the garden to her neighbour, 'I'll 'a to turn me britches an' shimmy this wik for we can't get near our vire for tryin' to dry the pit clothes out.'

Pit clothes took a lot of drying; men often worked in wet

conditions underground, and would come to the surface soaked to the knees in mud. On dry days this caked up on the walk home and could be hit off with a stick; on rainy days, with walks up to three miles long, the men came home like 'drowned rats', as the saying was. When there were two or three men in a household working, the family were lucky to see the fire.

The village had no drains and no dustmen. The privy buckets were emptied into holes dug in the garden, slops were thrown between the cabbages; all other rubbish landed on the ashmix, sometimes only a handy throwing distance from the doorways.

The ashmix consisted mainly of buckets of ashes, with empty tins, broken china, and bottomless pails. It was a 'play centre' for bare-bottomed toddlers, who piddled into the empty tins and made mud pies with dirt and ash. Except in winter, children were often bare-bottomed till they were old enough for school. 'Bless his little arse' was a mother's commonest form of endearment.

Older girls pillaged the ashmix for tins, bottles, and bits of china to play 'houses' or 'shops'. Nearby stood a great chestnut tree, one alone among a forest of oak; each triangle of its exposed roots was a girl's territory. A bit of rusty iron bed lath, balanced on a stone with a cocoa lid on each end, made scales. We sold 'brown sugar' (sandy earth), 'boiled sweets' (little stones), and 'currants' (sheep droppings). In the long hot days of August we made cool tents from damp green fern that grew thick among the oak trees, or played helter-skelter down the slopes on old sacks.

Here we sat and lay, amusing ourselves lazily popping 'snompers'. We picked spikes of the beautiful pink foxgloves growing in profusion among the fern; then took off each flower, trapping the air with thumb and forefinger, and pushed the ends together till they'd explode with a pleasant little pop.

Tiring of this diversion, we would search for five small stones roughly the same size. These would rattle about in a rusty tin until reasonably smooth, and then play 'jacks' with them. Town children call this 'five stones' but they buy them, neatly manufactured, from shops.

When we were very hungry and there was a chance of being called in for food, we would hint our presence to Mam by playing (near home) 'pigs, pigs, come to supper'. In this game, the other players turned their backs while a 'hidey girl' poked a piece of coloured china in a crack in a dry wall, between two marks. Whoever found it first became next 'hidey girl'. Often none of us could find it, not even the 'hidey girl'.

Life was wonderful except for one constant nagging irritation: hunger.

We knew that the wages our dads brought home from the pit were not enough to keep us out of debt, leave alone fill our bellies properly. We tried not to make matters worse by worrying our mothers for food. Everybody being in the same boat, we considered it good manners to refuse food offered by neighbours. The more the offer was pressed, the more vehemently we refused. Naturally enough, most of the stories we made up were filled with an abundance of delicious food.

But like other, less hungry, children we enjoyed ghost-stories too, and when the evenings grew shorter we scared the wits out of each other with them, until we were glad to run indoors before anything got us. It was nice to be indoors, safe from the cold. There was always a good fire. Most likely, on one side of it our Mam would be asleep with the baby on her lap, and on the other, old Great-Aunt with whom we lived. She was so crippled with arthritis, she just sat time away by the fire, and was smoked kipper-brown by the fumes.

If they were not at the pit, Dad and a couple of cronies would be arguing nineteen to the dozen about religion, politics, science, economics, or the fourth dimension. There they sat on their threadbare behinds putting the world in order. They sat the fire out, till the chill woke Mother up and she set about putting *her* house in order.

'Don't you men knew what time it is? Settin' there like a lot o' broody 'ens too idle to put a knob o' coal on the vire.'

She would plonk the baby on Father's lap, and rattle the poker between the bars, while the men, like scolded dogs with their tails between their legs, got out with as much dignity as they could muster.

Before she dozed off, Mam would have put our supper toast on the hob—just a few thick slices with the margarine spread only in the middle. No matter—toasted dry crust was delicious and we knew the art of chewing slowly to make it last. We kept very quiet so as not to wake Mam to supervise our bedtime wash. Into the little dark cold back-kitchen we sneaked, dipping our fingers into the well-used soapy water in a zinc bowl. We dampened the middle of our faces with our fingers; then we wiped off the loose dirt on a bit of towel hanging by on a nail. So up to the back-bedroom, three to a bed.

Then would come the best time of all. Our elder sister was our one-woman show. Her 'duet' rendering of *Madam will you walk* in high falsetto and deepest bass would give us hysterics. She could mime and mimic, and once did a 'Spanish' dance on the end of the bed, with a cracked soap dish for a castanet, turning it into a highly comical routine by scolding and smacking her elbows and knees for poking through the unmendable rents in the threadbare chemise of old Auntie's which she wore for a nightdress. Some-times our laughter brought Mam away from the fireside, and she would threaten from the bottom of the stairs to 'larrup us' if we didn't keep quiet. Sometimes our sister said some magic words, and turned the patch of striped ticking on the quilt into a flying zebra. We all got on its back and flew over the rooftops to a much better place than Peter Pan found. Our sister never stinted us: everything we wanted was there. Jelly, custard and tinned pine-apple to eat; a frilly pink silk dress with white shoes and socks for me; a real football and a little donkey for my young brother; dolls, marbles, proper skipping ropes with painted handles, and anything else we could think of.

'You be the best liar in the world, Bess,' we bragged. But our bellies rumbled.

As I dozed off to sleep in the warm safety of our shared bed, I listened to the plaintive wind in the forest trees which seemed to me to be the sighs of all the people that had died in our village, who wanted to come back to the Forest instead of going to heaven.

Dad

Mam was the light sleeper in our family of slug-a-beds. She acted as alarm-clock to get Dad out of the house by five in the morning, for early pit shift. It meant her getting up at a quarter past four, to light the fire and make his tea and toast. Surplus tea was allowed to get cold; then, unsweetened and unmilked, it was put in a bottle. This, with 'a snowl o' bread' and 'a marsel o' cheese', was standard diet for all the miners in our village. The bread and cheese was put in a butty tin, so the underground rats wouldn't eat it.

To us children our Dad was the fount of wisdom, kindliness and honour. Whenever we wanted his attention he became a child among us—slow, dreamy and always understanding. He never minded being woken up at any odd hour to help with a fretful baby, or to nurse a sick child. Once, when I had earache in the small hours, he took me, sobbing with pain, downstairs; he made up a good fire, warmed a brick in the oven to hold up to my head to try and ease the pain, cuddled me on his lap and tried to distract me with the tales of Brer Rabbit, all to no avail. His blackened, beloved old pipe, charred with the residue of strong tobacco, was the balm and cure for all his own pains, and at last in desperation, he gave it to me.

'There, my wench, thee have a few puffs o' feyther's bacca—that'll take the pain away.'

And so it must have, for I awoke in bed, late the next morning, with my earache gone.

If he had a fault, it was the spending of sixpence on a book while his ragged shirt-tails were hanging through the ragged patches of his moleskin trousers. He loved to discuss his reading with his cronies. The fireside talk we overheard between them was full of H. G. Wells, Einstein, God, Darwin, Shaw and Lenin.

The men were all well read. With a sweep of a pit-grimed fist they dismissed bogus religious cant—and, equally, the cult of material wealth acquired for its own sake. They filled the world's belly with its properly distributed abundance, and the world's soul with the beauty of man's and nature's genius.

Concerts in our village were rare, but once when Dad had been working in South Wales, he'd gone to hear some classical music played, and had found it a profound experience. And when he heard that a violinist and his accompanist were to give a concert in our chapel, he was full of anticipation.

The chapel was packed. When the violinist began to tune up his instrument, the hobbledehoys standing together at the back sniggered, and called out who was pulling the cat's tail.

I was flabbergasted when Dad, the most kindly and tolerant of men, went to the back of the chapel and, quietly but firmly, told them to behave or get out.

In my eyes, Dad could do no wrong; but, earthbound little pleb that I was, I too thought the music sounded like cats on the roof. I looked for distraction in the nimble acrobatics of the pianist's fingers. Then I studied her face and peculiar hair style, then down towards her feet. 'Oh, my gawd, 'ers showing 'er combs!' I thought. Above her high, laced boots, the like of which I had never seen before, showed a three-inch band of light grey ribbed wool.

I turned to draw Dad's attention to this shocking exposure; but I could tell by his face that, though his body sat beside me, his spirit was far away.

As soon as the clapping started I leaned over the back of him to my sister on his other side, and drew her attention to my discovery. She sighed and gave me one of her 'whatever shall we do with her' looks. 'You sawney hap' orth! That bain't 'er combs a-showin', that be the top of them woolly stockings 'ers a-wearin' inside they boots!'

'Was it a good concert, Dad?' I asked him, as we walked home.

'Beautiful, my wench, beautiful. I only wish we 'ad some vittles in the 'ouse. I shoulda' liked to 'ave exed 'em up for a bite o' supper.'

Dad was a very polite man, the sort to put himself out to listen to the King if he'd come up by our gate, just the same as he put himself out to listen to poor old George the simpleton. Dad was the only person who could 'talk' to George's deaf and dumb wife. As a girl she'd been sent away to learn the deaf and dumb sign-language, but this still left her with not a soul to talk to, until Dad sent away for a book on the subject and taught himself.

It was fascinating to watch the pantomime of their gestures, and to see the remarkable change that came over Liza Baa, as we called her. Her face lit up, and she would laugh and look like a young girl. She was as thin as a rake, for simple George came at the end of the job queues, and like all the other women Liza gave the lion's share of the food to her husband.

When funds permitted us to buy the corn, Mam kept a few fowls, but Liza had only one old hen, and that was a pet, treated as one of the family. People said the old hen spent the night perched on their iron bedstead. That wasn't true, but it did go in and out of the house for any crumbs it could find under her table—or on it. Never having heard the human voice, nor what words sounded like, Liza relieved her emotions by a sort of moaning and cackling. That old hen used to scratch and peck round Liza's skirts, cackling back in an answering sort of way. They thought a lot of each other.

When Dad got pneumonia Liza came to see him. After a few days in bed he'd struggled downstairs to ease Mam's lot in attending him, and he was sitting grey-faced and hollow-eyed by the fire when Liza came in carrying a dish. The news of his illness had got through to her slowly. Now, in her hands, as clawlike as the old hen's feet swimming in the broth, was her sacrifice, to speed Dad's convalescence—her old hen. She put the dish on the table. Dad looked at the skinny stewed bird, and then at the beautiful kindness in her face. He had to bend down to do up his shoelaces, and when he looked up he could only nod his thanks. He'd been struck dumb, too.

That illness, we always believed, came from the conditions in which he worked when he was forced to go to a pit three miles from home. He was sacked from the pit near the village after the owner heard of his radical views and told the manager to get rid of him. The walk to the new pit wasn't too bad—it was downhill most of the way—but it was a hard grind home for an exhausted man at the end of a long shift. Mam put a stop to our usual practice of running to meet him for pick-a-backs up the garden path; but to reassure us that all was well Dad would do a little clog dance at the door in his heavy pit boots. Sometimes, as a bonus, just to show us 'yore feyther hen't a old mon yet', he would put the top of his head on the table, a hand each side, and slowly stand on his head. Muddied, streaked with coal-dust and rain, tattered and tired, he brought his radiance in with him. All was well when Dad came home.

Sometimes, on Sunday evenings, Mam went to chapel and left Dad to mind us. The lovely fire she built up before she left would easily lull him, as well as old Auntie, to sleep if we let it. Once, when he had only my brother and me to mind, we did let it. Then we set to work on Dad's hair. Only the fringe was long enough to do anything with; and not much with that, until we had the wonderful idea of putting a bit of treacle on it.

We had, at the time, a supply of brimstone and treacle for blood purification kept in the cupboard by the fire. We sneakily dipped a moistened finger in the tin, and rubbed what we didn't lick off on to Dad's fringe. Then we made it into a myriad tiny plaits, and tied these into knots, a feat of some dexterity.

By then we decided it was time Dad amused *us*. Usually, the first thing Dad did when he woke up was to make sure his beloved old pipe was on or near him. But on this occasion he put his hand to the top of his head, rose slowly, and went over to look in the little mirror hanging by the door.

'You young varmints! You've turned your old feyther into a bloody 'Ottentot. Whatevera' you bin a-puttin' on my yud?'

Although we helped Dad to wash off the treacle, and laboriously undid the knotted plaits, he still had a regular coxcomb of hair, that wouldn't comb down flat. 'I'll see you two buggers don't ketch I nappin' agyun.' Dad never growled, but he had a try.

Taking a piece of chalk from his pocket, he turned the wooden chairs we weren't sitting on upside down. 'Now, then, you pair o' bright sparks, what be these, then?' and he drew with his chalk, on the underside of the chair seats, his versions of some tropical animals.

We got so engrossed with this activity that Dad heard Mam saying goodnight to Granny only just in time. 'Look out! 'Ere be your Mam a-comin'!' In two shakes of a lamb's tail, Dad had put the chairs back upright, and we were sitting in innocent idleness round the fire when Mam came in.

Before leaving for chapel, Mam always left the house as spick and span as she could. After tea, she would put old Auntie's red plush cloth on the table, trim the wick of the lamp, fill its blue china bowl with paraffin, and place it in the middle of the table.

This grand, plush table-cloth had once had bobbles dangling all round the border; but in winter, during our toddler stage, the space under the table had been our 'play area', and most of the bobbles had proved irresistible to our meddling little fingers. But it was still a proud possession.

One evening, as soon as Mam had gone, Dad told us to sit up round the table. Then he went into the back-kitchen and came out with something he called an 'oojah-board'. It was roughly heart-shaped, had a sharpened piece of pencil fixed to the underside at the front, and moved easily on some small castor arrangement. We had known for the past week that Dad had been whittling away at something for us.

Next he smoothed down a big piece of brown paper across one end of the table. 'Now,' he said to us, 'one at a time, shut your eyes, and put your hand on thic oojah-board, an' just let'n vind 'is way about on thic piece o' paper.'

The ouija-board moved with practically no help at all. After a count of ten, we could open our eyes to read the 'message' it had written. But we could make nothing of our squiggles.

'Trouble is,' said Dad, 'thic bit o' 'ood I made'n from is mahogany, an' thic bloody board's a-writin' in jungle language. 'Ere, let I 'ave a goo, I'll see if I can persuade'n to write a bit in English.'

Dad screwed his eyes up very tight, and seemed to go into a trance of concentration. Then, suddenly, apparently of its own free will, the ouija-board began to write—not all that plain, but quite legibly: *Look behind the soap dish*. We fell over each other rushing into the unlit back-kitchen to feel behind the soap dish. Sure enough, something was there—a round piece of glass, with a metal rim on it, and a handle.

We were dumbstruck, and even more so, when Dad said that upon his soul, if it weren't a magic glass! Sure enough, when he put the glass over the hairs on his forearm and told us to look through it, his arm looked like a cratered, miniature jungle.

Every now and again, old Auntie surfaced to wakefulness to ask us, 'what's goin' on', or 'what be you up to now?'

We were up to looking for tiny objects to put under the magic glass. It took us out by the door to pluck a leaf left here and there on the roses, and to look by candle-light in the garden-wall for little slugs or mosses.

We gathered quite a variety of objects to spread over the best plush cloth. Time was forgotten, and our excited chatter drowned Mam's homecoming footsteps in the yard. The table was a shambles.

'Well! I can't turn me back on you lot for vive minutes afore you've turned the place into a regular menagerie!'

'What's a menagerie, Dad?' I asked.

'A zoo, I think,' said Dad.

'Yus, an' you be bloody well right,' said Mam, gathering up the plush cloth to shake its contents on to the garden.

Mam was an energetic type, and loved a bit of bustle to things: tables must be scrubbed till you could see the grain of the wood, fire-irons polished till you could see your face in them, rag mats shaken till the dust flew, and husbands who sat still too long hustled into some sort of activity.

'I can't see 'ow you're ever goin' to learn anything wi' your yud always stuck in a book,' was a frequent scold of Mam's. Brought reluctantly back to earth from the pages of *Erewhon* one day, Dad scratched his head and observed with impartial dignity to Mam, 'Mother, 'tis a great pity thee 'asn't got my brains, or I 'asn't got thy energy, then one on us coulda' come to summat.'

However, like all of her sex, Mam had her illogical moments. One Saturday evening, she told my brother and me that, as Dad and old Auntie would mind the two little ones, we could go to Cinderford with her to get some shopping.

This had happened one or twice before, and we knew it meant a treat for us. In the tiny market place, lit with naphtha flares, was a long table covered with white oilcloth, and flanked by wooden benches, where faggots or peas (or both to the rich) were served. The stall-owner was a stout, homely-looking matron, with a white starched pinny over her black blouse and skirt. Perhaps to give her round, motherly face a touch of dignity, and a 'no good to ask for tick' severity, she topped it with a man's cloth cap.

Spaced at strategic intervals on the long table were bottles of vinegar, and pepper and salt pots. The delicious aroma those faggots and peas sent out to the entrance would stop us in our tracks like kids in the Bisto advertisement petrified on the hoardings.

If she couldn't stretch things to have a penn'orth herself, Mam would take my brother and me to the table, order a penny dish of peas between us, 'two spoons please', and would leave us while she looked for food bargains.

The thought of those peas turned us into a willing little pair of carrier mules, better than a bag of carrots could work on the real thing. Mam never mentioned the peas, but they hung in our minds' eye all along the mile-and-a-half short cut through the Forest.

Dear Mam, she was one of the world's frustrated spenders, and would peer into every shop, with her short-sighted eyes, 'buying' all sorts for everyone.

One of her favourite shops was a junk shop at the bottom of the High Street. Sometimes there was a pretty vase or picture that she would take in her mind's eye, and place in a variety of positions to make her own home prettier. Her sighs gave me the clue to her thoughts.

There was quite a hint of excitement in her voice that Saturday, when she asked me to read out the titles of four enormous dusty, important-looking books in the window.

'*The Circle of the Sciences*,' I told her.

'Goo in, and ex 'ow much they be,' she told me.

''Alf-a-crown,' I had to tell her, surprised by such an odd request coming from Mam.

We always knew when Mam had a nice secret, although we didn't always find out what the secret was. We sensed, sometimes, that it was something she shared only with Dad. We knew because of the way she would purse her mouth up, and try to control her joy with little twitchings of her lips. I noticed it was happening as we walked on up the street. She also opened her purse, took the contents into her hand, and did a lot of thinking.

We were thinking hard, too, of the market and the faggot and pea stall, and could hardly persuade our reluctant legs to walk past it, as Mam carried on without apparently noticing the place.

Without batting an eyelid, she told such a tale of woe to the butcher that he knocked down the price of a big cow's heart to one-and-six. Mam came out looking well pleased with herself. Then down to the grocer's for flour, sugar, some tea, and very little else.

We cut round a place called the Triangle, back into the High Street, where we didn't have to pass the market. I squeezed my little brother's hand in sympathy.

There was a cake shop a bit further down. Mam looked in her purse again. ''Ere you be,' she said to me, 'goo in and get a cake for you and Charlie to share.'

First we stared at the delectable array in the window, comparing size with exotic fancy trimmings, and mutually agreed that a cream slice would be the best buy. Mam broke it carefully in half between us.

Our faith in Mam, human nature, and the delicious wonders of life, returned. Mam hadn't even asked us to help her carry anything; one of the two straw frails she had brought was still empty. Well, it was till we got to the junk shop.

Then, full of pride, gracious as royalty ordering from Harrods, Mam went in and bought those four huge books for Dad. You could have knocked me over with the dust on them!

Mam put two of the books in the bottom of the frail with the shopping, and put the other two in the empty frail so that my brother and I could carry them, holding a handle each.

None of us had much fat to bring us out in a sweat, but what a huff and a puff we were in, and how our arms and legs ached. Had we been carrying those books for anyone else, Mam would have had a mutiny on her hands.

There was a lovely fire in the grate, and an air of expectancy indoors. Mam always tried to come home from such expeditions with something extra for supper.

'Kettle's a-boilin',' said old Auntie, and took the baby off Dad for him to wet the tea.

One by one, Mam heaved the books on to the table.

'They be for you, Dad. 'Alf-a-crown they was!' As usual I was precociously quick off the mark with any information.

Dad's mouth fell quite open, as he looked at those books with an expression that was a mixture of awe and bewilderment. No wonder! It was enough to make him awe-struck, Mam spending half-a-crown on books! His bewilderment was equally justified. Who could want books on science so out-of-date that the knowledge had become practically useless?

That was information to guard from her at all costs. Aware of Mam's scrutiny, he handled those books with as much reverence as if they'd come straight from the tomb of Tutankhamun. Then he looked up at her. 'Well *done*, Shuky,' he said, using his pet nickname for her. And the love in his eyes said volumes more than his words.

Mam was a generous-hearted woman. Possessions were easily procured from her with the wheedling tongue and covetous eye; but when she died, in her eightieth year, Father's books still had pride of place on the shelves in the alcove by her cottage fireplace.

Mam

I don't know how our Mam ever managed to keep five of us fed and clothed—let alone herself and our Dad and Great-Aunt Lizzie, whom we lived with. Right from the beginning of our lives we children understood that we couldn't expect to have as much as we wanted of anything, and must never ask.

Mam was all but defeated by the problem of keeping her brood clothed. She was thankful for any garment that anyone would give her for us, regardless of fit or suitability. I kept a piece of string permanently round my middle to hold up the odd assortment of drawers I had to wear. The boys at school used to chant:

> Sing, sing
> What shall I sing?
> Poll Mason's britches
> Be tied up with string!

A stout middle-aged neighbour once produced a pair of her faded blue fleecy-lined bloomers for me. My piece of string kept them up, more or less, but the crutch came down to my knees, the bottoms almost to my ankles. 'Thee'st look like one o' they sultanas from a harem,' said my elder sister, Bess. I crept unwillingly to school, well behind everyone else. Before I got there I hid in the ferns, took off the bloomers, and chewed a hole each side of the waist. I put my arms through the holes, and wore them like a pair of combinations.

Another of my most memorable outfits was a frock that Mam once made me by sewing up a leg-of-mutton style lady's costume coat. It had shoulders as wide as a guardsman's, and plenty of braid trimming. It was most unfortunate that, on the morning I was to wear this to school for the first time, one of my aunts, who was in service, sent me a parcel of ribbon pieces. I had a passion for beads and ribbons, and forgot the misery of having to wear that terrible frock in the delight of all this treasure. I begged Mam to let me take the whole lot to school, and rather to my surprise, my sister joined in. I should have suspected her droll sense of humour, but as usual I didn't.

'Let me do thee up like Mary Pickford,' she said.

I had a short, pudding-basin haircut, a snub nose, a mouth that the kindly would describe as generous, a pair of unremarkable small blue eyes, and a trusting belief in Bess's genius.

On the way to school we kept well behind everyone else, then stopped for her to transform me. Somehow she managed to tie round my head, in loops and bows and streamers, every bit of that ribbon.

'My Gawd!' she said, almost overcome by the results of her efforts. 'I reckon thee'st do look better'n Mary Pickford—more like a fairy queen. Dance round thic tree so I can see how thee'st look when they ribbons do flare out.'

As she watched me dance, she suddenly doubled up with an attack of collywobbles, hardly able to speak for the pain, and decided to go back home instead of to school. Smirking, dreamy full of self-satisfaction, I carried on. One and a half hours late, I pushed open my classroom door, confident that I would create a sensation.

I did. The class teacher stared as though something obscene had crawled up through the floorboards. The titters of the class broke into roars of derision. Why, I thought despairingly, hadn't it been I instead of Bess who was struck down with the collywobbles? She always seemed the lucky one.

Clothing us was the worst thing, but feeding us was quite bad enough. The best effort Mam ever made in this direction nearly failed, for reasons which I suppose were foreseeable.

Someone whose sow produced a litter gave her the runt. Its chances of survival appeared to be very small, but Mam hand-reared it to a fat pink old softie that came running like a child at her call. Nancy would rub her snout against Mam's apron in the intervals of slurping up the contents of the wooden trough Dad had made her. The friendly cadenza of her grunting was so expressive, Mam reckoned she could talk, and sat on the empty up-turned bucket by the pig's-cot door to fuss and spoil her for a bit, no matter how busy she was. If anybody left the garden gate open, Nancy came waddling up the path, expecting to come indoors for a neighbourly social half-hour, and sniffled dejectedly when Mam smacked her behind all the way back to the gate.

Poor Mam! She saved Nancy's bacon as long as she could, but she'd no answer when Auntie scolded her: 'Thy young 'uns'll be lucky to 'ave'er trotters to yut! If thee doosn't get the butcher to 'er soon, thee'la margaged'n all away.'

Mam had put one of Nancy's hocks 'in hock' to the grocer, towards payment for the bran, and the neighbours who'd given her their potato peelings were to have pieces. The butcher's services *had* to be ordered. For once I was speedy out of bed and off to school.

Mam was more courageous. It was she who cut the dried fern for the pyre to singe the bristles off Nancy, and she who filled the copper with water for scalding the singed offering. Mam made the sacrifice and did most of the work, but when it came to eating her plate of pig's fry, she felt the call to go down to the privy. Even Dad admitted ruefully that 'yuttin our Nancy nearly made us into cannibals'.

One Saturday afternoon in November we sensed that Mam was in a particularly good humour. Her mouth kept twitching at the corners as though it'd break into a proper smile if she wasn't careful. About four o'clock she pulled up her wrinkled lisle stockings, polished over the cracks of her only pair of down-trodden shoes, removed her sacking apron, put on her going-out costume coat, and announced that she was going shopping. Shops closed late in those days, and there were bargains to be had of meat and fish on the point of going off, and cheese too hard to stand another weekend in the shops.

Then she gave us our orders.

My elder sister was put in charge of the baby and making up the fire. After I had fetched in kindling wood, I was to spread a piece of newspaper on the scrubbed top table and clean our odds and ends of cutlery with powdered brick dust. I was also to help keep an eye on my younger brother and sister.

Then with dire warnings of what we should feel on our arses if we didn't obey these instructions, Mam made a sugar teat for the baby, took two straw frail bags, and was off.

The sugar teat was a couple of spoonfuls of sugar tied in a bit of rag and moistened by dipping into the kettle on the hob. The baby went to sleep before she'd sucked it down to the rag, so our elder sister, Bess, gave our little sister a suck on it, and promised my little brother and me could have one too if we would go and meet Mam when it got dark.

But first we must get the kindling. We didn't know the luxuries of topcoats or gloves, so I tied a couple of old woollen scarves from the nail behind the door round my little brother, and we went happily kicking among the autumn leaves for twigs and bits of fallen branches, breaking them into small lengths to go into the oven at the side of the big black-leaded grate to dry. Our dad got the miners' free allowance of coal so we always had a good fire.

I hated cleaning the cutlery and before starting arranged the forks and spoons into a row of 'piano keys'. On these I played my own tunes, singing an accompaniment of such excruciating tunelessness that my concert was brought to a sudden close by a clout round the ear from my sister.

It was almost a two-mile walk to the little mining town through the short cuts in the woods, and for us, in the dark, a much longer walk round by the main road along the edges of the Forest. Bess stuck a stump of candle in the bottom of a jam jar, and with thumping hearts my little brother and I set off, he holding the jam jar to keep his hands warm.

Almost all the trees in the forest were huge oaks—big enough for two witches to hide behind—but about half-way along the woodland path to the main road was a fine chestnut tree, and the weird hooting of a night owl seemed to come from its branches. My little brother knew as well as I that they pecked your eyes out in the dark. Taking the jam jar from him, I told him to keep his eyes shut, then the owl wouldn't be able to see him—walking myself with one eye open at a time, so as not to be wholly blinded at one fell swoop. The candle flame was flickering in pool of melted grease, almost at the end of its wick; my courage had almost given out too.

'Me boot's undone,' I lied, and bent down, fumbling, to gain time, trying to hide my mounting terror of the chestnut tree.

Just then Mam's chesty cough heralded her approach.

''Oo be there?' she called, noticing our little glimmering light.

'It only be me!' I was now brave as a lion. With Mam about, the witches and ogres would fly for their lives. Even Dad, who wasn't afraid of the dark or thunder and lightning, melted into thin air a bit quick when Mam got her dander up.

'Well done,' said Mam. 'I could do wi' a bit o' 'elp wi' these frails. They be feelin' a bit 'eavy now.'

That was a good omen!

You never knew with Mam. There were times when she had come home with a bag of broken biscuits, or a comic, or better still with a bag of toffee pieces that had given us hours of glorious chewings.

When we got in, we found that Bess had chucked plenty of coal on the fire, but it took a few deft pokings between the bottom bars by Mam to send it into glorious flames, licking at the black flue. The baby whimpered miserably with hunger, despite Bess's desperate jiggings.

''Er'll 'a' to wait a few more minutes,' gasped Mam, wetting a pot of tea from the big cast-iron black kettle on one of the hobs. She put a lump of fat in a frying pan on the fire, then took some liver from one of the frails. She suckled the baby and drank her tea with one hand, turning the frizzling pieces of liver and adding flour and water, salt and pepper, with the other, till the liver bubbled in a pan of thick brown gravy. Liver for supper! We sat small and quiet, trying to be scarcer than we were, lest by some movement we should destroy or hinder the chance of the feast to come.

The baby, already worn out with her hungry crying, soon went to sleep at the breast. Mam put her down carefully in a chair and dished up our supper. A small snippet of liver went on her own plate, and one a bit bigger was left in the pan for Father.

First we broke up our bread, carefully picking up any crumbs made in the process to dip in the gravy. Well-behaved above the table, we gently and joyfully kicked each other underneath it. When the bread and gravy were gone, we ate our liver, licking the gravy smears where the liver had been.

'Don't put your plates in the bowl yet,' said Mam. Then from a frail she took a piece of fancy cake, the like of which we'd never seen on our table before. Plain slab was a delicate luxury, and this was no plain slab! It had two yellow layers with a pink layer in the middle, and was sandwiched together with cream and jam. Mam put a slice each on our plates and it looked too good to eat. It seemed to me like an act of wicked greed to eat cake, jam and cream in one. I longed for a piece of bread to spread the jam and cream on, but I was a coward, and waited till Mam turned her head. Silently I signalled my idea to Bess. She was bigger and braver than me and was sitting on the other side of the table, out of reach of a clip round the head for such cheek.

'Wot you two up to?' asked Mam.

''Er do want another piece o' bread.'

I cringed away, but without a grumble Mam cut us all a piece.

With delicate care we all scraped our jam and cream on to our bread, picking up the tiniest morsel of cake dropped on the table with a tongue-moistened forefinger. We made our feast last a long time.

'Jesus Christ, I be vull as a egg!' said our little brother, rubbing his stomach through the big hole in the front of his jersey. It was the first time a grace had been said at our table.

'Get the flannel from the back-kitchen and rub round their mouths ready for bed,' Mam ordered.

When that was done, she fumbled in a frail and pulled out a doll's cup and saucer made of brightly-painted tin for our little sister, and a bag of coloured clay marbles for our brother. They accepted these gifts with the same puzzled delight that Cinderella must have felt when the pumpkin turned into a fairy coach. Then Bess and I gave them a pick-a-back up the stairs, and put our little brother in the middle of the iron bedstead he shared with us, and our little sister in the home-made bed next to our parents' bed in the other room. When we got downstairs again we found there was a packet of coloured crayons for Bess, who loved to draw, and a little round box of minute multicoloured china beads for me, and, glory of glories, two comics as well—*The Rainbow* and *The Sunbeam*.

'If you two be quiet, you can stop up for a bit,' said Mam, settling herself down in the chair by the hearth for a nap.

But where had the money come from to pay for all this? I'd heard her say in desperation more than once that she wouldn't be above robbing the bank if she know how to do it. When I was sure she was fast asleep, I whispered my fear to Bess.

'Doosn't thee fret theeself, you silly 'aporth. Our Mam could afford it. You know the bottom o'thic table leg our Dad'ave bin a-carvin' for Mr Jones? Well, thic Mr Jones was that pleased, 'im give our Dad seven-and-sixpence for doin' it. Course, our Mam 'ad the money, but you can bet'er got our Dad a' extra 'alf ounce o' baccy out on't.'

Well, what a lot of money to pay for a table leg to be mended!
True, Dad had been ages doing it, whittling away with a penknife,
a gouge and a chisel, to turn a block of wood into what looked like
a lion's claw wreathed with flowers. A few days previously, Mam
had sent me down to the shed at the bottom of our garden to tell
Dad to 'look slippy, the coal 'ad bin delivered'.

'Wot d'you think o' that then, my wench?' Dad had asked me,
holding up the almost finished carving.

'That's bloody good, Dad, thic rose and them leaves do look
just like the shape o' real 'uns.'

'Yus, I reckon your old feyther's done a bloody masterpiece
there. I bet thic Michael Anjeeloo oudn'ta' done it much better wi'
the sart o' tools I've got. I reckon Mr Jones' eyes'll pop out o' 'is
yud when 'im do see wot a good jot I a-made on't.'

'Yus, Dad, and if thee doosn't come and start getting thic coal
in, our Mam'll be making *thy* eyes pop out o' thy yud!'

We weren't wallowing in ill-gotten gains then! With my belly
full of liver and fancy cake, and my fingers decked with rings of
threaded beads, and *all of it paid for*, I heaved a great sigh of relief.
Bess and I sat quiet as angels in the golden light from the paraffin
lamp, transported into the world of Tiger Tim, Suzie Sunshine,
Marzipan the Magician, and the delicious adventures of The Two
Pickles.

We watched Mam till she showed signs of stirring, then tiptoed
upstairs before she could order us into the cold dark back-kitchen
to spoil a perfect evening with our idea of a wash.

Snuggling down under Mam's heavy home-made patchwork
quilt, we drifted into contented dreams.

Despite the fact that, unlike Dad, Mam never got her head stuck
in a book, she sometimes came up with an original idea that would
not have entered his head. Sometimes she thought it best not to
share with him, as for example, when she had the idea to go
scrumping some apples.

On this occasion, I was the lucky one to whom she confided her
hopes.

'Bain't stealin', really,' she said, 'you see, they've finished wi'
pickin' the apples now for cider an' suchlike, an' them what's left
on the ground only goes bad. You an' I could go arter dinner. 'Tis

Sunday, so there won't be a lot o' people about. We can take the colander to get a few blackberries from the 'edges of the orchard, in case we do see anybody. We'll pick some elderberries for your feyther's 'erb tea as well, so everybody'll be satisfied. Mind you, it's a smart step; two miles if it's a yard, an' it's uphill all the road. What d'you say then; d'you want to come with Mam?'

My greedy little stomach would not have owned me had I turned down such an offer. Apples to munch, apples to munch, it made my mouth water to think of them.

'Not 'alf,' I agreed.

With the colander held conspicuously, and two frails rolled unobtrusively under our arms, we started out after dinner, leaving others to wash up and mind the little ones.

We went through the woodland path, the way of us children, as far as the school. Without the busy hum of children's voices, and the comings and goings of little swarms of them in and out of entrances, it had the air of an abandoned beehive.

The hill was now less steep, and was dotted with cottages. 'Nice day', 'warm for the time o' year', and a few incurious stares, and we came to the road where we forked left. Here I was on unfamiliar territory.

''Ere 'tis,' said Mam at long last, as we came to a wide, five-barred gate with a path leading down through an orchard. Sure enough, speckled among the grass under the trees, were apples; pale green ones and rosy ones, some half-bad, and some nearly all good. There were also apples here and there on the branches.

Beside the gate was a notice—*Trespassers will be Prosecuted*. Even with her glasses on, Mam was very short-sighted, and I was too distracted by the apples to give it a second thought. There was one snag; we were in view of a man working on the land on the opposite side of the road.

Mam outlined our strategy. 'We'll just go in as if we've a right to. Don't pick any apples up yet. There's sure to be some blackberries round the meadows further on. We'll go an' pick some; then when we come back out, we'll fill the frails wi' apples. Wi' a bit o' luck thic man will've gone in for 'is tea by then.'

Sure enough, the gate at the other end of this long orchard opened on to a big field that sloped up on the right to a bank with a dip behind it. A few yards down, on the left, some huge blackberry bushes tumbled over the barbed wire fence that separated the meadow from a wild copse of brambles, nettles, and tangled undergrowth.

I had popped about two blackberries in my mouth, and one in the colander, when simultaneously Mam and I became aware of the bull, which had apparently been grazing on the other side of the bank, and was now coming to charge angrily at the intruders.

'Oh, my Gawd, quick! Get over thic wirc.' I had never heard Mam sound so alarmed. Without ceremony, or regard for the barbed wire, Mam heaved and pushed me over, then scrambled over herself. By then the bull was practically breathing down her neck.

Shoving, pushing, and pulling me in front of her, she gasped out to keep going; stumbling over a jungle of briars, nettles and other hindrances that clawed at us and stung. It was some yards before I looked up at Mam's face. It was pale ashen grey, lips and all, and beads of sweat had run down, misted up her glasses, and mixed with the blood from the scratches on her face.

'Was we in bad danger, Mam?' I asked.

"Im 'ould 'a killed us, but I reckon thic barbed wire fence 'ave 'alted'n. But be a good little wench and never mind the stings and scratches. The sooner we be out of 'ere the better.' Mam was so breathless it was an effort for her to speak at all.

Unable to see where we were going, we beat down a path with our arms and legs. At last we came to the end of the copse, and to a fence we could climb over on to the edge of a ploughed field. We skirted round this until we came to a gate. Over the gate, and we were on the grass verge of the road again.

'Oh, dear!' said Mam. 'What a sight you be! You do look as though you bin pulled through a 'edge back'ards.' She should have seen herself! We had lost the colander, but miraculously Mam had hung on to the frails. Very dispirited, we started home.

We were soon back by the orchard gate again. The man who had been working opposite was gone.

The apples still lay in the grass. Growing out of the hedge near the gate was an elderflower tree.

'Come on,' said Mam, pulling a few small branches of the berried elderflower to top the apples with, 'we'll dap in quick while we've got the chance, and fill the frails. Try and pick up the best ones.'

The damp grass had rotted the underside of most of them, but, noses to ground, we darted about under those trees like a pair of well-trained retrievers.

Urged by Mam to be quick, I did not even stop to eat one; anyway I intended, on the way home, to carry some of my load inside my skin. With the frails full to gaping open, we covered the apples with elderberry foliage, and were only yards from safety, when a man coming down the road turned into the gate. Our hearts sank.

With his boots and leggings, battered-brimmed hat above his weather-beaten face, he was obviously a farmer, maybe *the* farmer. Arms akimbo, legs apart, he stood blocking our way, and gruffly asked us what might we be doing in his orchard? His eyes were hard and angry.

So bedraggled were we by this time, he might well have mistaken us for a pair of gypsies.

The shape of the apples bulged out the sides of the straw frails. Red in the face as the rosiest of them, Mam tried to bluff her way out. 'We've just bin gatherin' a few 'erbs for the children's coughs in the winter; we didn't think we was doin' any 'arm.'

'Then you won't mind tipping your bags up for me to see.'

I felt deeply embarrassed, and sorry for Mam; we had escaped a bull, and as far as I could judge, had bumped into a pig. 'It's only a few 'erbs,' Mam lied lamely.

With that he picked up the frails, and tipped the apples out. Then he asked Mam for her name and address; she was near to tears when she told him.

'Pick up your bags, and don't let me catch you on my land again,' he warned us. Mam took her frails, and did not even bother to pick up the elderberries. Downcast and dejected, we carefully closed the orchard gate behind us, under the malevolent eye of the owner.

'The greedy, mingy old bugger!' I exploded, feeling that such a remark was safely above censure in the circumstances, 'all that traipsin' about an' 'ard work for nothin'!'

'Never mind,' said Mam, 'it could 'ave bin wuss. Thic bull might 'ave 'ad us. I only 'ope thic farmer's bark is wuss than 'is bite. I dread to think what'll happen if 'im do summons me. After all, 'twouldn't never do for 'im to let people come an' go on 'is land when they pick and choose. If 'im let one do it, 'undreds more 'ould do the same. The pity is that we got caught.'

Under some trees nearer home, Mam stopped, 'Might as well fill up these frails wi' these nice dry bits o' fire 'ood. They do 'elp to boil the kettle real quick for your feyther's cup o' tea on 'is early shift.'

A real mam our Mam was. Perhaps, on second thoughts, that farmer came to the same conclusion, for Mam heard no more from him.

School

Our village straggled up each side of a steep and stony track, an offshoot from the main road. Like London, we had our West End and our East End, our slums and our grandeur. The industrious, frugal, small-familied and childless couples, who'd saved hard to build their own places, lived in an extension of the village on the side of the main road. Their little palaces were mostly wooden or stone bungalows, with ingenious little architectural trimmings that sprang from competition between their owners.

One place was particularly attractive, inside and out. The couple had only one child. I once heard a bitterly envious woman saying, 'Aye, one of the ronk 'uns, 'er is. I'eard as 'er do tie a rag on a string and shove it up just before 'er do let 'er old mon get near 'er.'

In the gardens of the élite, snow-white washing danced on the clothes lines every Monday morning. The women never had to hide from the tradesmen and didn't patronise the packmen. Though they might give away a pair of well-polished, much-patched, worn-out boots, they were arid ground for the borrowers and cadgers. They kept primly to themselves in their prim little dwellings. They didn't laugh a lot.

At the top end of the village lived the feckless and the slum-mocky—and some wonderful women who had so many children they didn't know what to do next in the struggle to keep them clean, fed and clothed with the means at their disposal.

The hunger and the poverty at the feckless end, and in the middle (where *we* lived) got worse for us children when our sorely tried fathers, maddened to revolt by worsening conditions and short time in the pits, came out on strike. Soon there were no pigs in the cots, nor fowls pecking around the doors. No longer able to buy their bit of bacca, the men made themselves sick trying to smoke dried coltsfoot leaves. We children were often sick from the bitter acorns we tried desperately hard to acquire a taste for. With no pigs to snout them out, we scratched the earth away from a wild feathery-leaved plant for its bulbous root, called pignuts. Alas, these grew few and far between.

Tuberculosis followed malnutrition, and some of the village children were sent to sanatoria. Lucky things, we thought; but the rest of us had some good luck too—'they' started free dinners at school. I don't remember who 'they' were, but I do remember the dinners. Our Mam tried to get some sort of meat for Sunday dinner, but now it was meat *every day*—beautiful stews, corned beef, mince! And pudding as well—rice pudding made with milk, jam roly-poly, and (crowning delicacy) treacle pudding. This I liked above all else. We had one helping and never expected two.

One dinner-time 'they', who organised the dinners, came and had some with us. 'They' sat at a special table with the headmaster. When the tables were cleared, instead of telling us to dismiss, the headmaster stood up and said something I couldn't catch.

'What did 'im say, Bess?' I asked my elder sister.

She answered, with a sarcasm quite lost on me, 'Who do want some more treacle pud?'

Up shot my hand, surprisingly the only one. Puzzled, the headmaster asked what did I want? I told him: 'More puddin', please.'

There was silence while the whole school took the shock. Two hundred pairs of eyes gave me their undivided attention.

'You sawney 'aporth!' hissed my sister adding a sharp poke in the ribs.

The headmaster was equal to the occasion. 'We can't hold up the speeches of thanks at the moment, but no doubt Cook will find a bit of extra pudding for such an appreciative little stomach.' The joke went down well, but I wished I were dead; and when we were dismissed to the playground my sister turned her back on me, disowning me for my lack of manners. I hung back, trying to look invisible till I could get out and find a corner to hide in.

The headmaster was sitting by the door. As I passed he grabbed me on to his lap. 'Come on then, my little pudding girl, Cook's got a nice big helping for you.'

Dumb with mortification, I struggled off his lap. One more crumb of treacle pudding and I should have choked.

His name was Mr High, but in fact he was very short, and also very stout. His stomach protruded like a balloon blown up to bursting point. It was commonly said that if you could tap his navel, you would turn on undiluted cider. He was never actually sober nor ever completely drunk.

If he was a walking cider barrel, his wife was a tall vinegar bottle. They hated each other with cold, polite venom. They had no children, which may have been the root of the matter. It was a matter of opinion whether she had driven him to drink by her sour nature, or had acquired her sourness because of his drinking.

He was much the kinder of the two. As long as the pupils scraped through the low standards of learning required by the schools inspectors, he was not much concerned with our education. I think he considered the raw material at his disposal was not worth much cultivation.

When he required the labour, older pupils were sent to gather kindling wood for his home fires, sacks of bracken for his pigs' bedding, leaf-mould for his garden, and blackberries for his wife's preserves. These activities passed for nature study.

Mostly he treated us all with good-natured sarcasm, but now and again, when he was taking a class, he went into one of his tantrums. When he felt a tantrum coming on, the slightest misdemeanour, real or unintended, would set him off. Forms and desks toppled over as he dragged us out, clouting us round the ears with one hand, wielding his stick with the other. He threw our exercise books in the air, and pages came flying all over the classroom. It always gave me a fit of the giggles; I knew he would be likely to bring a chair down on my head if he noticed, so I always bent down to tie up my bootlaces during the hurricane. That way I got my whacks along my back. He never favoured anyone; we all got a hiding when he was in the mood. It did him the world of good—he was well-behaved for a long time afterwards.

Mrs High, who taught Standard Three, was a born snob; she only had time for the very small percentage of clean, tidy children. A runny-nosed, dirty, raggedy child like me appeared to contaminate her. She particularly disliked any child the headmaster especially noticed. (Poor woman! God knows what jealousies racked her soul.) On both counts I was doomed. When I reached Standard Three, at the age of nine, I was already Mr High's little pudding girl, and I was at all times an offence to the eye in the extraordinary assortment of clothes our Mam gave me to wear. But, by a piece of luck such as seldom came my way, I was out of the class again before the year was out.

As Mrs High took no interest in the scruffier members of

her class, I was able to spend my time drawing, doodling and composing rhymes in my exercise book; and one afternoon, when Mr High made one of his rare visits to Standard Three to look over our work, he picked up my book and said, 'How's my little pudding girl getting on?'

'I'll cop it now,' I thought, and wasn't surprised when he told me to come to the front of the class. However should I hold up my head again if he gave me the cane? It was a punishment rarely administered, which made the boys heroes, if they didn't yell or grimace, but disgraced a girl for the rest of her school life.

Instead of caning me, Mr High told me to read out some of my work to the class; and then he marched me into the top class, where Standards Five and Six were taught by Miss Hale. Bess was in this class. I waited while he had a little chat with Miss Hale; then I was told to step up on to her blackboard platform and read my poems out again. It appeared I'd done something clever. The pupils laughed a lot when I finished.

It took very little encouragement to inflate my ego, but later Bess said, 'It was your drawers. That leg with the 'lastic out was all 'angin' down.' And Mrs High's expression when I returned to her class damped down any further poetic aspirations and stopped me getting conceited.

Nevertheless, the following Monday I skipped Standard Four and was put into Miss Hale's class. It was soon obvious that I was an absolute duffer at arithmetic and sewing, but the humiliation of being bottom of the class in these subjects was made up for by Miss Hale's reading to us. She took us out of the classroom, over the hills and far away, with *Uncle Tom's Cabin, Black Beauty, Lorna Doone, Treasure Island*. This wasn't just 'doing the classics'—as she went along, we followed spellbound. Every day, life became richer. Learning new words was like having a key to free the imprisoned thoughts I'd been unable to express. And Miss Hale was always ready to listen.

Besides, she never commented on the weird unsuitability of our clothes, she never appeared even to notice the dried soapflakes on our necks, camouflaging the fleabites. Going to school now became a wonderful daily treat.

Another treat that came my way about the same time was when I was given a pile of schoolgirl magazines called *The Bluebird*. They came from Goggy, a boy who hadn't been able to go to work in the pits like the other boys, because he had so much wrong with him. His whole body was covered with taut, angry red skin as though he'd been scalded. His watery, raw-rimmed eyes were nearly blind. He had to wear special shoes for his misshapen sore feet, and even in these walking was an uncomfortable process. Inside this grotesque exterior was a wonderful young man, kind, intelligent, and purposeful.

He earned his living doing a paper round. Daily it took him over a large area of scattered cottages, single and in clusters, and it took him all God's hours to walk the umpteen miles on his tender feet. His wage was ten shillings a week. His widowed mother Mrs Protheroe acted midwife and washerwoman, or layer-out of the dead, to any villager that could spare a shilling or two for such services. She did it for nothing for those she respected if they had nothing to pay with. She made an art of frugality, wasting nothing, and kept herself and Goggy adequately fed and housed and very, very clean.

She and Goggy are both dead now, but they'll always be on the short list of those I have truly loved.

Anyway, Goggy gave me this treasure—this pile of schoolgirl magazines, which I had difficulty in hiding from the ravaging hands of the little ones, from the teasing destruction of older children, and most of all from Mam. Mam never read anything. Paper, to her, was something to be stuffed into holey boots, to spread on the table instead of a cloth, to protect the freshly scrubbed flagstone floor from our muddy tread, to lay fires with, or cut into squares for hanging in the privy. (The frustrations I suffered from reading unfinished snippets in there!)

The privy was my seat of learning. There I could stay for long sessions of undisturbed reading, and escape into fantasy. While my craze for those *Bluebird* magazines lasted, I became in turn Lil of the Lighthouse, Wanda of the Movies, the Heroine of St Catherine's, and even the Richest Girl in the School. Now and again, for a change, I was just myself.

Chapel

Mondays and Fridays we mixed with other children of the village at school, and on Sundays we met most of them again at chapel.

The chapel stood on a small natural plateau roughly in the middle of the village. We were told it was God's house, but we didn't think *He* would have much time to visit our chapel in person.

The chapel was looked after by a couple of the most respected villagers, and was kept clean and polished by Mrs Protheroe.

We knew we had to mind our P's and Q's in there, but it was a small and friendly house, with no pretensions of grandeur. It did not feel hollow and cold, nor at all overpowering. The windows were of plain glass, and bursts of sunshine brought out extra gleams on the wooden forms polished with such fervour by Mrs Protheroe.

It was quite pleasant to go there on wet Sundays and cold Wednesday evenings. We could still enjoy ourselves, and pass muster with the Sunday school teachers, even with our attention divided between them and our mischief.

The chapel did not have a ghoulish graveyard, either. Our Methodist preachers tried to take care of our souls, but the church, a couple of miles away, had to dispose of our mortal remains.

A simple place, our chapel, yet when the congregation joined together in a full-throated rendering of a favourite hymn, many of us shared a true communion with each other.

The women from the better-off end of the village and a sprinkling of the husbands were regular chapel-goers. Not so the other end. All too often the poorer women 'hadn't a rag on their backs good enough for chapel!'

We were the in-betweens in chapel attendance too, but every so often the love of music in Mam's Welsh blood drew her to chapel on a Sunday evening for the joy of the hymn singing.

'You can come with Mam, if you like,' she would offer me kindly. This would put me in a bit of a quandary. It didn't seem nice to refuse what Mam thought was a treat, and I knew it was likely that she would have a sweet or two in the bottom of her pocket to cure the fidgets brought on by the sermon.

Of course, in the hymn singing, there was the fascinating study of rows of faces, full of mouth-holes of infinite variety, pulled into the most peculiar shapes to get the tunes out. There was trying to count up to a hundred between the sonorous 'amens' of old Mr Matton; and there was the ribbon boss on the front of Mrs Griffiths' hat, which always looked as though it was going to fall off, but didn't. There were, too, mimes to make to other young sufferers in other rows, who had been conned into attending.

Some evenings I did go with Mam, but on other occasions the afternoon at Sunday school seemed more than enough for one day. Very few of us attended Sunday school for its own sake, but if we didn't put in a minimum number of appearances in the year, we wouldn't be included in the chapel treat.

But Sunday school—and attendances there—bucked up a bit when we had the novelty of a new teacher. This lady, Mrs Smith, was middle-aged with the gentlest voice and manner. I thought she had a beautiful face. She wore her hair in a bun, and when the sunlight came through the chapel window it lit up the tendrils of hair round her forehead into a golden halo. Instead of just reading from the Bible, she told us charming little stories. The boys tried to spoil it by asking her to read those parts of the Bible containing the 'dirty bits' they'd found out about. I felt very sorry for her, pink-faced and embarrassed, trying to ignore them. It was small martyrdom compared with what came later.

It was not an unknown sin, and men here and there committed it, but a woman? Never! Well, not until it came to light that Mrs Smith did. Yes, she was a female gambler! She put money on horses!

Secrets had a short life in our village. The preacher soon heard of this backslider brought into our midst. Justice must be done, and heard to be done, from the pulpit, in the Lord's name.

Unaware of all this, Mrs Smith took her seat among the Sunday-evening congregation. The chapel was much fuller than usual—sadists that we were.

Starting off in his low-pitched, holier-than-thou quaver, the preacher soon worked himself into a volcanic eruption of de-nouncement against those who committed one of the basest sins against their Maker—the sin of gambling. And who could be a greater sinner than a sister who had succumbed to this lure of the Devil?

So the ashes fell on her unprepared, defenceless head! There was a long dramatic pause, as long as he could manage to hold it without losing our attention. Then, again in low-pitched quavers, he asked the congregation to kneel and pray that the sinner in our midst might be brought back to righteousness by repentance and washed clean again in the blood of the Lamb. She must have been a compulsive gambler for she stopped coming to chapel. Dad never went to chapel, but he said he'd gamble a sovereign to a penny that Mrs Smith had more chance of getting to heaven than that preacher.

Chapel treat used to come on a school day, and as far as we were concerned the teacher might as well not have been there that day—our attention was on the classroom clock. Would it never come round to two o'clock? The rumble of empty stomachs was louder than the scratching of desultory pens, or the buzzing of lethargic bees and flies round the jam jars of wild flowers on the windowsills. Most of the mothers, knowing their offspring would get full bellies at the treat tea, gave them no food for the midday play break.

At last, when the hands of the clock said two precisely, the teacher would tell us to line up in front of the class and dismiss in a quiet and orderly fashion. Anyone disobeying would be brought back to class and miss the treat. We shuffled out as quietly as our nailed boots would allow, with never a whisper between us until we were clear of the school yard. Then, mad as a bunch of March hares, yelling and hooting at the top of our voices, we rushed as fast as our legs would carry us, through the wood to home.

Most of us were indoors only long enough to get our hair combed, face and hands washed, and stockings pulled up. We had nothing to change into. A few lucky ones had the paper curlers taken out of their hair, ribbon bows tied on, and fresh clean dresses. Then off to the chapel where we sat in rows on a grassy slope and the Minister came out to hear us say grace: 'For what we are about to receive may the Lord make us truly thankful.'

The words didn't do justice to our feelings. For many of us it was the only meal of the year that offered the luxury of eating as much as we wanted. And what a feast it was! For a start, what bread! Not bread like we had at home—kept for a few days before cutting, to make it go further, then spread only in the middle with lard, marge or lumpy mutton dripping, and strictly rationed to one or two pieces. *This* bread was oven-fresh, only a quarter-inch thick, cut from long squares and spread all over—corner to corner—with golden best butter. The Diamond Jubilee mugs were filled with scalding hot tea; and no one stinged with the milk and sugar. Like goddesses with cornucopias three village matrons bustled in and out of the vestry with an everlasting supply of baskets and enamel jugs. 'Don't know where the young varmints be putting it all,' they would laugh to one another, their kindly faces beaming under Sunday hats. As it was a chapel do, it had to be respected by Sunday hats, although they wore starched white aprons over their dark dresses.

Not until we all had agreed among ourselves that we 'wuz as vull as eggs' did we concede we were ready for a slice of bright slab cake. After such bounty we yelled our Thank-you grace.

Next we lined up behind the 'band'—that is, anyone who could play a mouth organ, tin whistle, a jew's harp, or even a paper and comb. We did a lap of honour round the village so that those too old or infirm to join us shouldn't miss the sight, and then down to the main road (where a motor car was still something to stand and stare at), to march singing at the top of our voices, in and out of tune, to the only farm in the district. Here the farmer let us have the use of one of his fields for our fun and games.

I was never any good at the egg-and-spoon, three-legged or sack races: after a flash start my stamina gave out completely. But I did win the penny prize in the bun-eating contest. For this a rope was fixed between two stakes and buns hung from it on a string. With hands tied behind our backs, we had to kneel down to catch and eat a bun. ''Tain't fair—'er do allus win cos 'er got a chops twice as big as anybody else's,' said the rosebud mouths I envied all the rest of the year. For once I was glad I'd got a genuine 'cake hole'. I spent my prize money straight away on an ice-cream cornet, giving the first licks to my little brother and sister.

When our games were finished, the grown-ups followed suit, frolicking like children, falling over in the sack and three-legged race, laughing and making fools of themselves to our huge delight.

Just when the running about and excitement had made us

thirsty and peckish again, the three matrons would be spied coming up the road with the remains of the bread and butter in baskets and a couple of helpers with big cans of cold tea. Then, before their legs were too tired to carry them, the very young and the very old took each other home, carrying with them bunches of cowslips picked from the meadow, thus leaving the field clear for the evening game of 'kiss in the ring'. This offered the one chance of flirtation that village convention allowed. Everyone made the most of it, and maybe when dusk fell the kissing lingered longer, and maybe the hugging got a bit tighter. But that was as far as it went; husbands and wives, sweethearts and lovers, went home in their proper pairs. A few men felt more manly, a few women more feminine, but some were more lonely than ever.

Another yearly treat run by the chapel was the Teetotallers' outing. Our virtuous reputation as teetotallers was quite unearned; we never had the chance or money to be anything else; except when some boys at school found that the headmaster hadn't locked the shed where he kept his barrels of cider. There, after school, he found five boys in a state of maudlin drunkenness when he was fetching his own supply. The boys were banned from the Good Templars meetings and from the outing; but being boys, it wasn't much disgrace. They would grow into men. Alcohol was only a sin for women and children. If a drop of cider did come a woman's way, she warmed it on the hob and drank it as 'medicine'.

The Teetotallers' outing was a grand affair. We could hardly contain our pride as we waited at the bottom of the village for the char-à-banc. What travellers we were! It was a good twenty-mile ride to our destination, a privately owned playground at Bishops Cleeve. We had the excitement of going through Gloucester, and also the privilege (as I considered—for the likes of us) of being allowed to pass through Cheltenham, with its grand Georgian houses and wide tree-lined roads.

Once, as we were going up Lansdown Road, Mrs Toomey saw her daughter, Emma, coming out of one of the houses, with some letters: obviously sent to the post by her employer. Of course it was unthinkable for the char-à-banc driver to stop so that Emma's Mam and her brothers and sisters could give her a hug and a kiss! But they caught sight of each other and waved frantically; and the other women made quite a do of how smart young Emma looked in her cap and apron, while Mrs Toomey fumbled around for something to dab her eyes with.

The playground we went to wasn't a brightly painted affair; everything had a weather-beaten drabness. But there were see-saws, roundabouts, helter-skelters, and swings. With our three-pence entrance fee, we had freedom to go on everything. A tea was laid on in a big wooden hut; not unlimited like the chapel treat tea, but all the same a satisfying number of pieces of bread and butter, a small fancy cake apiece, and two cups of tea. It was stylish too, for we sat on long wooden benches, and ate off trestle tables.

We squeezed the last minute from this outing; we left only when the early September dusk stopped play. It was very thrilling for those of us who could keep awake to see Cheltenham and Gloucester with their lights on. The older children nursed the sleeping younger ones and sang all the way home:

> Pull for the shore, sailor, pull for the shore
> Heed not the rolling waves, but bend to the oar

—our favourite hymn.

Teetotallers we may have been, but the after-effects of the swings, see-saws, and roundabouts, sent us reeling up our garden paths like a lot of drunken sailors.

One year, when I was about nine, I caught a strong dose of religious mania. It didn't last very long, and it was after I'd read a book called *Teddy's Button*. I kept my conversion a secret with God, because I didn't want to be laughed at, but the incredible improvement in my behaviour caused Mam to get quite worried. Well-behaved children were often marked for an early grave.

Actually it was a very handy time for me to believe in God and his miracles; I badly needed a miracle to fit me up with suitable clothes for Chapel Anniversary Sunday. Nearly everybody in the village made an effort to attend the anniversary, to see their daughters sing and recite in a service to mark the occasion.

Never backward to seize a chance to hog the limelight, I learned a fourteen-verse poem of religious platitudes, with which to try the Christian patience of the congregation. Its sheer length gave me the leading role, but I was desperately short of costume for the part.

Ideally, each girl should have been dressed all in white: a rare achievement indeed in our community. With my new-found faith in God's omnipotence, I thought this time I might be lucky. He could raise people from the dead, He could feed thousands on a handful of fish and three loaves; in that case He could provide me with some anniversary clothes. Nothing is beyond the power of prayer, and I prayed: morning, noon and night, promising God I would keep up my good behaviour, and would He please oblige me with an angel bringing a white silk frock, white straw hat (with ribbons), and white shoes and socks. White canvas shoes would do, I didn't expect buckskin. So that nobody would know of the arrangement, the angel could leave them in the fox-hole by the chestnut tree, and I would go out to play and 'find' them after school.

With pounding heart, I approached the hole every day; it was empty. Serve me right I thought! I'd been too greedy, asked too much. I amended my request. It could be a blue frock, a very plain hat, and brown shoes would do; and it wouldn't matter if none of it was new.

By Saturday, eve of the great day, I was still praying, but I would have settled for anything, provided I looked tidy. Nothing appeared, even though I raked thoroughly among the dead oak leaves, in case the angel had hidden my things from prying eyes.

I wished now that I hadn't given my brother the whole piece of orange peel that a girl had given me at school. I would have kept some for myself, had I known God was so mingy with His miracles. I looked up at the sky, and for Anyone who was looking I gave one of my awful scowls.

Reduced now to a weeping nuisance of self-pity, I went indoors and drove Mam beside herself by fretting about what I should wear on the next day.

Mam was so desperate that as a last hope she suggested we should try the Reddings. The Redding family were distant relations who had a small draper's shop, and in our eyes they were people of consequence. We had no friendship or contact with this grand family, who certainly wished none with us.

I was to go and ask them politely if they had any clothes to spare, as Mam couldn't get me any this week, what with Dad's pit boots falling to pieces, and her having to buy cough medicine for my little brother. 'Mind you,' she warned me, 'you might be unlucky, for people do say they be too mean to gi' you the time o' day.'

It was a long walk—over two miles—and I had time to ponder. Perhaps God had put the idea into Mam's head, for didn't He work in mysterious ways His wonders to perform? So I prayed again; all the way through the woods, along the main road, and through the straggling hamlet of Drybrook, till I came to the Reddings' garden gate. I was very thirsty and very hungry, but I tried to assume a polite and pleasant expression before asking for their bounty.

Old Mrs Redding answered my knock. She was small and bony, and she wore a voluminous black skirt, black blouse and a crochet shawl of red, blue and yellow. I thought she looked like a bantam hen.

All Mam had told me to say came out in a rush of supplication. The old lady didn't look very pleased. She didn't say anything, but hemmed and hawed in a very discouraging manner, and then went back indoors. She didn't ask me to step inside, but she didn't close the door either, so I waited hopefully on the doorstep.

After some time, she returned, carrying a bulky brown paper parcel tied so that the string would form a carrying handle. I could see the shape of a hat in it. I truly thanked her from the bottom of my heart, and decided not to take any further advantage by asking for a drink of water. I couldn't hurry through that hamlet quick enough to get to a quiet piece of road and undo the string, and see what I had got. I kept beaming skywards, my imagination full of white silk, lace and ribbons. But I was practically an unbeliever after I'd opened that parcel.

It contained two hats, one inside the other, and a frock. The style of the frock was all right, for I liked a bit of novelty; it was too big, though that didn't much matter either, but the colours! Black and brown! The top was made up of alternate squares of black and brown silk, like a chessboard, faggot-stitched together. The skirt was formed of three frills, two black, and a brown one in the middle. It was hard work, looking for a silver lining in that dress, but it *was* silk, and I was sure the skirt would make a big flounce if I twirled round in it. There were no shoes, but I supposed that my black boots would match the dress. Anyway, beggars couldn't be choosers.

The hats were a better proposition. They were identical in shape, made out of bands of straw braid. Both had faded to a dusty dark grey, but where the ribbons had been removed, I could see one had been a bright pink, the other cream.

I was suddenly inspired—I would undo the braid and turn it to the clean side on the pink hat. No, better still, I would unpick the braid from *both* hats and sew it in alternate stripes, clean side uppermost. I forgot how hungry and tired I was, as I hurried home to get on with my project.

Mam was pleased I'd struck lucky. She'd been fortunate too, while I was out. Gladys's mum had given her a basin of home-cured lard, and she spread some on two thick slices of bread for me. It was delicious with a sprinkle of salt. She let me finish up the tea in the pot, and then brought out a pair of brown sandals. They were not new, and the backs had been trodden down, never to stand again. They were also a bit too big; but providing I shuffled along without lifting my feet, I could manage. I was thrilled to bits. Hitherto my footwear had always been boots—often nailed boots; sandals were dainty and glamorous.

My spirits were high enough before Mam showed me the nearly-white socks that Mrs Brown had given her to go with the sandals. 'Thy cup runneth over,' I thought to myself.

The snag was Mrs Brown's stuck-up daughter, Eunice; she might throw it up at me about Mam asking for her old shoes. 'You never *cadged* 'em, did you, Mam?'

'No, that I didn't. I just 'appened to mention that you 'adn't a shoe fit to wear tomorrer, and she fetched them sandals and socks and gave 'em to me.'

Comforted on that point, I rummaged around looking for sewing cotton. The reel was nearly empty, but Mam let me pull threads from a treasured wash-stand cloth she used when the babies came. But the threads weren't very strong. I cut the pink and cream braid on the hats into pieces, sewed them together and wound them round into a hat shape, putting in a fixing stitch as often as the thread would allow.

Frayed edges were much in evidence, and my little brother said the hat looked like a 'busted bee skep'. In my eyes, it was a creation of no mean beauty. Mam let me stand it, for safety, on the wash-stand jug in her bedroom.

Because I could only shuffle along in my sandals, I started for chapel well before time. We had to wait in the little vestry; then make a grand entrance into chapel. When I arrived, a few girls were there already, among them Eunice.

I detested Eunice. I couldn't understand why God singled her out for so many favours. She was a cribber at school, put the blame for her own misdeeds on other children, and gave weak-minded cronies bites of bread and jam out of her lunch box. When she had a fight, she was downright spiteful.

There she sat today, clad from top to toe in white, except for the pink rosebuds and blue forget-me-nots round her straw hat. She had long brown curls as well, and a pretty face. There couldn't have been much left for her to ask God for. It didn't seem fair!

Gladys, my best friend, was there, and she too was nearly all in white, but I didn't mind about her. Gladys could have been dressed in fairy gossamer, and I wouldn't have grudged her it. She was kind and nice to everybody, especially me. She patted the place on the wooden form next to her for me to sit down.

All the glory I had felt in my sandals, white socks, and straw hat (which I'd thought quite passable with the frayed ends at the back) vanished. Compared with the others, I was going to look a proper gypsy. I just managed to hold back the tears and make a concentrated study of my whitish socks.

Presently Nell Wills shuffled in. It wasn't her shoes that handicapped *her*. It was her dress!

Nell had eleven brothers and sisters. A couple of the girls were in service, and a couple of the boys worked down the pit when there was any work. All the same, it was a miracle where Nell's mum had found the money to buy the white material and lace edging for Nell's dress. Considering Mrs Wills was mother of twelve children, she hadn't much notion of relating the shape of the dress to the body's needs. It was just a straight tube with two smaller straight tubes sewn in for sleeves, and a hole left in the top for Nell's head to go through.

The lace edging had gone round the neck and sleeves, but only two-thirds round the narrow skirt bottom. This had been made even narrower by a one-sided tuck, so that the lace might fit. The whole gave an interesting lop-sided effect, and it also made it nearly impossible for Nell to walk. Still, it did have the glory of being all white. I would gladly have swopped my dark flounces for it.

'I like your frock,' purred Queen Cat Eunice to Nell.

Nell was equal to the taunt. 'Yes, my mam paid four-and-elevenpence for it, brand-new at the Bon Marché.' Nell was the sort of red-haired, brother-toughened girl you didn't call a liar!

Any pleasure I'd anticipated from reciting my poem had evaporated before I took my seat, conscious that my outlandish appearance spoilt the show.

Several girls said their pieces. Eunice, who could play the piano and had a surprisingly sweet voice for such a nasty person, sang a solo to her own accompaniment. The audience was obviously highly impressed, but now we fell from the sublime to the ridiculous, for it was my turn!

I started off well enough, and everyone suffered me with quiet politeness. Too quiet; I could hear a faint crackling noise coming from my hat. It was difficult to concentrate on my pious poem, wondering what was happening up there on my head; and it became even more difficult when I saw the big ribbon boss on Mrs Dee's hat begin to shake. She was shaking too, with suppressed laughter. She was enormously fat, and her face went the same colour as her strawberry pink frock. One of my aunties had once brought home from service a funny-shaped dish, and had made in it something called blancmange. As I watched Mrs Dee, she reminded me of the saucerful of that lovely pudding my auntie had given me, and I forgot my lines.

Like the rippling of a breeze in a cornfield, her laughter spread to everyone in the audience. I knew now what they were laughing at—my hat. The inadequate stitching must have come undone, and I could picture the braid standing up in a spiral above it.

The poor choirmaster, who'd spent patient weeks coaching us for this day, was sticking his chin in and out in nervous bewilderment at this collapse of events. I felt terribly guilty, but the whole thing seemed so comical. So I had a fit of giggles and laughed till the tears came, then sat down. The closing hymn was 'Jesus Loves Me'. Even if I hadn't been so choked up, I wouldn't have had the nerve to sing it.

I was in no hurry to go home, for I'd caught sight of Mam's red, embarrassed face in the congregation. On this special Sunday there was jelly for tea, but not even for this quivering delicacy would I go home; at least not till Dad had put in a good word for me, as I knew he would once he'd heard all about it.

I didn't have much trouble avoiding people after chapel. No one seemed to be aware of me. I hung back in the vestry till everyone had gone. Now I wanted to indulge in my panacea for all my troubles, a day-dream in the Forest. I knew a special little bank among the ferns and foxgloves formed almost like a seat. In this green enchantment, I could grow rich, beautiful and successful, paying my debts with unstinted magnanimity. Besides, I also wanted to have a good cry.

I had reckoned without Gladys. She was waiting outside with Florence Cassons, who was almost as nice as Gladys. The sympathy on their faces was too much, and I started blubbering there and then. They put their arms around me. 'Doosn't thee cry,' comforted Gladys, 'I reckon they all enjoyed themselves.'

Florence was a rather special sort of girl. For a start she lived nearly a mile from the village, at Nelsons Green, where their only neighbour was an old witch, but Florence wasn't a bit afraid of her.

To take my mind off my troubles, Gladys suggested that we should walk part of the way home with Florence, but first she'd run indoors and tell her mam. She returned with some pieces of string and tied my sandals on firmly with deft fingers. I could now lift my feet without leaving my shoes behind. My spirits lifted too. I put my 'model' hat on the end of my sandal, and kicked it back to the Devil. Florence caught my mood. 'Let's 'ave a goo on the swing tree!'

The swing tree stood beside a large shallow hole in the woods; one of the branches of a huge oak had half broken off, and was hanging by its bark and woody sinews. The end hung low enough for us to reach, hold on to, and after a quick run, let our feet off the ground and swing over the hole in a circle back to the tree. Gladys didn't want to be a spoilsport but she was a bit worried about her best white dress.

Florence had a new blue frock, but ran on to the tree for first go, without giving it a thought. She was half-way over the hole when she lost her grip. Her fall was broken by the thick carpet of dead leaves in the bottom of the hole, and by her dress which was caught in the rough end of the branch. But she'd ricked her ankle, and it hurt badly to put her foot to the ground.

I felt I was a jinx, bringing trouble and calamity to everyone. What could I do to make amends? 'Will your mam gi' you a good 'iding for ripping your frock?' Gladys asked anxiously. Florence nodded—up and down, and sideways, since she couldn't be sure.

'*You* needn't come,' I said to Gladys, 'but *I'm* goin' to take Florence all the way home.' Perhaps old Mimey the witch would have me, but I'd have to risk it, *and* her geese! My sister, Bess, had told me in strictest confidence that they weren't really geese; but people Mimey had bewitched. Perhaps she would turn me into a goose. If she did, *I* wouldn't stick my neck out and run at people to frighten them.

Even the grown-ups reckoned that Mimey was a witch; hadn't Josh Pudge lost his leg in the pit after she'd cursed him for stealing one of her fowls?

If only I could save poor Florence from a good hiding as well! I was quite a skilful little liar when I put my mind to it. I concocted a story about a ferocious dog chasing us. In our rush to escape, Florence had stumbled over a tree root.

To my great relief, Gladys bravely said she'd come all the way, or at least till the geese started for us.

Actually the geese were grazing on the far side of the green, and took no notice of our approach at all. Mrs Cassons did, and came running out from her garden to see why Florence was limping. Florence began to cry and her mam was so concerned about her swollen ankle that I only had to tell a little fib that Florence had fallen down. There was Mrs Cassons comforting Florence and telling her not to worry about her dress—she could mend it so that it would hardly show!

Now we had a bigger surprise. Old Mimey the witch came out with two pieces of blackberry-jam tart still warm from the oven— one for Gladys and one for me. I was too scared to be good-mannered enough to refuse such generosity. 'Go on, try it,' she cackled. Gladys hung back, but I took a bite, partly to humour old Mimey, partly because I was almost permanently hungry. The pastry had a melt-in-the-mouth lightness, and there was a thick filling of sweet, juicy blackberry jam.

'It's the best tart I've ever tasted,' I said truthfully. 'My mam's a wonderful old tarter, but you're an even better'un.' This compliment pleased her so much she laughed until her dewlaps shook, and you could see the dirt embedded in her criss-cross wrinkled neck.

Despite our welcome, we left Nelsons Green behind as fast as we could. Gladys hadn't touched her tart. 'I can't abide blackberries cooked,' she said, 'you 'ave it.'

'Be you quite sure?'

She nodded. I couldn't have taken it off anyone else without much more persuasion. But I knew Gladys's mam was rich enough to give her bread and jam and any time she asked for it; we wouldn't have dreamt of that in our family.

Filled with tart, I wasn't worried if there wasn't much for tea at home. I left Gladys at her gate and made my way to our cottage. Bess and her friend were playing hopscotch on the play-flattened hard earth outside our garden gate.

'Thee bisn't 'alf gonna cop it off your mam for makin' sich a gawbee o' theeself in chapel,' Bess's friend warned me.

I waited until I was inside the gate with the catch down, then pushed out my purple tongue at them.

'Pooh, I don't care, I've just 'ad *two* pieces o' jam tart to yut.'

'Fibber!'

'No I bain't. Gladys an' I took Florence Cassons wum, cos 'er sprained 'er ankle, an' old Mimey the witch gi'ed us the tart. Gladys wasn't 'ungry so 'er gi'ed I 'ers.'

'Thee'st what? Thee'st yut vittles off old Mimey! Thou silly cooten thee! Now thee'lt die at twelve o'clock tonight. 'Er only gi' thee that tart to pizen thee!'

This dramatic comment from her friend made my sister's eyes widen to their fullest concern. The bit of flattery I felt at this was soon dispelled as she calmly went on playing hopscotch. I walked soberly up the garden path. So I was going to die then. What a day it had been! Dying seemed a fitting finish to it. But anyway, midnight was a long way off.

Mam had saved me a saucerful of jelly, and a couple of yards off the end of her tongue to go with it. I let her lather herself out, without my usual impudence of sticking up for myself. Gloating in my martyrdom, I thought how sorry she would feel when she found me dead and cold in the morning.

Bess slept on the outside of the bed, my little brother in the middle, and I on the side against the wall. That wall gave me claustrophobia for life.

The other two were soon fast asleep. I listened fearfully for the chimes from Great-Aunt Lizzie's wall clock downstairs. It kept time right to the second.

I heard it strike eleven ominously. 'Matthew, Mark, Luke and John, bless the bed that I lie on. Two at my head, two at my feet, they will guard me while I sleep.'

The top of our iron bedstead was jammed against the wall, and so was my side; still I supposed angels didn't need any room as they weren't solid like us. I wondered how they would come to fetch me—through the tiny window, or through the walls? I tried to picture what it would be like to be dead. I wouldn't be able to feel anything, smell anything, hear, taste, or see anything. I was already in the pitch dark, so I knew what it was like not to see. If I couldn't do all those things, and my body had to be left behind, anyway, to go down the pity 'ole, there didn't seem much left worth taking. It was wicked to be afraid of angels; but I was. I put my head under the heavy patchwork quilt. I didn't want to see them coming into the bedroom.

The next thing I heard was Mam's irate voice threatening to come upstairs and 'larrup our arses if we wasn't down in two shakes of a lamb's tail to get ready for school.'

Her nagging voice sounded like the chimes of heaven. I wasn't dead; I was still here! I hugged my little brother fiercely.

'Pooh,' I goaded Bess, 'I bain't dead. I be still 'ere.'

Obviously the two pieces of blackberry tart still rankled, for she said: 'Ow d'you know you be? You might only think you be!' Then, jumping smartly out of bed, she hid behind the door as Mam rushed in. When Mam had finished with my bare behind, I knew I was still alive all right—and fairly tingling with it.

Great-Aunt Lizzie

The cottage we lived in was the property of my Great-Aunt Lizzie, and she slept in our tiny parlour, having long been too crippled with arthritis to get up the stairs. Apart from her iron bed, there was a wooden chair and a chest of drawers in her room. This chest, of mahogany, with fine glass knobs, was the grandest piece of furniture in the cottage.

Old Auntie lived, with rigid independence, on her old age pension of five shillings, for which munificence she frequently and fervently thanked Lloyd George. She did accept a share of our garden produce, but more than paid for this by helping all she could with the housework, although her gnarled and misshapen hands made her slow and awkward. Often she would drat the infernal rheumatics and wish it to Halifax. We didn't know where this was, but it sounded dramatic.

Whenever she sat down, there was always a baby to go on her lap, and her voluminous fusty black skirts were our refuge when Mam was after us for some mischief. She wore black cloth boots, with shiny toe-caps that didn't protect her corns from our clumsy feet. Often, accidentally, we made her cry out with pain. She forgave us anything, and one of the treats of our lives was the weekly share of scraping out her Nestlé's milk tin. With a teaspoon each, two or three of us would take a turn on the sparse leavings till the tin was as shiny and clean inside as a new one.

Another of Auntie's bounties came after the annual visit of a middle-aged relative. He always brought her a quarter of humbugs and a few apples. This visit was not regarded by her as one of goodwill. She disliked the man over some episode in the past, and besides, she knew he had taken out an insurance policy on her life. 'I bet I be aggravatin' the varmint, lastin' this long,' she would chuckle, ' 'im do only come to see if I be on me last legs. " 'ow be you?" 'im do ex I, but what 'im's a-really sayin', by the look in 'is eyes, is " 'ow dare you kip goin' on and on, an' costin' me tuppence a year for 'umbugs?" Durn me if it ain't a reg'lar tonic to me to aggravate'n so. I do feel quite perky agyun arter 'im a' bin 'ere.'

The sight of the apples and sweets perked us up too. One of the apples was cut up and shared between us as soon as he had gone. The other few Auntie stored among her laying-out clothes in the chest of drawers. It was another great treat when she cut up one of these between us, though they always tasted of camphor balls.

The Almighty, in whose existence she had implicit belief, had been more generous with her life-span than she'd anticipated. So every couple of years she paid a village woman sixpence to launder her laying-out clothes, because the coal dust from the fires got into everything. She wouldn't give our mother the task, as Mam was not the most skilful of washerwomen.

When she got into her eighties, Aunt Lizzie would gently chide the Almighty for His tardiness in collecting her. 'I be getting useless down 'err now, and me laying-out things'll be wore out afore I, if He ben't careful.'

From her memories, and from what Dad told us, we learned a lot about her life. When she was eight years old, the eldest of four, her mother had died with the baby in childbirth. Her father worked in a stone quarry for a pittance. Straight away, with help from neighbours, little Lizzie tried to run the household. When a near-blind widow came to live in the village, and was willing to step into the role of stepmother, it seemed like an act of providence. Lizzie, now gone nine years old, thought differently. She was a better judge than her elders, and saw behind the veneer of pious goodness the cruel, greedy hypocrite her stepmother turned out to be. Too late, Lizzie's father found his mistake. So he decided it would be best for all concerned if his little wench went into service at once.

A job was found for her as scullery-maid in a manor house nearly thirty miles away. Her clothes were tied in a bundle at each end of a stick on her father's shoulder; and they set out at dawn to walk the distance. When Lizzie's legs could carry her no further, a night's shelter in a barn was begged from a farmer. The next day they tramped on, and when at length he'd handed her over to the cook, Lizzie's dad turned, with tears in his eyes, for the long walk back.

Her former life was soon almost obliterated by her new below-stairs world of dungeon cellars and labyrinthine passages, and by her lowly status among the small army of servants. In order for her to stand at the sink and reach the mountain of pots and pans she scoured, she had to get on a box. But she was not born to be a scullery-maid for long: her sturdiness of spirit, and her intelligence and shrewdness, saved her.

By the time she was sixteen, she was head housemaid, owned a locked cash-box containing golden sovereigns (her hoarded wages), and was soon to become, by a series of tragedies, a woman of property.

She had judged her stepmother rightly. Food that should have been fairly shared among the family had mostly gone down her gullet, until she became a hefty seventeen stone, while Lizzie's younger sisters and brother became thin as matchsticks. The two little girls died of consumption, the brother developed a bad cough, and the father—perhaps no longer wanting to live—just died to get away from his problems. He left two dwellings which he'd inherited: the cottage he lived in and the smaller one next door. One was left to Lizzie, and one to her brother, who became our grandfather.

Lizzie paid for, and attended, her father's funeral. Afterwards she promptly turned her stepmother out, and decided to make a home for her brother and look after him in a way he'd never known. It was no good wasting love on the dead, but she had an abundance for her little brother.

The cottages were in poor repair and seemed like hovels to Lizzie coming from the manor house. She enquired around for the cheapest skilled labour to do the repairs. She did the unskilled labouring herself. She mixed mortar and wheeled it in by the barrow-load; she fetched and carried in the role of builder's mate, till her hands bled and it was agony to straighten her back. The builder reckoned it was the hardest money he'd ever earned, keeping up with her. When the building was finished, she still had enough money left to buy some bedsteads; she intended to earn her living by catering for lodgers.

She took in three middle-aged miners—a widower and two surly bachelors. Lizzie fed them well, did their washing, kept the cottage spotless, and expected (and got) their weekly board money each Friday on the dot. She paid twopence a week for her brother to learn to read and write at a dame-school in the village, just as her father had paid for her before she left home. And she started to dig the garden, but her lodgers took the spade from her hands. Lizzie's rabbit pie, meat dumplings and treacle roly-poly were well worth a bit of digging. When, at the age of eighteen, she took and married the fifty-year-old widower, nobody was surprised. She was considered staid and mature far beyond her years.

Now he shared her bed, Lizzie could take in another lodger. This was a gentle bachelor, John Webb, a safetyman in the pit. His kindness helped her when, at the age of twenty-three, she was widowed by a pit-fall. Five years later, John Webb summoned up the courage to propose marriage to her.

She loved John Webb with all her heart and fretted that she could not bear him a child. She grew quite beautiful; and, in her old age, she would often recall the day they went to Speech House fair. She wore a pale-green silk bustle dress, with parasol to match. She pinned extra side-curls to her own abundant brown ones under her Dolly Varden hat. 'It had a wide pale-green ribbon to match, and a big pink rose in every dip in the brim. Lady Webb, they called me, after that day; and John held my arm and walked me about as though I were the Queen herself.'

When he was twenty-one Lizzie's brother married, and settled down in his cottage next door. Now he was off her hands, and with little to hinder them and a tidy nest-egg of golden sovereigns, John and Lizzie decided to sail to America and seek their fortune. It was the time of the California Gold Rush. Lizzie was too prudent to sell her cottage. She gave notice to her lodgers and let it.

Off they went, sailing steerage class from Southampton, and then travelling across America by covered wagon, till they reached California and a gold-crazed miners' camp. Gold there might be, thought Lizzie, and again there might not. But men needed feeding and housing. Let John try for the gold; she would ensure their living by running a boarding-house. She chose only the more respectable types for her lodgers, and her venture prospered well enough to make up for John's practically barren claim.

Lizzie picked some gigantic oak and chestnut leaves, and put them between the pages of her enormous family Bible. Some day, when she returned to England, her friends would marvel at them. That day came sooner than she had dreamed. John Webb had never been robust: now his pallor had turned to yellow, and he lost his appetite. A doctor diagnosed cancer, far advanced. It was unthinkable to Lizzie that John should be buried in foreign soil;

she was not sure that the Almighty had stretched his jurisdiction as far as America. She sold the boarding-house, booked a more comfortable passage home, for John's sake, and brought him home to die. They'd been away two years, and she was now almost penniless. So once again she earned a living taking in lodgers.

Her brother still lived next door and like her was, in the local idiom, 'a reg'lar scrat'. He did all available hours in the pit, kept a few sheep and pigs, and was always at the ready to earn a few coppers extra if the chance came his way. Somehow he was always finding the time to enlarge his cottage. He was now the proud father of a baby son, and wanted to become a man of property. But his frantic, tireless striving had taken toll of his doubtful health. All Lizzie's efforts at building him up had been dissipated by overwork. She became very worried about his cough and his thinness, but he was a married man now, and no longer her beloved responsibility.

Gathering acorns for his pigs' winter feed, he went into the forest in pouring rain, and caught a chill which flared into pneumonia. In less than a week he lay dying. 'Kip a eye on me little boy,' he said to Lizzie. He loved his young wife very dearly, but regarded her as a feckless young girl compared with his practical sister. Lizzie would have taken the baby to bring up as her own, but the young mother wouldn't part with him altogether. Instead, she took her baby son home for her parents to mind, let the cottage at one-and-sixpence a week, and herself went back into service, to earn her keep and his. This baby, Charles, was to be my father.

After three years she married again, another miner, and came back to her cottage. There she gave birth to eight more children; and Great-Aunt Lizzie was three-quarters mother to Dad and half-mother to the rest of them.

As he grew up, my father Charlie became her idol. He was impractical, dreamy, clever, and utterly kind. There grew between them a bond of affection such as I have never seen. She forgave him his wild atheistic talk for she knew he wouldn't hurt a fly. She forgave him his foolishness in marrying a Welsh girl she couldn't really like, because he had the needs of a man. He'd gone to work in the Welsh coal-fields because of the slump at home. When he married, Lizzie let her cottage again, and went to join him in

Wales, where she rented a cottage to share with him and his new wife. Soon there was a beautiful baby girl named Elizabeth—my sister Bess.

When the slump hit the Welsh coal-fields, they all came back again and settled in Great-Aunt's cottage. Though seven more children were born, it was unthinkable that we should move. Over the years we broke most of her treasured china and ornaments. On Sunday afternoons her red plush cloth was put on the table, and we little ones sat underneath and pulled the bobbles off. When she was still able to get upstairs to bed, one or the other of us warmed her old bones at night.

One thing we were not allowed to put our mischievous hands on was her best hat. It was a big-brimmed black straw. I don't know what trimmings it had started out with, but over the years Great-Aunt had sewn on to it every black trimming that came her way. There was an ostrich feather, cartwheels of black tulle, bits of lace with jet beads, rosettes, bows of black ribbon, bunches of black cherries and a bird or two. Sacred, nebulous, amorphous, it resided in its own special cardboard box, to be brought out and worn for the significant occasion.

One such was a chapel anniversary at which I recited a poem. Despite her crippling arthritis, she decided to come. Dad was no chapel-goer, but he gave her his arm; and with her walking-stick in her other hand, and allowing an hour for a three-minute journey, they made it. She was so pleased with my performance, that she gave me the honour of carrying her hat to her room afterwards. I laid it carefully on the bed.

Despite Mam's efforts, we always had fleas, but that summer we were infested. They were torture to Great-Aunt Lizzie; for by the time she had reached one bite to give it a good scratch, 'the tarnation critter' would bite somewhere else. She bought boxes of Keating's powder to sprinkle under the feather beds, and in the patchwork quilts. It made us sneeze, and itch worse than the fleas. She used to blame the cat for the fleas, for she was always catching him on her bed.

After the efforts of the day she decided to go to bed early. But soon she was back; she opened the kitchen door and stood there forlornly holding a battered black object.

'Me 'at! Oh, me 'at! I thought as 'twere that dratted cat on me bed, so I gi'ed 'im a whack wi' me stick. The pestering critter never budged. I'll teach him for once and all, I thought. So I really laid into 'im wi' me stick summat cruel. No wonder 'im didn't muv. 'Twere me 'at I was whackin'.'

The sight of that bedraggled hat with the ostrich feather limp and broken, the birds moulting, the cherries plucked, the bows undone, the roses picked, was too much for Dad. He just had to laugh, and it set us all off. She even forgave him for that.

'Never mind, Auntie,' my sister soothed her when she got her breath back, 'I'll mend it for you so no one'll notice, even if it takes me a week.'

We all knew how clever my sister was. 'All right, my wench; and it'll be doing you a good turn too, for I be leaving you that' at in me will.'

I'm not telling anyone what my sister said about that, behind Auntie's back of course. Sure enough, though, she did wonders to restore that hat, but poor old Auntie was never again well enough to go out in it.

Granny and Grancher

Until I was about ten years old, Granny, Dad's mother, lived in the cottage next door with her second husband, Grancher. Like our Dad, Grancher was a miner, dour, handsome, uncommunicative. Granny bore him seven daughters, and he greeted the news of each birth with a resigned grunt and a spit into the back of the fire.

But Granny kept her trump card under her pinny until the last moment of her child-bearing years. Then, belatedly, she presented him with a baby son. Mam said Grancher nearly fainted when he was told, and that Grancher went upstairs and kissed Granny and his little son.

He nearly turned into an ordinary human being after that.

In some ways, we were lucky to have such a grancher; he never gave us a cuff round the earhole, or shouted at us. But we were aware of his prickles, like a hedgehog, and even as toddlers developed a sort of radar to avoid contact with his chair or person. His wooden chair was the only one with arms on, and it was sacred to his use. In the winter, when there was no gardening to be done, and not much work in the pit, Grancher dozed away the time by the fire chewing his cud of twisted tobacco.

Lively Granny would be off into our house for a quat and a chat; and then we children used her place as a play house. So long as we didn't kick into the rungs of his chair, or make physical contact with him, Grancher completely ignored us, and would not have turned round if we had been walking upside down on the ceiling.

When any of my aunties came home from domestic service in the winter, they used him as a clothes airer for the stockings and blouses they wore for meeting their local beaux.

One autumn I sat for three weeks, after school hours, on Granny's steel fender, 'atching out a cuckoo!', and I don't think Grancher noticed I was there. This was a ploy my sister thought up to get rid of 'our little misery guts', as she called me.

'See this 'ere fir cone,' she said to me in her special confidential whisper, 'well, that's where the cuckoos do come from. That pink down there in the spikes is the blood. Now if you do sit on Granny's fender, an' kip a-turning this fir cone round by the fire, a dear little cuckoo'll 'atch out. But don't tell anybody what you be doin', or the spell'll break.'

So there I sat.

Luckily for me somebody in the village killed a pig, and gave Granny the chitterlings. These had to be cleaned in a zinc bath on the table, for we had no sinks, taps, or running water. The smell drove Grancher out; he must have found a couple of pennies to go down to the pub with. Granny's sense of smell was almost nil, due to a severe illness earlier on; but she kindly said 'that I might like to run out and play wi' t'others, till the wust o'smell was over.' I explained that I couldn't. It didn't matter about telling Granny our secrets; she was like father, and did not pooh-pooh our ideas. *She* believed in miracles.

'Well, I never knowed that afore. You do live and learn summat every day,' said Granny. 'I s'pose young Lizzie told thee that?'

'Aye, Granny, 'er did.'

'Mm, I thought so.' Granny took the cone, and solemnly held it first to one ear, then the other. Sadly she shook her head. 'I be a-feared thee'lt never 'atch a cuckoo outa' thic 'un, 'im's addled. But still, thee doesn't wanna disappoint Lizzie; thee tell 'er thic cuckoo 'atched out all of a sudden and fled up the chimley afore thee cust cetch'n. I must say Lizzie's a sharp wench, 'er can 'atch a cuckoo outa' all sarts. Now, thee take some big taters from thic box in the back-kitchen, thee'lt find Lizzie an' t'others roasting taters at the back of old Ben's pig's cot.'

Granny never knocked down our childish illusions.

Granny's kitchen was as friendly to us children as our own, and the big fender round the hearth more familiar to my behind than any chair.

In the middle of the mantelpiece, the tea was kept in the Mazawattee tin, with its picture of a plump, bespectacled granny, and a little girl, the living spit of her, enjoying a cup of that famous brew. On each side were two other pretty tins. One, with a monocled dandy on it advertising Sharp's toffees, acted as filing cabinet for Granny's important papers; the other was her home safe, often rifled to find a spare ha'penny for one of us.

In the centre of the room was a big, scrubbed-top table, on another wall, a big chest of drawers. On the top of this chest was a photograph of a slim girl with her hair piled up in Edwardian style. Her tiny waist was accentuated by the fit of an ankle-length skirt, her close-fitting white blouse was high-necked, with leg-of-mutton sleeves. I thought the girl was quite beautiful, but I tried not to look at the picture too long in case Granny should notice, and start to think of Elsie.

Granny had produced some fine, handsome girls among her bevy of highly individual daughters, and if, at times, one seemed to have more imperfections than another, Granny still strove not 'to make poop o' one an' pudden o' another'.

Despite this, a stronger heartstring had attached her to Elsie; gentle, ladylike Elsie; delicate, difficult to rear, and treasured the more because of it.

With a natural aptitude for fine needlework, and a remarkable neatness in her own appearance, Elsie soon rose high in the ranks of domestic service. It was lucky, for she had little stamina to keep her going in the rougher, menial jobs.

The cough that had plagued her chesty childhood persisted, and one day Elsie just quietly fainted at her mistress's feet. The doctor was called, and advanced tuberculosis diagnosed. The servant was no longer worthy of her hire. Elsie was not the responsibility of her employers, and she was sent back home to 'recuperate'.

Granny was too familiar with the scourge of consumption not to be in great dread about her daughter. Up till then Granny had suffered much, humbly accepting 'Thy will be done', but she would not accept that it was the will of the Lord to take Elsie from her. He had blessed her with this special sibling, and Granny was willing to go to any trouble to save her.

A sofa-bed was made up for Elsie by the fire, and Granny became her round-the-clock vigilante; taking a day-time nap, when she could, on the bed upstairs, while Mam or a neighbour kept watch. At night Granny 'managed' with Grancher's chair, and another wooden one to put her feet up on.

'I'd be thankful if thee'st 'ould spare a bit o' thic for our Elsie.' With desperate candour, Granny asked for, and was willingly given, a share of any little delicacy that might find its way on to a neighbour's table. Elsie got the first pickings from the neighbours' gardens, the finest piece of liver from a new-killed pig, the best white meat from the breast of a sacrificed hen. All but Granny could see this bounty was in vain.

When the sun came out, Granny would pillow Grancher's chair, and carry her lightweight darling to the door. 'Is Mam's little wench feelin' better today?' On its thin stem of a neck the emaciated little face would nod brightly. Even when Elsie was too weak to pull the slipped shawl back round her own shoulders, Granny clung on to her desperate illusion of hope. Everyone around her waited with apprehension for the end. They did not have long to wait. Against Granny's heart, the little bundle of bones, convulsed with her last blood-flecked cough, gave up the struggle.

"'Twas terrible. We thought your Granny's reason was gone. 'Er sat that queer an' quiet, 'er might as well've been made out o' stone. 'Twas only days arter, when somebody said 'er reckoned the Almighty 'ad took Elsie to 'elp'n look arter all the little young uns they 'ad up there in 'eaven, 'er bein' such a good zart o' wench, that your Gran broke down and cried. Then we made 'er a nice cup o' 'ot tay, an' got 'er to yut a morsel o' vittles. But 'twere a long time before your Granny got herself right vut forrad agyun.'

Granny had never had the chance to learn to read or write, and she believed implicitly whatever she was told by religious Bible readers, whom she considered her betters by reason of their superior education.

But, education or no, in the year of the great drought she was generally credited with ending the water shortage. Rainless week had followed rainless week, and the spring that filled the well had died to a trickle. Women, children and men not at work queued for hours to fill a bucket.

Though by no means a finick about cleanliness, Granny did have her standards. Having turned her drawers inside out twice, in lieu of a change, she told Grancher that he must help her bring water from 'the splashes', as she *must* 'dab out a bit o' washin'. Going to 'the splashes' meant carrying a zinc bath half a mile, mostly down a very steep woodland slope, to a small valley stream that was still running.

Granny and Grancher struggled back up with the bath of water, seeking firm footholds, trying to hold the bath level, to take a rest, as there was no means of balancing it until they reached the top. Somehow they got home with most of the water in the bath, until they were negotiating the garden steps down to the cottage door. Right there, the handle came off Grancher's side, and every drop of water spilled out, mostly on Granny who was going down the steps first, and the rest over the tiny stone-flagged yard.

For a minute or two the shock of the cold water robbed Granny of the use of her tongue. Then, with a withering look skyward, she announced: 'If cleanliness be next to godliness, let 'Im see vit to send us down a drap more rain.'

During the night such an almighty thunderstorm blew up we thought the end of the world was coming. We hid our heads under the patchwork quilts, whilst torrents of rain found its way through every leaky cottage roof.

'I shall 'a' to be more polite 'ow I do ex fer things in the future,' said Granny.

Granny's voracious appetite for anything of interest that came her way made her as excited as any of us children when there was talk of a magic lantern show to be put on in the chapel. She always tried to find us a ha'penny, but not even her munificence could stretch to the tuppence each we needed as entrance fee to the magic lantern show. She suggested we might go and ask Mr Riley if he wanted some acorns picked up for his pigs. Mr Riley owned a fair-sized piece of ground by his cottage, and had turned it into a piggery. Letting the sows out to snuffle around for their own acorns was only possible if someone was there to see they didn't wander off.

Mr Riley supplied some big zinc buckets, and offered tuppence a bucketful. That year the oak trees had shed a poor crop, and it took a lot of scratching about in the sodden dead bracken and leaves to find the acorns. Oh dear, an acorn didn't go far to fill up the space in a bucket!

My sister had to have her eye on me all the time to keep me going. I was more interested in looking for the extra small and extra large acorn cups to make a doll's tea-set. Mam wasn't very pleased with me either, for the sodden leaf mould had soaked my boots, and rotted the uppers from the soles. With the bad economy of poverty, Mam had bought my nailed boots from 'Jacob's, the diddler'. He sold rock-bottom quality at rock-bottom prices. The thick 'leather' soles of my boots turned out to be compressed cardboard.

'Fat lot o'good,' Mam sniffed, 'spilin' sixpenn'orth o' shoe leather to earn tuppence.' We picked up five penn'orth altogether, and Granny made up the difference. Father mended my boots.

Come the great evening we were all set to go, Mam and the baby as well, but there was a bit of a hold-up with Granny's garters.

For everyday comfort Granny wore her stockings, slop-stocking fashion, rolled down round her ankles. Skirts were ankle-length, so it was no odds to anyone, but such informality could not do for chapel. 'Goo an' ex your mam if'er 'a' got a bit o' 'lastic or string or summat, fer I can't lay me 'ands on nuthin' to kip me stockings up wi'.'

Mam frantically rummaged about for something, but had to call out that she couldn't find a bit o' nothin', not even if she wanted to hang herself with it. Granny wasn't beaten. She pantomimed to one of us to sneak the laces out of Grancher's boots, as he sat, apparently asleep, by the fire. It was a fearsome delicate job, but we managed it.

Although we were early, the front seats in chapel were already filled, and soon the place was packed. A stage had been improvised for the magic lantern show, and between it and the audience the chapel dignitaries waited with an air of importance. The audience waited, too; and waited and waited. The sniffs and coughs grew louder, but we sat stoically on. We'd paid our money: we expected results. One or other of the dignitaries kept going to the door on a fruitless errand to see if anyone was coming. At length one of them had to announce there must have been some sort of hold-up, and the show would be late.

Granny left her seat, and went over to whisper something to the young man who played the chapel piano. The next thing, he was thumping out *Little Brown Jug* and Granny was up on the steps, singing a lively rendering of it and dancing a cross between a sailor's hornpipe and an Irish jig.

She clapped her hands to the rhythm, and beckoned the audience to join in. Her choice of song in this temple of teetotalism caused the dignitaries to get a bit red in the face, but the audience loved it, and sang at the tops of their voices. Grancher's bootlaces didn't hold up, but who cared? Other impromptu turns followed, and by then I'd caught the mood of the evening. My exhibitionist tendencies came to the boil. Bubbling up and down on my seat, I shouted out, 'I wanna sing a song, I wanna sing a song!' And someone came to lift me up on the stage. Mam tried to pull me back. 'You can't go up on that stage. They'll be able to see your britches, and they be the colour o' the turnpike road where you bin playing on the ashmix.'

She was too late; I was up there. Anyway, at five years old the state of my drawers meant nothing to me. I only knew two songs right through—*Twinkle Twinkle Little Star* and a lewd, comical ballad taught me by a fun-loving auntie. The innuendoes, Greek to me, were ripe and fruity. My auntie had shown me just the right moments to ogle my eyes, shake where my hips would grow, and stamp my feet. I stood up there and let them have it. It brought the house down. The audience stamped, clapped and hollered for more. They threw halfpennies, pennies, and even a silver three-penny bit on to the stage. Quick as a monkey, I scrabbled up the money and, holding out a fistful, shouted proudly to my mother: 'Look, Mam, we shan't 'a' to 'ide in the back-kitchen from the baker, Saturday. I got enough money to pay 'im.'

Poor minister! Worried by such goings on in the chapel, he feared the house really would come tumbling down about our blasphemous heads. So he tried to put things right by mounting the pulpit, and getting the audience singing some well-loved hymns.

The evening ended in a mellow glow. Nobody asked for their money back, so all felt virtuous for contributing to the chapel funds. An old neighbour about summed it up when she observed to Granny: 'Well, s'welp me gawd, Liz, I enjoyed meself that much I'd forgot what I went there var in the fust place!'

When Granny and Grancher moved to another village we seemed much poorer, although we were actually two shillings and fourpence a week better off—that was the rent Dad let her cottage for. It had belonged to Dad's father, and when Dad was twenty-one it became his. He married at twenty-one, and he and Mam lived with old Auntie; but Granny thought he should have his own cottage, and told him she would find somewhere else to live, although she was still struggling with great hardship to bring up his brood of stepsisters. Dad wouldn't hear of it. 'It be thy 'ouse, Mother. I shall never make no claim on't; and I don't want it mentioned again, nor you ever to feel beholden to me for it.'

Thirteen years later, by their own scrimping, and with a loan from their daughters in service, Granny and Grancher were able to put down the money on a tiny cottage a few miles from where she was born. It was situated on a hillside, with a panoramic view of the beautiful Wye valley. Every day, till the end of her long life, Granny would stand and gaze long and gratefully at her riches.

When my father was killed in the pit (that was when I was thirty) Grancher and Granny were in their late seventies; but it wasn't his age that kept Grancher away from the funeral.

'I shan't come. I couldn't stand to see that good booy put under the ground.'

It was a lot for Grancher to say all in one go.

The Doll

If the chapel treat was the highlight of our life in summer, Christmas was the pinnacle of our winter delight, though most of the joy was in the anticipation. Every year for many years I spent weeks getting excited about a hopeless dream. I wanted—oh how I wanted—a doll. I knew it was quite impossible for Mam and Dad to buy me one. I had no luck praying for one, and it wasn't any good asking Dad to put a word in for me in that quarter, because I'd heard him and his butties argue and come to the conclusion that there couldn't be a God, or at any rate not one who worried about us as individuals.

But Father Christmas was quite a likely benefactor, though he too had his limitations. *My* dad had explained to me that as Father Christmas was such an old man, with his long white beard, he couldn't be expected to carry big things for all the children. I should have to wait my turn for a doll. Meantime I must be satisfied with something small, like a penny box of beads, and an orange if I was lucky. My turn for a doll seemed a long time coming.

My patience ran out one autumn when I was nine years old. Gladys, my best friend, who already had a nice doll, was given the most fantastic doll you ever saw. I didn't begrudge Gladys anything—she let me nurse her doll, and dress and undress it. But that was like being a nanny, not the same as having your own baby. The new doll was the size of a child, had long hair, eyes that opened and shut, and wore socks and shoes. Gladys's dad had won it at Barton fair. The doll was much too grand to play with, and was put on display in their cottage. All the village children, and quite a few grown-ups, called at Gladys's home for the privilege of seeing it.

As far as I was concerned, matters regarding a doll had now come to a head. I couldn't help Father Christmas's decrepitude— he would *have* to bring me a doll this Christmas. I gave him plenty of warning by shouting my request up the chimney weeks in advance of the usual time. Towards Christmas I started to write notes to him as well, with a stub of pencil given me by a neighbour as payment for running errands.

I was puzzling out how best to put my case to him with the limited spelling and vocabulary of a nine-year-old, when Dad came in. I told him I was making a bargain with Father Christmas: providing he brought me a doll this time, he needn't bring me anything else ever. But it had to be a doll big enough to sit on my lap, and have hair, and eyes that opened and shut.

'I be a-feared 'tis no good thee exing Feyther Christmas for that sart o'doll, my wench. 'Im do only take that sart to the rich people's young uns,' Dad warned me kindly.

'You do want to tell the silly old bugger off then. Tell 'im they rich people can afford to buy dolls for their children. It's the likes o' we lot 'im do want to bring the best toys to. Why ever 'aven't 'im got more sense than that?'

Father, who usually had an explanation for everything under the sun, scratched his head and admitted himself 'proper flummoxed'.

Bess said I'd be lucky to get anything if Father Christmas overheard me calling him a silly old bugger. Just because she was gone thirteen years old, and would soon be going into domestic service, she fancied herself too grown-up to ask Father Christmas for anything. Anyway, then she would be rich enough to buy anything she wanted, for my auntie in Bristol was getting her a job with the fantastic wage of five shillings a week.

With hope only slightly diminished, I continued to shout my order up the chimney, and to send up my notes when the draught was strong enough to stop them falling back into the fire.

My little brother fell asleep on Christmas Eve long before I did. I kept poking him awake to keep me company, but it was no good. I must have been awake for hours, when I heard stealthy footsteps coming up the stairs. It must be Father Christmas! Should I look, or shouldn't I? I had the patchwork quilt pulled right up to my eyes—he wouldn't notice, if I just took a peep. I suddenly felt terrified.

It was a bit of an anticlimax when I saw my sister in the doorway! 'Oh gawd! I thought you was Feyther Christmas!' It seemed to me that she was hiding something behind her back.

'If thee doosn't go to sleep Feyther Christmas wunt come at all,' she scolded me.

'I can't,' I wailed, 'thee'lt 'a' to 'it I over the yud wi' the coal 'ammer.'

I banged my obstinate head into the bolster. 'Go to sleep, you silly little bitch,' I told myself crossly.

It was my excited little brother who poked *me* awake in the morning. 'Look—Feyther Christmas a' brought I a tin whistle, a orange, a bag o' marbles an' some sweets.'

I sat bolt upright, like a jack-in-the-box. My doll, my doll! Had Father Christmas brought my doll?

At the bottom of my piece of the bed was propped the ugliest apology for a doll one could ever hope not to see.

It looked for all the world like an old, darned, black woollen stocking, lumpily stuffed, with a bit of old ribbon tied tightly round the foot to form its head. The eyes were two odd-sized buttons, and it grimaced from ear to ear with a red woollen gash of a mouth.

After all that cajoling up the chimney, after all the notes I'd written, fancy him bringing me a thing like that! He must think me a horrible little girl to treat me so, but I couldn't be that horrible! Mam came in, looking a bit anxious, but she said, bright enough, 'Well then, Feyther Christmas didn't forget. 'Im did bring a doll for you.'

'Yes, an' 'im can 'ave the bugger back.'

Mother looked crestfallen. 'It won't break, like one o' they china dolls.'

'It's ugly, an' boss-eyed, an' got no 'air, and 'ow would you like it if the angels sent you a babby as ugly as *that*?'

Then I pulled the quilt over my head, to show I had cut myself off from the season of goodwill, and everyone concerned with it.

But Mam hadn't. After a bit she came back and sat on the bed. She didn't say anything, and my curiosity soon overcame me enough to have a peep at what she was up to.

Her baby boy, born a year after my little brother, had died; I thought he'd gone to heaven to be pampered and fussed over by the angels. Mam had kept a few of his baby clothes, though in general the women in our part of the village pooled their baby clothes to help each other out. Now she was dressing my doll up in a flannel nightdress, a bonnet and a piece of shawl. Held up in Mam's arms and cuddled against her neck, it looked like a real infant from the back. I was tempted to be won round. Mam left it, all snugly wrapped up, on the bed, while she went to get breakfast.

I and the doll were soon downstairs with the rest of the family, sitting at the table. Mam was in a specially good humour with me. We didn't have such things as bacon and eggs even on Christmas Day, but as a great treat old Auntie had given us half a tin of Nestlé's milk to share out on our toast. As if that were not enough, she'd given us each a shiny new penny as well. I felt warmed and loved again. I made a bit of sop in a saucer, with a drop of my tea and a bit of the bread and milk, and pretended to spoon it into my doll's mouth, before taking her out.

I knew that other children might laugh at her ugliness as they did at Lil Wills's poor little looney sister, so I decided to take her for a walk on my own. Miss Phillips, whose cottage garden adjoined ours, was just coming back from the ashmix with an empty bucket.

'My, my, Polly!' It looks as though Feyther Christmas 'a' brought you a real big doll this time. Let me 'ave a look at 'er.'

I loved the inside of Miss Phillips' neat, tidy cottage, but none of us were much taken with her—she nagged us for playing noisily, and wouldn't let us play ball where we wanted to. I gave her one of my ferocious scowls to put her off, but she insisted on following me and unwrapping the piece of shawl to see what I'd got.

'Oh my gawd, that'un 'ould do better to frighten the birds off the gyarden. I reckon Feyther Christmas musta took 'im from a crow's nest.'

How dare she? I bridled like an insulted mother! I doubled my scowl, and threw in my monkey face for good measure.

'Never mind,' I said to the doll, when we were out of earshot. ''Er's a nasty old bisom, and your mammy 'ouldn't change you for all the money in the world.'

Miss Phillips' insults cemented my feeling for my new charge. From then, she became the object of my affection.

I had taken squatter's rights of the narrow space between Dad's shed at the bottom of our garden, and the old stone wall of Miss Phillips' garden. Here I played whenever I could. Only my little brother, baby sister and my best friend, Gladys, were allowed to come in without special permission.

One hot, humid summer evening I was minding the two little ones down there, whilst Mam was doing some washing, when an ominous rumble growled across the sky, which had suddenly gone very dark. Almost simultaneously came a vivid flash of lightning that made my little brother jump. Mam had a morbid fear of thunderstorms: she screamed from the doorway for us to come indoors at once. I picked up my toddler sister and shouted at my brother to hurry; we got indoors just as the rain started to come down in a torrent. Mam took us to the coal hole under the stairs. Even here the tiny back window let in the lightning flashes, and the thunder seemed to be concentrating on knocking our cottage down.

Then I remembered! 'Me doll, me doll! I've left her down the bottom of the garden!'

Mother promised me she would be all right, and when the storm was over she would dry her out on the fender. The storm lasted past our bedtime, and though the rumbles got quieter and there weren't so many lightning flashes, Mam wouldn't let me put my nose outside the door.

She promised that Dad would fetch the doll in when he came home from his late shift at the pit. In the morning there was no doll on the fender when I got up. Mam had forgotten, but she ran down to get it before I could put my boots on. She came back with the disintegrating remains.

'Bain't no good you carrying on: it fell to pieces in me 'and.'

Despite a halfpenny and a few currants in a piece of paper, I was still sniffing back the tears when Gladys came to call for me.

'Never mind, Poll,' she said. 'We'll give her a lovely funeral. I'll go back 'ome and ask Mam if we can 'ave some flowers to put on the grave.'

She came back with a bunch of sweet-williams and an old straw hat. ''Ere, you be the chief mourner, you can wear this.'

We decided to hold the funeral in private. My little brother would probably only cry, and there was no one else worthy of the honour of attending. Gladys spoke a long sermon, then walked round the grave three times chanting, 'Ashes to ashes, dust to dust, if Gawd won't 'ave her, the devil must.' Then she put a handful of earth on the remains, and we filled up the grave and put the flowers in a jam jar on the top.

'O' course the devil *won't* 'ave 'er,' said Gladys.

It was nice of her to say that, but I never had a doubt where my beloved doll would go.

1926

No matter how crowded, it was a rare cottage where the occupants did not squeeze up to find room for the cripple, the simpleton, or even the 'bad penny', seeking the solace of companionship round somebody else's fireside.

When it was time to die, the good doctor had to let ill alone. As long as old Foresters could crawl to the chair by the fireside, they did so—poking the fire to life not just for the warmth and comfort, but to see their young days dance again in the flames. When the time came to give up the ghost, they prayed to do it in their own beds. They dreaded being taken to the workhouse—a brick and mortar reality—more than they dreaded the thought of the hell fire they had only heard of.

I once went to visit a dying old man, taken in mercy to the hospital from his neglected hovel of a cottage. Still alive, after the shock of an all-over bath, a pedicure, a manicure, and a fresh white bed-shirt, he lay between snowy sheets in the warm comfort of the bright ward, waited on by kindly starched nurses, but I could read the desperate message in his eyes before he struggled to gasp out the words, 'Please take I wum to die!'

Unless they slipped away without warning, there was never a shortage of sitters for the vigil hours of dying. When it was a child, hands were wrung, tears coursed down cheeks, and the sighs were strong enough to bear the little dead spirit to its rest without a wind from Heaven.

Poor Tilly Toomey was forced to bed a fortnight before the end. Despite a rota of bedtime sittings from her neighbours, there were times when Tom, her husband, had to take a turn. Tom Toomey had never been reckoned a patient sort of man.

'I bin a good wife to thee, ain't I, Tom?'

'Aye, that thee 'ast, Till.'

'I brought up thee young 'uns the Lord spared us as best I could, didn't I, Tom?'

'Aye, aye, my wench, thee didst.'

'I allus tried to 'ave zom vittles o' zom zart on the table when thee'st come wum from pit, didn't I, Tom?'

'Yus, yus, thee didst.'

'An' I allus tried to 'ave a clane shirt putt by for thee for funerals, didn't I, Tom? There's one in the top drawer, ironed ready, but thee must air'n a bit to wear for I.'

'Aye, aye, all right, 'oman.'

'An' I tried not to oversalt the bacon when I cured the pigs, didn't I, Tom?'

'Aye, aye, that's all right enuff, Till—but do stop thee frettin' about they things now. Thee save thee strength to get on wi' thee dyin'!'

Unless it was a matter of life and death the doctor was not called to our house—we were ages behind with the quarterly five shillings he charged for his services. In dire necessity a shilling or two would be scraped up from somewhere to get him to call, and he never let anyone down, God bless him.

Mostly our Dad cured us with his home-made potions. He gathered elderflower, yarrow, camomile, and other wild herbs, dried them and stored them in brown paper bags for his bitter brews. Constipation, coughs, colic, sickness, diarrhoea, sores, fever, delirium—whatever we had, out came the dreaded brown jug, and on the hob it went with its infusion of herbs. No matter how ill I was feeling, I used to feel I would rather die than drink that brown liquid horror. Death was at least an unknown quantity: the taste of Dad's herb tea was not. Vicious as a polecat, I would screw myself up into the wooden armchair and battle would begin. Dad rounded up his helpers—Granny from next door, Mrs Skinner from the other side, Mam, and old Great-Aunt Lizzie, who was too crippled to do much except her share of the scolding. A clothes peg was fixed on my nose.

'Now 'er'll 'a' to open 'er chops,' said Dad. 'You 'old 'er arm Mrs Skinner. You, mother, 'old t'other. I'll 'old 'er yud still, and when she do open 'er chops to breathe, you get a good dose down 'er gullet. If we can get it down 'er, and 'er to bed for a good sweat, 'er'll be right as ninepence in a day or two.'

Desperation gave me superhuman strength. Somehow I would twist my head aside just as Granny was about to pour. Eventually some of it would find its target, but what Granny could get down, I could bring back up.

'Well!' gasped Mrs Skinner, 'I don't know about getting '*er* in a sweat. It's brought us lot out in one!' She mopped her forehead with a corner of her sack apron. 'They do say it's good 'uns the Lord do take first, so I don't see why we be bothering to drench that varmint.'

I was put to bed in disgrace, but Mam made me some toast tea. We were sometimes lucky enough to get an orange at Christmas, but lemons were a luxury we never saw. For feverish sore throats Mam toasted a piece of bread to near blackness, put it in a jug and then poured boiling water over it. When cool, this rather acrid drink was strangely refreshing to a parched throat.

All of this happened in its usual sequence when I was twelve and got scarlet fever. By the time the rash erupted and they guessed what was wrong with me, I was very ill and the doctor had to be sent for. Dad borrowed Mr Skinner's bike to help to do the two-mile journey quicker. On the way back, he made a long detour to the little town; then, before the doctor arrived, came rushing breathless up the stairs. From his pocket he pulled a thin oblong parcel wrapped in brown paper, unwrapped it, and showed me something I'd coveted without hope for years—a box of water-colours.

'There,' he said. 'Thee'll be able to paint to thee 'eart's content when thee'st do get back wum from thic hospital. See—Dad'll hide the box behind this picture so no one'll know about it. Now you hurry up an' get better, an' back home quick, for your old dad.'

I was sent to the Cottage Isolation Hospital, where I nearly died. But seven weeks later I tottered up our garden path on spindly, emaciated legs, 'a sorry sight for sore eyes', as Mrs Skinner put it.

My convalescence was not helped by the fact that the men were out on strike again—it was nineteen twenty-six. The strike was really a desperate cry for the status of manhood—to be able to do a full week's work in the pit, to be paid enough to fill the bellies of their families. The women stood four-square behind their struggling husbands, the older children sensed it would have been better if they hadn't been born, and apologised by being quiet and undemanding.

Some city people, mostly working-class and sympathetic to the miners' cause, offered to take miners' children into their homes to ease the burden for a while. One day two ladies came to our cottage and said one of us could go. As I was still terribly thin, it was decided to send me in a party going to London.

Mam was a dab hand at cadging anything that was going for her family, but she spoke no more than the truth when she told them I had nothing fit to wear to go in. From the pile of shoes and clothes collected by charity, they found me a dress and a pair of black boots. Both were brand-new! Alas! the boots were too narrow for my feet, broadened by wearing well-worn left-offs. A quart may not go into a pint pot, but my feet had to go into those boots. The cotton lock-knit dress was a narrow, shapeless tube in a hideous design like grey-black snakeskin. Luckily my tight boots only enabled me to mince along, so I couldn't come a cropper by taking a full stride in it. A neighbour contributed a hat. It had been a good one in its time, a brown velvet with a wide brim lined with green velvet. Someone had cut most of the brim off, and left a shaggy edge to prove it. The crown was on the big side—I had to wrinkle my forehead up to raise it for vision. Mrs Skinner, in a fit of generosity, gave me her cardigan. Mam cut off the frayed cuffs and hemmed them, and darned the holes. The shoulder seams came down to my elbows, and it reached long enough down to hide a lot of the dress. Nevertheless, a cardigan was considered a very modish item.

In full regalia, on the morning of my departure, I felt I was dressed to kill. It helped me to bear the torture of walking a mile in those boots. Mam came with me to where the party of children would board the char-à-banc for the journey to the station. The other twenty-four children had already arrived when we got there. The two ladies who were to be in charge of us for the journey to Paddington exchanged a meaning look when they saw me, and seeing the rest of the children, mostly little girls, I guessed why. My self-satisfaction ebbed away fast. They all seemed remarkably clean, and by our standards, dressed up to the nines. Some of them had little cases or cardboard boxes. Like aristocrats, almost imperceptibly, they left a little space each side of me in the char-à-banc.

I didn't care very much. I just withdrew into the delightful daydreams my imagination had conjured up for the outcome of the journey. I thought chiefly about my favourite page in my favourite comic, *The Rainbow*, which was about 'The Two Pickles', a curly-haired brother and sister who lived in a lovely house. They had a pet dog, Fluff; their father seemed to have plenty of money; their mother never got irritable like our Mam. Reading about the Pickles' mummy, I forgot that our Mam worked and worried over us all day, never had a new rag to her back, never went out for her own pleasure, and did her best against terrible odds. I took all she did for granted, but I noticed she wasn't often gentle and soft-tongued. I'd made up my mind that the lady who was going to have me in London was just like the Pickles' mummy.

My self-centred imagination pictured a house like theirs but without any Pickles—I was going to have her all to myself. She would buy me a pink silk dress, white shoes and socks, and call me 'darling' and 'dear'. We should eat off a proper table-cloth with lace round it, and have liver every day for dinner, and fancy slab cake for tea. Her husband would always have a pocketful of change, from which I would have frequent pennies for sweets. I dwelt so much on these fantasies that I came to believe in them. God knows my rose-coloured glasses had been knocked off enough times, but I never learned. Anyway, the fact that I was going to London was enough to make me believe in fairies.

London was the centre of the universe. Kings and scoundrels had hallowed her pavements with their tread. In the classroom London had seemed a world away. I'd never expected to go there in all my life. I knew I would feel a more important human being when I did.

It was a great surprise to find out how big England was: the train from Gloucester seemed to be going on for ever. One of the girls, called Florence, asked the lady escort in our carriage if perhaps the train had gone through London and forgotten to stop. By the way the lady laughed it appeared Florence had made a fool of herself. She didn't feel herself so much above me then, and began to talk to me. She was very tidy, but extremely plain—a droopy sort of girl, chinless, round-shouldered and very thin.

When we got to Paddington I couldn't see it. Like an insect to a man's hand, I couldn't recognise the whole object because of its size. The little bewildered tribe of us were shepherded into a sort of cattle pen. Outside it waited a lot of people, our prospective hosts. One by one the children were led out as people decided

which of them to take into their homes. As the numbers thinned
we huddled in the middle. Soon only two were left: Florence and
me. 'O God, don't let me be last!' I prayed.

After a pause, Florence was taken out. But it seemed that the
stomach of charity was not strong enough to take me. I hung my
head in shame. I was not only unwanted, I was a nuisance. To
make it worse, I couldn't hold back my tears. I wiped them away
quickly with the sleeve of my cardigan. As I stood there alone, a
thin young man with a very kind face and manner hurried up to
me. 'Come on, kiddie,' he said, 'I know where we've got a nice
home for you. Are you hungry?'

I shook my head: I'd never felt so full up.

Off we went. He took me to a large building in Westminster.
On the way we passed Westminster Abbey. 'You must come and
see it inside,' he said kindly. 'You may never have the chance
again.' We went in, and I sensed his appreciation of its wonders by
the way he gazed about. But I was too ignorant, and too worried
about his problem of getting rid of me, to make the most of my
chance.

I think the building we went to must have been Transport
House. He took me up some stairs, and told me to sit in one of
the big fat chairs in the most luxurious room I'd ever seen. It had
huge windows. I looked out at the traffic, trying to regain my sense
of reality. 'Shan't be long,' the young man promised, and went
away, leaving the door open.

Presently a young lady walked by, and looked inside—looked
again, harder—then came back with a couple more. Gradually a
small crowd of people was hanging around the doorway. Some of
the girls clucked their sympathy at the sight of me; some could
hardly stifle their laughter. One kindly girl put a banana in my
hand, another followed with a piece of chocolate. One came up
with a bag of peanuts, while another tied a wide blue ribbon round
my neck in a bow. They were well on the way to making a proper
monkey out of me, but scuttled away guiltily when the young man
came back and gave them an angry look.

'We've a nice home for you to go to in Kent,' he said, trying in
his goodness of heart to give the impression I was someone special
instead of something scorned; but he didn't fool me. I felt very
tired, and I thought Kent was at Land's End and a further journey

away than the one I'd already done. My big ideas about this adventure hung like a penance on my spirits. Just as well if I slipped off the edge when I get to Land's End, I thought.

We went to a railway station and into a restaurant, very palatial with potted palms and snowy table-cloths. We sat down, and he ordered himself a cup of coffee, and for me a glass of milk, a ham sandwich, an apple and a bun. He seemed quite at home in such magnificent surroundings. I was glad he took a newspaper out of his pocket to read, for I didn't feel at all at home. The ham sandwich was delicious; so was the milk. Four plates I thought— one for each item! I'd never seen an apple served on a plate before; the knife beside it seemed quite superfluous. I ate the apple, peel, core and all, of course; the bit of stalk took some chewing, but I felt it would have been rude to leave it on the shiny white plate. I couldn't manage the bun; but I was sure the young man would be hungry before we got to Kent, so I put it in my cardigan pocket for him.

Presently he peeped from behind his paper and saw that I'd finished, so we went out to get on our train. The journey was over in no time. We were now in a place called Plumstead, he told me. He stepped out briskly. I hobbled along, trying not to hinder him; but my feet had swollen so badly inside the tight boots that walking was agony.

At last he stopped and knocked on the door of one of a long row of identical houses. A plump woman with a kind face opened it. 'I've brought you the miner's child you asked for,' he told her.

Her face fell at the sight of me. 'Oh dear! you've brought a girl. It was a boy we asked for. It's a bit difficult with the accommodation, you see.'

Perhaps it was the combination of my hangdog look at this response and the supplication in the young man's face that made her say, 'Oh well, now you're here you may as well stay. We'll manage somehow.'

A fervent 'Thank you' from my escort, and he was off like a shot before she changed her mind. I don't blame him. And God bless him, wherever he is.

My hosts, Mr and Mrs Couch, had two daughters and a son aged eleven, seven and thirteen. They were working-class people of very modest means. Mr Couch had a job at the Woolwich

Arsenal. Their budget must have been stretched very thin to let me in, but these warm-hearted people made me feel the luxury of being welcome.

When bedtime came that first evening, Mrs Couch washed my feet, now bleeding and blistered from the tight boots. Her kind concern soothed my bruised spirits as much as the Zam Buk ointment soothed my feet.

I stayed with them for five months, and during that time other kindly people gave me clothes. The local children treated me as a novelty, but in the nicest possible way. It was a strange new world of bricks and pavements, of the luxury of going, for a penny, to the public baths for a weekly hairwash and bath, tasting new exotic foods like Yorkshire pudding and stewed prunes, and waiting with excited apprehension for the gas stove's pop when the tap was turned off under the kettle. It was a happy and interesting interlude.

When I got back home, plump, well-dressed, with a brand-new accent, my family marvelled at the change. It soon wore off, of course, and so did the accent and some of the extra weight, but it was a long time before I ceased to revel in the joy of being back—back home with my very own family and friends, back at school which I loved, and back in my beloved Forest again.

A Death

Now I was back at school in Miss Hale's class, every day was a fresh delight. In the dreaded sewing lessons Miss Hale put me to paint pictures for the classroom wall—I had a little talent for drawing and painting. Tidily dressed, I even earned some respect from the boys. But it didn't last long.

Our Mam had been taken ill with something in her leg which swelled up angry red and shiny. The doctor ordered her into the new cottage hospital, recently built in the Forest, about three miles away. My sister left her job in service, and she now ran the household, with what little help she could cajole or bully out of undomesticated me.

Before breakfast I walked a quarter-mile to get two buckets of water from the well. Then we had tea, and I needed no persuasion to take a cup into our beloved old Great-Aunt Lizzie before I went to school.

One morning she seemed very tired as I tried to wake her for her tea. I slipped my arm round her shoulders to ease her up on her pillows. How well I knew every furrow of her dry parchment cheek, and stale-sweet fusty smell of her unwashed old age.

'Come on, Auntie. I'll be late for school.'

With great effort she opened her eyes. 'Ta, my little wench—I'll drink it later. I be so tired.'

I kissed her, shouted to Bess that Auntie would want another cup later, as she was too tired, and ran out to school.

On my way home at dinner-time I called in at the grocer's, on Bess's instructions, to get a loaf. I had to ask for it on tick. This always made me squirm inside, using my ingratiating, begging-for-credit manner. Once I was outside with the loaf achieved, I skipped for joy. Now I had the lovely long walk home in the dappled sunlight that filtered on to the woodland path through the great oak branches.

In a clearing, a little further on, a tall plateau of slag from a disused mine tempted me to run up it, among the golden gorse bushes that bloomed on its grey bulk. A rustle in the branches of a nearby oak made me look up to see a red squirrel, bushy tail fanned out behind him, nibbling at something between his paws. I wished he could come down and talk to me.

I forgot the time—a habit that frequently got me into trouble—and so trouble was what I expected when I saw Bess hurrying towards me. I ran to meet her, holding up the bread as a plea for mercy. Her face was tear-smudged, and her eyes red from crying. 'You'll have to go back to the shop and ask for some tay and sugar. Old Auntie's dead, and we'll have to have some in the house,' she sobbed.

She couldn't be! The thought that Auntie could never feel sunshine or shade, see colour, or hear sound again, was not to be borne. I judged death by my own standards, and didn't reason that Auntie rarely moved from the fire, and took ages to turn her dry old bones just to look through the window. We children had, for years, brought the world into her on the end of our prattling tongues; and the seasons' offerings, to put into jam jars of water, for her to bury her old nose in and say, 'My, they be purty flowers, and smell so scenty.'

Of late, I'd sat, quiet as a mouse, keeping her company when her mind wandered. She saw, and talked to, people from the past that were all round her, but invisible to me. When they were gone, she would feel lonely if there were nobody real in the room. We made up most of her world, and she was a dear and integral part of ours. She cherished and protected us in babyhood and early years, and as we grew older we cherished her.

'Go on,' said Bess, 'you'll have to get some tay an' sugar. It wun't be respectful to 'er if we can't put a cup of tay when they do come to see 'er laid out.'

I turned back, wrestling with this first attempt to understand death. Asking for tea and sugar on tick now seemed unimportant. Only when Mr White, the shopkeeper, vehemently shook his head, did I burst out crying. Auntie must not be disgraced! When I could speak through my sobbing, I told Mr White what had happened.

Life is full of surprises. 'That's different,' he said. 'I respected that old lady. She never asked for one penny of credit, not like *some* I could mention. If everyone was like her, only spent what they could afford, life would be better for the likes of me. Here, take this tay and sugar out of my respect. I shan't put it on the bill.'

When I got home, Mrs Protheroe and an old lady we knew as Granny James was there. Mrs Protheroe, efficient, kindly and helpful, had washed Auntie and dressed her in her laying-out clothes. Granny James had picked the finest flowers from her garden. She was now throwing out ingratiating hints for a keepsake, eyeing, with a covetous glance, one of the few good pieces of Auntie's china we children hadn't broken. Granny James's cottage was a regular magpie's nest of china and pretty nick-nacks, mostly garnered on the excuse of 'something to remember the dear departed by'.

They'd brought out Auntie's bits of food. The sight of her sugar-basin, partly used-up tin of Nestlé's milk, and half-eaten small loaf, and the thought that now she would never eat them were so poignant, I felt desperate and lost. For the first time I couldn't run to Dad to put the world to rights. But he was there. He'd come home from early shift at the pit a few minutes after Auntie had died. Still in his pit clothes, he sat staring into space.

'Don't thee fret thyself, my boy,' said Mrs Protheroe. ''Er went as peaceful as a lamb, dear old soul. 'Er's in a better place now; of that I be sure.'

But her words couldn't reach him. I knelt down by him, waiting. At long last two tears—the first I'd ever seen on his face—rolled down his pit-blackened cheeks.

After the death of a villager, a service was held in their memory at the chapel, three Sundays later. I was surprised to see Dad getting himself as clean and tidy as possible to attend the service for Auntie. He never went to chapel, and indeed held the opinion that in general organised religion was the opium dealt out to the masses by the cynical few, to obtain for themselves their own heaven on this earth.

Father was my truth. Father was my yardstick to measure the world by. How could he go to chapel for something he didn't believe in?

''Tis a okard question, my wench. But you see, though thy old Auntie died, 'er be still living in people's minds—people who do think different than we. 'Tis to please them that did respect and love Auntie in their way that I be a-goin' to chapel.'

I don't remember thinking about death before Great-Aunt Lizzie died, and I was equally incurious about birth—retarded, you might say. If I *had* any curiosity about it, I expect it was

damped by the taboo nature of the subject. Up to the age of
elevent or twelve, waist to knees was unmentionable; later than
that, it was neck to knees.

It was no wonder, really, that working-class mothers put the
poison in for Nature where their daughters were concerned. After
all, they were obliged to send them out into the world at the age of
fourteen, with their bodies unprotected except by fear of men and
God. And despite all the evidence Nature provides for the country
child, it never occurred to me, or other children that I knew, to
connect the two sexes with having babies.

When my sister came home on holiday from service at sixteen
years old, she was charged with the delicate task of filling in this
gap in my knowledge. I was then twelve.

Poor Mam got it in the neck from me, then. She was completely
puzzled why I refused to speak to her, or even to Dad if I could
help it. I cried most of the time and was sullen and dejected. She
thought I was outgrowing my strength, and got me some iron
medicine.

But before this, when I was ten years old, and my little sister
was born, it did occur to me to wonder where the nurses *got* the
babies to bring to the cottages. Sometimes it wasn't even a nurse,
but only Mrs Protheroe, so she must have been in the secret,
too. It was obviously something they kept to themselves. After
pondering about it for days, the 'truth' suddenly hit me on the way
home from school.

In my excitement, I forgot my task of collecting kindling from
under the trees to light tomorrow's fire. Instead I sneaked in with
an armful of old cabbage stumps that Mrs Skinner had thrown out
on the ashmix, and these I thrust into the oven in the side of
our old-fashioned range to dry. Mrs Skinner had come into our
cottage for a 'quat and a chat', and to coo over the new baby, lying
in Mam's lap by the fire.

'I do know where babbies come from, Mam,' I announced
proudly.

Mam's face reddened. She began to poke the fire, and go into a
fit of coughing. 'Go an' fetch the little 'uns indoors,' she gasped.
But I was not to be put off from my moment of glory.

'Let me tell you first where babbies do come from,' and I stood
my ground inside the door. 'Well,' I explained, indicating a large
flat surface with my hand, 'there's the sky,' then indicating a lower

surface, 'and there's the earth. Well, you see, the angels do come to the edge of the sky wi' the babbies an' 'and 'em down over to the nurses at the edge o' the world.'

I knew babies came from Heaven, for they were all 'little angels' when they arrived at the breast, although as soon as they could walk they became 'reg'lar little devils', 'aggravatin' tarments', and 'dirty little toe-rags'.

But before the women could comment on my theory, an acrid smell of burnt cabbage issued from the oven. 'You lazy little slummock, you,' shouted Mam.

Handing the baby to Mrs Skinner, she pulled the stumps out of the oven and whacked them with much vigour but poor aim at my flying figure—down the garden path, over the gate, and out into the forest for some proper kindling wood.

I felt it was very poor thanks for such valuable information; but perhaps Mam was upset that I had shown up her ignorance about babies in front of Mrs Skinner.

Scandal

Folk in our village were short of most things, but sex at least was a luxury not denied them, though someone is reputed to have said, 'It's too good for the poor.'

In spite of the care taken by the mothers of the village to instil virtue in their daughters, sometimes, now and again, a problem child would grow in our midst. Such a one was Lollie Blackman. In summer Lollie's main occupation was looking for lovers coupling in the tall green bracken. More than once she'd been chased for her intrusion by a furious, trouserless swain. Mothers threatened their children with good hidings if they went further than the garden gate to play with her; but I had no idea at the time why Lollie was so black-listed.

Although her own mother naturally saw her in a more kindly light, even she was glad to pack her off to service when she was thirteen. It was then generally forecast that Lollie would soon be home again with her belly full of more than good food. This didn't happen as soon as expected, but promising news reached us through her mother after very few weeks that Lollie had left her place in Cheltenham and gone to London.

She was rather a swarthy girl, with straight black hair, heavy black eyebrows, and sallow skin. A couple of years later, when she came home again, she had frizzy, buttercup-yellow hair, a pink-and-white complexion that must have taken a half-pound of make-up to achieve, her own eyebrows replaced by two thin, pencilled arches high on her forehead, and butterflies painted on the calves of her legs. Other, more natural, eyebrows were to shoot up much higher than Lollie's from the surprises she had in store for them.

Chapel was the last place anyone expected Lollie to turn up, but she did. She had decided 'to open our cake-'oles' with a preview of the outfits purloined from a string of mistresses. You could indeed have put a baker's basket of buns in the open mouths of the congregation as she swept in wearing a pale lilac chiffon tea-gown, with wide wing sleeves that reached the floor.

Slowly she undulated up to a seat in the front. Wafts of perfume stronger than high-church incense filled the tiny chapel. The preacher might just as well have gone home. He was an old-fashioned, ranting, Bible puncher. Usually the congregation thought the halfpenny they put in the collection well spent watching him 'work hisself into sic a lather 'e could have shaved his whiskers off wi' the froth on 'em'. But this Sunday he didn't get a look in.

'Pity thee'st warrn't at chapel today. Thee'st missed seeing Madam Butterfly,' a neighbour said to our Mam. The women regarded Lollie as a big joke, but they were soon laughing on the other side of their faces when their husbands began disappearing.

'I dunno where Tom be got to. 'Im went out to feed the pig a hour agoo, an' I an't see nothin' on 'im since.'

'Must be along o' my Ern, for 'im a' cleared off somewhere too.'

'And our 'Arry! I been a-waiting for 'im to vetch I a buckut o' wayter from the well this last half-hour.'

'That's funny. Ben offered to goo an' get I a bit o' kindlin' wood, an' I should think 'im's a-waiting for the tree to grow.'

'They be up in the wood, sat down, a-watching Lollie Blackman take 'er clothes off,' piped up a young bystander.

The wives moved off as one woman towards the wood, but they didn't creep up quietly enough. All they saw was the scuttling movements through the tall dense green bracken.

''Ere, I 'a' got thee a nice bundle o' vire wood,' said one of the men sheepishly to his wife a bit later.

'Oh, thee 'ast, 'ast thee? Well 'ere's a bit o' stick from me to go with it!' And his infuriated spouse whacked a piece of it across his buttocks.

Next day she was gossiping in a neighbour's cottage and the neighbour said, ''Asn't thee better pop up wum to see what they mon be up to? 'Im might be up in the wood again to see Lollie Blackman.'

'No fear. I 'ticed the varmint upstayers meself afore I come out, an' I've tied un to the bedpost.'

All the women now kept an eagle eye on their husbands' movements. 'I cawn't even go to crap wi'out exing 'er permission,' grumbled one of the poor wretches. Men left the use of the little bucket privies in the gardens for the women and children, themselves going out to the woods for their own calls of nature, to the 'manhole', as it was called—a large natural hollow where they kept an old spade.

Lollie didn't come home again for a long time. It was quite a sensation when a detective came to ask her mother for Lollie's address. He drew a genuine blank, for though Lollie often sent her Mam a parcel or a few shillings, she put no address in.

Then one fine day she just managed to stagger up the hill to her Mam's cottage in time to get into bed and give birth to a beautiful half-caste baby boy. During his birth Lollie entertained everybody within earshot with her opinions of men and of nature's method of reproduction, in words that would have raised a navvy's eyebrows. The advent of this little dark stranger brought a touch of cosmopolitan sophistication to our village. After a few weeks Lollie was off again, leaving the baby behind. Her mother's delight in this piccaninny grandchild must have added years to her life-span. As to the rest of us, the whole village doted on this little novelty of a child and made a regular mascot of him.

Lollie was an exception. The standard of morals among the village girls was very high. It was a rare thing for one of them to come home from service in trouble. If she did, she was forgiven. One more younger child had to sleep at the bottom of the bed to make room for her return, and the family food was shared out a little thinner.

Poor Sukie was a different kind of exception. She never got into service. She lived alone with her widowed mother, who kept her porter ale in the teapot, and kept having swigs 'o' cold tay'—no one was fooled by this.

Sukie's father had died in the asylum soon after she was born. Some reckoned his brain had been turned by sheer aggravation when his wife, in middle age, gave birth to yet another girl. They'd already had a brood of daughters, who'd all gone into service, or died, or married away from home.

Sukie went to school, but there was too much of a draught between her earholes for her to learn anything. She had a desk in the corner of the back row and slept through all the lessons, except when a pupil was ordered to prod her awake to stop her snoring. She attended school till she was twelve. After that she spent most of her time wandering about in the woods, sort of singing to herself. When she was hungry she gathered up a bundle of kindling wood and took it to someone's door. If they hadn't got a bit of bread or a cold potato to spare they might pull her a carrot or turnip from the garden.

Taking pity on her, the elderly widowed landlady of the village pub gave her a shilling a week and a daily meal to do some cleaning and scrubbing each day. Some days Sukie started down the hill and forgot where she was going, but someone was sure to notice and start her off down the right track again.

Alas, in the course of time Sukie began to emerge from her forest wanderings with her drawers in her hand.

'Come 'ere you silly wench,' the women would scold her gently, taking her into their back-kitchens to put the drawers on again. They put no evil construction to this habit of hers, until her obvious condition proclaimed it.

'Dirty, low-down skunk, whomever 'im is,' they said in disgust.

'If I could ketch un, I'd casterate the bugger wi' a red 'ot poker,' threatened her mother.

But none of the village men was in danger of being recognised as the child's father—it was such a poor, wizened little creature, it didn't look like anyone.

Sukie hadn't the sense, her mother was too fuddled with porter ale, and they lived too near starvation, to give the extra coddling such a poor starter needed. He just lay and cried weakly. Mam let me go and see him, because I liked simple Sukie a lot. I thought he looked much more like a monkey than the new babies brought to our house, but I was very upset when I heard he'd died. Mam told me Mrs Protheroe had brought him, not a nurse, so I gave that good lady a piece of my mind for taking him to poor Sukie instead of to our house where Mam would have looked after him properly.

After two more babies, the village matrons decided that Sukie was a moral danger. They had her put away in an Institution in Bristol. With no woods to wander in and with nobody to care whether she had her drawers on or not, poor Sukie soon pined away and died.

Before long two other misguided characters moved into the lime-light of our little stage. 'A bright pair o' beauties they two be!' the respectable housewives sniffed. I didn't consider Tilly Pudge and Minnie Meadows bright or beautiful, but they were a friendly, relaxed pair, always ready to pour a cup of tea for anyone who dropped in. Mind you, it didn't pay to accept if you were the fastidious sort. A dirty cup would be taken from a cluttered table, swilled out with a suggestion of water from the kettle on the hob, and wiped with the corner of a dirty sack apron. If there was any condensed milk left in the tin under its hovering flies, you got a bit, scraped out with a spoon that had probably been licked by the cat and a mongrel dog and a variety of bare-bottomed toddlers.

Minnie and Tilly lived in adjoining cottages, but were always in each other's places. With them, housework was an afterthought rather than a habit. They were too friendly by nature to be disliked, but were often gossiped about by more efficient house-wives. At ten years old or so, I found the gossip enthralling but largely meaningless.

'I don't think as they've washed their curtains or rubbed a rag over their winders since they got married.'

'Just as well, if you ask me. I for one wouldn't want to see what goes on in *their* places.'

'I don't know why their old men puts up wi' such a pair of good-for-nothin's.'

(So far so good for 'Big-Ears', but then would come the sort of thing that continually baffled me in grown-up conversation.)

'Doosn't thee worry. They be good for *summat* and that's all some men do think about.'

'Judging by the looks o' their two men, thee bist right there: both on 'em be like skinned rabbits, thin enough to pull dru 'ole in a colander.'

'I've 'eard they be so mad at it, they do get down in broad daylight, 'avin it on the mat in front o' the vire.' Came a time when the 'two beauties' took a great fancy for going into the forest for kindling wood, a job that normally fell to the children's lot.

'Don't tell me they two 'ould bother to frizz their 'air, wash their vit, and put on a clane pinny just to vetch a bit o' virewood.'

'It's sticks they be arter all right, but not 'ooden ones. Mark my words, they'll be coming back one day wi' more than they bargained for, and serve 'em right, I'd say.'

'What say we go for a bit o' wood in the same direction and see what we canst ferret out?'

One night I woke suddenly in the small hours to hear Mam trying to rouse Dad—'Wake up, wake up, you great cooten! I can hear a woman screamin' as though 'er's bein' murdered!'

I heard Dad bundling down the stairs as fast as he could go, moving clumsily in his half-asleep state. I didn't let Mam know that 'Big-Ears' was awake, but lay still as a mouse beside my little brother and sister, who slept soundly on. It wasn't long before I heard Dad come quietly back upstairs.

'*Was* it somebody bein' murdered?' said Mam.

'It might be a couple o' murders before the night's out, but I 'ouldn't lift a finger to stop it if it were.'

''Twas that pair o' beauties then, I'll warrant,' said Mam.

'Aye, thee bist right there, Mother.' I heard the iron bedstead groan as he got back into bed. 'Seems that their two men got wind o' their antics and instead o' goin' on to the late shift, they doubled back quiet in the wood and watched to see what they two 'ussies got up to. Sure enough, when the kids were asleep, them two sneaked out to get up to no good wi' a couple of men in the ferns. I reckon by the time Micah and Absy a' finished wi' their hides tonight they'll be too sore to lay about wi' anybody for a long time to come, an' serve 'em right.'

I couldn't make head nor tail of this rigmarole. Whatever was it the two beauties were out in the wood for instead of being nice and warm in bed? And why was Dad, the kindest-hearted man in the world, so nasty about them? The illogical behaviour of grown-ups was too puzzling to be worth worrying over. I snuggled down against my little brother's warm back and went to sleep.

Going to Granny's

It was a Sunday, it was a lovely day, my brother and I both had tidy boots to our feet; and Mam's fine row of summer cabbages had all turned into firm big-headed specimens at the same time, with one among them a regular king.

'I'll tell you what, if you two'll be good young 'uns and weed they couple o' rows o' onions for me, you shall take a cabbage over to Granny and Grancher's, after dinner.'

Granny had been gone for many months, and we still missed her badly; but Mam drove a hard bargain. Weeding the garden was always a horrible job, but weeding onions was the horriblest. The weeds were so many, and the onion spikes were so like the spikes of the grass around them that had to be pulled out. But we had been over to Granny's before, so we decided it was worth it. 'Now mind where you be puttin' your feet,' warned Mam, and left us to it.

Now and again the gentle breeze wafted to us the smell of our Sunday meat cooking, promise of delight to come, with cabbage and taters.

We eyed the gooseberries still left on the bush for Mam to make a couple more tarts with, but decided they were too well placed in view of the window to risk a foray. 'Stick at it,' said Mam; coming up to empty a bucket of slops between the rows of taters.

'Stick at it,' I mimicked, softly, in disgust. Time went so slowly weeding onions. The birds in the trees seemed luckier and freer than we. They just swooped across the blue ceiling of the sky, with no one ordering *them* about!

Then it happened. A bee, perhaps overladen with pollen, paused to rest on my head. It got in a panic when it lost its foothold in my hair, and turned me into a jack-in-the-box sort of lunatic with its frustrated buzzing. I was sure to be stung, and I feared that out of all proportion to the pain it would cause. Rushing blindly about, screaming and beating myself about the head, I danced over the garden, not caring where I was putting my feet.

By the time Mam, Dad, and our neighbours had rushed down

the garden to my aid, I had been brought to a halt. With my eyes shut for terror of the bee, I had run into the rope swing Dad had fixed up for us at the bottom of the garden. Stretched to its full length, it had brought me staggering back, caught in a rough rope noose. The bee had stopped buzzing.

'Doosn't worry, 'im's died,' said Dad, picking its remains carefully out of my hair.

''Er might 'ave 'ung 'erself on thic swing,' said Mam worriedly.

''Twas wuth a tanner to see 'er a-caperin' about; better'n they monkeys in the zoo any day,' laughed one of the neighbours.

'Yes, and our Mam can get a bloody monkey to weed 'er onions, as I shan't do 'em agyun,' I sniffed.

Although it was Sunday, which made my language doubly sinful, I got away with it. I was excused as being in a state of shock. Our neighbour brought in her jar of goose-grease for Mam to rub some in my sore neck. This, with the effect of a plate of Sunday dinner, quite cured it.

'Rub your shoes over, and wash your hands and faces, whilst I go and cut the cabbage,' ordered Mam. Out of the garden she came, with the biggest, finest specimen from the row.

As well as generosity, there was an element of show-off in the gesture. Mam and Grancher had been keen gardening rivals. Who could dig the first feed of new potatoes had been the main competition between them. Grancher was an old hand at the game, and he knew a dodge or two; Mam was green-fingered with a deep, inborn love for growing things.

The narrow, paved yard, running the length of our two cottages, was divided by a four-foot wall. Access to each doorway was by a narrow garden path that circumvented it. As far as I can remember, Grancher never crossed this demarcation line to see what Mam got up to in her garden. But she wasn't above looking round *his* garden for horticultural hints, after she had popped into Granny's for a bit of a squawk.

Come February, whilst Grancher was at work, Mam followed the horses, a shovel under her arm, and a bucket in each hand. She wheeled in barrow loads of leaf mould from the forest, and when we had a pig, the cleanings from her cot were like treasure trove to Mam.

The first day there was no frost in the ground, she would dig a trench, and fill the bottom with her rich compost, then a bit of earth, and then the potatoes, before covering them down with a lovingly patted top layer of earth.

''Tis the smell of all that muck they taters can't stand. That's why they do push up so quick, to get a breath o' fresh air,' was Father's diagnosis of their remarkably early germination.

If it looked like a frost, Mam covered them with twigs and bits of dried fern till the danger had passed. When Mam knew she had a good start, she would call across the garden to Grancher, in all innocence like, to ask him how his taters were comin' on. Grancher never gave her more than a grunt and a shrug, but they were enough for Mam to read the signs.

Come about Whitsun time, and Grancher would come to the wall, clear his throat loudly, and put a sample of his first diggings on the top. Out Mam would go and give fulsome praise to such an achievement, knowing that Grancher, apparently standing indifferent in his yard, was smirking with self-satisfaction.

'I 'aven't tried mine yet. I'll 'ave a dig at one later on,' Mam would say. We had seen her, gently, oh so gently, scraping away the soil under the haulm, and burrowing with her fingers to feel the size of hers. She would wait until he came out into next door's yard again, then put *her* offering on the wall. Grancher couldn't resist having a look. If Mam's were smaller he would grunt quite kindly over them; if they were bigger, he spat into the corner of his yard, and stumped up the steps to his garden.

'I'll bet Grancher 'ant got a cabbage like this in 'is gyarden, but don't you two tell'n I said so.'

As the crow flies it was about a mile and a half to Granny's. For us, up hill and down dale, it was nearer two and a half. Mam watched us from the gate until we started down the steep wooded hill that took us from her view. Negotiating the wavy little footpath at such an angle, carrying a big cabbage, proved a bit awkward. I decided it was big enough to make its own way with a rolling start from me. It kept leaving the path to get lodged in the ferns, or against the trunk of a tree. It looked a bit battered by the time it got to the bottom. Never mind, I stripped off the broken outside leaves, and left them as manna from heaven and a nice change of diet, for the insects teeming busily among the leaf mould.

It was lovely down in the narrow valley, watching the little stream we called 'the splashes', where Granny and Grancher had fetched the water. It bubbled clear and gently over the pebbles.

On down, a bit out of our way, was a place where watercress grew. Should we get some for Granny? Yes, it would be a good idea, because afterwards we could take our boots off to wipe away the mud with some fern. Then if we had our boots off, we might as well take off our socks and paddle our feet in the water.

We didn't manage to get any watercress, but we got mud inside and outside our boots. 'My vit do veel all squelchy,' I said, as we started up the hill the other side.

'An' mine do,' said my brother.

'Never mind, our Mam wun't know, they'll be dry by the time we do get wum.' Coming through the leafy branches, the hot sun made ever-changing, lacy patterns on our bodies.

'Phew, I be as 'ot as a fresh 'osses turd. I be a-goin' to zit down,' and my brother, suiting action to words, chose a spot where a swirl of dead leaves had made a soft place among the fern at the side of the path. I was feeling a bit hot and bothered myself, handicapped as I was by the cabbage which seemed to be getting more heavy and awkward with every step.

'It's your turn to 'ave a go carrying the cabbage,' I told him tartly.

'Ben't my job to carry'n; you be the biggest, an' our Mam give 'im you to look arter, not me.'

'Snakes do live in dead leaves. You do want to watch out, you might get bit to dyuth lyin' there.'

A bit of danger, real or imaginary, *did* add some spice to life. We carried on to the top of the hill a bit quicker after that. Once on the flat, we soon found a good shady place to rest; on a carpet of moss big enough to stretch out on. This place, we reckoned, was half-way to Granny's.

'We shouldn't lie 'ere, really. This moss is fairy ground, by right.'

My brother took little notice of this; he wouldn't admit to believing in fairies. I wasn't quite wholly convinced myself, but I was always looking for signs of the little folk in the woods. A bit of self-persuasion, and a lot of imagination, helped.

After all, there were all those fairy tales, and pictures of fairies, in the books at school. Perhaps if we lay very quiet and pretended to be asleep, some fairies might come to look at us, like the Lilliputians did in *Gulliver's Travels*. After a few minutes, I felt something on my hand; was it a fairy? No, a careful peep only revealed a ladybird; perhaps the fairies had sent her to see what we were. They'd never come out now, with two giants about.

'Come on!' I poked my brother sharply in the ribs; he really was asleep!

It wasn't much further to walk to the edge of that piece of the Forest.

Now the really adventurous part of the walk lay before us; a big stretch of rough grassland, with a cottage dotted here and there. Here, ferocious dogs might come bounding out to snarl, and threaten attack on the two strangers.

If the cantankerous old gander spotted us, he would bring his flock of wives to hiss warnings at us from the end of their out-stretched necks. There was also an old black-and-white billy goat; true, he was tethered, but more than likely he would break his tether just as we passed him, and chase us. There might also be a couple of children about, bigger than us; you could never be sure if they belonged to a friendly tribe. Luckily, there were mostly grown-ups about too; busy in the gardens, or just standing looking at the work to be done. In a last resort, these could be yelled to for help.

We emerged from our ordeal with nothing worse than slightly faster beating hearts, and some kindly nods from an old man leaning over a gate. Down over the bank, and we were on the main road, and only a few minutes from Granny's place.

The main road went steeply downward in a horseshoe bend to meet another road which led to the River Wye. We did not have to go many yards down the road before we took the little path leading to Grancher's garden gate. A steep bank sloped from the main road to the back of the cottage, which stood, snug from the worst of the winds, on a narrow plateau. It was fronted by a garden terraced with little dry-stone walls to stop it slipping down altogether into the sharp incline below.

The level ground extended to the gate, and to a bit of garden to the left of it. Here Grancher was busy, to our surprise, among a patch of flowers. We expected no enthusiastic welcome from Grancher, and were certainly not prepared to be beckoned over, and asked to tell: 'What d'ye think o' they, then?'

We had no words to express what we 'thought o' they'. 'They' were about twenty different species of dahlias, and each seemed incomparably beautiful until you looked at the next. Grancher's rough hands, embedded with pit dirt scars, knotty and gnarled with work, made a perfect foil for their loveliness as he cupped each bloom to show them to us.

Which was the best, the modest pale salmon one, blushing pinkly at her petal tips, or that purple majesty, the size of a tea-plate? Soft yellows, mauves and pinks, brilliant reds, proud as a rich sultan in his harem, Grancher showed off his beauties; and his hands trembled with the ecstasy of it all.

'Oh, Grancher! They be the best flowers I've ever seen!' And so they seemed.

We decided we would give the cabbage straight to Granny. Just then she came to the door. 'Hello, me butties, is Grancher showin' you 'is dailies, then? What a lovely day you've 'ad to come over! Just see the river from 'ere. There! What d'ye think o' that? Ben't it a beautiful sight? All they fields and trees, and ups and downs, for miles and miles.'

It truly was a fantastic sight, but wasted on two hungry little morons, who were much more excited by the view of the plate of fancy cakes on the table.

Even before she had moved from next door to us, Granny had sometimes been wealthy enough to buy off the baker seven fancy cakes for sixpence for Sunday tea. Like the dahlias they were all special, but there was one extra special, the cream slice, and that presented problems.

With the mad generosity of grown-ups, Granny always offered the plate of cakes to visitors first. In the case of my brother and me, it would be to the one who had finished their bread and jam first. Granny always gave us two pieces of bread and jam, and even offered us a third.

The bread and jam was delicious with a cup of hot, sweet tea. It was too good to gollop down, yet we had to keep a wary eye on each other. We sought a fine balance—to get full enjoyment out of the bread and jam, yet to finish it just in time to claim the cream slice. This particular Sunday the angels themselves seemed to be keeping a special watch over us. There were *two* cream slices on the plate.

When tea was over, Grancher turned his chair to the fireplace, cut himself a cud of his black twist tobacco, and picked up the *News of the World*. Grancher could read, and Granny could not, but when they were on their own, with a bit of cajoling from

Granny, he would read her some of the juicy scandals. I expect Grancher could write as well, but I do not remember seeing him ever put a pen to paper. Correspondence was a problem for Granny. Whatever the contents of a letter she had to get it second-hand.

Perhaps the great highlights of their lives as they grew older were the occasional letters they received from America. Pride and heartache overwhelmed them when they talked of 'Our Olive'. Olive, the eldest daughter, had married a young man of property, and they had gone to America to seek their fortune. The young husband had gone over first, to find work, and somewhere to live. Their first baby, Nella, was six weeks old, when, two months later, Grancher escorted Olive and her baby to Portsmouth, so that she could sail to join her husband.

Not only Grancher, but anyone of any age who could read, was roped in to read Olive's letters for Granny, until she knew them all off by heart. A second daughter was born to Olive, and, as they grew, photographs of them were sent home.

'To think,' Granny would marvel, 'that we 'ave got two little American wenches for granddaughters! But, oh, I'd give me right arm jest to 'ave 'em sit on me lap for vive minutes. P'r'aps one day we will see 'em, f'r our Olive's husband be doin' well out there, an' when they can afford it, our Olive's goin' to come back to see us.'

Granny and Grancher kept this hope even to their deathbeds, but Olive never managed the journey home.

We had eaten our tea, we had viewed the landscape, we had admired Grancher's dahlias, and we would have liked to stay on. But Mam had told us not to be late, and it was time to go.

Granny told us to thank Mam for the cabbage, and gave us each a kiss and a piece of paper containing a bull's-eye and a clove sweet. Feeling very content, we pointed our noses towards home.

When we reached the main road we had a little conference. Should we retrace our steps the way we had come, or seek new adventures by going the long way home, all round the road? The possibility of seeing a horse-and-cart, some strange faces, perhaps even a car, decided us to go round by the road for a change.

Before long we had cause to be pleased with our decision, a chance to gaze over the hedge and take a long look at Liza Ward's donkey. This animal had a small claim to fame. His mistress ran a one-woman hire service with this donkey and a cart. To advertise her services, she had taken part in a carnival, dressing up the donkey's legs in two pairs of her open-legged calico drawers, with frills round the bottoms. To add to its ladylike appearance Liza had tied a wide ribbon round its neck, and trimmed the straw hat through which its ears poked, with a band of red roses.

A few derided her for 'makin' a numbskull out of a poor dumb animal', but most of the spectators thoroughly enjoyed the joke, and business boomed for Liza. We moved on a bit quick when Liza herself came out of her cottage.

We passed a few stragglers out for a Sunday walk, but did not see one horse-and-cart, let alone a car!

The ferocious animals that might have escaped from a zoo, and were lurking behind each cottage to pounce on us, never materialised. Still, we had a nice cool dabble in the horse's trough beside the road near Mirey Stock. Being Sunday, we could not watch the slag-filled carts crossing the bridge from Waterloo pit to the slag heap.

But look, danger *was* at hand! In a little clearing among the trees on our left, some gypsies had made a camp. Gypsy women were all right, when they came, laden with babies, to sell clothes pegs at the door, when Mam or Dad were about. But gypsy *men*, with their dark skins, squatting round a fire, whittling at sticks with shining sharp knives, they were a different breed altogether! Gypsies stole children, and sold them in faraway places; if they got hungry enough, they would even make a stew of you, and give your clothes to their children to wear! This was more adventure than we had bargained for. With fear to stoke our engines, we ran like the clappers to the other side of the road, and along the grass verge until our very breath gave out. Rather to our surprise, the gypsies had ignored us.

Now they were behind us, and the first houses of our village were in sight. The welcoming sight of Mam coming out to look for us gave us the energy to hurry up to her. We took our places, one each side of her skirts. She clucked at us like a broody hen in a coop away from her chicks, when they run too far from her feathers.

Though I loved our visits to Granny's, it would have been even nicer if she had still lived next door. She was that rare thing, an ally for ourselves among the grown-ups. We missed the extra refuge of her cottage. This loss was brought home to me most powerfully one Saturday in late November.

'Just my luck,' said Mam resignedly, 'your feyther's got a good wage this wik, so 'is boots 'ad to goo an' bust open agyun. They be past 'im bodgin' up any more an' I might as well try an' get a pair for you as well, for your'n ben't much better. It's a nice day so I'll take the little'uns wi' me. Now mind you do as I say whilst I be gone. Get they forks and knives clean till I can see my face in 'em. Kip a good fire goin', an' put some taters in the oven for supper when we've bin gone about an hour.'

'I'll mind the babby,' I offered. Mam loved her children, and on reflection, felt her youngest offspring would be safer with her, than left to the tender but absent-minded and inefficient care of a Peter Pan sort of daughter, who was old enough to have, but was sadly lacking in, 'a bit o' 'omanhood'. Bess was by now away from home, in service, and besides, there was no old auntie to keep an eye on things.

I didn't press the offer; I had exciting prospects in store.

Also I realised it might be a bit of a ploy on Mam's part, to take three small children. The town tradesmen could not afford to be sentimental, but the wistful eyes of children would sometimes get a bit extra dabbed on the scales.

Mam was only a little woman, and the big plaid Welsh shawl her mother had given her nearly enveloped her as well as the baby. She carried the baby in it, Welsh fashion, after the manner of the gypsies who carried their babies as they brought pegs to the door to sell. I think the warm body of a child must act as a recharging battery to the mother's body. Women seem to be able to carry children for distances long after one would expect them to drop from fatigue.

I felt a small sense of guilt, watching the little convoy go down the garden path. It was soon dispelled by the thought of the book, which I knew father had 'hidden' on the top shelf near the fireplace.

For once I had the house, the fire, and a book to read, all to myself!

I spread some newspapers on the table, tipped the contents of the kitchen drawer on to it, got the brickdust and rags from the back-kitchen, and gave our odd assortment of cutlery an enthusiastic, if not very thorough, rubbing over. I banked up the fire; lumps in the front, small at the back; then I stood up on a chair to reach down the book.

Very little printed matter that came into our house was censored from us, but obviously Dad had considered *Coffin Island and Other Stories* by Edgar Allan Poe, a little macabre for young readers. It had been printed like a thick magazine, with a lurid cover illustration of a skeleton hanging from a dead tree, near a church, on a moonlit night; and lurking in the shadows were weird, ghoulish creatures.

A bit scary, but nothing to worry about, with the lovely autumn sunshine streaming in through the window, and a cheerful fire to sit by. Not time to put the potatoes in the oven yet.

Feeling as lucky as a cat shut up in a dairy, I pulled my chair up to the fire, rested my feet on the steel fender, and plunged into my feast of horror.

Very soon I was both repelled and fascinated. I feared to go on reading, yet dared not stop. Even the dancing flames of the fire could bring no cheer to the black mood of every page, although they brought enough for my young eyes to read by. What kind of mind could the author of this horror have possessed? The warm entrails of a fresh-killed corpse could have been his inkwell.

Only when the flames began to flicker down, did I notice that the daylight had quietly gone. The window was no longer a frame for the sunlit garden and distant trees; it now framed the black mourning of the night.

Outside the reach of the fire the little room had grown dark. Fool, greedy fool! So anxious to settle down with my book, I had not had the forethought to bring the lamp in from the back-kitchen, to put a spare bucker of coal by the hearth in readiness for making up the fire. Nor had I fetched the potatoes from the box in the back-kitchen to go in the oven.

And now I couldn't! Not only Poe's murderers and corpses were gathering in our little dark back-kitchen, but all the witches and ogres from my own mind's store had joined them. They might even now be coming behind my chair, waiting to pounce; to put their claw-like talons round my throat.

Mam, Mam, hurry home Mam, before the flame from the fire dies down, and I am left in the black pit of darkness, and they can carry me away! If only Granny had not moved from next door, or the young couple who had taken the cottage had not gone out for the evening!

Somehow I must find the courage to lift the poker from the fender and break the last bits of black coal into more flames, but take care not to turn my head or take my eyes from the printed page to acknowledge 'them', who I could now sense were in the darkening corners.

In those days damp courses were uncommon, and our cottages were breeding grounds for cockroaches. Though, perodically, Mam attacked every crack and crevice with Keating's powder, Jeyes' fluid, and boiling soda water, she could not stay the infestation of these pests.

They never emerged in daylight, or by lamplight, and never came up to the bedrooms. But when the family were in bed, and all was dark, out they came, to forage up the walls, in the rag mats, and even across the clothes line on the ceiling. We children hated them, and would never come downstairs in the dark, unless Mam or Dad preceded us with a lighted candle. Mam made her wallpaper paste with a flour mix. Now as the cockroaches looked for sustenance, their movements made faint crackles behind the paper. Only, to me, it wasn't cockroaches; it was the stiff black cloaks of fearsome witches brushing against the wall.

All the time, the glow of the fire went down until there was barely enough to read by. Concentrating on the page was less horrific than allowing my mind to dwell on the lurking horrors, crowding now right up round my chair. The draught from under the back-kitchen door came straight from graves freshly opened by fiendish vandals; I could almost smell the bodies.

Old Auntie's corpse had been laid out in the little narrow room adjoining. Now her spirit knew all about my wicked sins. Now she knew how I had crouched down on the mat by the fire, slyly waiting to steal the remainder of the sodden chewed crust from my little brother's hand, while he lay asleep on her lap. Now she knew that I had dipped my finger in her sugar basin. All my bad deeds came to the surface of my memory. Perhaps old Auntie didn't love me any more, now that immortality had opened her eyes to my sins.

I dared not raise my eyes, for old Auntie's ghost would not lurk behind the chair, or in the corner. No, she would come white and wraithlike, and scold me with a forbidding skeletal finger, to my face.

The fire was almost out. Only Mam could save me now, and it seemed that Mam would never come. Never? Wasn't that the creak of the garden gate? Wasn't that sound the sound of voices? The dear, familiar tones of Mam and the little ones? Yet not till Mam's hand closed on the doorknob to enter, did I find the courage to move.

Dispirited by the high price of boots, tired out, with aching arms and painful varicosed legs, hungry, her patience tired by the weary whimpering of the little ones, Mam's misery flared into righteous anger, as I scurried to light the lamp and fill the coal bucket.

The dead fire, the oven empty of the warm, roast potatoes she had used to encourage the little ones as they soldiered on through the woods, the selfish thoughtlessness of a daughter old enough to know better—all this should have got me the sort of hiding I deserved, if Mam had found the strength to give it me.

But she was almost in tears. 'Whatever 'ave you bin doin'?' she wailed. Mam never read a book herself. Her own life was too full of conflicts and troubles, work and excitement. It was no use trying to explain. Abject with guilt, I now tried to help her.

'I'll tell you what you can do, you lazy hussy, you can go up to Joe Meek's an' ex'n to let me 'ave a shillin's worth o' meat. Tell'n I'll pay'n for it next Friday wi'out fail. Thanks to buying you some boots, which you don't deserve, as well as some for your feyther, there wasn't a penny left for any meat for tomorrow's dinner.'

The relief at being safe, and secure in Mam's unimaginative presence, receded sickeningly at the thought of this new threat. All the horrible fiends that had fled at Mam's homecoming would be waiting out there in the dark; darkness now made even more sinister by the shadows thrown by the light of the emerging moon.

With a boldness brought on by terror, I begged that my little brother should go with me. Such a heartless request, on top of my other shortcomings, nearly made Mam explode. 'Wasn't 'is poor little legs nearly droppin' off, as 'twas, from 'elpin' to carry 'ome my boots, and vittles for the likes o' me, too idle to get off my arse to keep a bit o' fire goin', let alone put a tater in the oven for their hungry bellies?' Shame on me!

Ashamed I was. I had no case to plead for mercy, no grounds to give Mam some defiant cheek to try and dodge the errand. Her righteous wrath, my normal cowardice, and a spur from my conscience sent me out into the night, a poor match for the intrigues of Poe's imagination.

My throat was tight with terror by the time I had reached the garden gate. I decided to walk down the middle of the rough cobbled path that surrounded the village. If I kept too near the dry-stone garden walls, God knows what weird-faced apparitions might pop up over them. If I walked too near the ditched bank bordering the forest, I might be within arm's reach of the monsters and ogres hiding behind the trees.

I mustn't break into a run, even if my trembling legs could manage it; *that* would be acknowledging the retinue of evil spirits dogging my footsteps, waiting to pounce. Where, oh where was I going to get the courage not to run past the chapel?

There it was, half-way down the hill, a black sinister shape against the moonlit sky; just as on the cover of the book. Even the tree was there, a nearby oak, leafless and dying, its branches turned into creaking talons, from which hung the skeletons I knew would be visible when I got near enough.

It was such a long way to the next cottage gate, all of a hundred yards. Carry on, feet, one in front of the other; eyes, don't look to left or right—cows can see each side as well as in front—oh! I'm glad I'm not a cow. I've passed the chapel, I'm still safe, now if I can keep on to the bottom of the village, I shall hear the blessed sounds of men's voices in the pub, and see the light in Mr Meek's window, the first one up the main road, and my destination.

Mr Meek's family had grown up. He still worked in the pit, ran some sheep in the forest, and was a spare-time butcher, as well as doing a bit of local preaching. It needed a Christian spirit to be a butcher in our village; there couldn't have been much profit in it!

Now I was hoping he would be a very kind man, and let Mam have a shilling's worth of meat.

Fear must have lent me a pale and tragic air. Mrs Meek won him round to letting me have some bits of meat wrapped up in newspaper, in no time at all. I was sorry to step outside their warm little lamplit kitchen. Now I had again to run the gamut of terror.

I had the pleasure of knowing Mam would be relieved and pleased that I had got something for our Sunday dinner on tick. But I wished it had been a lump of cheese, or a bag of taters; anything but meat—meat was dead flesh—dead flesh came off corpses. The soft, newspaper-wrapped bundle felt obscene and revolting under my arm; just the bait to bring the evil spirits, witches, and ogres crowding back on to my trail. Why, tonight of all nights, was there not a singular, solitary soul about to keep me company? It was more terrifying than ever to pass the ghostly chapel again as I went up the hill. Better to risk the long arms of the forest ogres, than the ghost of Poe's skeleton, hanging from the dead tree, creaking eerily in a light night breeze.

Don't look right; don't look left; just look straight ahead, at the little square of diffused lamplight coming through the paper blind at Mrs Protheroe's window.

Walk in the rain-formed ditch near the bank; this was the furthest I dare get from the chapel without getting too near the trees. It was a night shelter for an old ewe, which got up in lumbering fashion and broke the quiet with its loud peeved baaing, and sent me sprawling into the ditch, parting me from the parcel of meat under my arm.

Perhaps I would have died of fright there, had Mrs Protheroe not come out of her cottage just then, with a lighted lantern, to make sure her fowls were shut in. The well-known, shadowy figure, and the little bobbing light were a beacon that gave me the whimpering courage to retrieve my parcel, the paper now broken in places so that I must touch the raw, dead flesh.

Quietly sobbing with relief, I found the strength in my rubbery legs to hurry up the hill whilst Mrs Protheroe was still about. She listened at my plaintive approach, and, holding up her lantern to see me by, enquired kindly: 'Be that you, Polly my wench—what's the matter?'

'I fell over a sheep; I didn't know what it was,' I sniffed. 'The meat's come all undone,' I added forlornly.

'Come on in a minute, and I'll see to it for you.'

Inside, in the sparsely furnished, spotlessly clean little living-room, a bright fire burned in a shining grate. By it sat Goggy, snow-white hankie in his misshapen hand, catching the fluid from his chronically watering eyes, as he read one of his favourite books by Jack London.

He turned the book over, to give me his kind attention. Mrs Protheroe rewrapped the meat in clean paper, and then asked Goggy if he would take the lantern, and escort me to our garden gate. She had sensed how scared I was. Without demur, Goggy got up from the fire, and we went. On his tender malformed feet, it was slow progress, but what did that matter? Goggy could talk of shoes and ships and sealing-wax, of cabbages and kings; and he asked me how I was getting on at school.

To this damsel in distress he was indeed a knight in shining armour.

'Good night, Poll,' he said kindly, holding the lantern at arm's length to light me part-way down the garden path.

'Good night, Gog, and thanks a lot,' I called back.

Only a few yards more of dark gardens, and I was indoors again; into the cosy lamplit room, with a fire that Mam had magically coaxed into a cheery blaze. 'I got a bit o' meat,' I said, proud to have redeemed myself a little.

I could tell Mam was mollified, though her tone was still a bit sharp, as she bade me sit on the corner of the steel fender and have a good warm. We'd all have to wait for our suppers as, thanks to me, the taters were still hard in the oven. However, she spread us all a piece of bread to be going on with.

Like a soldier home from the wars, I had no grumble. I was so happy to be back, safe and sound, in the tiny fortress ruled by Mam.

Party's Over

In families like ours, there were only three important birthdays in your youth; the one marking your arrival into the world; the fifth, which meant you could go to school and leave a bit more room under mother's feet; and the fourteenth. This birthday meant, for a daughter, that she was old enough to get her feet under someone else's table; in the case of a son, that he could follow his father down the pit, thereby lessening a little the wrinkles in his mam's purse, but adding a few more to her brow from worrying about his safety. For girls, going into service was our only future. There was no employment for us in the village, and leaving home at fourteen was common to us all.

We didn't expect folk outside the family to be interested in birthdays. Top-form teachers, and especially ones like Miss Hale, were an exception. Every year, a batch of young faces above the wooden desks were replaced with new ones. Often the back of a departing child would bring an involuntary sigh, no doubt in some cases, a sigh of relief.

One playtime, a few days before my fourteenth birthday, Miss Hale kept me in the classroom. She wanted to know if I had one special chum. I had two, Gladys and Dolly. Gentle, even-tempered Gladys, with whom I never quarrelled, and Dolly, more my own sort, peppered with flaws, with whom I frequently fell out of friendship and back in again. I had just made up after a row with Dolly, so her name tripped out first on my tongue.

'Well, what I would like you to do,' said Miss Hale, 'is to ask your parents' permission if you can come home with me next Tuesday. It will mean getting back fairly late; but tell them I'll be in charge of you and see you get home all right. Tell your mothers to dress you up in your best bibs and tuckers.'

It was a mystifying request, but I would have done anything for Miss Hale. Every time I thought of it, I overflowed with pride and conceit, because she had let me paint brilliant scarlet poppies on some black satin cushion-covers for her home. She had brought the oil paints to school for me to do it in drawing-class. Miss Hale was a wonderful painter, and I knew she could have done the poppies much better herself. Besides, she gave me the remainder of the paints to take home for myself, *and* some brushes.

Father said that sort of paint was expensive. He sat down one evening, and had a go with me trying to paint a picture. His was so much better than mine, that I told him he should have painted the poppies for Miss Hale.

Mam was very impressed by the invitation, and determined by any means in her power that I should go tidy to school that day. She let me wear her treasured white silk blouse, given her by one of my aunties in service; and, if some of the rest of my plumes were borrowed, at least I went to school decked out in fine feathers on my fourteenth birthday. Dolly's mam had done much the same for her.

Our school had a small, railed, concrete play-yard for the infant classes. The rest of the school ran loose in break-times, to play on a dirt area hardened by pupils' boots; and on a small, natural greensward which reached to the forest's edge. But there was no hopscotch, leap-frog, skipping, or tag, for Dolly and me that day. Social butterflies must not get grubby.

When school was over, we stayed behind with Miss Hale, until an unfamiliar quiet enveloped the cluster of grey stone buildings. It was a two-mile walk to the house to which Miss Hale had recently moved. No doubt Dolly, as well as I, was hoping for the honour of carrying her case.

Neither of us got it. A car, a real *car*, with a man driving it, came up to the school gates. It was as big a surprise to us as the pumpkin coach was to Cinderella.

Showing no surprise, Miss Hale ushered us out of school, and into the two back seats. Dolly and I were too overwhelmed even to whisper our amazement. We just widened our eyes and nudged each other. The two miles were gone in no time. We stepped down from our seats with more than a touch of grandeur, then stood back politely while Miss Hale had a few words with the driver.

After our cottages, Miss Hale's house seemed of palatial size; it was of red brick, and looked nearly brand-new. Inside, all seemed very grand. We had a wash in a little sink with a tap and a small pink towel, so clean and pretty we wondered whether to use it or wipe our hands on the legs of our drawers. Unlike the bucket privies we were used to at home and at school, Miss Hale's house had a water lavatory with a chain to pull.

When we were ready, Miss Hale took us into the dining-room. Our eyes nearly popped out of our heads at the sight of the table. It was more like a picture than reality. Only a few spaces of white lace cloth showed between the pretty, flowered plates and sparkling glass dishes, filled with an assortment of tinned fruit, jelly, and blancmange. There was ham, brown *and* white bread-and-butter, a pink-iced cake, and even fancy iced biscuits. Our mouths watered, yet it seemed wrong to destroy, by eating, such a work of art as that tea-table.

'Come on, girls, pull yourselves up to the table; you must both be hungry by now.'

I had always regarded Miss Hale as a very special lady, but even I did not realise how near to the style of a queen she lived. She rang a little bell, and almost at once the maid came in with the tea. I knew the maid, although she was a few years older than I, and came from another village. Had I met her on a woodland path, I would have said ''ullo, Jean' to her, bold as brass. But here, in Miss Hale's house, and seeing her all dressed up in a black dress, with a little lace apron, I didn't have the nerve.

Of course, Miss Hale was quite friendly and easy-going with her, and told her to bring in a jug of boiling water to put in the teapot for a second cup. Mam had told me to be careful to mind my manners, which to me meant eating as little as possible, and that very daintily, but Miss Hale just kept putting stuff on our plates in a manner that showed we were expected to eat it up, and who disobeys a school-teacher?

Everything tasted so delectable there wasn't much of a problem with leftovers. In lieu of social polish, our appreciative appetites served as grace and thank you to our hostess.

In response to Miss Hale's bell, Jean came in, and cleared the table. Then Miss Hale fixed up what she told us was a ping-pong net across it. She gave us a little white ball, and a small round wooden bat each, and tried to show us how to play table-tennis. At first, much to our dismay, we sent the ball flying against the walls and ceiling. We were improving, and happily absorbed trying to master the skill needed for some nimble scoring, when Miss Hale told us the car was waiting to take us all to the pictures. The pictures! What a rich layer-cake sort of evening we were having!

But this evening, there was no walk through the woods. It was an occasion, a state arrival, in a motor car: stately seats, too, the dearest in the house, in the front of the balcony, at one-and-six a go.

The picture was called *Ben Hur*, one of the great silent classics. The hero, Ramon Novarro, was unbelievably handsome. So, as far as our immature experience allowed, we ran, with him, the gamut of his sufferings and achievements. We wept for the cruelly treated galley-slaves in the great Roman Navy ships; we held our breath for the famous chariot race; we sat in awed reverence, as the hand of Christ passed over the face of the old harridan, transforming her back to innocent beauty. Billions of Hollywood dollars had been poured into this melting-pot of hokum, and Dolly and I made the most of the feast it provided.

When the show was over, and the lights came on, it was difficult to readjust; I did not feel myself at all. Miss Hale asked us if we had enjoyed ourselves. 'It was wonderful Miss,' we gulped, still husky from our weeping.

'Good night, miss, and thank you, miss,' we chorused when Miss Hale left us at her gate, while we were driven on to the village.

After exchanging good-nights with the driver, we walked up the rough track to our garden gate. Our stomachs were still happily digesting all the luscious food, and our minds were full of Ben Hur. Or, rather, mine, and, I suspected, Dolly's were full of Ramon Novarro. I had fallen in love with him, so it would be silly to find out if Dolly was laying claim to him as well. We both held our counsel; it was not the time or place to fight about whom he belonged to just then.

Accompanied as I was by the spirit of that brave, noble charioteer, I was sure there would be no witches or such-like hanging about behind the hedges or down the garden path tonight.

Mam and Dad were sitting by the fire, waiting to hear all about our visit to Miss Hale's. My tongue now ran on nineteen to the dozen about the wonders of the evening; the car rides, the lovely house, the food, the ping-pong game, the pictures.

'Well,' exclaimed Mam, 'all I can say is that Miss Hale's a thorough good 'oman to go to all that trouble and expense just for you, and because it's your birthday!'

Just for me! It had all been for my benefit! As I began to realise this was indeed so, it seemed the most wonderful surprise of it all.

On my very last day at school, I said goodbye to Miss Hale, and took a long look round at the familiar classroom, waiting until the school doors were locked behind me. All the rest of the children had gone when I walked slowly home through the Forest, a solitary mourner for my schooldays. The bony finger of poverty was pushing me out into an alien world, away from the little corner I knew and the family I loved.

Yet, since I had no choice about leaving, at least I was determined to be mistress of my own fate. I had heard about domestic service in Bristol or Cheltenham from older girls in the village. *I* was going to go to London.

A few weeks before my birthday, I'd answered an advertisement in the *Daily Herald* for 'a general maid fond of children'. I'd got the job, no doubt because of the very flattering testimonial supplied by Miss Hale. The address sounded very grand—a hundred and fourteen Mildmay Park Road, Stoke Newington. The people's name was Fox.

Mam was very concerned that I should be aware of my own status. 'You'll be a young 'oman,' she said, 'now you be goin' into service, and you'll 'ave to start bein' called by your proper name, Winifred. That's what you was baptised and registered by, not the paltry name of Polly your Dad give you.'

I did not want to be a young 'oman, a Winifred, I just wanted to stay a Polly. But I could not do that, so what did it matter what I was called? I promised Mam I would let my employers call me by my proper name.

Mam didn't get too alarmed about my going to London, as I had an auntie working in Westminster as a cook, and one of Dad's butties from the pit had told Mam in all seriousness that if I was to walk towards a place called Marble Arch, which was in the middle of London, on my half-day, I would be bound to bump into her; so she thought I wouldn't feel too lonely up there.

She did ask, very grumpily, where I thought the money was coming from to pay my fare all that way. As I was starting off at the big wage of six-and-eightpence a week, I wrote to Mrs Fox asking if she would forward my fare and deduct it at the rate of two shillings a week. I would still have four-and-eightpence left, and that was a lot of money to get used to all of a sudden. She sent back a pound by return.

In fact I was becoming a young person of means. For going-away presents I had a variety of things from several neighbours.

Two properly hemmed handkerchiefs, the first I had ever owned, that had sprigs of flowers in the corner. After a lifetime of using the inside of my skirt hem or sleeve, when no one was looking, it seemed sacrilegious to use these dainty, ironed white squares for wiping my nose. Then I had a comb with all the teeth in; a camisole, edged with lace, in good condition (I had nothing to fill it up with then, but the giver remarked that I would soon grow into it); and a much-battered tin trunk that looked very presentable when Dad had banged out the biggest dents with a hammer and Mam had worked herself into a sweat polishing it. Girls going into service had to provide their own black dress and white cap and apron, and this was a problem. Luckily Mam was able to make a swap. A young miner's wife, expecting her first baby, exchanged her maids' dresses for Mam's treasured wash-stand jug and basin set.

Wonderful as these gifts were, they didn't compare with what was in the brown paper parcel given me by Miss Hale—one of her coats, a hat, and a pair of shoes. Mam said they were as good as brand-new, and must have cost a mint of money.

So, a couple of weeks after my birthday, Mam rose at five-thirty to light the fire, that I might have a good warm, and some hot tea and toast, before we started our walk to the little station-halt a mile away. A good many ladies slumbering peacefully in their beds would have stirred uneasily in their sleep had they known what was on the way to try them.

Despite all my newly acquired material wealth, I'd never felt so poor in spirit. My little sister had woken when Mam called me, and now she sat on my lap, sipping my tea and nibbling little bits of my toast. To part from her warm little body seemed as terrible as parting with my head on a scaffold. I would have to wait a whole year before I could claim a holiday, and come home to my family again. A year was eternity!

The little room I sat in seemed the most desirable place on earth. I looked at the big black-leaded grate Mam took such pride in shining. In the oven door was set an emblem, a smiling face surrounded by rays—*smiling*, when I was going away! Sometimes

Mam had made me clean the big steel fender and the fire irons with a damp rag dipped in the ashes from under the fire. 'Shine it till you can see your face in it' was her order, and a very sour, sullen face it reflected by the time I'd finished. Now I thought how lucky I would be to stay at home and rub a real sparkle into it. The dresser Dad had made stood there showing off the pride of Mam's household possessions: a teapot, jug and sugar basin got with labels saved from tea packets. The few wooden chairs, the well-scrubbed table, the rag hearthrug, old Auntie's two vases, showing angelic cherubs caressing beautiful Grecian ladies, standing at either end of the mantelpiece with the tea caddy in the centre, the religious texts, hung on nails around the walls, were no longer inanimate objects but *friends*.

Mam was much more chatty and friendly than usual and didn't appear to notice that I only nodded my head to her remarks. My throat would choke up so. My young brother had woken early and come downstairs. 'I be comin' to 'elp you carry your trunk to the station,' he said.

'Well,' said Mam, 'we'll 'a' to be goin' soon or you'll miss your train. I'll pop in and ask Mrs Skinner to kip an eye on the two little'uns. You be gettin' your coat an' 'at on. One thing, you be startin' off nice and tidy. The people you be goin' to work for will think you've come from a nice respectable 'ome, wi' clothes like that on.'

Miss Hale's hat was a head-hugging cloche with rosettes of brown ribbon over the ears. It had sat nicely on her fluffy, thick golden hair, but on my plain brown basin-cut bob it came so far over my eyebrows that I had to lift it continually to see where I was going. The brown coat had fur collar and cuffs and one big fancy button at the waist. True, the cuffs came down to the tips of my fingers and the hem nearly to my ankles, and there was room, as the bus conductor says, for one more inside; but—'Never mind,' said Mam, 'now you'll be gettin' your bellyful of good food, you'll soon be fillin' it, an' it'll last you for donkey's years.'

Mrs Skinner came in to fetch my little sister, and promised to keep an ear open for the baby, who was still abed. My flesh, where my sister had nestled against me, seemed to tear as Mrs Skinner took her.

'My, Polly, you do look a proper young 'oman in they clothes. If I didn't know 'twas you, I could pass you on the road wi'out recognisin' you.' This was not surprising, since very little of me was visible.

My tin trunk was a good deal heavier than its contents. Mam and my brother insisted on carrying it between them. I was dressed in style, and I must be sent off in style. I walked behind them and felt ashamed of my reluctance to go out into the world and get my keep and be a help to the family. Before he'd gone to work on the late shift, Dad had come upstairs to say goodbye. 'Be you still awake, old butty?'

'Yes, Dad.'

'Now I don't have to tell thee 'ow much your mam and I wish we could kip thee at 'ome. We don't worry about thee bein' a good wench; we know thee won'tst do anythin' to let thy old Mam and Dad down. Our worry is that the job might be no good. Now mind what I do say: if they do work thee too 'ard, or not give thee enough vittles, or be bad to thee in any way, thee drap us a line and we'll scrape the money up some'ow to get thee wum. O' course, thee'st got to remember thee doesn't know much about the sart o' 'ousework they people do want, so be willin' to learn and do thee best. 'Pon my soul, if thy old dad don't envy thee a-goin' to a place like London. Just thinka' the sights, an' the wonderful things they 'a' got up there. Mind thee'st kip thee eyes open, and remember it all to tell thee old dad about when thee'st come 'ome for thee 'olidays. A year do seem a long way at thy age, and it'll seem a long time to we at 'ome, but just you think o' the excitement when we all come to the station to meet thee.'

I had thought *this* journey to the station would be exciting too, all those weeks ago when the pound came from Mrs Fox for my fare, but as I walked behind Mam and my brother I could only think about Mam's shoes, and how they were downtrodden and worn out completely on one side. Her shapeless lisle stockings hung in loose folds round her thin ankles. Perhaps my new mistress would give me some left-off clothes to send home, as some of my aunties used to for Granny. I noticed, too, the thin knobbly legs of my brother, emerging like matchsticks from the legs of his patched trousers, and I remembered a time when he'd fainted and gone into a coma. Dad had run, like one gone mad, for the doctor. When the doctor came he said something about malnutrition, and I looked it up in the dictionary at school. Under-nourished, that's what it meant. Well, now I would be able to do something about it. Surely I could send home at least a shilling a week; that would pay for three extra loaves. Perhaps I could send more when I'd repaid the pound.

We passed the well and its bubbling spring, where I'd gone so often with a bucket; past the old slag heap, where poor crippled Absy David was killed by a fall as he scratched for tiny coals to keep his fire going; past the wood we called the Hain, where blackberries grew, the best always out of reach, but plenty left to blacken our tongues for weeks, and to scratch our legs to smarting, bloodstained soreness, and sometimes enough for a blackberry tart, when Mam could spare the sugar; past the old beech-tree in the bluebell wood—here, one rare and joyous Sunday, Mam had taken us for a picnic, a real picnic, lighting a fire, boiling eggs in a tin saucepan, and making a jug of tea with the water when the eggs were done.

On we went, up to the slope by Nelsons Green, and in a moment we should be able to see the station. Oh, if only some magic act had made it disappear! No, it was there. And so, miraculously, was Dad!

There he was, emerging from a side track on to our path. His face was grey with fatigue, and smudged with pit dirt embedded in the wrinkles, but his eyes shone with pleasure as I ran to him, delighted at the surprise. He was sweating, for he'd made a long and hurried detour.

'Bless my soul, I can't be a-kissin' thee wi' all that finery on. I'll spile it all wi' this pit dirt. But give I thee trunk. I don't think it'll matter if I puts 'un on my shoulder: Mam can dust'n off wi' 'er pinny on the station.'

Oh what a lucky girl I felt to be so loved! Full of pride, and misery, of good intentions, and fear of what was in store, full of overwhelming love for everyone and everything I was leaving behind, I stood bemused, watching the train chug to a halt. The little platform became the edge of the old world, the world I had known, as a child in the Forest.

PART II

In the East End

It seemed to me as though time itself paused a moment with that train. As it chugged away, the picture of the little group I was leaving behind etched itself through a blur of tears into my memory.

Although the plush upholstered seat in the train seemed most luxurious, I felt I had been sucked into an iron demon caterpillar, with a mad engine for a head, shrieking and puffing with indecent haste to take me away from home.

When we had gone past Gloucester station, all seemed lost. But I mustn't cry, oh, I *mustn't* cry, lest the woman sitting opposite should notice. She had not looked up from the book she was reading.

The train ate the miles up like a rapacious locust. Insatiable, it went on and on, in what seemed to be an everlasting journey. I was able to recognise that Swindon wasn't Paddington despite its size and bustle. After Reading I began to feel nervous. Surely, when I had been to London before, during the General Strike, it hadn't been quite so far as this? Perhaps the train had hurtled past London! I plucked up the courage to ask my travelling companion.

I think that lady might well be described as a retiring sort of person. She had retired into anonymity behind her book for the whole journey. I can't say a twinkle came in her eye exactly, but her mouth did crack open a bit like a smile when she assured me that we had not passed London, and would soon be at Paddington. I could tell she didn't come from my part of Gloucestershire by the way she spoke.

Mam had told me I was to mind not to move off the platform, or speak to a soul until Blodwen, whom my new mistress had arranged to meet me, introduced herself. Apart from what I had learned at school of the great and glamorous history of London, I had also gleaned from hearsay that it was full of thieves, pickpockets, and white-slave traffickers on the look-out for lonely girls. To be on the safe side I sat on my up-ended trunk on the platform, kept my hand in my pocket firmly clutching my handkerchief with the two-and-ninepence in it, and looked such a picture of misery I don't think I'd have stood a chance of being abducted if a slavedealer had been about.

Soon all the other passengers had hurried purposefully off to their destinations.

'Campin' out for the night, then?' the engine-driver's mate called, as the train I had come on shunted out of the station.

'Where d'you come from, then?' asked a pimply-faced young porter, in a manner that showed he had no hopes of me as a potential tip. He didn't look anything to be afraid of, so I answered him, 'Gloucestershire.'

He looked me over with insolent deliberation. 'That's where the cheeses come from, ain't it?' He made it sound like an insult. 'Wot yer got in there,' he said, nodding at my trunk, 'a few swedes to gnaw at?'

I was spared any more of his baiting by the approach of a young woman who seemed to know immediately who I was. She must be Blodwen, who worked for a friend of my new mistress. Blodwen didn't look like my idea of a maid at all. Her good looks were hidden, rather than accentuated, by an overdose of lipstick, rouge, powder, and mascara. She had the first cropped hair I'd seen, and she wore a flapper-length black satin coat fastened with one big fancy button. She was in high-heeled black court shoes, and pink silk stockings. I was very impressed.

The porter wasn't. 'She come up to skivvy in the same place as you, then?' he asked her. Like me, he was ignorant of the fact that she really longed to be taken for an actress, and she was stung to the quick that he saw through her. So she advised him tartly, 'Mind your own bloody business! You clear off, and go and count your pimples!'

This, I realised, was a young woman of authority.

'You know it's Jews you've come to work for, don't you? Watch out they don't try to get most of your wages back selling you something. How much money have you got with you?'

I told her: two-and-ninepence. 'Jesus! is that all?'

I couldn't make her out. It was a lot of money, and when I thought how badly it was needed at home, I thought she had a cheek. Especially when she added, 'Lend me a shilling for our fares, gal. I'm broke. Don't tell your missus. She gave me our fares, but I spent some of it on stockings to meet you, mine had a ladder in 'em.'

I gave her a shilling; one-and-ninepence was plenty to last me a week. Then I'd really be in the money, even when the two-shilling deduction was made for the pound advanced for my train fare, I'd still have nearly five shillings left. Six and eightpence a week seemed like riches to me. I thought afterwards it wouldn't have been right for a self-styled actress to go about with a ladder in her stocking. She found my old tin trunk a handicap to her style, too, but somehow it had to be got to Stoke Newington.

The first bus conductor was not sympathetic. He wanted to know if we'd got lost from a safari expedition—his bus had no room for big game hunters' equipment. 'Good job we aren't. With you looking so much like a monkey we'd have shot you,' Blodwen spat at him.

The next conductor let us, and the trunk, on, but enquired sarcastically whose dead body it contained. 'A bad-mannered conductor's,' Blodwen informed him.

Much to my dismay, for the further we travelled into London the more hopelessly lost I felt, we had to get off that bus and get on another. The first conductor we approached let us put the trunk on his bus. He had a crony sitting near the door.

'D'you reckon,' he said, in a loud, mock-confidential whisper, 'that I've caught 'em red-handed with the loot? You've 'eard ain't you, about that break-in at the Tower? 'Alf the crown jewels stole, and *that*'—nodding to the trunk—'is where they be 'idden.' This style of banter continued, with much apparently good-humoured repartee from Blodwen. But when we and the trunk were off the bus, and it was starting off again, she held out her hand with the coppers for the fare still in it.

'Bloody pair of smart alecs! We put one over on you,' she hollered after them.

Although much of my attention had been focused on Blodwen, marvelling at her self-possession, I had also been aware of the concrete jungle getting thicker round us. It seemed a mad place, where they had drowned the sky with the silhouettes of houses, houses so squashed together that they hadn't left room anywhere for a blade of grass, let alone a tree. Coming from a village where one door meant one dwelling (even if it were a one-up one-down cottage with a lean-to back-kitchen), I couldn't make out why Londoners wanted such huge places to live in. I mistook a block of flats for a single house. I'd never heard of people living in layers.

They had buried the earth under concrete, and instead of growing flowers for colour, the London women painted their faces. They were a clever lot—all of them—for how could they find their way about in such a maze? What a clever girl Blodwen is, I thought. I knew I should never be able to find my way out of London by myself.

'This is it—Mildmay Park Road,' announced Blodwen, as we turned into a road of tall, drab, narrow houses.

All I could think was it ought to be ashamed of itself, swanking with such a grand-sounding name. Misery Dark Road would have been a more appropriate name; it would at least have had the virtue of honesty.

'That's where I work,' said Blodwen, pointing to one of the houses. 'It's only three doors away from you, so I'll look out for you when you're shaking the mats in the back-yard. You look up to the top windows to see if I'm waving. You're having your half-day same as me, Wednesday. I go to the Shoreditch Olympia mostly; it's only sixpence for a seat in the gods, and the programme lasts three hours! It's Mary Philbin in *Drums of Love* next week.'

By now we had stopped, and Blodwen was knocking at the door. Never mind about the drums of love! My own heartbeats pounded in my eardrums—the moment had come, I had arrived at the threshold of my career.

For a moment a curtain was drawn back a little on a ground-floor window for an unfriendly, indifferent face to see who was knocking. Then another face looked out from a top-floor window.

'Here's your shiksa!' Blodwen called up. Then to me, 'Now mind, don't tell her I borrowed that shilling. See you Wednesday— I'm off now—these buggers always want you to do them a favour if you hang about.'

I had known Blodwen less than an hour, but it was terrible to see her walk away.

The door was opened by a woman whom I judged to be in her early thirties. She had very black hair, dark eyes, and sallow skin. She looked a bit foreign. I had wondered what Jews looked like; I had only heard of Shylock and the ones in the Bible. Meanwhile she summed up what was visible of me. The too-large coat and hat Miss Hale had given me got her first attention. 'Such a coat, and such a hat, on such a girl! How come?' said her expression, as though she price-tagged them by instinct.

Though I had thought the road was shabby, I was impressed by the width of the stairs, and its fancy-patterned oilcloth with no cracks or bare patches. At the top of the first flight of stairs she told me to put my trunk down on the landing. 'That's your room—that's ours,' pointing to the doors, 'and this is the lavatory.' She opened this door, and there I beheld a flush toilet with a chain, a roll of toilet paper on a holder fixed to the wall, and a warm little rug for your feet. Fancy that! A posh lavatory stuck up in the middle of a house! As we went on up, she showed me in the corner of the stairway a little sink with a tap over it. 'That's our water,' she said. I was duly impressed by these unheard-of conveniences, and I thought, well, I've got a job with people of quality after all! A rum lot, as well, I added when we got to the top of the house, and she showed me a very small kitchen, the living-room, and the parlour. My new mistress explained, 'It's better this way, then it's quieter for the woman in the bottom half of the house.' 'Fancy,' I thought, 'I've got an upside-down job in half a house!'

The master was out, but the two small children of the household were playing quietly in the living-room—a boy toddler, and a girl a couple of years older. They were beautiful, with dark curling hair and huge brown eyes. Even though they were plump and well dressed, they were a vivid reminder that I might never see my little sisters and brother again.

This time I couldn't stop the tears, but Mrs Fox, my new mistress, seemed to understand. She took me downstairs to my bedroom, and told me to have a little wash and then come upstairs for my supper.

I had heard too much about being in service from my aunties to expect much in the way of sleeping quarters. My room seemed a novelty just the same. It was the home of the family junk; travelling bags and hobby kits, dressmaking dummies and the spades and buckets of seaside holidays. In places the junk was stacked to the ceiling, but space was left for a little iron bedstead, and a small marble-topped washstand. There was a row of hooks behind the door for hanging clothes.

Mrs Fox had told me to put on my black afternoon dress and white apron. I kept trying to staunch the tears with the flannel and water in the washstand bowl. A black frock seemed to suit the occasion. I was in mourning for my lost self. I was in a strange new world—in a different role—with entirely new people to adjust to. My childhood was dead—now I was the skivvy—I was near to wishing she were dead too.

I was given my supper in the tiny kitchen while the family ate in the living-room. It was strange to be considered not fit to eat in the same room as other human beings. It was a good supper, a thick soup with butter beans in it, but loneliness and misery had taken away my appetite. How delicious, in comparison, seemed the remembered slice of marge-spread toast given me by Mam and eaten as a member of a family.

I was glad when I was told to go to bed; now I could squash my face into the pillow to smother the day's pent-up tears. Dr Johnson may have found in London 'all that life can afford', but all I could think was, 'what a bloody 'ole to come to.'

Having from time to time worked for Jewish people, I have a soft spot for them. It has been my experience, however, that they do like to think they have a bargain. Poor Mrs Fox, with six-and-eight a week to pay in wages, plus my keep, certainly had no bargain in me.

As far as domestic skills were concerned she had drawn a blank. Her standards of spit-and-polish were very high, and she lost a fair bit of fat showing me, by example, how to do each chore. On the first morning, I don't think she had the breath left to tackle the stairs, so she sent me to a special cut-price Jewish shop for some eggs.

Through the kitchen window overlooking the street she pointed out the direction. From there it seemed simple enough—second turning on the right past the chemist's, then first on the left till I came to Bloom's stores. I felt very proud of my achievement when I found the shop.

Bloom's stores seemed to contain things from all over the world, packed higgledy-piggledy into a long, dark-brown interior. There was only a very narrow space in front of a counter piled with goods for the customers, four of whom were already lined up inside. Pickled herring, paraffin, candles, cakes, matzo meal, washing-soda, pulses, spices, fats, flours, foreign-sounding food dried, tinned or packed, and eggs at fourteen for a shilling! The smells were indescribable confusion, once inhaled never forgotten!

A little old woman, almost indistinguishable from the surrounding brownness, hindered rather than helped by a similarly brown little old man, had got themselves in a right tangle. They searched their haphazard stock for some item for the first customer.

Despite the spectacles perched on the end of his long nose, the old man kept knocking things over in his futile effort to find what the customer wanted. With supplicating outstretched hands, the old woman begged the rest of us not to go away.

I was in no hurry—I found the whole spectacle very funny, and became most interested in the success or failure of the search. But I never found out the result.

Eventually the old man pushed by to ask what I wanted. 'Seven eggs for sixpence,' I told him. He seemed so disappointed he couldn't sell me anything else it was just as well my mistress had only given me the bare sixpence! The trouble was, he gesticulated his disappointment so strongly, he knocked an egg off the top of the box on to the floor and it broke.

I think those eggs must have come a long way, and taken their time about it; probably across the sea. Their insides were so pale, with a slight suggestion of green, that it was difficult to tell the yolk from the white. It must have been one from this shop Mrs Fox had given me for my breakfast. As I ate alone, I was able to pop down to the lavatory with my mouth full and pull the chain on the contents. I wasn't fussy about food, but those eggs took some swallowing.

As soon as I stepped on to the pavement from Bloom's stores, I knew I was lost. I couldn't remember from which direction I had come, and to my uninitiated eye, all the houses looked the same. I hurried a few yards in one direction, panicked, then tried the other way. I asked an old lady the way to Mildmay Park Road but she just ignored me. I did think of going back to ask the shopkeepers, but they seemed to have enough troubles of their own when I'd left them.

I had been used to taking my bearings by the different characteristics of familiar trees, banks, grasses, mosses and ferns; each woodland path was so different. Streets were all the same. Even when I summoned up the courage to ask other passers-by for directions, it was more by luck than by understanding that I got back into Mildmay Park Road just as an irate Mrs Fox was coming to look for me.

I proved what a duffer I could be when I had been there about three days. The family were going out for the afternoon and evening, and I should be on my own. To make sure I wasn't idle, Mrs Fox gave me a list of jobs to do. Before they went, she herself boiled up a bucket of soda-water on the gas stove. I was to take that stove to pieces, all of it, the top, and the oven, and thoroughly scrub all the parts in this soda-water; then wash out the kitchen and a flight of stairs. After that I could go in the living-room and clean the silver and brasses.

Gas stoves, in those days, were made entirely of black iron. I was completely ignorant about gas except to know that it was an explosive element, and that the jets made a little pop as they were turned off. I was scared stiff of them. However, I did as I was told and took the stove to pieces in my fashion, thoroughly scrubbing each piece in the soda-water, then piling them up on a wad of newspapers put ready on the little kitchen table. It was quite a pile-up by the time I'd done the last piece, and a thick topping of grease floated on the bucket of water, now barely lukewarm. What the gas company had put together, I had pulled asunder.

I was soon in a sweat, more from apprehension than from my labours, as I tried to fit the thing back together. I was very scared that if I put the wrong piece in the wrong hole I might blow the kitchen up. I decided to leave the bad alone, and scrub the floor and stairs down. It would have to be in fresh cold water as I couldn't heat any up. First I must empty the bucket, so I tipped the greasy water down the little sink in the corner. At least, that was my intention, but the sink only gave me its half-hearted co-operation. Some of the water disappeared, but the rest stopped, dark and greasy to the rim of the sink.

'Oh, my Gawd,' I panicked, 'what've I done now?' I'd ruined the sink as well as the gas stove! It was the first sink I'd ever had any dealings with; how could I know they suffered from constipation? Suddenly I remembered the hymn we had been taught in our teetotaller's meetings:

> Pull for the shore, sailor, pull for the shore
> Heed not the rolling waves, but bend to the oar

I bent to wash the floor and stairs with my bucket of cold, grease-speckled water; trying to rally out of my despair with a quaking rendering of that hymn. My tears splashed into the bucket. Too daft to think of pouring this bucket of water down the lavatory, I left it to decorate the landing.

I had one straw of hope left—I would clean that silver and brass as it had never been cleaned before, in an effort to make amends.

It was getting dusk, and I should need to see what I was doing. I had seen Mrs Fox put a light to the gas-mantle, so, taking a match, I followed suit. I struck the match and pushed it into the mantle, which instantly disintegrated, as daintily as snowflake powder, on to the mat.

Now, I *had* done it! Equating fragility with expense, I thought I must have bankrupted my wages for months. Only, how would I have any wages? I'd get the sack; nobody could be expected to put up with such a booby. What would I do? I'd no money to get home, even if I'd known how to get there.

Then I thought of Blodwen. I'd only seen her once, when I was mat-shaking in the back-yard, and her face in the window had been as welcome as sunshine after rain. Desperation made me think—I would go and knock on the door of the house where she worked, and throw myself on Boldwen's mercy. I ran down the stairs, and left the front door ajar. With a heart pounding at my own boldness, I knocked on the door of number 108. All the windows were in darkness. I knocked again, and again, and again. It was no good—they must all be out. I got back just as a draught caught the front door and it banged shut in my face.

I was now locked out. Perhaps it was as well, really. At least I couldn't do any more damage out here! I didn't feel I had any right to be stuck on the pavement either, though I stepped apologetically out of the way of passers-by. They took no notice, of course. It was as difficult to be conspicuous in London then as it is now. The time passed in a kind of black limbo, between the sins I had committed indoors, and the retribution to come.

I must have had water on the brain; I started to cry again as soon as the Foxes walked up towards me. To my incredible surprise and relief, Mrs Fox seemed more annoyed at my miser-able reaction than she did about my misdeeds. If she had not been my mistress I would have loved to hug her in gratitude. She put the stove back together in no time, and pooh-poohed the idea that a gas-mantle was a precious object. Then she got me to ladle the greasy water out of the sink, and put a packet of soda into it. She boiled up a kettle on the reconstituted stove, and poured it over the soda. After some gurglings and belchings the sink relieved itself, and me.

In a back-handed way, that calamitous afternoon did me a good turn. I still had the silver to clean, and I was allowed to stay in the living-room with the family while I did it. The children watched me, and in no time I was making them laugh with silly rhymes, and drawing things in their crayon books. The silver took a long time; but, after that, I was allowed in with the family to keep the children company. Soon the Foxes were able to go out for an evening, knowing I would keep the children happy and safe.

The next day was Wednesday, my half-day. As though she hadn't been kind enough, Mrs Fox gave me the four-and-eightpence wages due a day in advance. I still had my one-and-ninepence, and I decided to ask Blodwen to take me to a post office so I could put a three-shilling postal order in my letter home. Those three shillings seemed like a silver lining showing through at last.

I was ready to go down when Blodwen knocked at the door. She was made up to the nines again, and wearing a new pink silk blouse. 'Come on, gal, step it out. I want to get meself a new hat to match this blouse, before we go to the pictures.'

I don't suppose it's practised now; but in those days, if you paused outside a shop in the East End to look at the window display, you were literally pulled inside, and cajoled, beseeched, and nearly threatened, to buy something. Resistance was difficult, but Blodwen managed it. 'Get off,' she threatened, 'or I'll put my bloody shoe through your window.' Eventually, after much window-shopping, and peering into the interiors, Blodwen decided on a shop to get her hat. It was a small shop, run, apparently, by one assistant.

Hundreds of hats were piled in a long trough-like counter, for the customers to pick and choose. The fashion then was for head-hugging felt hats in the style of a Roman soldier's helmet. There were several colours, and various trimmings.

The prodigal son couldn't have got a more effusive welcome than we did from that shop assistant. It seemed that her shop had the very hats that could have been exclusively designed for two such young ladies.

Had I been buying a hat, I would have suited myself in a matter of moments. But not Blodwen. She tried on hat after hat for so long that I began to feel quite sorry for the assistant. Not one of them was exactly what Blodwen wanted. Could she try that pink one in the far corner of the window? The one so difficult to get at?

Desperately determined to make a sale, the poor woman

wriggled herself through the window display to reach it. My stomach couldn't stand any more of Blodwen's brand of sadism. 'I'll wait outside for you,' I told her.

She came out of the hat shop just in time to catch me being frogmarched into the next-door gowns and mantles emporium by two saleswomen; despite my entreaties that I had no money to spend.

Blodwen got hold of me by the back of my coat collar and yanked me away. 'You can be had up for kidnapping you know,' she threatened the two women. 'Come on, let's get a move on, the bloody picture'll have started.' She hustled me down the street.

'Did you buy that hat out of the window?' I asked.

'Who said anything about buying a hat?'

My puzzled response to this remark got me an impatient shove. 'Wait till we get out of sight of here, then I'll show you.' And show me she did. Two hats, one pink (but not the one from the window) and one brown were in her shopping bag. 'This one's for you,' she said, handing me the brown one.

'D'you mean to say you stole them?' I asked incredulously.

''Course I did,' she laughed, 'that's why I got the silly old bloodsucker to get that one out of the window, so's I could pop these in my bag. Ten-and-six she wanted for that pink hat in the window—bloody cheek—she must have seen me coming! Daylight robbers, that's what they are.'

I put the hat back in her bag as though it were a live viper. Oh dear, whatever would my Mam and Dad have said if they could see me now going out with a thief, and a Welsh one at that? Mam was very proud of being Welsh, and depicted them all as a cut above anybody you could find in Gloucestershire. When she had a bit of a shindig with Dad, didn't she always taunt him that 'she indeed had come from a respectable family'. I'd never be able to tell Mam about Blodwen.

We didn't have a policeman in our village but in a place the size of London they probably had a couple of dozen. Any minute I half-expected the hands of a pair of them to come down heavily on our shoulders.

I was glad when we came to the picture house; the police'd never find us in that great place.

It wasn't exactly the gods; it was steps that served for both purposes. Peanut shells and sweet wrappings crackled under our feet, as Blodwen found us a space to sit. The tang of orange peel fought with tobacco and the warm body odour rising from the stalls and balcony.

Between the films there were live turns, and these had just started. I was bewitched with surprise and delight; soon stolen hats, my domestic shortcomings, and even homesickness faded from my consciousness.

There was a troupe of Japanese jugglers, made exquisitely miniature and deft by the distance. Next came three trim girl dancers, tapping out their lively dances with identical precision. I was spellbound.

Anna Rogers, the fifteen-year-old wonder girl, came next. She seemed uncannily clever. She must have been. She was only sixteen when I saw her name on a playbill in South London five years later.

'Not bad turns this week,' observed the sophisticated Blodwen. '*Not bad!*' They were magic people, so clever, so beautiful! Aladdin himself couldn't have been more dazzled, when the Genie's lamp transported him to the treasure cave, than I was that first night in the Olympia picture house, Shoreditch.

The film, *Drums of Love*, was completely lost on me. The heroine lying about on skin-covered divans, languishing for whatever it was she was missing, didn't have my sympathy.

Before she emerged into the spotlight of public gaze, Blodwen had to make up her face again. How drab and insignificant everything seemed, compared with the world of stage and screen!

The ladies' cloakroom smelled dusty, and stale with cheap perfume. 'Can I wait outside, on the steps?' I asked Blodwen, as she daubed on the Phul-Nana. She nodded absently, then tried to add yet more mascara to her eyelashes.

I stood alone on the steps that led up to the paybox. I was storing into my memory the wonder of those stage turns, so that I might tell Dad and Mam, if I ever got home again. My musings were interrupted by two young lads, apparently in a state of agitation.

'Eh, miss! Our friend's fainted down that alley. Will you come and see if you can 'elp him?'

'Oh dear, poor boy,' I thought. I had seen children faint in school and be carried to lie down by the stove near teacher's desk. Teacher would roll up her coat and make a pillow, and sponge the child's face with cold water.

So, I had started down the steps with them, when Blodwen came out and demanded where the hell was I going? The boys melted into thin air.

Anxious to help, I was all for taking Blodwen down the alley to find the fainting boy.

'Jesus! It's me that's going to faint, being landed with a turnip-head like you! Honest, gal, you're greener than my Mam's cabbage after she puts the soda in. *Don't* you *ever* go anywhere with anybody, especially boys that you don't know.'

If Blodwen found me a puzzle, I found her peculiar notions were puzzling, too. What harm could possibly have come to me going down a back-alley to help a boy who'd fainted? From my gentle father, and the kindly men of our mining village, I had learned nothing to make me beware a man's advances.

But I didn't argue with Blodwen. I was so glad of her company, and so grateful for it, that I felt it only fair to do as she told me. Except for taking a stolen hat; I had to draw the line somewhere.

Despite the weekly excitement of my half-day, and the fact that sometimes I had to go over my chores only twice to pass muster, I was terribly homesick. I had been used to playing with, picking up, and generally loving, two little sisters and a brother; and receiving affection from them, from my parents, and from my playmates. Much as I liked the two children of my master and mistress, I was sensitive enough to realise that I could not show them the warmth that I could express at home.

After many weeks, when I could find an odd corner to myself, I still let the tears run. I knew exactly what the expression 'a heavy heart' meant. Mam wrote to me every couple of weeks. These letters were my lifeline; pieces of paper to treasure, to keep alive the hope that one day I would get back home.

That day came. When I had been with Mrs Fox for about three months, I had a letter from Mam saying my four-year-old sister was ill again with pleurisy.

I was learning to live with homesickness, but I could not contain this additional blow. When my little sister was two she had been for a spell in a sanatorium, and had become brown, plump, a picture of health. But each winter since, she had had this terrible illness. How could she get better, if I weren't there to help run upstairs with the hot linseed-meal poultices for Mam to put on her as fast as Dad could make them?

I was so distraught that I could not speak coherently when Mrs Fox asked me what was the matter. She took the letter and read it. My grief went to her kind heart. 'You shall go home,' she said. 'Pack your clothes, and I'll get Blodwen to take you to the station. Have you got your train fare?' I shook my head; I had not saved up enough in the time. 'Never mind,' she said, 'I'll make it up. When your little sister is better, promise you'll come back and work for me.'

In view of my deficiencies, her request was one small proof of the Jewish ability to stand suffering. I promised her that I would. I would have promised anyone anything without a scruple, as long as I could get home to my little sister. But I had no intention of coming back.

Kind Mrs Fox! She made up a parcel of warm vests and clothes from her children's plentiful store. I took all her kindness; and I'm ashamed to admit I never even wrote to her.

Blodwen said she would miss me, and insisted on me taking the brown hat home. She told me of all the people she had known in Wales who had got over pleurisy. She got me, quivering with fear lest I miss the train, into Paddington with time to spare.

I told her she was better, and more like an actress, than Mary Pickford. I felt so grateful to Blodwen, and all I had to give her was a compliment.

The train, which had seemed so mad to take me away from home, did not go half fast enough as it huffed and puffed its way westward.

An Old Lady

When I reached Cinderford, and began the walk home, I realised how much I had seen, how many new sights and sensations I had absorbed in those few months in London.

I had seen a mountain to measure a molehill by. The little shop, whose window had contained a lifetime's indulgences of sweet-tooth delights, where the decision how best to spend a penny had kept me drooling with anticipation for a quarter of an hour, was now just a pokey little sweet shop.

The endless greensward to the old brickworks was but a quarter-mile's walk of rough open sheep-grazing pastureland. The single-line railway track that cut across it, with Wimsey Halt station shelter for waiting passengers, was as small and poor as a child's plaything. Everything seemed to have shrunk in that forest clearing; all the better for my hurrying feet to get me home and to my little sister's bedside.

The old magic came back as I entered the last part of my walk, through the forest surrounding our village. There they stood, the oaks, unchanged and beautiful, living statues of nature's architecture. Even Sir Christopher Wren could fashion nothing to match them.

Now I was back home. But oh, how pitiful, how small, home seemed! How little and worried Mam looked, as she took me straight upstairs to my sister. ''Er've'ad the crisis; 'er's on the mend, thank God, so doosn't worry now,' Mam comforted me.

Sweat-dampened strands of dark hair clung to the forehead of the little, wizened, wasted face in the bed, bereft of the plump contours of healthy childhood, all mouth, and great, sad, heavy eyes.

I, great, blubbering, homesick coward, had come back home, penniless and jobless, to lessen still further the chances of comfort for those I professed to love. As I sat on the bed and hugged her, I made a resolve. I would get a job at once. If it was the worst place in the world, I'd stick it for at least six months. I wrote right away for another job; this time, in the Cotswolds.

Prepared now for the heartache of home-sickness after my first short-lived job, but determined to stay in this one for six months whatever the conditions, I put down one hundred and eighty-three lines on a piece of paper—every night I could look forward to crossing one off.

Now one hundred per cent willing, if not very able, I started my job as general maid to an old lady in the Cotswolds. I was fourteen years old and just emerging from my first childhood—she was ninety-one and tottering into her second, so we got on pretty well together. Her treatment of the long string of unfortunate girls who had preceded me had given her a local reputation for being a 'cantankerous old tartar'.

Actually age had softened the old tyrant quite a bit. I was the first maid allowed to sleep in one of the bedrooms. The others had had to make do on an old palliasse on the floor of the attic. I found this out when she poked me awake with her walking-stick in the small hours to tell me there was a burglar up there.

If there was I didn't intend to disturb him.

With lighted candle in hand I climbed up through the trap door. I banged about a bit to give the illusion of inspection, clambered down and firmly announced, 'Not a sign o' a skerrit of any sorts up there ma'am.'

Because of her rheumatics I had to act as 'kneel in' for the old lady's prayers. I thought she had a fat chance of getting to heaven with that attic on her conscience and two spare bedrooms in the house! But she was old and pitiful, so just in case there was a God up there listening I put in a plea for her on the quiet.

She was a proper old termagant for waking me up in the night on one pretext or another. Eventually she asked me to sleep with her in her big four-poster bed.

I had to undress her at night. It was a long business—nature's whittling had left very little under the voluminous layers of clothes. Her false teeth came out first—then her false hair which was attached to a goffered white headpiece in the manner of Queen Victoria. After I had removed the layers of day clothes and helped her on to the night commode, I had all the rigmarole of dressing her up for the night. Woollen vest, flannel chemise, nightgown, bed jacket and bedsocks; lastly a white silk scarf over her poor little balding head tied under her chin in case she died in the night—she didn't want the indignity of being found with her mouth agape. After that it was gently heaving her up into the great four-poster bed.

Before I could get in, I had to go through the nightly ritual of making sure every door downstairs, even the one at the bottom of the stairs, was chained and padlocked. As the windows were lead latticed, I kept assuring her that Tom Thumb couldn't get in, let alone a burglar. It was a bit disheartening after all that trouble to be poked awake a couple of hours later to do a bit of exorcising. She used to wake up saying she was having horrible visions and the only way I could get rid of them was for me to walk slowly round the bed three times saying prayers.

She had a great dread of dying and confessed this to me one day.

'Don't you fret about that ma'am,' I comforted her, lying like a trooper on the spur of the moment, 'my old Great-Auntie come to me in a vision and told me'twas like goin' to sleep in a coal'ole and wakin' up in a palace.' The times I had to tell her that fib, adding bits I 'remembered', to convince and further reassure her.

At first I ate my food in the kitchen, but she had to ring her bell so often for me to mop up the mess she made, that soon she sacrificed dignity for expediency and said I could eat in the dining-room with her. 'Don't go getting big ideas that you are a lady's equal,' she warned me. Such a remote possibility had never entered my head!

My old mistress had to live on a very small pittance allowed her by her nephew in London. She was childless, and had been a widow for many years. Her sea-captain husband had left his money invested in German railway stock. It had gone up in smoke in the First World War.

Every year the nephew came down to make sure she had not altered the will leaving the cottage and its contents to him. Her longevity was obviously getting on his nerves, but he was still getting a bargain.

The cottage was a gem of Cotswold stone with lattice windows set in a quarter of an acre of walled garden. The kitchen was separated from the dining-room by the parlour. The access door from the kitchen to this middle room was kept locked, so I had to run across the yard with the food. In a downpour the gravy got watered down a bit.

The garden bloomed with the glory of an English cottage

garden. It seemed to contain a little of everything: winter jasmine to autumn chrysanthemums—with crocuses, daffodils, narcissi, lily of the valley, primulas, pansies, snapdragons, Canterbury bells, sweet williams, carnations, pinks, mignonette and lavender, some cultivated, and some which had sown themselves of their own sweet will in unexpected places. Also there were a green and a rosy apple tree; red-, white- and black-currant bushes; white and dark pink raspberries; three sorts of gooseberries and four rows of strawberries.

In the spring the rows of young vegetables were like fancy stitching on the earth's dark petticoat—rosettes of baby lettuce; the feathery stitch of young carrot tops; spiky stitch of spring onions, and the dainty embroidery of red-edged baby beetroot leaves. An old man came two days a week for a shilling a day to keep it all in order. He made up for his small wage by nicking a lot of the produce. Very conscious of the capitalist structure of our society, I turned a blind eye to this until I felt he was overstepping the mark, and robbing my old mistress who was also poor. I ticked him off. Fifty-fifty from then on, or I threatened to spill the beans.

Though the old lady ate very little herself it was still a struggle for her to pay my one pound a month wages. 'Don't you fret ma'am, a plate o'taters wi' a knob o' marg would suit me fine for dinner,' I often told her.

In those days the baker's man called every day. Twice a week she took a fresh batch loaf from him, sometimes still warm from the oven. To sit with her in that dining-room with the sun streaming through the lattice window, watching the japonica blossoms nod against the panes, eating crusty buttered newly-baked bread, and drinking tea made with fresh spring water from a silver teapot, feasting the eye on a standard tea-rose through the open door, made up for a lot of my life's drawbacks.

There were other pleasures too. I never had any time off, but once a month she sent me into Stroud to get a freshly laundered headpiece from a little widow woman who did the hand laundry. At the same time I could send a postal order home to Mam and buy myself black stockings or a pair of shoes. To save her the tuppence fare I offered to walk—and so had three miles each way that was sheer delight from start to finish.

A white rose growing over the remains of a tumble-down cottage had gone into ecstasies free from the pruner's knife. In late spring, wall-flowers, tawny velvet to brilliant flame, burst from crevices in dry-stone garden walls. Sometimes a lady in one of the gardens would bid me a pleasant 'good afternoon'. Of course, they didn't know I was a mere skivvy. It was nice to be spoken to as an ordinary human being.

As well as the wonders before my eyes, I had all the wonders of a dream future to ponder on. I never stinted myself in this field. A dawdler by nature, I didn't have to worry about stepping it out, as a neighbour from a nearby cottage got my mistress tea on these occasions. This same woman had 'obliged' when there was a gap between the arrival of a new maid and the departure of the last one. All the same I mostly got a tart scolding for my lateness.

In my early days there, on Sunday mornings, I had to help my mistress up the hill to the nearby church, leave her at the door and be there to collect her when the service was over. Later on she sent me in her stead, sitting in for her in her pew, six rows from the front. There was too much to be done for me to attend morning service. I went in the evenings instead.

Regurgitated through the rector's monotonous sing-song, I found the words of the Bible illogical and meaningless. 'Blessed are the meek for they shall inherit the earth.' I wondered when? The snobby lot sitting in the front few rows looked as though they had got a good whack of it, and there was nothing meek about *them*. I found no comfort for my spirit in the service, but I found an object for my romantic notions on the organ stool. He was young, incredibly handsome, with a profile like Ivor Novello's and so remotely inaccessible that he was just right for my daydreams.

I evolved a wonderful daydream around that young organist. I sat in a lovely cottage on top of a hill with a cliff-face going down to the sea. In a delightfully cosy room with frilled muslin curtains, a glowing fire, a table laid with the daintiest of teas on a snowy-lace cloth, and a baby like a living doll in a cradle by the side of the hearth, I waited for the young organist—now transformed to a bronzed young sea captain. Smart as paint in his uniform, he was hurrying up the cliff-face to the baby, home and me. Never a thought as to how this situation came about, or how my daydream would continue, intruded upon my mind.

Next to crossing a tick off my piece of paper every evening, I looked forward to going to church. Until one evening, perhaps by some kind of telepathy, the young man turned his head and seemed to look straight into my eyes. It was a cool, patronising stare, as though he'd sensed the boldness of my thoughts. I felt terrible, like a criminal caught in the act. I nearly keeled over in the pew with faintness.

After that, I persuaded my mistress to let me give her a proxy sermon at home. She didn't really like being left alone, so she agreed. Because she couldn't kneel down, I had to kneel on a higher chair than the one she sat on, to give the illusion of a pulpit. Imitating the intoning manner of the rector, I crucified the words even better than he did, but she was well satisfied.

I love the courage of old age, illogically struggling on with the daily grinds of living when they're no longer important. What mattered a few cobwebs to my old mistress? Yet she told me that the cottage must be spring-cleaned, starting with the dining-room. I had never heard of spring-cleaning, but I soon knew all about it, and how!

First the polish had to be made. Under her supervision, I boiled up a mixture of beeswax, vinegar, and linseed oil. Polish is a misnomer for this product, it's the elbow grease necessary to rub off its dulling patina where the shine comes in.

The dining-room was not large, but it was very crowded. Apart from ornaments, pictures, and knick-knacks, there were a good many items of furniture. One wall was almost taken up with a magnificent Chippendale bookcase, usually kept locked.

Now I had to take every volume outside, open it, bang it shut in case it had gathered dust, then rub the leather covers. It was a lengthy business; every time I went outside, the fresh beauties of the garden, the view of the gently undulating hills and valleys, and the warmth of the sun, made me slower than ever.

The dining-table had been made from a huge slice of mahogany, and had no join. If that table is now in the possession of some lucky owner, they can thank me for helping with its preservation. Drops of my sweat went into the polishing of it. I have swept enough dust under the carpet in my time to fill a few window boxes, and concentrated my energies only on the parts of objects that showed—but there was no dodging this job! It was too big to take outside, and under the old lady's strict eye, perfection was the target.

The old man who did the gardening helped me to hang the faded carpet over the clothes line. She sat on a chair by the door to make sure I whacked the hell out of it. Then it was laid on the flagstoned yard, and sprinkled with a thick layer of salt and used tea-leaves, saved for the purpose. It was left like that while we had our dinner. Then I had to brush off every tea-leaf with a small hard brush, and go over it with a cloth wrung out in a bucket of water laced with vinegar to restore the faded colours, then hang it on to the line to dry.

I had to scrub the tiled floor underneath three times with hot soda-water before I was allowed to polish the surrounds till the sunlight brought a sparkle to the tiles.

Every job took ages. I had all the time in the world. My mistress was irritable because hers was running so short. She would ring her handbell angrily, and threatened me with her walking-stick for my dallying. 'Ketch me first,' I thought.

She did one day. I'd found a copy of *Uncle Tom's Cabin* in the attic during one of my burglar-hunting excursions. She never gave me a minute's peace to read, so I hid it on a shelf in the kitchen cupboard. All my chores in there were done slapdash quick, so that I could have a read. The tap-tap of her stick across the yard warned me of her approach.

One day I got so engrossed in the part where Eliza braves the frozen river with her little son in her arms that I was indeed deaf to the world around me, the scalding tears falling on a pile of plates already inadequately wiped. I came smartly back to earth with a stinging swish from her walking-stick across my behind. She'd had a lot of practice, so was quite a markswoman despite her age. My uncontrollable fit of crying against the cupboard door, for I'd not yet found out if Eliza got safely across, took my old mistress by surprise. She was quite contrite. I didn't bother to enlighten her—she might find me with my head stuck in the cupboard again!

In those days, maids were two-a-penny, yet enticing a maid away was common practice. On one occasion, the old lady's nephew, his wife, and his two daughters came to stay for a week.

The day before they left to go back to London, the nephew's wife came into the kitchen, all smarm and charm, to tell me I'd be much happier in London working for them. She gave me a stamped envelope addressed to her, for me to let her know when I'd be coming. I was not to tell the old lady.

When she went out, I stared into the little mirror in the kitchen to see if I looked as big a simpleton as she took me for.

Another relative tried it on too. She was quite a charming

maiden lady, who had been left very well off and lived in a small select house somewhere in Sussex. I can't think why, but she reckoned I was just the sort of girl she'd been looking for. If I went to her, I would be more than a maid, a sort of lady's companion. She had a local woman to do the rough work. She also hinted that if I stopped with her, it would eventually be much to my material advantage.

Even the rector had a dab at it.

I was picking runner beans for dinner one day, when he came up the garden path after a visit. He stood there, humming and hawing about the weather and God's bounties of the earth, but he soon got onto his own tribulations. The housemaid was leaving the rectory; if I wanted a better job, it was mine.

I haven't much time for the clergy on the whole, especially those who get up on a Sunday morning to cleaned rooms, lit fires and a good big breakfast cooked for them by the meek in heart in the back regions of the house.

'No thank you,' I told him.

All this again was said behind my old mistress's back, which killed the notion from the start, as far as I was concerned.

Though I had some loyalty to my mistress, some pity, if not quite affection for her, it didn't stop me giving her my month's notice when the six months was up. I should have to wait another six months before I had earned the annual two weeks holiday she allowed. But I knew I couldn't bear the separation from my family that long.

She autocratically pooh-poohed the idea. I told her I meant it, and she must start looking for another maid. She did nothing of the sort. She gave me a sort of bribe, a fine wooden needlework casket, with a sampler in it, which she had worked at the age of six. I felt I could not accept it and gave her my notice in writing. I had heard my aunties say this made it legal. She threw it on the fire. Two more weeks of longing to get home went by, and it was my afternoon to walk into Stroud. I was upstairs getting ready when I heard footsteps on the yard, and got the surprise of my life to see my elder sister, Bess, standing there.

'Where be the old varmint?' she asked.

I nodded towards the dining-room door.

'I be come to fetch thee wum.'

'I can't come,' I wailed, 'she's got nobody yet to take my place.'

'Nor likely to, you sawney hap'orth, as long as you be muggins enough to stop 'ere. Where's your things?'

'Up here,' I told her, 'but my box is in through the kitchen there.'

'Chuck thee things out through the winda then. I'll put 'em in thee box and thee canst run away then.'

Now I can't say I needed a lot of persuading to do as she said. Her very presence, so strong a reminder of home and family, and the knowledge that they too were anxious to see me, stilled the small voice of conscience.

I wrote a little note to say that I was running away and put it beside the tea-caddy, where the woman would be bound to see it when she made the tea for my mistress.

The sight of the old lady nodding by the fire—her hands veined and thin as the claws of a plucked chicken—began to give me second thoughts. But she stirred and sharply ordered me to be back before dusk. I didn't answer. For a while, a little while, I could escape from servitude. I was going to see and touch my little sisters and brother, my Mam and Dad, and the dear familiar sights of home.

Cheltenham Spa

I decided to get another job to better myself. This time it was in Cheltenham, that aristocrat of towns, where in the 1920s everybody who wasn't a servant was a somebody; including the snooty little Pekes and Pomeranians, creatures rated much higher in their mistresses' eyes than the servants.

Again I was to be the only maid, and still at five shillings a week, but I thought I was making headway into a more sohisticated and plentiful world. In fact, the only thing I found more plentiful was the work.

Although my new master had been among the sons of gentlemen at Cheltenham College, it had not managed to educate out of his nature a patronising distaste for servants, and all the 'lower orders'. Ironically, he had married 'beneath him'—a pretty, calculating nurse. She had thought the private-ward appendix patient was worth more than nursing, and after his discharge, she manipulated him into marriage.

They had both been 'had'. The business he had inherited on the death of his widowed mother had come to a poor pass under her mismanagement. But he and his wife shared the same snob values. She had married to get into the middle class—and be damned he *was* middle class—upper middle class old chap, actually. They were determined to cut some sort of figure, even if it was on very thin ice. The coming of their two children, a boy then three years old, and a girl of six months, had aggravated their situation.

They were in need of a strong young fool—one who could be house-maid from six till one for cleaning the house, then parlour-maid for waiting at table, then nanny for the children's afternoon outings, then washerwoman in the evenings. They needed a creature that would run on very little fuel and would not question her lot. Instead, they had me; but at any rate I *was* a fool.

I soon found my new mistress's sharp tongue a more efficient goad than my old one's walking-stick. I became quite a nimble worker, especially as, on the spartan diet she provided, I had no surplus flesh to hold me back.

Every Wednesday, after I had washed up the lunch things and cleared up the kitchen, I was free until ten o'clock. This arrangement held good for alternate Sundays too.

There were other girls from our small village working as maids in Cheltenham. One of these, Dolly, who had been a special friend at school and had shared my fourteenth birthday party, had taken the trouble to write to Mam for my address. Then she wrote to me, saying she would call for me on our next Sunday afternoon off; we could go to the pictures together.

My employers had taken their children off for the day, making a great deal of fuss piling into the rather grand car they could ill-afford to run. I had been given a long list of jobs to get through before I went out, and madam informed me she had left my lunch under a traycloth on the kitchen table. I tackled my jobs with a will, heartened by the thought of spending my afternoon off with Dolly. I was scrubbing the basement passage—the last of my chores—when she rang the door bell. It was half past two.

'I thought it was supposed to be your 'alf-day! I finished work at 'alf past twelve! My missus didn't even let me do the washing-up after dinner! You should finish work at one o'clock on your 'alf-day; it's the law.' These observations were made in a very loud voice, and with a jerk of the head upwards that implied 'and I 'ope them buggers upstairs be listenin'.'

'They be gone out for the day,' I told her. 'Never mind, I've only got to eat me dinner, and change; that wun't take me long.'

'It certainly wun't take thee long to yut thee dinner!' Dolly gasped, when she lifted the traycloth.

Rigor mortis had already begun to set in on the tiny cube of stale corned beef; the dry outside was curling up with mortification for having bothered a clean plate. Sitting in a lonely state on another plate was a wizened apple.

'What's that s'pos'ed to be, your 'ors d'urvies?'

'No, that's my dinner.'

'The old cow! Where do they kip the vittles 'ere?'

Before I could tell her where the larder was, and that it was locked, Dolly had discovered both.

'Not left you even a bit o' bread to fill up the carners! You shoulda' seen what I 'ad for my dinner. But I won't tell you; it'd be croo-el! Never mind; we'll go round and see my cousin Olive in her job afore we go to the pictures.'

Dolly's cousin, Olive, worked as a parlour-maid in a private boarding school for small boys. 'I 'ope it's cook's Sunday off. Miserable old faggot 'er is; don't like the maids 'avin' any friends in the kitchen.'

We were lucky; cook was out. The five maids on duty were just about to sit down to their tea, laid on one end of an enormous, well-scoured, wooden table. Each girl's plate was rationed to three thick slices of bread and marge, a dab of red jam, and a good-sized wedge of pale currant cake. The kitchen-maid poured out their tea, and a cup each for Dolly and me. I tried to look uninterested in the feast about to be consumed, but when Dolly realised a cup of tea was going to be our lot, she told them about my 'dinner' and what a 'starve-guts' job I had landed myself in. Five pairs of kindly sympathetic eyes gave me their full attention; and each took a bit of her cake and bread and jam and piled it on to a plate for me, saying what a shame it was.

It was too much; I burst out crying. I wasn't sure whom I was feeling sorriest for; myself—or those five kind girls, barely allowed their identities under the uniform caps and aprons.

I was too choked up to eat much, but they put their offerings in a paper bag, and insisted I took it with me. When we got outside I unjustly accused Dolly of letting me make a fool of myself.

It was heaven to go inside the warm dark picture house, where tear stains did not show. Here I could exchange my lot for one of the glamour queens of Hollywood. Afterwards I returned to reality, and said good night to Dolly. Cheltenham seemed an aloof and cold place to walk through.

Indoors again, I sat on the edge of the narrow iron bedstead that practically filled my tiny box-room, and ate the remains of my food parcel.

Every day, by breakfast time, I had done a couple of hours hard work. I had the appetite of a growing girl nearing fifteen years. My mistress bought my bacon separate from theirs; it was narrow streaky rashers cut very thin, and one of these was put out each morning for my breakfast. But, for my bread, I had to go into the dining-room. 'One, two, or three slices?' the master would ask, somehow implying by his manner that it was an act of charity to give me any. Sensing it to be grudged, I was too proud to ask for three, too hungry to stick at one. I always compromised, 'two, sir, please.'

Despite her toffee-nosed ambitions, or perhaps to show off her status, the mistress had remained friendly with one of her nursing colleagues. This was an exquisitely pretty young woman. I thought her pink-and-white complexion, and her golden-haired, blue-eyed beauty, must surely be the equal of Mary Pickford's. She looked as though butter wouldn't melt in her mouth. Once she came in her nurse's uniform, and I thought 'ministering angel' a very apt description. Sometimes she came to lunch; on these occasions the master gave her a lift to the house in his car.

One afternoon, the mistress was downstairs in the dining-room, and I was upstairs just completing my weekly turn-out of the lounge. Through the lace curtains I saw the master's car draw up, and him handing Nurse Hale out. Not wishing to emerge into the hall just as they were coming in, I waited in the lounge, and heard the front door quietly open and close. A little longer—for them to pass through—and I came out. But they were there! Very still, very quiet, and *very* close together!

In fact, it took them a whole minute to get unstuck from as passionate an embrace as ever Rod la Rocque and Vilma Banky could manage. I was shocked; so shocked you could have knocked me down with the feather duster I was carrying.

Fancy! The likes of her! So beautiful, so *nice*, wanting to be kissed by the likes of him—someone the likes of me would turn her nose up at—an ungentlemanly man in gentleman's clothes! I suppose he must have had considerable hidden charm, but I hadn't cottoned on to it.

By the colour of their faces, they had had a bigger shock than I. Oh well, their business was none of mine. Even my own wasn't, for when the master and mistress had been discussing me with visitors while I was still in the room, and I had ventured to correct them on a point, I had been told that servants didn't have eyes or ears for their betters' conversation and activities. So the surprised lovers went into the dining-room, and I went on with my work, and nothing was said.

The next morning, when I went in for my breakfast, I realised that the master's maxim about servants' eyes and ears was not strictly true. Instead of his usual enquiry, he gratuitously suggested I might like *three* slices of bread, *and* he gave me a big smile with the offer! I recognised the insinuated bribe with its suggestion that I might be capable of blackmail, and the tacit admission that he'd been aware of my hunger. I looked him coldly and squarely in the eye.

'No, thank you, two as usual, sir,' I replied; and the piece I went without was by far the most satisfying.

On the Farm

Six months was the limit of my endurance as far as the Cheltenham household was concerned. I escaped to home as soon as I reasonably could, and determined never again to look for a job where my employers were trying to keep up an appearance beyond their means.

But as I couldn't stay for long to add to the burden of the little ones, I knew it could be only a brief respite.

After two pinch-belly jobs, the chance to work in the house of a remote hundred-acre farm in Wales seemed a good idea. It would be no progress moneywise; the wage offered was still only a pound a month, but 'farmhouse' surely meant bowls of big brown eggs, sizzling home-cured bacon, thick creamy butter on home-baked bread, and mugs full of frothy milk still warm from the cow.

It also meant being 'a strong willing girl'. Well, I was willing, and farmhouse food would make anyone strong, surely. Best of all, I shouldn't have to wear the hated caps and aprons, and I would sit down to meals with the family.

It was two miles to Little Rowan Farm from the nearest bus stop, but I only had to walk up the lane. My clothes were now packed in my new, large four-and-eleven cardboard portmanteau; it wasn't very heavy. The mud was the big hindrance; it was February. Recent snows had melted, and the red clay soil was a nice mud-pie consistency. I gathered enough on my shoes, and on my portmanteau when I put it down for a rest, to fill a fair-size window box.

There was still enough light for me to pick my way round to the back of the farmhouse. The front of the house was in darkness, and the porch door in the middle was obviously not for general use. I had already acquired the back-door entrance habit, anyway.

This back-door was a stable-fashioned one, with a separate top and bottom half. It was wide enough for a horse to get through. When the top half was opened at my knocking, I took in a picture of living, primitive even by my standards.

I looked in on a long, narrow room, ceilinged with black oak beams the size of a small tree. Where the dark shadows revealed them, the walls were distempered in ochre. A small window at the far end was covered with a roller blind to shut out the night. On an enormous table was a paraffin lamp. By its soft light, and the flickers from the hearth, I saw a few oak shelves, ebony black with age, arranged with odd cups, saucers, and plates. A crudely made settle, covered with shiny black oilcloth, was pushed up hard against the wall facing the fireplace. This fireplace was merely a cavernous hole in the wall, surrounded by slabs of stone. From a chain fixed to an iron bar hung a huge witch-type black cauldron. Half a small tree trunk sulked smokily in the middle of the fire, and a big black kettle stood just nudging the flame on the hearth.

The man half-dozing in a wooden armchair by the fire might have been John Bull himself. His eyes were closed, but one booted foot was gently tapping the rockers of a wooden cradle on the floor. The cherub baby in the cradle had the same bright ginger hair as himself.

A couple, obviously the baby's parents, sat with their backs to the door; between them a bag, for the feathers each was plucking from a chicken. In the wall, just above their heads, a little iron door marked the bread oven.

Just inside, and to my right, a boy about my own age was skinning one of a number of moles on the lid of a wash-copper built into the corner. His hands were like swedes.

In the opposite corner was a stone salting slab; above it, on the wall, hung the remains of a flitch of bacon covered with the grey salty rime that preserved it and protected it from flies. Here and there, on the stone-flagged floor, sacks were laid in strategic places to catch the dirt from muddy boots.

It wasn't a prepossessing place, yet its very ugly homeliness bore a comfort. I was sick of snobs.

I didn't feel uneasy to sit at the supper table with such people, but my notions of farmhouse food were knocked on the head at once. It was most unfortunate that I had an absolute abhorrence of cheese in any form. Supper at Little Rowan Farm was a choice— dry bread and cheese, or dry bread and broth from the cauldron, or dry bread and skim milk. It had one saving factor—the bread was unlimited. I chose broth with mine. This had plenty of pepper and salt in it, and a few bits of onion, easily seen floating in its pale grey slightly greasy depths. There was a faint flavour of bacon, but a vegetarian could have eaten it without much trouble to his conscience.

The others all had bread and cheese and cider. We didn't get up from the table until my new mistress (a fervent chapel-goer) had said grace. Privately, I told the Almighty that I didn't feel all that thankful, and my amen wasn't very enthusiastic.

After supper, with warm water from the kettle on the hearth, I washed up the supper things in a big chipped enamel bowl, after wiping the table down. Bert, the mole-skinner, showed me how to use the water pump in the back-yard. Then we fetched the milk-separator from the bitterly cold dairy. I gathered that I was supposed to be overawed by this newly acquired modern contraption. Buckets of milk were poured into the capacious top, and out of one spout came the cream, and from the other, thin bluish skim milk. The bowls of cream were taken into the dairy for butter making; the skim milk was for our domestic use, and for the animals.

By the next evening, I knew that the old man was the baby's paternal grandfather. He was a widower, and had five married sons and two married daughters. They all rented farms, and he stayed a little time with each one, applying his skill to helping them at hedging, haymaking, cider-making, mangel-chopping, and so on. He treated life like a fat, juicy steak, something to get stuck into, and, even at the age of seventy, any woman's behind that came within his reach was for slapping. Having him under her roof was torture to my Calvinistic, chapel-besotted, over-refined mistress. Only the obvious adoration that mother and grandfather felt for the baby made the arrangement possible.

Bert was another of his grandchildren, one of six orphaned by the death of their parents. He and his brothers and sister had been shared out among the others; and my employers had certainly got a bargain.

From the age of nine, when they had taken him in, he'd been made to earn his keep by pre-school and after-school chores. Now he gave them full-time assistance, and didn't get a penny in wages. The only coppers he had to spend were the few odd ones he received for his moleskins.

While I was there, an Act of Parliament was passed, obliging his uncle to pay him a minimum of one pound a month. He never saw this money either; they banked it for him. And after that, the sight of Bert standing still for even a minute was hard for them to bear.

His body and soul were held together by the plainest of food; his clothes were patched-up cast-offs of his grandfather. The trousers' waist came nearly to his armpits, and the tattered matching jacket reached to his knees.

I had worn too many queer left-off garments myself to laugh at his comic appearance. My own shortage of working clothes was eased by a kind middle-aged woman who lived in a cottage up the lane. She gave me the dresses she'd worn as a VAD in the War. I was slim enough to hook up the twenty-inch waist, and tall enough for the skirts to come only to my ankles. They were made of stout khaki with brown trimming.

I had long hair tied back with a ribbon, and I was nearly sixteen years old. It was 1930, and the current fashions then were shingled or Eton-cropped hair, and short dresses showing fancy beribboned garters.

One autumn day, I nipped down the field in the hope of finding a walnut left under the tree in the corner. As I searched, a huntswoman rode up. She reined in her mount at the side of me, and in a loud, assured 'county' voice, called to a male rider a few yards away: 'Do come and have a look at this. Isn't it quaint?'

She stared at me with such insolent amusement that I realised I was the 'it' referred to. The blood rushed to my cheeks, but I stared back. Her heavily rouged and powdered face was covered with a black net attached to a hard black hat. She rode sidesaddle, and her shining black boots were almost covered by a long black hobble skirt.

Talk about the pot calling the kettle black! She looked ridiculous, but I had better manners than to say so out loud. The man drew up and she repeated her remark.

'Beautiful, I'd say,' he observed, and touched his riding hat to me. Then he snubbed her further by bidding me good morning with a warm smile that was more than polite. 'Good mornin' and good 'untin',' I replied. And to the disappearing back of his companion I wished, 'Good riddance, and I 'ope you come a cropper in some cow muck.'

For a few minutes a gentleman had made me feel like a lady.

I worked a year on that farm, and the dinners only varied by the nature of the potatoes—waxy in their early summer youth, floury the rest of the year. The swedes, boiled in a big iron saucepan, tasted always the same; and so did the home-cured bacon, sizzling in a heavy black pot next to the saucepan. Day in, day out, weekdays and Sundays, it was always the same, and it never tasted less than delicious. Hunger was a good appetiser, for our breakfast was always thick toast and margarine, with plenty of sweet tea.

Nothing that could be taken to the market on Tuesday was ever used at home. The cracked or soft-shell eggs were given to the men for breakfast. There were never enough dud eggs for Bert or me!

But this didn't worry Bert. Once he knew I could be trusted, he confided in me that when he found where the hens laid off, he just broke the shell and swallowed the eggs raw.

He was quite a sturdy lad, and I felt sorry for him. Sometimes, when I was doing some chore, and no one about, I let him put his arms round my waist, and maybe a hand would creep up and cup a breast. I had begun to feel a need to be caressed; but not by Bert. He wasn't my style at all.

When the master, mistress and baby went off with their wares in the pony and trap to market, I fed the ducks and fowls, did the cleaning, and cooked dinner for Bert, the old man, and myself. On market day we lingered a little longer over it, but one day, Bert had a lot to do and took himself off early.

The old man stretched out his legs, patted his round paunch, belched heartily, and with a wicked twinkle in his eye, suggested I forget the work and go up on the bed with him for a slap and a tickle. I thought the idea outrageously funny, and nearly fell about laughing, he wasn't my type either. The old bull stumped out, a bit aggrieved at my reaction.

Things like half-days off were never mentioned down on the farm; but I used to enjoy my weekly two-mile walk to the village shop. I didn't enjoy it so much on the way back, for a bag of tea, sugar, flour, and salt, plus a gallon tin of paraffin, took the dance out of my footsteps. I was quite a strong girl now, for if Bert had his egg bonus, I was a secret cream dipper every time I went into the dairy.

As I shut the farm gate behind me, and set off down the lane to the shop, my spirits rose. For the next hour or two, unsupervised by my mistress's sharp eye, I could belong to myself. The shopping bag and the paraffin can couldn't weigh down my spirits. Oh, lucky, lucky me! To be alive and sixteen years old, and walking up a Welsh country lane on a perfect May morning. Look near, look far, all was a transport of delight.

On the left was a tree-ringed pond with a couple of horses grazing. Close by stood two ancient oaks, no longer leaf-bearing, gnarled and distorted with sylvan senility; a regular granma and grancher of trees. Beyond them, in the far distance, the Sugar Loaf dominated a mountainous skyline. As I walked, I would note where the primrose clumps grew thickest on the banks. I could wheel the baby there later, and then pick and bunch them for market.

Mrs Jones was shaking her mats. 'Mornin', gal,' she called out cheerily. 'Indeed to G-o-d, this bit o'sun shows up the cobwebs. Mind you step in for a cup o'tea on your way back, look. Be a good gal, and bring me a tin of Nestlé's milk. Tell Dai I'll pay 'im Friday.' On an after-thought, 'and two Oxos to make the gravy look as if it's got a bit o'meat in it.'

Yes, Mrs Jones, righto, Mrs Jones! Anything to oblige Mrs Jones! It was that sort of a morning, anyone would have obliged anybody for anything.

A farm labourer on a bicycle passed me: 'Mornin', my lovely,' he beamed; he too had got the mood of the day. I heard Mrs Jones call out to him, 'How are you getting on now, Gwillum?'

'Not very often; the old gal won't let me!'

In broad daylight, rabbits turned the land into a conjuror's hat, appearing by magic, and disappearing again after short ecstatic sessions of grass nibbling. They wagged their rounded powder-puff behinds in careless defiance of their enemies.

To the shop I trod the light fantastic; but homeward was a plod, weighed down as I was by my load. I was thankful indeed to reach Mrs Jones's.

Apart from her big black-leaded grate, I can't recall anything special about the dark brown inside of her cottage. But I do remember the Welsh cakes she gave me with a cup of tea—flat, round, currant-sprinkled, melt-in-the-mouth morsels, tasting then like manna from heaven. We had an unspoken agreement not to mention these stops for refreshment to my mistress; and my load seemed lighter for the rest of the way.

'There's a time you've been,' my mistress would say tartly. 'I thought you'd forgot yourself and gone to Abergavenny by mistake! Well, fill the lamps, and then you'd better get on straight away peeling the swedes and potatoes for dinner. You won't have time now to scrub out the dairy first.' I never minded her scolding; I felt sorry for her. She hadn't enjoyed the glory of my four-mile walk.

Long before I picked primroses for market, I was put gathering snowdrops, even the first few hardy ones that peeped up through the snow here and there. They were one penny a bunch, and cheap at the price if you took into account the aches I suffered as my frozen fingers thawed. But the sheer joy of gathering wild flowers made up for it.

Because of our simple diet, only onions were grown in the vegetable garden; potatoes came from the field. But there were also a few gooseberry bushes. I didn't expect to get any of these cooked, but I did look forward to eating a few ripe ones. I was disappointed. The mistress shared the job of picking them—again for market—with me, and somehow, under her forbidding eye, I didn't have the nerve to pop one into my mouth.

However, I made up for it with apples. Bert and the master gathered these, and stacked them in a huge mound on the flagstones by the back door, while they waited their turn to borrow the cider press.

Old Fagin himself couldn't have criticised the sly speed with which I pinched a few on my way to the privy. I knew the pale greeny-yellow ones that were sugar-sweet and juicy.

At first, my extra calls of nature were shams, just simply to sit enthroned in the privy, juicily munching and watching the tell-tale cores float out of sight down the stream. But after the apples had been there a week, I had to dash down the garden path in earnest, too quickly to bend and snatch one up.

'I see you got the back-door trot; perhaps you should eat a few green apples to have a good clear-out,' Bert sniggered in my ear.

I had my own back on him later. Myfanwy, the postgirl, brought our letters on horseback. She was nineteen and very goodlooking, and seemed to me like a member of royalty, sitting up there so casual and at ease.

We saw her only rarely, and then usually with my letter from Mam. Bert told me enviously he had never had a letter in his life. I bided my time and wrote him one. I wrote it backwards so that he would have to hold it up to the mirror to read. I wrote, 'Important message under stamp on envelope—tell no one—a secret admirer.' Under the stamp I printed, 'April Fool.'

On April the first, when he and the master came in for dinner, I gave Bert the letter. I regretted it the moment I saw the joy and excitement it caused him. His piled-up plate of dinner was usually the highlight of his day, but it got cold while he painstakingly made out the writing in a piece of old spotted mirror by the door. Then gently, after licking the stamp wet with his tongue, he carefully peeled it off, not noticing there was no postmark. I wished I hadn't seen the hurt, and the dreadful disappointment in his face, when he got the message. I was as near to tears for my tactless cruelty as he was, but I couldn't rub in his humiliation by showing my pity.

That summer, the hay had been cut and turned by pitch-fork over and over to sun-dried perfection. The master had the countryman's feel that rain was on the way. Could the mistress spare me to help him and Bert get the hay into the rick?

I was careful not to let her see how much I would love to go. I even scowled to put her off the scent. She seemed to think that, in Heaven's name, life must be a cross to bear, not something to make light of. Humming and hawing a bit, she agreed, reluctantly.

The master let me climb into the waggon behind old Bonnie, the carthorse, whose back was wide enough to dance a hornpipe on. She made nothing of getting up the short steep bank to the gate of the meadow. Bert swung the gate open, and immediately we were at work.

Now it was my job to level off and tread down the forkfuls of hay that the master and Bert loaded from either side. In no time at all, all of us except Bonnie were sweating profusely. The men could strip to their shirts, but not take them off, with such a mistress in charge.

I, of course, had to sweat it out in my ankle-length old VAD dress, but at least I had the sleeves rolled up above the elbows. I didn't care anyway; it was lovely to be out.

The master said I was doing the job as well as any man. High praise, indeed, for when she was about, he was almost as dumb as Buster Keaton.

He and Bert kept pitching up the hay, and I kept treading it down. The load got higher and higher. The ground seemed a perilous way off, especially when the top-heavy load swayed as

Bonnie got on uneven ground. Eventually I was using a pitchfork to take it from the loaders who could no longer reach. But, at last, when I was letting out little squeals of apprehension, the master and Bert threw ropes up to me to let down the other side and secure the load. There was no way for me to get down until we got to the rick and the ladder. While the men had a pause and put on their jackets, I sat, queen of all I surveyed, on a throne of golden hay, crowned with a red-spotted hankerchief corner-knotted. As far as the eye could see, my pastoral domain was of exceeding beauty.

However, my regal dignity was sorely tried as Bonnie gingerly felt her way down the steep slope from meadow to lane. Talk about Cleopatra on a camel! It couldn't have been a bumpier ride. The master looked happy and quite boyish, as he laughed up to reassure me I was safe.

We felt a spot or two of rain; getting that hay in so neatly on time quite went to the master's head. When the waggon got to the rick, he told me to step off the top on to the hay that was already stacked there, and wait while Bert and he unloaded. I could have a little rest up there. I caught on when they took away Bonnie, and the empty waggon, *and* the ladder. I was stranded.

'There's plenty o' rats in that stack to keep you company,' guffawed Bert, 'there's nothing they like better than running up women's skirts.'

'That's how she shoulda' trod that hay down on the waggon,' laughed the master, as I jumped up and down like Nijinsky, and screamed with panic.

The noise brought the mistress out; the grins dropped from their faces, and with a show of serious concern they placed the ladder against the stack. But the mistress had her suspicions. She stood there, while they turned their backs to me as I descended, though the length of my skirt was modest enough. I followed her indoors, turning behind her back to poke my tongue out at the miscreants. I guessed the master was in the doghouse for a bit.

Nature had been trying hard to push me into womanhood, and she was having a bit of a struggle. Now, after half a year on the farm, she was eventually winning. A frugal but healthy diet, plenty of exercise, sound sleep, early rising, early bed, no worries, and the fresh air from the mountains filling the lungs by day and night. It had its effect; I was blossoming out very roundly in the right places: a fact that, unknown to me, hadn't escaped the watchful eye of the young man who owned the next farm. He had even wasted his time hanging about on his land next to the lane, to watch me on my weekly walk to the shop.

If his name cropped up at the farm, my mistress gave a disapproving sniff, for he was known as 'a bit of a wild lad' who rode a motorbike, and stayed out half the night in Abergavenny town. He was twenty-six.

I had been allowed to go into Abergavenny once for a spending spree, with three months' saved-up wages. I sent a postal order home to Mam, and had plenty left for shoes and a few everyday clothes, plus a pale-green silk dress and a wide-brimmed lacy straw hat with green ribbons. When the year was up, and I due for a holiday, I intended to impress the boys back home. Then an unexpected opportunity came for me to wear my new finery.

Two things happended. The old man went off to stay with another son, and the new chapel minister invited my master and mistress to stay on after Sunday evening service, and to take supper with him.

These blessings put my mistress in such a transport of good humour that she told me I could have some time off to go to Sunday-evening chapel. Poor Bert would have to be the Christian who did all the chores! 'Six days shalt thou labour' had to be overlooked in his case.

Normally, I'd have preferred to stay at home and help Bert rather than listen to a Sunday sermon, but I wasn't going to miss the chance to try out my new clothes. Saturday morning I washed my hair and put it in curling papers.

The master and mistress, with the baby, started for chapel well ahead of me, which gave me the chance to pinch a dab of her Pond's Vanishing Cream to put on my snub nose. As I looked in her mirror, I blushed rose-pink with pleasure. Oh, it couldn't be me! That pretty girl, in a lovely dress, with brown silky curls, and round face framed in lacy straw!

Bert was so surprised he nearly stepped back into the bucket of pig-swill he'd been stirring. He looked quite hungry at the sight of me.

Freedom to walk out in the hedgerowed lane normally meant that I would indulge in a hop-skip-and-dance routine when out of sight of the farm. But today I walked proud and sedate like a young lady of quality.

On the very corner of the lane was a farmhouse that looked in the front as grand as a manor, although the back was the usual quagmire surrounded by barns, stables, and pig-styes. Just as I passed, a girl about my own age picked her way carefully to the gate. She was carrying a Bible, and was obviously in her Sunday clothes. Not having seen her before, I didn't venture to speak. She, however, had seen me often as I carried the paraffin, and knew that I was the 'help' at Little Rowan Farm. She did similar work on a grander scale. She was Welsh and friendly, and talkative. Her dad was a miner too, in Abertillery. She was the eldest of six, and her name was Letty Meadows. We had a lot in common, except that I thought her name and herself much prettier than I.

The chapel was a mile further on past the village. It was a minute building of grey stone, not important enough to have its own churchyard, but set in a neat grass plot just off the road. It was almost filled. Considering the sparseness of the local population, it proved how popular chapel attending was in Wales.

The service had not yet begun. My master and mistress were up front, talking to the new minister. Filled with gracious superiority by the minister's attention, my mistress beckoned me to her and introduced me as 'our maid'. I thought the description savoured of swank, and wasn't in the spirit of Jesus as taught in chapel. I was glad to return to Letty on the back seat by the door.

She was no more interested in the sermon that I was; neither were a couple of likeable-looking lads, in the seat in front of us, who weren't taken in by the apparent indifference Letty and I showed to their head-turnings in our direction.

'I wonder if they'll follow us after,' whispered Letty hopefully.

In unspoken agreement, we didn't hang around the chapel door, but hurried off down the road, to escape surveillance by our elders.

'Don't turn round, but, indeed, they are following us,' said Letty, well pleased.

Gauche and unsure like dog puppies, bold and diffident by turns, they whistled the popular love ballads of the day to us, and shouted out compliments disguised as sarcasm.

We answered and encouraged them in the only ways we knew— tossing our curls, giggling to each other, and even looking round to acknowledge their presence. Suddenly, a tuppenny bar of chocolate fell, from mid-air, in front of our feet.

'Which one do you like best?' asked Letty. Highly flattered at getting any masculine attention at all, I didn't feel too fussy; also it was most likely that they were both after Letty. So, to be on the safe side, I lied, 'I don't fancy either of 'em.'

After about half a mile, the boys had got up to within a few feet of us; but they hung back a bit when they saw our neighbour farmer waiting at the kerbside with his motorbike. Much to my surprise, he started to push his motorbike, and walk alongside us. Surprise is not a strong enough word for what I felt when he asked *me* if I would take a pillion lift home. I could only suppose that he didn't have the nerve to ask Letty. She was so much prettier than I, and I then judged feminine attraction simply by the face.

I was not enamoured of mine. 'More like a Chink's dial!' I used to scold my reflection—high cheekbones, squat nose, wide mouth. That I had grown to five feet six inches tall, with a tiny waist, and lovely feminine proportions had quite escaped my notice. If I sound immodest, it's because I saw, many years later, some snapshots taken at the time. And if a modern sixteen-year-old miss thinks I was ludicrously retarded, I *was*.

'Take Letty instead,' I offered haughtily, for I wanted none of his charity.

'There isn't room for the two of you, and it's you I asked,' he said firmly, and quickly added, with some tact, 'Letty hasn't so far to go as you.'

'Go on, gal, have a ride,' urged Letty. I was so convinced of Letty's superiority, there was no need to feel pity for any slight, even unintended. Anyway, she had the two beaux behind her to choose from. I was also inwardly excited beyond measure at such a turn of events. So I couldn't resist accepting my moment of glory.

I took off my hat, and sat as gracefully as I could on the pillion. My heart was in my mouth, for more than one reason, when the motorbike chugged into life.

When we turned off the main road into the lane, the ride became very bumpy; but as soon as he got to the first gate on his land, he stopped and wheeled the bike inside. 'I'd like to walk you home the rest of the way,' he said.

At first he politely left a stranger's gap, bridged by mutual physical awareness between us; but suddenly, on pretext of an imaginary stumble, he took my arm. The pressure of his strong hand, firm yet gentle, pretending to hold me up, was very pleasing. But I was unpractised in coquetry, and it took nearly half a mile more before his arm got round my shoulder, with my head gently pressed against his chest.

The strong curve of a man's right arm is surely the dearest haven for a woman's head. By the time we had reached the horse-chestnut tree in the lane opposite Little Rowan, his arm had got down round my waist.

My instinctive woman's guile had been awakened during our walk, and I made a show of reluctance when he suggested we sit down under the chestnut tree. But slowly I allowed his tender male dominance to persuade me, and we were on the soft grass, he with his back against the trunk. Now I felt as helpless as a seedling that cannot resist the lure of the sun, forced by the very basis of its nature to grow, to bloom, and to seed.

I let the young man take me in his arms, tilt my unresisting face to his, gently brush my lips with his, searching for, and finding for both of us, such a profound sweetness as I had never dreamed of. Everything beautiful I had ever known, or thought of, had lain dormant for this moment, to be awakened in this kiss. A kind of reverence came over us.

I could feel the pounding of my heart and his. It was just a kiss—no more. But for me, new to the taste of love, it was enough, more than enough. The young man pulled me to my feet, and even the touching of our hands was ecstasy, and unabated till we reached the porch. Then, tenderly, as though I were made of gossamer, the young farmer kissed my lips, my forehead, and my work-roughened hands. 'I'll watch for you,' he whispered, and was gone.

It seemed as if I floated round to the back-door. I wanted no supper. The cream pan did not tempt me to dip a finger. I could live without bread and drink tonight, for I had tasted nectar. I was sixteen and I *had* been kissed.

But Bert, poor Bert, still a clod-hopping mortal, *he* needed some supper.

I was coming out of the dairy with the cheese for him when he clumped in through the door.

'*I* saw who brought you home tonight.' His voice sounded dour and accusing. 'When he realised I'd spotted him, he told me not to tell my uncle.'

He told him not to tell his uncle! One minute I had been floating on the airy pinnacle of ecstasy, a Venus adored, and now I was the disowned beggar-maid, someone ashamed to have been seen with.

To have been escorted to the door of the Kingdom of Love, to have had my hand kissed like a queen, and then to have been snubbed so, and snubbed in front of someone like Bert!

At sixteen, black was black and white was white; it took years to merge them into grey. Lover to traitor, nectar to dust, I was still too full up for any supper. For now I was stuffed up with outraged feminine pride. By the time I got to bed it was overflowing from my eyes in two salty torrents.

Hitherto I had loved to waken in the morning to the pungent farmyard odours flavouring the new morning air, air that had come across the sea and over the top of the Sugar Loaf mountain. The soft feather bed did not compete too strongly with the new day beckoning through the window.

The waking sounds of birds and beasts, already heralded by the cock-crows near and far, gave importance to each day.

Come on, then, fowls! Fly from your perches, gobble up your scattered breakfast of golden corn.

Lumber ungainly up the lane, you cows, through the creaking, five-barred, wooden gate, into the rested field.

Don't wag your tail right off, old sheep dog, just because you are being let off your chain to manage, almost on your own, the moving of a hundred silly old sheep. Good dog, yes you *are* a good dog.

Stop your scolding quack-quack, you upstart ducks. I've got a lot of other jobs before I come to pull up the door of your pen.

Skinny sinuous cats, which of you were fighting like two Lucifers in the night? More ratting, and less tomming, you jealous Romeos. But here's your milk, all half a bucket of it, skimmed of course, to share between the six, seven, eight, oh, the lot of you.

There, I've seen to you all, but my heart's not in it any more; it's lying like lead in my side, and nobody knows, and nobody cares. I wish I was a cat, a sheep, a cow or a duck, you are somebody. I'm nobody, a proper nothing. No, I *am* a somebody;

I'm Polly Mason, and I'll show him, oh, I'll show him! I'll walk by him, haughtier than any queen, if I ever set eyes on him again.

Set eyes on him again? Well, of all the cruel nerve! There he was, talking to the master by the granary door, and I must pass them to fetch some wood from the stack near the dog's kennel. I concentrated as much venom into the look I gave him as I then knew how to muster.

I threw the wood on the fire with enough angry carelessness to wake the baby, morning-napping in the wooden cradle on the floor. This brought me a sharp reprimand from the mistress to watch what I was doing.

I though my master and mistress looked at me a bit quizzical when we were eating our dinner, but they made no comment on my behaviour.

It had not been the habit of the young farmer to call on my master, but now, to my annoyance and embarrassment, I could not help seeing them talking on several occasions. Once I was unlucky enough to answer the door to his knock. Luckily, the mistress was in the kitchen, for he held out his arms as though he would grab hold of me, and his eyes were as soft and begging as a spaniel's.

Let him do his underhand begging; I would not give him a bone if he were starving. I took great care to make myself scarce, and never to glance in his direction when he was about.

The village shop now delivered by van; I was half-glad, half-sorry that my weekly errand was finished. The exhilaration of feeling free for an hour or so was shadowed by the thought that I might bump into *him*.

It was a very cold autumn day when the shopkeeper forgot to bring our paraffin. We needed it for the lamps; I must put a move on with my chores and fetch it before dark.

On the way, I saw the cause of my misery walking behind a horse-drawn plough on his land some fields away. Away from the busy bustle of the farm, a deep sense of melancholy came over me. I would have to go away. I resolved to give in a month's notice the next day.

Hurrying home, changing the heavy can from one hand to the other to speed my progress, I was brought to a heart-pounding halt by the young farmer. He had been waiting behind the hedge near the last gate that bounded his land. He had stepped out in front of me and stood barring my way. Though already rosycheeked from exertion, I felt the blood rush to my face, and away from my legs.

I tried to side-step and pass him; I wanted none of his hold-in-the-corner attentions. With sheer strength he took the paraffin can from me, put an iron-grip on each of my shoulders, and backed me towards the gate. His manner was desperate and beseeching.

'Why do you keep hiding and turning away from me?' he begged, holding me in his arms against my will, and trying to find my lips with his.

Had I been a girl of true spirit I would have smacked his face and told him I was as good as he; and if he could not acknowledge openly he found me attractive, he could keep the secret all to himself.

Up till then my life had not done much to nurture such a spirit. I was full of inward pride, the sort that would cut off its nose to spite its face; the sort of pride that made a great fuss over the little it had to be proud about. I could not bear to put into words that hurt his slight had caused me. A week before, his kiss had made my body melt, yet now I felt as unyielding and unfeeling as the gate I was pressed against.

Puzzled and upset by my obstinacy, his ardour turned to anger; he let me go and walked back through the gate.

My mistress did not seem unduly upset when I gave her my month's notice. Though willing, I was not a particularly able servant. I found watching the floating myriads of dust particles highlighted in a shaft of sunlight through the window more amusing than polishing it off the furniture. Besides, I was getting a big girl with a big appetite; I was gone sixteen years old, and might be wanting a rise soon on my five-shilling-a-week wages. A livelier fourteen-year-old girl might be cheaper and easier to train.

I wrote home and told them I was leaving my job. Mam told a neighbour, and the neighbour put this item of news in her letter to her daughter who was working in London. By this means, before I had left the farm I had a letter from my neighbour's daughter telling me she could get me a job any time. It would be working for Jewish people, as she was, and the wages were very good, ten shillings a week, and they did not mind if you did not wear caps and aprons. Her address was in Aldgate.

Supper was eaten in high good humour the evening before I left the farm. Bert and the master had taken all day to walk some bullocks into Abergavenny for sale, and they had fetched a very good price. Bert was as high and mighty as the Prince of Wales, with a new cap the guv'nor had bought him, and the master and mistress were oozing with good humour.

'We did wonder a while back,' smiled the master, winking at his wife, 'if we were going to have you for a neighbour in time. Poor Dai took a proper fancy to you, you know, neglecting his own place, finding excuses to come across to see me. I knew who he'd *really* come to see. Mind you, he asked me all above board if it would be all right for him to take you out. I could tell by the way you looked at him he wasn't going to have any luck. You could have done worse, you know. There's many a girl round here would jump at the chance of him.'

The piece of broth-soaked bread I had just spooned into my mouth waited there to be swallowed; to go down with the surprise, the shame, the remorse and helplessness I felt trying to cope with the multiplicity of emotions these remarks had waked.

What an upstart! What an intolerant misjudger of character! What a fool I had been!

I like to think that if I had been a free agent, I would have jumped up from the table and run to make some apology. It is self-delusion. I had not the grace of character, the wit, or the experience to handle the situation. I had burned my boats, and I had fallen out of love. All the same I took remorse to bed with me that night, and it allowed me very little sleep.

The next morning I could have started my homeward journey early by catching a bus in the village. My mistress suggested I might help out until after dinner, and then catch a bus from a different direction. Instead of going down the lane, it would mean a walk of about three miles through a part of the surrounding countryside I had not seen. The master could give me explicit directions. It seemed a reasonable request, and I willingly agreed.

She put me to clean out all the fowls' cotes, and I worked at it like a Trojan. I shovelled up their droppings from the wooden floors into a wheelbarrow to heap in a corner of the garden. Then I pumped buckets of water, added some Jeyes' fluid, and sloshed out the cotes, perches, walls and floors.

By dinner-time I was having a proper farmer's farewell. I had muck up to the eyebrows, and my old working clothes and shoes stank of it. When I had washed and changed for my leave-taking, I rolled them up in a soiled pinafore and squeezed them down by my other clothes in my case.

I felt very little tugging at the heart-strings when I turned my back on Little Rowan Farm. The beautiful baby, now able to toddle from chair to chair, would hardly miss me, for I had been allowed little time to nurse or play with her.

The master came into the lane to point out the directions. I thanked him, waved goodbye to my mistress and the baby over the gate, and shouted 'cheerio' to Bert who was off up the lane to some chore in a field.

The weather was not dry underfoot. It rarely is in autumn, but the fields had nearly all been grazed, so the damp grass was short. The air was clean and sharp, just right for a long walk.

There is a great luxury being in open country all by oneself. I had hurried enough to put down my case, and rest against the knotty trunk of one of the trees; then I took a sort of mental bath in the tranquillity of it all. I could see sheep and cows in some distant fields, so I reckoned the farm which I had been told to pass would soon be in sight.

And so it was, the house almost hidden among its old barns. The only signs of life were the busy scratching hens close to the farm, a few geese a little further afield, and some pigs snuffling and grunting in a small fenced enclosure. Then a chained farm dog must have scented my coming on the wind. Strangers to bark at must have been a luxury, for he appeared to intend alerting the whole district by his yelping, snapping frenzy and straining at his chain. It made me quite nervous.

So, instead of going on to the forecourt of the farmhouse to get on to the path, I thought I would get out through the field-gate.

That field-gate was obviously the way the cows were taken in and out, too. Each side of it, the ground was churned up into a deep quagmire of mud and cowpats. It was impossible to open the gate without going through the mud; the overgrown hedges were not negotiable either.

Nature's commonsense department must have temporarily run out of stock when I was fashioned. I never thought of taking out from my case my already muddy farm shoes. I kept my best ones on, thinking that by a mad dash and a jump on to the barred gate I could skim the mud without getting really involved with it.

I did have the foresight to throw my case over the hedge first. A sharp run, and I was brought to a halt ankle-deep in mud so sticky it sucked my shoes under, and I stepped out into the morass in my stockinged feet. Well, I was not going to leave the shoes behind; they were brand-new and had cost my nine-and-eleven. I fumbled about for them in the glutinous mud, getting lots on my coat as well as my hands, to rescue them. Then I squelched on until I had fastened the gate behind me, and went to my case.

The catch had come undone from the bump it had got. After cleaning myself up as best I could, I changed my stockings. I put my old farm shoes back on; a lot of the dirt from them was now on the soiled clothes I had wrapped them in. Then I wrapped up my muddier new ones the same way. The case catch was very obstinate after my ill-treatment, but at last I got it to click into place.

I had not yet reached the status of owning a handbag, let alone a mirror, but I did not think I looked too bad. Nobody much would notice my feet on the bus, and the mud on my coat might be dry before then.

There was the path, anyway, leading down a steep hill. In places it was quite tricky negotiating the downward path with a case, but presently my concentration was broken by a living fire of beauty to my right. On the sides of a large natural gorge, trees of many varieties had taken root through the years. Unnaturally sheltered from the wind, they had retained their leaves very late, and the slanting rays of the sun burnished what was already a breathtaking feast for the eye. I stood and worshipped the vista, and felt the inadequate loneliness of the human spirit when faced with something it cannot measure up to.

The case resting against my leg reminded me I had a bus to catch. Goodbye, goodbye, beautiful lonely place!

I made it to the lane at the bottom of the path in nimble good time. Opposite was another farmhouse, much smaller than the previous one I had passed. A kindly-looking middle-aged man was sitting on a tree stump, just inside the gate, chopping pointed ends to hedge stakes. A gentle word to the collie sitting by his feet restricted it to a mere attempt to wag its tail.

It seemed a suitable opportunity to ask the time and how much further it was to the main road, where I hoped to catch the bus to Monmouth. He pulled out his pocket-watch on the end of its chain, and appeared to make some mental calculation.

'You've got nine minutes left, my gal; you'll have to step it out sharp, there isn't a minute to spare. Mrs Morris lives just a few yards up the main road, she'll tell you if the bus is gone.'

The man had looked a bit like my Dad, and this reminded me with a joyful rush that I was going home. Step it out? Yes, indeed I could, or even run, case and all. I did not intend to miss that bus.

I could not have imagined that man rushing to catch a bus anywhere. Farms seemed like self-contained islands bounded by their own hedgerows, miniature universes, no relation to the far-off busy cities that could have been on another planet.

I emerged on to the road just in time to wave the bus down as it was going past. A bit out of puff, I clambered on. There were two empty seats, one at the back, and one right up the front. The back one by the door would suit me fine; with the bus so full I would have to put my case up on the rack. In my thoughtless excitement I lifted it upside down, the catch flew open, and the back-seat passengers got a shower of the contents.

One of my muddy shoes hit a small boy on the side of the head; he opened his mouth to cry, but forgot his intention watching my mortified retrieving of a pair of muddy bloomers from a man's bald head; and the mad grabs I made to stuff such an unladylike cascade of belongings back into my case.

The bus door was shut, and the bus already moving, or I might have jumped off and thrown myself under it. Mustering no dignity whatsoever, I took my case to the seat at the front of the bus, and squeezed in with it somehow.

Certain that I was the object of contemptuous surprise, or at the best, pity, I could only pray that all my fellow passengers would stay on at Monmouth, and only I would have to change to the bus going to Cinderford. I was not quite lucky; two witnesses of my humiliation got on the Cinderford bus, and they travelled on when I alighted at the bottom of our village.

Nothing mattered now. I was back on familiar ground, back to my own identity, back among the friendly people of home.

'Well, well, 'tis Polly, ben't it? I s'pose thee bist wum for a 'oliday, my wench?' said Granny Herbert.

'No, I've left me job. Joy Barker a' got me a job in London not far from 'er.'

'Well, I'eard as thee wast workin' on a farm, and seems thee'st brought a fair bit on it wum with thee.'

'That's nothin',' I bragged, still not knowing about my mud-smudged face, 'you should see what I've got in my case.' Oh, how funny it was now, in the telling to Granny Herbert.

'Thee bist a cough drop sure enough,' she chortled, 'come thee on in an' 'ave a cup o'tay.'

I shook my head.

I had not been able to write Mam what time to expect me, but my feet itched to get up the hill to home. I felt I could already smell the special tarts Mam would have made for my home-coming, and see the little ones, on their best behaviour, sitting patiently, or running to the gate to see if our Poll was coming, so that tea could at last begin.

London Again

After three years in service, feeling now a woman of the world, I was more sensibly resigned to my lot.

Though I could not quite manage to leave the little ones and my loved surroundings dry-eyed—there was compensation in the feeling of excitement wondering what was in store for me in my new job in Aldgate.

Very much was in store for me! Without crossing the water I seemed to have landed in a fascinating foreign world where living was punctuated by exclamation marks. 'Such a bargian!' 'Such a shmatte!' 'Such a vedding!' 'Such a gefilte fish!' 'Such a shiksa I got now!' A place of 'eins's, zwei's, drei's, vier's and fünf's'. A way of life where Momma was indeed the queen of the gas stove and the preparing and cooking of food for her 'children' was the holy rite of her life.

'Taste, Vinnie, taste!' Borsht soup and gefilte fish, noodle soup and strudel—salt beef—and farfel pudding, chopped liver with hard-boiled eggs and onion served piled up on matza biscuits. We Christians can get our salivary juices running with the smell from a fish and chip shop—but oh there is an ocean's difference in that fish and the dish of fried cutlets Momma cooked for Shabbes.

Only the freshest, firmest, finest fish would do for her, and only the best Rakusens frying oil to cook them in—brought by long practice to the exact right sizzling temperature. Oh those plump forefingers of hers, prodding the endless supply of fish and chickens on the innumerable stalls down Petticoat Lane. If only the breath that was wasted in arguments with foregone conclusions as to the proper price for wares offered could have been caught and bottled!

Meat was meat (until all that koshering business of soaking it in water and salt had emasculated it) and milk was milk, but if they partook of one they must not partake of the other until four hours had elapsed. Never the twain must meet, nor even the dishes they were served on. The meat ones were kept in the scullery—milk ones on the dresser that took up one wall of the big kitchen. Washing-up was done in two separate bowls—if one had so much as caught sight of the other both would have been excommunicated to the dustbin.

The standards of hygiene in that Jewish household could have passed in an operating theatre. Some of their fastidious habits rubbed off on to me and remain with me forty years later.

I ate most of my meals from the large kitchen table with the family. Shabbes was the exception. The thirty bentwood chairs round the massive table in the dining-room were often inadequate to seat the tribe of relatives who came to nosh the salt herrings with onion rings, gefilte fish topped with boiled carrot, hard-boiled eggs, salad and fruit. Fish, fruit and water—or lemon tea—occupied the no-man's-land between milk and meat so no one had to fast four hours if they didn't want to. Apart from plenty of silver candlesticks to hold the candles lit for the Shabbes there was little in the way of ornaments—just as well for they would have come a cropper with all the pantomime of gestures that accompanied the conversation and laughter. As the visitors kept piling down the basement stairs to the dining-room, greeting each other with 'good Shabbes', all I could say under my breath was 'good riddance'—the washing-up seemed endless.

When was a domestic servant not a domestic servant? When I was the shiksa in that Jewish household. I was not expected to wear cap and apron—I shared a bedroom with daughters Leah and Becky until Leah married—leaving late-born Becky, aged eleven, the only unmarried daughter. If the family were talking in English on non-personal matters I was allowed to chip in with my say. In the workshops that occupied the two top floors of the house, the sons, daughters and in-laws provided most of the work force, for Momma had produced seven children to go with the three already born to the widower she had married. When business was good they would work fifteen hours a day—and I worked fifteen hours a day for their domestic comfort.

I had practically no time off except to be a chaperon companion to Becky when she went to the pictures. Dear beautiful little Becky—she came to treat me like an older sister and I only had to tell her how I would love to see a picture and she made sure I did. When the summer heat drew out the bugs from the walls—despite all the spirits of salt Momma made me paint in the crevices of the iron bedsteads—they got on the snowy-white duvets. Becky and I would have penny bets on a couple of bugs as to which would reach the highest point of the wall first, then fell asleep before finding out.

Once when I received a letter from home containing the sad news of the death of a childhood friend, I was distraught with grief and could not hide it. Instead of eating my breakfast (which I took with Momma when the family had gone up to the factory or off to school) I wept into it. Momma couldn't read or write, but between my gulps she begged me to tell her what was the matter. The tears came in her own eyes, and as an older friend to younger friend she told me about the death of a little sister of hers many years ago which still grieved her. She let the work go and shared and halved my sorrow with me. She was my mistress and my employer—but such a universal mother was she that I could not help feeling she was also a bit of a Momma to me.

I learnt to hold on to my ten shillings wages as grimly as Scrooge, for Leah was always trying to sell me a bargain. Mind you, I learnt this lesson painfully. It was when Leah beguiled me into buying a pair of her high-heeled upper-crust-style size four-and-a-half shoes for my plebeian broad size six feet. Somehow I managed to squeeze into them, and like a pig on stilts I hobbled in conceited agony trying to keep pace with Becky on the way to the Brick Lane Palace cinema. As soon as we were in our seats I took off my shoes for the comforting freedom of a carpet of peanut shells, cool orange peel and sweet wrappings. The ugly sisters stood as much chance of getting into Cinderella's glass slipper as I had of getting my swollen inflamed feet back into Leah's left-offs. I hadn't got into the habit of buying silk stockings so it was barefoot through the streets for me—my feet feeling as conspicuous and big as Darling Clementine's!

'Serve you right,' Becky scolded me. 'You ought to know by now that Leah could sell a side of bacon to a Rabbi if she put her mind to it.'

Leah was forced to give me up as a customer for her clothes— she was very slim and determined to remain so despite Momma's hysterical wailings at the sight of what Leah left on her piled-up plate. Momma extracted some comfort piling all the family's left-overs on to my plate. Leah remained slim—I grew plump. Leah just had to admit that 'it didn't quite fit' when I stood, arms in a rigid back stretch position unable to reach upwards or forwards, a six-inch gap between buttons and buttonholes on a coat she was trying to flog me for a week's wages. Once in the cause of high fashion Leah did manage to get a quart into a pint pot. It was when she got married and was determined to make her short fat Momma look elegant for once. This meant strait-jacketing Momma into a corset at least two sizes too small. It took four of us to pummel and push small mountains of adipose tissue inside a few hooks and eyes at the top—only to cause it to burst out when we fastened the ones at the bottom. Poor Momma—in the couple of hours it took us to get that corset fastened up she had groaned and sweated pounds away under the strain—we were a bit slimmer ourselves too.

'I'm dying,' she gasped when Leah had finished dressing her in a fashionable outfit in which she was cruelly uncomfortable. Momma survived the wedding day—but it must have nearly killed her having no room for the grand nosh-up after the ceremony.

The three unmarried sons were nice decent young men—but they could not resist my new voluptuous curves for a bit of free pinching practice. Of course, young Jews must not take a surreptitious interest in a shiksa's flesh, or allow one to have a pinch more than another. They kept a wary eye on each other, but it was still dodgems for me when they were about. With Lew it was imposible. He was only eighteen years old but already engaged to a very sweet pretty girl. She lived far out in the suburbs—they could only meet twice a week and his masculinity was on the boil all the time. He tried to assuage it a little by kissing me at every possible opportunity. When he caught me with my hands full it was difficult to dodge him so that he didn't get my lips. It was impossible to feel mad at him—he was like an over-sexed puppy full of joy and daring. He would come into the scullery on pretext of sniffing appreciatively over what Momma was stirring on the gas stove and take a quick nip at the back of my neck. It made me a bag of nerves even if it did add a spice of flavour to the day. He was always on the razor's edge of discovery—his very daring made me laugh, quite undoing the value of the terrible scowls I gave him to warn him off.

Father's words, 'We know thee'lt be a good little wench and not do anything to let thee old Mam and Dad down', was a very effective chastity belt for locking out temptation. It was lucky Lew's father didn't know about his attentions. 'Poppa' was a highly orthodox little Jew. The bronchial asthma which racked him made him small and thin, and I sometimes wondered where he had room to keep all the terrible coughs which sent him into purple-faced paroxysms. Sometimes there was only me about when the old gentleman was taken by a spasm so cruel it seemed determined to choke him there and then. In a dilemma of pity I did not know whether to offend the dignity of the man by putting my arms round his shoulders to steady him—being only a shiksa and a maid at that—or whether to stand helpless and endure the watching. I often did the former—he gave no sign of feeling offence. Every January and February when the London fog was at its worst, his elder sons paid for him to stay in a nursing home in Bognor.

Fifteen-year-old Moishe rejoiced in this escape from the Talmud. Every evening, black cap on head, he was made to study it for a long period. When his father left the room for a coughing session Moishe read the comic folded between the pages. Not being religious myself, I didn't blame him—what with his school homework he didn't have much time for recreation—as long as the old gentleman thought Moishe was religious that was all that mattered. I had a very soft spot for handsome Moishe—didn't he put on the records I liked over and over again on the old wind-up gramophone whenever he could? What could be better than Richard Tauber singing *You Are My Heart's Delight*, to gild the spirits of a seventeen-year-old romantic?

Blessed with little initiative of my own, I stayed with the Cohens over two years without thought of getting another job, or of asking for a rise—they hadn't thought of that either.

However a girl from our village had found a job in a young lady students' college hall near Tottenham Court Road—she wrote to me recommending I get one there too. A vacancy for a kitchen-maid was coming up, the wages were twelve-and-six a week, the food excellent and plentiful, half a day off a week—and a whole day every third Sunday. The only snag was that I'd have to wear servant's uniform—which meant spending my bit of savings on the hated stuff and forgoing a visit back home before starting there.

Mrs Cohen offered me fifteen shillings a week to stay on. However the old restlessness had started to work again, and whatever pangs I might feel about leaving this household—especially dear Becky—I knew that as long as I was in service I could never be more than a migrant worker at someone else's table.

College Hall

After my own home, I had found the Cohens' kitchen hugely spacious; but the kitchen at College Hall was like looking through a magnifying-glass. The whole ground floor of the Aldgate house would have fitted into one corner of it. No expense had been spared to equip it with steamer trays, cooking stoves, and a hot-plate big enough to hide Ali Baba and his forty thieves. There were sinks for this and sinks for that, some big enough to have a bath in. The only thing the planners left out was a pair of roller-skates to cut out the walking.

As well as the kitchen proper, an enormous scullery, a walk-in larder, a servery, a servant's hall, brush cupboards, staff cloak-rooms, and the grandly large student's dining-room occupied the semi-basement floor. There were twenty living-in maids, four daily women, and two cooks; not your ordinary cooks, these were lady-cooks, who ate in their own private quarters, spoke with upper-crust accents, and had *Cordon Bleu* qualifications.

In charge of all the domestic arrangements was Miss Delaine, so grand and remote in her office we hardly ever saw her; then nice, kindly, middle-aged Miss Robson, the bursar, and genteel Miss Mander, the secretary, engager of staff. I suppose Dorcas, the telephonist and receptionist was next in the hierarchy, but it was difficult to know where to place her. She fetched her meals from the servants' hall on a tray, and ate in the privacy of her cosy little room by the front door. She wore a bottle-green uniform, with cream cap and apron, while we kitchen-maids wore blue print dresses, and the house-maids and parlour-maids black. Dorcas looked down her nose at the rest of us, and she was a tale-bearer to Miss Mander of every little misdemeanour, or short cuts to the housework, she could discover. She was thoroughly disliked by all the domestic staff. There were about eighty lady-students, mostly upper middle-class by birth.

The place was a sea of bums and bosoms, a vast hen-house with no resident cockerel. If something remotely personable in trousers came through the doors, it was he who had to do the dodging! We three kitchen-maids were even grateful for the sour masculine grunt the sole man about the place, old Spackman, gave us. Spackman arrived only to disappear again to stoke and feed the incinerator and boilers at the end of a labyrinth of underground passages.

I doubt if 'old' Spackman was more than fifty. His calling seemed to have dried up his tongue, and given a patina of ashy greyness to his hair, skin, clothes, and outlook. He seemed safe enough in this female jungle.

Though the students had a centrally heated, carpeted bedroom each, with a bathroom between three, we maids did not do so badly. True, we were three to a room, and only had mats by our beds and no central heating, but being highest up we had the most panoramic views of the roofs, and we had two bathrooms between us, with hot pipes to dry our stockings and smalls.

Being able to have a bath nearly every day was a novel luxury I wallowed in, literally. At the Cohens', the whole family, as well as I, had to troop down to the public baths once a week, and get back before it was time to light the Shabbes candles.

This was the first job in which I had official and recognised time off. My half-day rarely coincided with that of the girl who had got me the job. No matter, I was very happy to slip off to the pictures, and change identities with the woman star of the film.

Knowing I was considered plain as a child, the idea had stuck, and as a rule I gave practically no thought to my appearance. I was still under the illusion that men fell in love with a pretty face, and I never assumed that my figure would hold any attraction for them. Yet I had a tiny waist, and a long period of good food and plenty of work had developed me nicely in all the right places.

My fellow-workers used to scold me for my lack of interest, so to placate them one half-day off, I decided to dress myself up. I had washed my hair, and I let one of them put it in curlers. After my bath, I decided to put on a dress bought a long time ago at a jumble sale. It was in navy lock-knit wool with pale blue striped trimming in the yoke. I had to tug and pull at it a bit until I had smoothed it over me as closely fitting as a second skin.

A bit tight, I thought, but never mind, it was not far to walk to the Dominion, Tottenham Court Road, where a film starring Clark Gable was showing. I combed out my hair, now a silky cascade of wavy curls to my shoulders, and finished my ensemble with a navy-blue beret perched, as was the fashion, on one side of my head. Neither of my room-mates was there to approve the transformation. Only one of the cooks was in the kitchen, and she opened her mouth in considerable astonishment as I walked through the door. She looked as though she were going to say something, but must have recollected she was a lady and just stared at me instead.

Along Tottenham Court Road a lot of other people, especially men, seemed to be pointedly staring at me too. A pair of them, in the City gear of bowler hats, dark suits and gold-headed canes, stopped in their tracks, raised their hats, gave little simultaneous bows, and smiling in the most complimentary manner, said something in a language I thought was Latin.

I was not quite sure if this pantomime was for my benefit at first but then a bus passed, and a young man holding on to the rail at the bottom of the stairs, called out to me to 'wait for him'. He was a perfect stranger!

There was so much head-turning in my direction, I got quite worried that something was amiss. Oh, there was Kath, my room-mate. 'Hey, Kath, is there anything wrong with me at the back? People seem to be staring at me, I wondered if something was showing.'

'I should think something *is* showing, practically everything you've got! It's that dress, it's a mile too tight.'

I decided to go back to College Hall and change. I was waylaid by a street photographer already developing the picture he had taken of me. It cost me sixpence. I looked at it, and thought all I needed was two French blokes and we could have gone straight into one of those apache dances.

Kath came back shortly after me, and drew some of the other maids' attention to my plight. One of the more sophisticated ones took my measurements, 37–20–39, and in that frock! 'Crikey, no wonder some of their eyes was poppin' out!'

I had a new awareness; I was a little richer than I had thought, but almost clueless how to spend my wares. Also after seeing the film I was only interested in someone like Clark Gable.

Life was very comfortable in my College Hall job. My only pangs came when I scraped out all the custard, milk pudding and gravies, that were left in the cooking utensils after dishing-up. If only, by some magic means, I could send them home! I bought wool, and knitted vests and jumpers for my little sisters, and sent

Mam an occasional postal order, little enough, yet I was always broke the last week of the month.

When my Sunday off came around I did not care if I were broke. London was outside the door, I had long strong young legs, and like Felix I could keep on walking. Freedom to go out was still precious enough to be exciting.

I was going to say I followed my nose, but that would have taken me skywards. I just put one foot in front of the other, and everywhere was fascinating. People, and shop-windows to gaze at; the quiet of the City, still with cobbled side streets, and dark little shops with bottle-glass windows.

Sometimes my Sunday-off meanderings took me through some of London's magic names, Fleet Street, Lincoln's Inn, Cheapside and Shaftesbury Avenue, where the pictures of the actors and actresses appearing in the theatres were displayed outside. They actually appeared here *in the flesh*! Names like Jack Buchanan, Elsie Randolph, Margaretta Scott, Isobel Elsom, Gladys Cooper, Fay Compton, Nigel Playfair; names that had a fairy-tale remoteness about them, when I had seen their photographs on bits of paper torn from newspapers and periodicals and hung up in our privy back home.

How lucky was I, Polly Mason from the Forest of Dean, to be able to tread these hallowed streets.

I had no money to buy food, but the physical hunger never got sharp enough to make me turn round until a clock somewhere reminded me I *must* be in by ten o'clock. It was no problem finding my way; I would ask some kindly-looking woman, she would tell me what bus to catch, and I just walked the bus routes back to Tottenham Court Road. I knew my fellow kitchen-maids would have left me more than enough supper in the hot plate to make up for my missed meals.

I had no one to share the emotions my secret love inspired. I tried desperately to write it all down. When I left College Hall, I consigned a pile of scribbled efforts to the incinerator.

The young lady residents were allowed to go on the roof of College Hall, a privilege which was barred to us domestics. To reach the roof the students had to pass the end of the corridor where the maids' bedrooms were. One day I was just coming out on to our back stairs, when a student came down from the roof. She was a Canadian, and apparently not very familiar with the then rigid English class system. She started to talk to me. Our conversation became so animated she followed me down our staircase until she came to the floor where her bedroom was. We were still talking and laughing when Miss Mander came by. Her smile for the student was pretty chilly, but the look she gave me was a real freezer.

The next day I was summoned to Miss Robson's office for a lecture in proper decorum for kitchen-maids, which most certainly did not include their talking in a familiar manner with any of the students.

Having choked on this bitter pill nearly all night and not being able to swallow it, next morning I asked to be allowed to speak to Miss Robson. Hurt pride had puffed me up on to my very high horse, which has no bridle, alas, and now I was ready to give *her* a lecture, and my month's notice to go with it.

That morning I did not go into prayers, which were attended by everyone resident in the main hall. That omission alone would have got me summoned to Miss Robson's presence.

At ten o'clock I was told by one of the lady cooks that Miss Robson would see me, but first I must put on a clean apron and cap.

'Come in,' called Miss Robson, and I stood squarely in front of her, my head held a bit on the high side. She asked me why had I not attended prayers that morning, and reminded me once again that I had been seen talking and laughing on the stairs with one of the lady students.

Now, yet more incensed than in the first interview, I told her that she had got it a little bit wrong. The young lady had got into conversation with *me*. Secondly, if I was not fit to talk to the students, how could I talk to God, who I was under the impression was considered a good deal superior to any student.

'You do not talk to God. You pray to God, and pray that He may listen to you,' Miss Robson reprimanded me, but her tone was not unkind.

'Well, even if I'm praying to Him, if we're all good enough to do that together in His presence, why aren't we good enough to talk to each other?'

Miss Robson gave a deep sigh, and then a kindly-meant lecture on humility. She herself would have to curtsey to royalty, we all had our place in society, and ducks could never be happy trying to pretend they were swans. Far better for me if I knew my place and made the best of it.

I agreed with her that College Hall was a very good place for the servants, but she could now offer mine to a more deserving girl, as I was giving my notice in there and then.

It is a credit to this good lady that she tried to persuade me to alter my mind. I very firmly refused her kind offer. After my previous jobs I thought perhaps I had cut off my nose to spite my face, but I felt a kind of glory in my rebellion. I sang *The Red Flag* as loud as I dared among the clatter of the pots and pans, and thought of my Dad and all the downtrodden workers in the world, and nearly cried.

On my next half-day off I went to look for another job. One of the maids told me about a domestic servant agency in the Edgware Road. The lady who ran it gave me three jobs to apply for, the third one with some apparent reluctance. 'I don't think it is really your sort of job,' she mused. It was for a domestic help in a bed-and-breakfast hotel in a terrace not far from Paddington station. It was the nearest on her list, so disregarding her comment I thought I would apply there first.

The terrace ran from Edgware Road to Lancaster Gate. The tall houses looked elegant on each side fronted by a row of trees in a narrow, grassy, iron-railed enclosure. I hoped at once I would get the job; the trees were an unexpected bounty.

The number I wanted was a corner house, another good omen, for it added to the illusion of space. There was a short flight of steps up to the front door, and a longer flight of steps down to the area and the back door.

Oh well, I was not a servant there yet. Still smarting from my 'telling-off' at College Hall, and in militant mood, I rang the front door bell.

The Boarding-House

I had the physical advantage of looking down on the lady of the boarding-house, for it was she, a Miss Lowry, who answered the bell.

Frizzy, light sandy hair topped a pale, flaccid face; even the freckles on it looked anaemic. Her short neck seemed to have run into her bosom, which in turn appeared to have run into her flabby belly. An unbaked dough sort of person.

She had a very friendly manner, which did not alter when I told her I was after the job as maid, and not applying for a room.

No, the post had not been filled; the wages were fifteen shillings a week. Time off, from three p.m. to seven p.m. on every alternate day; off duty from seven p.m. the other days.

Seven p.m. till when?

That would be entirely up to me; I would have my own key to the front door.

Uniform?

No, as long as I looked smart and clean in an overall.

She gave me all this information standing in the small hall inside the front door. My own key of the door! My own key of the *front* door! I was just coming up to twenty-one, and now I really felt like it! No hated caps and aprons! Fifteen shillings a week, and all that time off! A tree outside, as well! And that lady in the domestic agency saying she didn't think it was my sort of job! I felt sick with apprehension lest I did not get it.

'You would share a room downstairs with the other maid; she's older than you, a funny sort in some ways, but I think you would get on with her all right. Would you like to see the room?'

The room was small and drab, in a drab basement, next to a drab kitchen. One other small basement room was let to a permanent boarder, and Miss Lowry herself had the big one.

When she opened the door at the narrow end of the hall leading to the basement, the concentration of hot ashy fumes from a coke boiler nearly made me choke.

I did not care if the room had been as black as a dungeon, and the air like fog; it was a small price to pay for the privilege of using the same door as everyone else.

Did I think the job would suit me? I felt the question should have been would I suit the job? She appeared to have taken me on there and then. I gave her Miss Robson's name and address for a reference and explained I must work out my notice. However, if I heard no further from Miss Lowry within a week, the job was mine.

Two weeks went by, I heard nothing, the job was mine. Lucky, lucky me!

One more week to go. It was the morning of my twenty-first birthday, a fact I had barely taken note of. There had never been any spare money for celebrating birthdays, even with a card, in my childhood; so birthdays have never been important to me. When I was summoned to Miss Robson's office, my heart sank. Perhaps Miss Lowry had been slow in writing for a reference, and now Miss Robson was going to say she could not give me one?

But, no. There was Miss Robson giving me a friendly smile and handing me a little parcel for my birthday. I was so surprised, I did not know how to thank her properly, before she asked me if I had found another job.

I told her I had, and where it was, and that I would have a key of my own, and lots of free time. I did not mean to be unpleasant, I just wanted her to know how lucky I was. Surprisingly, she shook her greying head sadly.

'Well, Winifred, I don't care for the sound of this job; they haven't applied to me for a reference, which is not a good sign. Now I want you to think it over carefully. I've engaged a replacement for you, but that doesn't matter; you may still stay on until you find a more suitable situation.'

The bad name of the Paddington area obviously meant something to Miss Robson, but I had no idea why she should take this attitude. Because of this my thanks were somewhat insincere.

My parcel from Miss Robson contained scented writing-paper and envelopes. When I expressed surprise to the other two kitchen-maids, their surprise was even greater that I had not mentioned my birthday, and the twenty-first at that! Hadn't my family sent me a card? Oh, what a shame!

By teatime my misfortune had spread through to the other girls, and I was being made much fuss of. I wrote home post-haste, sending the money for Mam to send me a birthday card to shut them up. And so she did, by return, a grand one, with a big gold key on the front. I was thrilled and pleased to receive it.

Lest you think me entirely ungracious—when a few weeks later the domestic staff at College Hall went down like ninepins to a scourge of 'flu, I went round there for over a month and spent all my spare time working like a Trojan wherever I could best be put to use.

When all the staff had recuperated, Miss Robson, herself ill with 'flu, sent me a written message that there would always be a job for me at College Hall as long as she was in residence.

My helpful attitude brought me the reward again of the excellent College Hall food, an item that was lamentably short at the Terrace; and I was able to take some of it back to Joan, the other maid.

Miss Lowry shared her room with an enormous neutered tom cat which she adored. Most mornings she would send me up to Ginger's, a butcher in Edgware Road for three penn'orth of cat's meat. The best of these pieces she kept for the cat, and the rest, with a penn'orth of pot-herbs, made the stew for our dinner. For breakfast we had the same as the boarders, a piece of thinly cut streaky bacon, and a fried egg. We also had toast, and any of the marmalade left on the boarders' trays. After dinner we sometimes had a swiss bun, then three for two pence, as a sweet, or maybe, one of Miss Lowry's rice puddings.

The rice puddings of College Hall would not have owned one of hers even as a poor relation. College puddings were made with a cupful of rice, two cupfuls of sugar, and two quarts of top-grade milk, steamed for eight hours until milk and rice had changed into a thick pinky-yellow cream with a rich golden skin on top.

Miss Lowry used a cupful of cheap rice, a couple of spoons of sugar, a pint of water with a dash of milk, and she cooked it until the rice grains had swollen enough to make a nodding acquaintance with each other.

The rest of the day we had to subsist on tea and toast, and go easy on the bread for that. About that time a sweet named Mars Bars came out, and most days Joan and I kept going on one each. Miss Lowry had her own cache of goodies in her room.

After Joan and I had taken the eighteen trays round on my first morning, you could have knocked me down with a feather duster when she said, 'Come on, cocky, we'll go back to our bedroom,' where we sat down on our beds. From under hers she took a wind-up gramophone and played several times over her repertoire of three records—*Laugh, clown laugh, Charmaine,* and *My Diane.*

After the brisk efficiency of College Hall, I got into quite a sweat waiting for Miss Lowry to come and tell us off.

'Don't you drop yer drawers frettin' about '*er*', Joan sniffed, puffing away at the first Woodbine of the day.

I had not cottoned on then that Joan had some kind of hold over Miss Lowry. I never did find out quite what it was, but it was something to do with a man. Had Miss Lowry's highly religious father found out about it, it would probably have brought on the threatened heart attack. Mr Lowry was not supposed to know the reason why his daughter could charge such high prices for bed and breakfast. Nor, at that time, did I realise why Miss Robson had been so opposed to my new job.

Sometimes it was difficult for me to know whether Joan or Miss Lowry was my boss. It was a delicate situation for Miss Lowry. Joan being rather lazy, the only way Miss Lowry could get Joan's part of the staircase paint washed down was to threaten her with the sack. Although Joan made dark hints about letting out secrets, she seemed to prefer to flounce up the stairs with a bucket of hot water into every stair-tread corner, rather than pack her case, get Miss Lowry into hot water, and clear out. Nevertheless the little mystery remained.

I stayed at that Paddington boarding-house for eighteen months, and my eyes were opened to life styles and personalities which would have been completely alien to anyone living in our village. For boarding-houses come second only to asylums in collecting a rich and varied population of human eccentrics.

Of the eighteen rooms for letting, eight were occupied by 'permanents'. The cheap top-floor rooms mostly served as nest-boxes for eggheads—students of one kind or another. Judging by the bags under their eyes and the fact that they were permanently broke, they were also studying the more gaudy aspects of London's night life. When we had the 'Room to Let' notice over the door, it was always like a little adventure to answer the bell. There was a constant stream of overnight visitors for the rooms—couples, usually, with anonymous names and faces, and little or no luggage.

Many of the permanents I still remember vividly today. A maid, like a barber or hairdresser, makes good blotting paper for the outpouring of human feelings. Absorbing snippets of auto-biographical confession came my way, from the lonely, the un-happy, the angry, and the kindly who had no family of their own.

Miss Player and Miss Wills, who occupied ground-floor rooms, were night-club hostesses. One was beautiful, the archetypal dumb blonde, thick as a brick and the ideal cure for any tired business man. Her beauty and youth gave her the security of ten pounds a week as the mistress of a wealthy man. The other, Miss Wills, was a sad example of what many Miss Players grow into. She was fat, common, aimless and suicidally unhappy. The days of being kept were long over for Miss Wills, and she only remained in her job because Miss Player would have left too if the manage-ment sacked her. The Miss Players of this world are a club-owner's dream.

Then there was Miss O'Rory, who had a room on the first floor. She suffered from bronchial asthma and was arthritic as well. Despite her poor health, she never missed her daily walk. Winter and summer she wore an ancient Harris tweed coat and battered brown felt hat, yet no one could ever have mistaken her for a member of the lower classes. She was one of the eight children of an Irish rector, and having been a rebel had become separated from her family. She bragged that for many years she had lived in the South of France as the mistress of a famous artist. Yet, when the Jubilee of George V took place, she insisted that I, who should have been on duty, place a chair by the front door for her so that I could pop up to the Edgware Road to see the procession. Old and broken-winded Miss O'Rory might have been, but she was a thoroughbred.

Mr Davis, who had a big room on the same floor, was some-thing in the city. He looked the part too when he left each morning for the Stock Exchange complete with bowler hat, brief-case, spats and umbrella. As he went away at weekends and was one of Joan's 'breakfasts' I saw very little of him, and wasn't much bothered about that.

It was quite different when Mr O'Brien arrived.

'Ooh, isn't he *lovely*!' I enthused to Joan after I had taken in his breakfast.

There he was asleep with his crinkly dark wavy hair against the white pillow, his long dark lashes and pinky-bronzed face contrasting so nicely with his silky blue pyjamas. He looked even better when he opened his blue eyes and smiled at me. His room smelled sweetly of scented soap, and a single rose in a glass by his bedside table just completed the picture.

He looked like a film star, and I told Joan so. She gave one of her sniffs—she was always giving one of her sniffs about somebody, and said: 'Well, what d'you expect, 'im being one o' them?'

One of them? What did she mean by that, and sounding so contemptuous? Perhaps it was because he was an actor.

I didn't ask Joan to enlarge on her comments then, but I found out what she meant one morning when I took up Mr O'Brien's breakfast. Another male head was poking out of the bedclothes beside his.

'Bring up another breakfast tray, please,' said Mr O'Brien.

Bring up another! Indeed, he shouldn't have one. I marched downstairs, plonked down the tray, and told Miss Lowry I wasn't going to wait on the likes of him. I did not properly know what 'the likes of him' meant, but if inexperience and intolerance are the parents of judgement, I had plenty of both.

Poor Mr O'Brien, he had to go.

Eventually Mr Davis left to marry a middle-aged woman of Amazonian proportions (she could easily have carried him off under her arm!) and his place was taken by Angela Mandcope. Her arrival in London was given a line or two in the gossip columns of the evening papers, for she was a well-known artist from South Africa. Her nephew, a former student resident, had recommended the place. Angela Mandcope was divorced, about forty, small, dark, attractive-looking, restless and chatty.

She was very friendly to us, but somehow I couldn't take to her. Every day she was visited by a very upper-crust young man who was quite good-looking in a thin, fair sort of way. His name was Neville.

She had her hooks well and truly into him, having met him on his uncle's estate in South Africa. Mrs Mandcope asked if I would like to pose for her sometimes in my free time, in the nude of course, and I wouldn't mind Neville wandering in and out, would I?

By now, I was getting used to eccentrics and their odd ideas, so I declined quite politely. But her next offer left me temporarily speechless, despite the fact that I always was and always will be a 'chopsy mouth'.

Neville, she told me, was the only son of a lord, she and he were passionately in love and wanted to get married. There was no hope because this noble lord demanded that his son should marry someone who could produce male heirs for the family fortune and name. Mrs Mandcope could have no children.

Now, if Neville could present to his father a bonny healthy son he could prove was his, whom they could then adopt, Neville reckoned that his father would assent to the marriage. Neville agreed with her that I would do very nicely to bear his baby. Of course, when I could no longer work I should be comfortably kept, have the baby in a good nursing home, and be paid a lump sum of at least a hundred pounds. If it should be a girl, I could keep the baby if I wished.

I was so shocked and hurt by this proposition, I could not answer her. I walked down to the basement wounded to the heart.

I felt defiled through no fault of my own. How often, to myself, had I pictured myself married. My husband would be someone kind and wise like my father, whose grey eyes would have crinkly corners, who would have the manners and presence of Clark Gable. There would be a house with pretty curtains and cushions, and nice lace-edged cloths for the table. Then one day there would be my own babies, precious bundles to love and dress up and dote upon. A dream of future love, tied up for the present in the ribbons of hope. Now these romantic notions had been raped by suggestions so cold, so heartless, so insulting, I was hurt beyond measure.

That the conception of a child could be arranged like a business deal, and that that child, one's own flesh and blood, be handed over to someone else for money! The icy shock brought on a mood of cold fury. Master Neville had better not come near me! After a few days my mood softened. Perhaps he knew nothing about it. She was a lunatic, and desperate to make a good matrimonial catch; such people should not be judged seriously.

I was on duty one evening, cleaning and filling up the cruets at the kitchen table, when Neville himself came down to the kitchen. He had the air and ingratiating manner of a man about to ask a favour.

Let it be for a pot of tea and toast for two! Please God, don't let him repeat her monstrous suggestion to me! But, after some humming and hawing, and admittedly with some diffidence, he broached the subject.

Cruel in my scorn, I told him that I would have smacked his face but that I had more respect for my hand. That even if his father were a lord and he fancied himself a member of the privileged classes, it did not give him the right to consider I was as debased as himself and Mrs Mandcope. What's more, for his information, people who did menial tasks and were forced to wait on their inferiors had warm blood in their veins, and deep feelings, and were, 'inconsiderately, perhaps', part of the same human race of which he thought himself so superior a member . . . etc., etc.

He went upstairs in a very different mood from the one he came down in. He was pale-faced, ruffled and shamed, but I had no pity for him and certainly none for her. I was thankful that Mrs Mandcope left the boarding-house almost at once.

I was soon to learn that infatuation can make fools and villains of us all, and that my judgement might have been more tempered.

'Number seventeen,' Joan told me one evening. 'Mr Gordon's back. You'll like him, he used to have number twelve until he went to Canada. He's been gone a year; but now he's back to get a degree. Not a hap'orth of trouble, and a proper gentleman.' High praise indeed, from Joan! I was glad he was one of my 'breakfasts'. I looked forward to seeing this paragon.

At seven-thirty sharp I knocked at number seventeen. A deep, male voice answered sleepily, 'Come in.' I saw his forehead and cow's lick of dark hair first; then his whole face emerged from the blankets.

My dream man! Kind, grey eyes with crinkly corners, well-marked but not too bushy eyebrows, a straight firm nose, and a mouth full enough for tenderness, but firm enough for a strong character. A nicely balanced mixture of Clark Gable and my Dad!

A pipe and tobacco pouch lay on the bedside table, a tweed sports jacket and haversack hung behind the door. A real masculine aura. His voice had a Clark Gable drawl as well, and his smile was even more knee-weakening as he sat up and said: 'Good morning, ma-am.'

I floated all the way downstairs. It must be Fate, to bring a man looking like my ideal lover to this very place. Joan had given me a start in the build-up; now I had seen the façade, and I proceeded to stuff Mr Gordon with every virtue known to the male sex. I worshipped him. Had he said to me, 'Winnie, I fancy you should get on the roof and chuck yourself off this morning,' I would have willingly done it to please him.

If he was aware of my adulation, he did not show it. He did not have to; a few words from him went round in my mind like a record with the needle stuck in a groove until he spoke to me again. Each room had a numbered box in the hall which the tenants could change to 'in' or 'out'. I was sad when his box said 'out', and a love-lorn droop when it said 'in'.

He slept three floors above my basement room, but was as remote and desirable as a Hollywood film star. I had put him on a pedestal, a god of my own making, so that I might have the exquisite torture of being hopelessly in love. It kept me easily immune from the skirmishing attacks on my virtue that were inevitable in a setting like a Paddington terrace boarding-house.

To have Mr Gordon in number seventeen redressed the balance for all the wicked men in the world. It didn't occur to me to question what he was doing about sex. He never brought any girls home. I imagined he was living in a state of pure celibacy until Miss Right should come along.

Then Joan dropped a bombshell—she quietly gave in a week's notice. I already knew that Joan was a woman of means. She had been awarded £400 many years ago, as a result of an injury. She had saved up a nest-egg from her wages to go with it, and was going into partnership in a shop, with her married sister. She was very thrilled about this venture, and as a bonus washed the whole of the staircase paintwork from top to bottom before she left.

From the same domestic agency that I had come from Miss Lowry got a replacement maid; a girl named Rosie, and anyone less like a rose would be hard to visualise. One could picture her a thin grey little rodent climbing out of the Paddington Canal and nearly turning into a girl. Had she filled her narrow lungs with a good gust of fresh air the shock might have been disastrous. 'Narrow' is the word that comes to mind to describe Rosie physically. She had a long thin pallid face, well sprinkled with pimples and blackheads; her nose was long and just kept her small grey eyes apart. She looked as sly as a ferret.

Narrow, physically, she may have been; but her mind and her morals were as broad as her horizons stretched. She was engagingly frank, even to her own disadvantage.

She was engaged to a baker's roundsman, and as willing to pop into bed with him as with any other man who gave her the chance. Sex to her was like fish and chips, enjoyable, but nothing to make a fuss about. In the male-female spectrum I would have placed her and Mr Gordon at opposite extremes.

She had been at the boarding-house about a fortnight, when Mr Gordon was about to go up to his Lancashire home for the long summer vacation. Instead of going out on her evening off she must have gone upstairs. She came down about an hour later to get ready to meet her regular boy-friend. As she changed, she gave me a running commentary on Mr Gordon's sexual powers and habits in bed. At first, her words would not, could not, sink in. I looked at her ugly little face, skinny straight figure, and her general air of having knocked about an awful lot.

Was Mr Gordon, that god among men, so bereft of female companionship that he must have the likes of *her*? His modesty seemed fantastic; he was worthy of the most beautiful woman in the world! *I* was a few notches better all round than Rosie; he could have *me*; oh, if only I knew how to go about this business of sex!

So disheartened was I, that I almost finished with men before I started with them. Yet his face, with his crinkly-cornered eyes, his nose, his mouth, his pipe-smoking tweedy air, the way his hair grew in a cow's-lick from his forehead, was to haunt my memory for many years.

A Job for Life

Between going to the pictures, and happenings in the boarding-house, my life did not lack its little dramas. But I gradually became aware of something sinister and unwholesome happening in the streets of London. Sometimes I saw bands of black-shirted youths marching about led by a politician named Mosley.

Their choice of black for a uniform seemed evil in itself. Most of them wore jackboots and marched like the German Nazi soldiers I had seen in the newsreels. They seemed full of anger and hate and were looking for something to vent it on.

Why were they allowed to darken our streets? What did they want? 'They're taking a leaf out of that Hitler's book; they want to destroy the Jews,' some said. But why?

What had the Jews done to them? I thought of my life in the Jewish household at Aldgate. There they were, working like beavers, wishing no harm or unkindness to anyone. If I had to choose whom to live among, I would run back to Aldgate quick rather than mix with the sort represented by that black-shirted lot of bullies.

I was put more in the political picture one evening when a group of young people came to the front door. Their spokesman was Sheila Lynd, daughter of the writer Robert Lynd, and the group were distributing anti-Mosley leaflets. She stayed half an hour, explaining his devious methods of trying to get political power. She asked me if I would join an anti-Mosley rally in the East End the following Sunday.

It would be my half-day off and I was in just the mood to vent my anger on someone. That Mosley and his black-shirted crew would do nicely. Let any one of them dare lay a finger on a hair of my Becky's head!

Yes, I would join a young Communist group going down to the East End to stop the Mosley march through there. Among the group with Sheila Lynd was a good-looking fellow who promised to call for me.

By now, with Joan's departure and my infatuation with Mr Gordon turning into a sad memory, I had had enough of the boarding-house. I was fed up; I was ready for a change, ready for some adventure. I gave Miss Lowry two weeks' notice. I had decided to find digs or a room for myself and take a job as a waitress.

Sure enough, on the Sunday afternoon, the young man called for me with a few more anti-Mosleyites. We got on the underground at Praed Street.

When the train stopped at Edgware Road, a much larger contingent got in. A young man among this group seemed to have taken it upon himself to act as spokesman. He waved his arms about and spoke rather loudly, and in my mean fashion I mentally labelled him a 'bighead'. He was accompanied by a beautiful, quiet sort of girl, whom I took to be his girl-friend.

'Fancy,' I thought, 'a nice ladylike girl, and so good-looking too, going out with a show-off like him!'

He was quite a handsome young man, and when I momentarily caught the look he gave me I did note that he had nice, big, soft brown eyes.

'Hiya, Greening,' he addressed my companion.

'Hiya, Syd.'

'That's Syd Foley and his sister,' my escort informed me; not that I was interested.

Before I lost my escort in the mêlée of crowds and foot and mounted police at Aldgate, he had told me a political meeting was being held the following Thursday over a pub in the Shirland Road, Maida Vale. I was off duty that evening and I was keen to go.

Mixing with this group of young left-wing idealists gave me something else to think about, and helped take my mind off Mr Gordon. Some of them belonged to the Labour League of Youth, some to the Young Communists League, some to the Peace Pledge Union, and some to all three!

They certainly had a love-hate relationship with society. They loved the exploited, and hated the exploiters and aggressors. They all seemed to seek goodness, but were hot-headed and blinkered up to the eyebrows with political prejudices.

On Thursday I was among the first comers and took a seat at the end of the front row of chairs. Quite a small crowd turned up—the last of the stragglers was that talkative Syd Foley off the train. Before he took a seat at the back, his glance seemed to sweep casually over the attendance.

I had absorbed quite a bit of political groundwork as I sat on the corner of the fender at home listening to Dad arguing and discussing with his butties. On politics at least I was inclined to question statements before swallowing them whole.

One speaker exhorted us to shop at the Co-op where profits were redistributed as dividends to the customers. I had tasted Co-op cocoa! What, I demanded to know, were the salaries of the highly paid Co-op officials? They seemed to me to be in the capitalist managing director's bracket. Down with such salaries, and higher dividends instead, was my resolution. No wonder the Co-op prices couldn't compete with Lewis's cut-price shop in Church Street. Whilst I was at it, I had a go at high-salaried socialist politicians—they were capitalists too, selling ideals wrapped up with the gift of the gab. They contributed nothing materially to society, but liked to enjoy the high standard of living of the 'enemy'.

A university graduate dealt with my points—he wrapped up the answers in so much verbose intellectual flannel that I was all at sea and wished I'd kept my mouth shut.

During the meeting I had exchanged a few words with a nice cockney girl sitting next to me, and when it was over we walked down the stairs together. I noticed Syd Foley joined us—he and the girl appeared to know each other.

Compared with his behaviour in the train, he kept very quiet, leaving the chatting to us as we walked up Warwick Avenue to the Edgware Road. Here I had to turn right for my walk back to the Terrace, and my companion left for Kilburn. I bid them both good night, having taken it for granted that Syd was escorting the other girl home. To my surprise he too wished her good night and asked if he might walk on with me. I told him where I worked and said if it wasn't taking him out of his way I had no objection. Oh, it was on his way, he said (the fibber).

We talked politics right to the door. I did fumble a bit unnecessarily in my bag to find my key, but he just said good night without a hint of wishing to see me again. I was a bit piqued, but not much bothered.

The next morning on the mat inside the hall was a hand-delivered note addressed to me. Would I perhaps consider going to the pictures with him? He had found out the telephone number of the boarding-house, and would ring for my answer that evening. We arranged to go to the pictures on Saturday. I asked him to come at half past six.

When I was sent to the butcher's on Saturday morning for the cat's meat, I made a few purchases of my own—a thick lamb chop, half a pound of sausages, a gammon rasher and some bread rolls. I had noticed when we walked down the Edgware Road that when the wind blew against Syd's mac he looked as thin as an exclamation mark!

Miss Lowry always spent Saturday night at her father's home in Neasden. Rosie hung around the kitchen with her mouth drooling while I cooked Syd's meal. I plonked a sausage between a bread roll and told her to make herself scarce. After Mr Gordon I couldn't afford to have her hanging about.

Syd was prompt in arriving, and showed a gratifying appreciation for the unexpected meal—the lot went down. I excused myself and went into the bedroom so he could pick up his chop for the last juicy fragments instead of trying to worry them off with a knife and fork. I had noticed that the cuffs of his jacket were on the verge of fraying—he was obviously not a young man of means.

I dabbed on some extra perfume—June Night was the name. Rosie kindly offered to wash up.

'I thought you would like to see the film at the "Select",' said Syd as we approached the Edgware Road. The 'Select' was a tiny cinema known locally by two other names, 'The Flea Pit' and 'The Hole in the Wall'. Seats were sixpence, a shilling, and one-and-six. I didn't need to be clairvoyant to know where we would be sitting. I thought of his coat cuffs. I'd like to pay for myself, I said, putting my sixpence down for the cashier. There was no embarrassed argument from Syd. Contrariwise I thought: mean bugger, he'd better watch out if he's one of the wandering hand brigade.

We had been sitting inside for a long time before he shyly put an arm round my shoulder and drew my head near to his. This was nice—I felt protected and very content. When the lights went up for the ice-cream sellers he reached into his pocket and brought out two apples—the sort the barrow boys flogged at knock-down prices, small, wizened, but still sound enough to eat.

We both managed to appear very uninterested in ice-cream, and settled back down until 'God save the King'. Syd didn't kiss me, he didn't even ask for one on the doorstep. All the same, he asked for another date a few evenings hence. By then I hoped to have found some digs.

I found my digs on the top floor of a slummy house in Molyneux Street which ran parallel with the Edgware Road. It was smelly and dark—some of the tenants lit a candle at night and put it on a shelf on the landing, but there were still plenty of dark corners for the bugs to take a walk. My room was the smaller of two rented by an Irishwoman for eleven shillings. She charged me eight shillings for mine. 'Mrs' Flaherty was fat, fair and fortyish—and she certainly had a weakness for 'a dhrap o' the hard stuff'. She shared the room with her little daughter Annie, then six years old. 'Mrs' was a courtesy title only—she had never married.

For my eight shillings rent she reckoned to include a pint of paraffin each week for the little oil lamp and small iron contraption I could cook on. They both gave off more smoke than an Indian on the warpath. Instead, I bought candles, and an occasional seven-pound bag of coal to light a fire in the tiny grate. I had no key, and Mrs Flaherty often helped herself to a piece of candle or a knob or two of my coal.

She worked hard as a cleaner in two or three pubs, and she was soon asking me to keep an eye on Annie so that she could work evenings as well. I think she was addicted to the smell of alcohol. I reckon a match would have ignited a couple of inches from her mouth.

It wouldn't be fair to describe my room as a black hole of Calcutta, it was more of a dark greyish-brown. Walls, ceiling and floor merged indiscernibly into this colour, undisturbed by the rickety chest of drawers, small table, two chairs and narrow iron bed. Ugly as it was, it was a haven compared with the big brightly lit clean teashop in Oxford Street where I worked as a Nippy.

I was terrified by my job. There are good waitresses, they keep calm, there are bad waitresses, they keep calmer: 'Sod the customers, let 'em wait', and there are nervous, anxious-to-please hopelessly inefficient ones—I was one of the latter.

The working hours of the staff were staggered so that the maximum number were on duty during the rush hours, yet it was still grossly inadequate.

My five tables seated twenty diners. At twelve noon, from shop counters, offices, machine shops and the pavements, customers rushed in like the hordes of Babylon. They were always in a hurry. Sensible waitresses took the orders from one table at a time, ignoring the desperate tuggings at their skirt and the beseeching, urgent voices. They were cruel to be kind. I tried to be kind by taking twenty orders, so jumbled up by the time I reached the service counter that most of them were forgotten.

A great many of the items on the menu were pre-cooked at a central depot and kept hot or cold in a honeycomb of metal compartments along the counter. The counter hands filled them up from the back, the waitresses taking out their orders from the front. Often they were empty, as in the mad rush the four or five counter hands tried to cope with the myriad orders for this or that on toast which they had to prepare behind the counter, as well as mixing and dispensing all drinks, hot and cold.

The customers turned us into impatient despots, we turned the counter hands into wild-eyed viragos threatening to remove our entrails with the knives they brandished. Upstairs, in the steamy noisy bedlam of clattering crockery and cutlery, the washers-up screamed out invective about the ceaseless demand for clean replacements. It was like being on a treadmill in Hell. None of my customers ever actually had a seizure but some came near it.

We did not get much stamina from the food provided with the job. The staff took their lunches at half past ten or eleven o'clock. A tiny portion of tough red meat (I wonder if it was horse?), some greyish potato that had been put through a mincer to make it appear more palatable, and a small mound of worm-shaped rice pudding for afters of a quality even worse than Miss Lowry's—this was a typical meal. It cost us one-and-six a week. Two shillings a week were also deducted for our uniform, from our wages of thirty-one shillings. It took us six months to pay for, and we were immediately made to order another set. Then there was our insurance stamp, and it was automatically assumed we would contribute threepence a week to the employees' sports ground somewhere in the suburbs.

It was the firm's policy to place waitresses in a teashop a bus ride from their home address—this meant a couple of bob a week for fares. For tea, which was free, we got some bread and butter and a penny bun. The cups of tea that went with it were the best I've ever tasted.

If we worked in a teashop that closed late, on evening duty we were allowed threepence-ha'penny off the menu for our supper. We could augment this by buying extra at discount prices. Hunger made me a spendthrift. I often had only one pound left to pay my rent, coal and candles, off-duty food, black stockings for work, entertainment and saving up for holidays. 'You should be like me,' said one of the girls. 'I often earn myself ten shillings a time going out with some of the customers.'

Yet a good percentage of waitresses were cheerful, well-balanced girls.

My weekly day off frequently came on a Sunday. They were halcyon days. After his dinner, Syd called to take me out. I had always found London a place of wonder and interest, but I had only been looking at the casket; Syd showed me the jewels inside. The museums—British, Science, Victoria and Albert, the National Gallery—treasure troves of exhibitions, free, or paid for with a pittance. He took me to the gods at Sadler's Wells. Syd had an innately cultured mind, and he had been to Grammar School. I followed in the wake of his deeper, richer appreciation. But he had desires of the flesh as well as the spirit—he wanted to take me to bed. He was barely twenty—I was two and a half years older.

I remembered a verse I had once read:

> There was a young lady so wild
> She kept herself pure undefiled
> By thinking of Jesus
> Venereal diseases
> And the dangers of having a child.

I sensed the implied sneer, but I thought the young woman had a sensible idea of self-preservation.

I wasn't worried about Jesus. I was, however, concerned with my own self-respect, and very scared of getting pregnant. I was at the same time very curious about this mysterious world of sex. For many months Syd cajoled and sulked, while I kept up my defences.

One winter evening Syd took me for an unsuccessful swimming lesson. Seeing him so near to nakedness gave me courage—I gave in to his demand.

There was no light in my landlady's room—she had told me she was spending the night away. We sneaked upstairs—no need for a candle, enough light filtered through the window to undress by.

Syd tactfully looked at the view while I got into bed. I squeezed up close to the wall and buried my burning face in the pillow. Syd had assured me he would take no risks. Presently he got in beside me—thin and bony though he was, it was very uncomfortable in the narrow bed. Fear, prudery, inexperience and above all the horrifying thought of Mrs Flaherty discovering us turned me into a cold, unresponsive object.

With no encouragement from me, Syd too lost his nerve. We were two failures together. We buried our faces in each other's necks like lost babes in the wood. But it was nice to have each other's company, holding hands in the dark.

Above my head my romantic dreams started floating away—the handsome desert sheik carrying me off from the tent where I was held prisoner, Clark Gable in the Edgware Road realising that the girl turning the corner into Molyneux Street was the very one he wanted for his next leading lady. These dreams dissolved for ever.

Now thirty-five years married, we know we found our way. It has been a most rewarding partnership. We started our own family tree, branching sturdily. We made our own dreams.

No Pipe Dreams for Father

To my friends

A Washing Day

It was the worst day of the week. It was washing day and the signs were ominous. True the weather was dry, but it was worried by a spiteful icy wind. Mother was already in a lather carrying buckets of water through our little living-room to fill the copper in the dark back-kitchen. Old Auntie was irritated at the small amount of rainwater in the brick-lined covered well, outside the front door, that housed the precious water from our cottage's guttering.

Old Auntie was a washer of the old school, a believer in starching, blueing, and plenty of rinsing. Mother, who would work like a Trojan at the dollying and scrubbing, had no time for such laundering refinements. She was glad to get it washed at any price. Intolerant of each other's methods, they were as likely to come to the boil as the whites in the copper. They would have a row before the day was out, and treat each other to a list of their respective shortcomings in all directions.

The fire in the big black-leaded grate had the miseries, too, suffocated as it was by a huge black iron saucepan full of swede and potato peel and coarse cabbage, boiling to add to the bran in the bucket for the pigs' dinner. My sister had been packed off to school in a bad humour because the pair of drawers old Auntie had made her from some striped flanellette 'is showin' all down below me frock'.

My toddler brother was crying to be picked up. Mother, heavy with child, could hardly find room to squeeze with her loaded buckets between the table and chairs. The last thing she wanted was an unco-operative three-year-old who had soaked up the atmosphere of tension and irritability.

'Now get from under my feet,' Mam warned me as I stood by the copper while she tried to poke the fire beneath it to a blaze. Determined to help, I threw a pair of my sister's black woollen school stockings into the copper among the whites when Mam had to rush to the kitchen. The saucepan of pigs' food had tipped into the fire, and poor Auntie had not the strength in her rheumaticky old hands to straighten it.

'I'll get the little varmint outside,' said old Auntie, and wrapping me up in a parcel of old scarves, she shoved me outside with a couple of currants in a piece of paper. With a mutinous scowl I sat on top of the stone steps leading up to the garden. My nose was level with a group of early narcissi and their perfume drew it to their white-petalled beauty and the thin scarlet edgings of their trumpet centres. At three years old I felt 'drunk' for the first time, intoxicated by a little piece of nature's living artistry. The coldness of the stone step on my bum soon sobered me up and I crept indoors again.

Old Auntie had poured the saucepan of pigs' scraps into the bucket with the bran, where it waited to cool enough for Mam to take it to the pigs, and now she had got my little brother on her lap, soothing him to sleep. To sit over that steaming bucket would be just the job to warm my bum, I thought, and I knew that her arthritics and having my brother on her lap would prevent her stopping me for a bit. I ignored her warnings and edged myself over the bucket. Just a little too far: my behind, and a whole lot more of me, got a warm-up as down I went into the mushy smelly contents. Wedged a prisoner, there I sat till Mam rushed out from the back-kitchen and truly hotted up my nether end with her soapy hands.

'That's all I be short of, a yup more washin',' Mam wailed as she peeled my clothes off. 'I know what we'll do,' said old Auntie, 'we'll shut the little toe-rag up in the front room.'

The front room was a narrow slip of a room which contained old Auntie's single bed, her finest piece of furniture, a mahogany chest of drawers with glass knobs, a small wooden table under the window, and a couple of chairs. There was also a hanging basket over the window, from which grew a trailing plant much cossetted and watered, and old Auntie's family Bible.

Re-dressed in what Mam could find me, I was pushed inside and the door locked. Kicking and banging brought no response. Presently, from the back-kitchen, I could hear the two women's voices raised in argument. All the washing in the copper had boiled to a dingy greyish-blue. Mam had fished out a pair of ruined, once-black, woollen stockings, and now each was blaming the other for putting them in with the whites. Suddenly Mam exclaimed, 'I'll warrant it was that little tartar in the front room what done it. I'll give 'er the good 'idin' of 'er life, that I will.'

Mam's mood made Auntie act in defence council on my behalf till she had cooled off. 'Leave 'er be till we 'ave finished the weshin'! Anyroads, non ont'll need the blue bag for a bit.'

Unrepentant, my martyrdom increased. 'I'll rip your bloody plant down if you don't let me out,' I yelled as they came within earshot. 'Doosn't take any notice on 'er,' advised old Auntie; ''er can't reach up to touch'n.'

I couldn't, but there was the chair to climb on, and the little table. Not quite tall enough, so I took the chair, and from it reached the Bible off the chest of drawers. It was a huge illustrated volume with metal clasps to shut it. I struggled and heaved it on to the table, then tiptoed to reach some of the trailing foliage and ripped at it with all my energy.

I knew I was in for a good hiding, I intended to have my hide's worth! When they opened the door, I intended to get under the far corner of the bed. They would have to drag me out! My apprehension soon changed to hope when I heard the sound of Father's heavy pit boots across the yard. I put back my head, opened my mouth, and began to howl piteously.

'What's all this then? What's goin' on?' asked Father as he unlocked the door and picked me up in his dirty pit clothes. 'That's right,' said Mam sharply. 'Make me a bit more weshin', as though the little 'ussy ain't made me enough already.'

I sniffed and sobbed as tragically as an Ophelia, whilst Mam listed my misdemeanours of the day, interrupted by a little scream of horror from old Auntie. 'Me plant, me plant! Er 'ave ruined me plant!' I clung tightly to the refuge of Dad's neck whilst he inspected my horticultural rape.

'Now, doosn't thee fret, Aunt. I 'a' bin meanin' to prune thic plant f'r a long time. Thee see, 'im'll shoot out better'n ever now.' Father put me down and followed Mam into the back-kitchen. There was some whispering, and sounds of kissing going on, and Mam came out looking all soppy with her mouth twitching at the corners as it did when she had a nice secret all to herself.

Dad sat down at the table, took my little brother in the crook of one arm and me on the other knee, and began to eat his boiled-egg tea. Times were hard, but never in my life did I ever hear Dad complain about whatever Mam could muster up for him to eat. Enthroned on his lap I ate the bits of crust he broke from his own bread and butter and dripping in the yoke of his egg, a bit for my brother and a bit for me.

Naughty, undeserving, I drank the tea he poured into his saucer, but I remember . . . I remember . . .

Early One Morning

The feather bed, made from plucked chicken feathers by ancestral grannies, was warm and soft. My sister, little brother and I slept in its dents as cosy as beans in their fur-lined pods. Winter and summer, Mam had quite a job prising us out of it.

From our little back bedroom it was hard to see what season it was. The bottom of the tiny window rested on the garden level of the cottage above ours, and weeds often obstructed our minute view.

On school mornings our Mam kept calling up the stairs threatening us with the stick on our behinds to start out with, and very likely the same from the headmaster at the other end, if we were late for school. We became quite expert at measuring the irritation in Mam's voice, and we mostly timed our jumps out of bed just as she started up the stairs. We thought of a good ploy to fool her by banging our boots on the wooden floor without actually leaving the bed, but it did not always work!

On summer mornings, once up, it seemed just as good as being in bed. My sister and I washed first, in the little dark back-kitchen. Our little brother could take his time; he was still too young for a stint of water carrying before breakfast.

My sister had a proper yoke with a bucket at each end, and I had two wire-handled tins. Mam would be getting our breakfast, toast done in front of the fire bars and kept warm on the hob, while we went down the garden path, then through the gently sloping woodland, and down to the well at the side of the main road. Converging from other paths, we could hear the voices of other children on the same errand.

The pure, exhilarating morning air, the sunshine benediction, and the thought of the warm toast to come, plus our sleep-renewed energies, often drove us mad with joy. In those days, wild sweet days, we had the privilege to behave like lunatics. We could yell our heads off, take running jumps into the lush green fern between the trees, make drums out of our buckets with banging sticks, and pause to look at all the wonders along the way.

'Look at this bloody yup under 'ere!' The flat upturned stone revealed a mass of sluggish wood-lice. Poor stupid things, hiding from the summer's day! Whatever did they do all day! Unlucky creatures. Lower the stone again, very carefully, not to squash them. Oh, how lucky I was, born me instead of wood-lice!

'Eh, thee come 'n zee wot I 'ave found. The cu'st 'a some, there's plenty a growin' just 'ere.' We picked and relished the pale green juicy sharp-tanged leaves of something we knew as woodsorrel. It often sharpened our imaginations as well as our taste buds.

'Coo, I just zeen a girt great fox over there, wi' blood round 'is chops. 'Im 'ave 'id behind thic tree over there.'

We knew it was not true, but in an ecstasy of terror we would run screaming down to the well. Fear-tightened throats were soon eased with cupped handfuls of sparkling spring water. In the mossy stream from the well overflow we observed the progress of the black spot in the frog spawn, via the tadpole to the endearing ugly croaking frog; a fairy prince, of course, under a witch's spell.

Water slopped out of our containers as we raced to pluck the rare white foxglove amid the myriads of pinky-purple ones growing among the ferns. These special ones were for Teacher.

By the time I heaved my tins on to the back-kitchen table, the water content was well down.

Toast in hand, and off up the hill to school. Spring brought the leggy lambs running up to their mothers for short and urgent sucking sessions. We saw the afterbirths, we knew that hens laid eggs and that baby pigs came out of the mother sow, but we never doubted that we were young, God-like creatures, mysteriously deposited under the gooseberry bush to be brought to our mothers in the midwife's bag. How I scolded Mam on one occasion for just lying in bed all day with our new-born baby when she should have been getting our tea. That she must be there to keep him warm seemed a poor excuse.

Autumn brought the fluttering leaves, piled by the winds into the banks of confetti to jump and roll in and scatter back to the winds.

Winter seeped through our boots, aggravating our itching chilblains, but they were soon forgotten in the snowball pelting with our 'enemies'. Icicles made lovely lollyices to suck, but summer mornings were the best of all, mornings to recapture when I listen now to the evocative genius of Beethoven's 'Pastoral' Symphony, taking me back to the well-springs of my childhood, to fetching water from the well.

No Pipe Dreams For Father

I stood with uncharacteristic patience whilst Mam tied up my pinny into a sort of pocket, put old Auntie's pension book in it, then made it extra safe with two large safetypins. I was going on a very important errand and well aware of it!

'Now mind,' old Auntie warned me, 'if thee dost get playin' about and lose me pension book I'll never let thee 'elp to scrape out me Nestlé's milk tin agyun.'

It was an unnecessary caution; I had every intention of making a sedate bee-line down the rutted track to the post-office-cum-shop at the bottom of our village. I intended to keep well to the forest side of the path to resist the distracting temptations of other children engaged in the ordinary pastime of playing. I was six years old and for the first time trusted alone for this very important mission.

I had old Auntie's livelihood in my pinny; her old age pension book from which she could draw five whole shillings a week. It was a fortune—even old Auntie thought so and was apt to give as much praise to Lloyd George as she did to the Almighty for His munificence. She sang God's praises every Sunday and dratted the devil for the rest of the week.

It was fair shares really, considering that a life of hard work, absolute honesty, and much kindness to others, had left her at seventy-six years old a housebound arthritic with only enough savings put by to 'putt I under the ground dacent'. Rigidly independent of spirit, God knows how she would have managed had Lloyd George not come just in time with the five shillings a week old age allowance.

Fairly speaking, she could have accepted the little sustenance she required from us, for she had shared her home with Father from the day he had got married. We children had broken many of her treasured ornaments, kicked the legs off her best table, piddled on her feather beds and trodden on her rheumaticky toes.

Mother had kept her lap filled with a succession of babies to be hushed and comforted to sleep. Father revered her and we children adored her; this squared our books, for never by the slightest imputation did she make *us* feel indebted to *her*.

Too crippled to walk down to the post office to draw her pension herself, this task was entrusted to Father, and on this particular Friday afternoon I was going to meet him at the post office on his way home from his early shift at the pit.

Friday was a very special day for us children. It was pay day! However short work was at the pit, Mam always insisted Dad must have his shilling a week pocket money. Ninepence of this went on two packets of his beloved Stanfield tobacco, twopence on a slab of marzipan toffee for us children, and a penny on liquorice all-sorts for Mam and old Auntie.

Waiting outside the post office provided me with a lovely extra treat. In its little shop window was a shelf with a beautiful baby doll priced at half a crown. It had been there a very long time. Flanking the doll on each side was a doll's tea-set in a cardboard box and a set of doll's furniture in another cardboard box, each priced at sevenpence. I was pleased no one could afford to buy them, for it meant that I could 'pretend' play with them. Magic worked in those days. I 'got' them out of the window and sat down on the grassy bank outside to 'nurse' the doll and 'arrange' the furniture using little stones as substitutes—then I pretend-drank my tea from the tiny cups, holding my little finger crooked in the manner my Aunties told me their mistresses did in service.

It was a wonderful treat, too, when I had Father's company all to myself. Father was a bottomless source of fascinating information, and all us children loved him to distraction. However, I got so engrossed playing with my pretend toys it was only when I noticed Father's mudcaked pit boots near me that I sprang up for my pitgrimed hugs.

I marched into the post office with him, my snub nose stuck even farther into the air; after all we were cash customers with a whole shilling to spend!

When we got home Mam shared out the marzipan toffee, and magnanimously letting her have Dad's company I ran out to play—out into the beautiful green forest when school holidays and summer days lasted for ever. Yet winter came with its ills and chills, thinning us out with its icy brittle fingers, etching for ever on the memory a trail of black figures bent against the cruel snow-flecked east winds carrying a coffin in front of them, and the matching mourning of leaden skies, the creaking moans of dark leafless trees, and the black tread marks in the snow. That winter I came close to the edge of 'the pitty hole' myself.

Though by no means a particularly sunny-natured child, my persistent grizzling one evening attracted Father's notice before he went off to the night shift. He picked me up on his lap, felt my burning forehead, and noticed my heavy eyes and quickened breathing with some concern.

'Mark my words, thic young un be a' sickening fir zummat. The best place for 'er is bed an' a bit o' quiet.'

He put a brick to warm in the oven, helped Mam to make a bed for me in their room and lit a fire in its tiny grate. When the fire had warmed the bedroom and the hot brick my bed, Mam gave me a washdown mustard bath and covered me with extra blankets borrowed from a kindly neighbour; my worried father went out in the darkness to walk to the pit.

When he came home in the early hours of the morning I was worse.

Father's only culinary achievement was invalid's sop and he proceeded to make me some. He poured some boiling water on a piece of bread in a basin, beat it to a cream, adding sugar, a little knob of butter and a drop of milk. When my normally greedy little stomach refused to touch the delicacy, alarm set in.

Mam made some invalid drink—boiling water poured on a piece of toast and allowed to get cold. My siblings went to bed with hushed voices and tip-toe manner.

'I be goin' for the doctor,' said Father.

For the doctor's and pride's sake two shillings off the arrears we owed him had to be multiple-borrowed from our impoverished neighbours, and Father ran through the woods to the doctor's house before going on his night shift.

Old Auntie, who had given up the struggle of getting upstairs to sleep, made a tortured ascent to sit with me whilst Mam did her evening chores and attended to the baby.

The doctor came, shook his head on my account, advised that the crisis would come shortly and my chance of surviving it was nil. His visit did not register on me; a black coma kept sucking me down. When I opened my eyes it was to unrecognizable surroundings. I could hear far-away voices and someone crying softly—'I be afeared we be gwine to lose the little wench, Maggie, fir I never

knowed anybody as bad as 'er is to get over it—and to think that
only a couple o' days ago 'er was threadin' me needle for me as
right as rain.' I could see no one, only weird terrible shadows on
the wall and a pair of fiery tiger's eyes gleaming in the corner
ready to pounce on me and eat me up. I must have screamed. Old
Auntie pounded the floor with her walking-stick. Mam rushed
upstairs carrying the oil-lamp. Some of the shadows disappeared,
the tiger's eyes became the fire's reflection on the top caps of a
pair of treasured boy's boots someone had given Mam for my little
brother to grow into. Mam had kept them shined and polished on
the bamboo what-not in the corner of the bedroom.

'Dad, Dad, I want our Dad,' I begged from this little oasis of
lucidity. Dad would make the witches' shadows go, and the tigers,
and save me from the black pit that kept sucking me down. Several
times I struggled to consciousness to see Dad's face—but he was
still down in his own black pit hacking on his knees for the coal
that nearly kept our bodies and souls together.

'Dad, Dad, oh I want our Dad'—and he was there—allowed
straight up to the invalid's bedroom in his pit dirt. That dear kind
face with the crinkles at the corner of his eyes, held my hands in
his pit-calloused ones. I was safe now. Dad was home.

'There there, my little wench, Fayther's wum, an' I'll stop 'ere
till thee bist better—now mind thee'st got to make up thee mind
to get better—for who's goin' to putt the taters in the dib 'oles for
'er old Dad, an' who's goin' to play wi' the babby whilst Mam do
get on wi' the washin'?—now thee take a sip o' thee Mam's drink
and goo to a nice nap and I'll stop 'ere by thee bed.'

I took some spoonfuls from him whilst Mam fetched him up a
cup of tea.

In the morning the doctor was amazed to find me still in the
land of the living.

I had survived, but only just. I could make no headway with
appetite or strength despite all the love and attention lavished
upon me. My ten-year-old sister filled jars of flowers to put by my
bed, Mam got little luxuries she couldn't afford to tempt my
palate, but best of all I loved it when Dad came up to sit with me,
to tell me stories or just to sit and read himself from one of the
books a pit butty of his used to lend him.

One Friday, Dad came up with a cup and spoon in his hand and
an expression of great pleading in his eyes. Beastly little daughter I

must have been, for this was an ominous sign. Dad was a great believer in herbal medicines and often brewed his own from the herbs he gathered. I thought they tasted terrible and my pig-headed nature made me the most unco-operative of swallowers, but I noticed what I thought was a book wrapped in brown paper in Dad's pocket. Perhaps Dad was going to sit with me for a long time.

With the patience of Job, and his own incredible gifts of love and encouragement, he got me to take eight spoonfuls of his little brew; then to bolster the undeserved praise he lavished upon me, he drank the dregs from the cup himself.

Then from his pocket he took the brown paper parcel, but it wasn't a book! He unwrapped it and put it on my bed. I could hardly believe my eyes. It was the box of doll's furniture out of the post office window!

'There then, that's fir bein' a good little wench. Now thee try and start yuttin' a bit better and then thee'lt be able to get up and goo out on the tump to play to thee 'eart's content wi' all the t'other young uns. Now afore I do go out to do a bit o' gyardening I'll 'a' me a little nap.' It was a little nap. As soon as he woke up it was always Father's habit to feel round for his beloved old pipe. He did so now, put it in his mouth, then took his baccy tin out of his pocket. There was nothing in it. He put it and his pipe back in his pocket, then sat sadly staring through the window.

I remembered—today was Friday, pocket-money day! Sevenpence for doll's furniture, twopence for marzipan toffee, a penny for liquorice all-sorts—there was only twopence left!

I looked at my Dad, and I looked at my present, and I wished that doll's furniture was where old Auntie sent the 'tarmenting devil', all the way to Halifax.

The Rivals

They had been rivals in love. If 'Hell hath no fury like a woman scorned' it has no greater rivalry than when two females set their caps at the same man! In the case of Vernie and Lydie, whilst enjoying the flattery of their attentions, the young man in question had been smart enough to escape his dilemma by marrying someone else altogether.

This mutual loss did not bring them together. Each blamed the other, and though they eventually acquired a husband each, they remained bitter enemies, ever trying to outdo each other, especially in the matter of dress.

Both were talented needlewomen. Chapel Anniversary was the highlight of their year and to outshine each other on that day was the summit of their ambitions.

Paris has its yearly bonanza of Haute Couture, and fifty-odd years ago our chapel had its fashion parade, too, on that important Sunday. Any girls lucky enough to be home from service on their annual holiday paraded the finery their hard-earned shillings had bought them for the delectation of the village boys, but the 'stars' of the show were always Vernie and Lydie. Much to Lydie's chagrin, Vernie was always voted the winner. 'Wonder wot they two show-offs'll turn up in this time?' was a frequent conjecture of the village women who could not afford such indulgences.

At seven years old, ribbons and laces, frills and bows met with my undiluted approval and a determination to indulge in them when I grew up and could earn some money. I was always happy when chance permitted me to sit on the corner of Vernie's fender and watch her sewing. Even her rag-mats had a glamour. She didn't just poke the bits of rag through the sack at random; she patterned the colours and once earned a spate of childish praise from me when she fashioned a black cat in the middle of one from scraps cut from a dead old woman's skirt. But it was her drawers and chemises I especially envied; on the legs of the former she threaded pink ribbon through slotted borders and added frills of lace. Her washing day was 'a sight f'r sore eyes', as one man remarked—the women were not so charitable. 'I bet they never even go on 'er arse; 'er do just dip 'em in the wayter an' 'ang 'em on the line to show off.' No doubt the shape that Vernie possessed to fill them, that went with a very flirtatious pair of eyes in a pretty face, didn't endear her to them either!

Lydie also was no mean looker and she had the advantage of a crowning glory of naturally curly auburn hair. Her luck, however, didn't last as far as her legs. They were fat and shapeless, with ankles that hung over the high-heeled shoes she wore on Sundays.

Having little sensitivity about how my 'social calls' were regarded, on occasions I took up my perch on Lydie's fender too, thus one summer becoming the innocent decoy of Vernie's underhand machinations.

'D'you know wot!' Vernie said to me one day a few weeks before Anniversary Sunday.

'D'you know wot!' she repeated, her eyes shining, hands clasped together in apparent ecstatic anticipation—'I be going to make meself a real classy dress f'r the anniversary, summat different. I be sick o' bright colours, I be goin' to wear black: a black velvut frock trimmed wi' black braid—I shall 'ave long sleeves to look different, an' a nice little close-fittin' black 'at an' I shall wear me pearls, 'an very 'igh-'eeled black patunt shoes.'

I was rather less than enthusiastic at this description. I thought black was the awfulest colour to wear and only fit for funerals.

Vernie enthused on—'Wot made I think on't was a picture of a actress—on a postcard; 'er 'ad lovely ginger 'air and thic black frock 'er was wearin' set it off summat lovely. I read somewhere as well that all the smart 'igh up women be goin' into black—they do reckon bright colours be too common. Oh I do wish I 'ad ginger wavy 'air, but I shall wear black just the same an' I'll bet I shall look smarter than all the t'others put together!'

My hitherto unqualified admiration for Vernie's taste, plus her persuasive enthusiasm, nearly brainwashed me into thinking it a good idea; she went on so much about it I knew the details off by heart before my belly told me it was time to go home.

I had to go by Lydie's cottage farther up the hill, near the chapel. I was passing her gate and got quite a surprise when she beckoned me inside from her doorstep.

'I've got a bit o' custard left in a basin if you'd like to yut it up?' Though my belly at that time was my god, and I took every opportunity to send it down an offering, it was ingrained in us village children not to accept from neighbours, who in general had pantries as bare as our own; but the temptation of custard, a rare treat for Sunday tea only in our house, and the fact that Lydie had no children to feed, made my scruples on this score give in without a murmur. 'Come on, set down,' Lydie said in a most kindly manner. She showed me a butterfly she was embroidering on a corner of a pillow case—the subject got round to sewing, then to the Anniversary Sunday—then to the problem of what to wear for that grand occasion?

Without much prompting, and automatically imitating Vernie's fervent manner, I told her all about Vernie's plan to wear black. 'Vernie said—ooh 'er wish 'er'd got ginger 'air cos then 'er'd look like that beautiful actress in the photo 'er got the idea from. Ginger 'air like you got,' I added artlessly.

I had finished the custard, and was further astounded with a piece of bread and jam. Meantime Lydie skilfully got all the details of Vernie's forthcoming outfit from my mouthy chatter.

To augment the pittance they could get from their husbands' meagre earnings—both Vernie and Lydie tramped the surrounding country in the autumn to earn their pins and needle money. They gathered acorns at 2d. a bucket under the forest oaks for a local pig-keeper—and had their own blackberry territories. The 'Jam Man' came in the evenings to the main road at the bottom of the village with his horse and cart to buy this wild fruit. He was a proper Shylock; having no competition, he paid very stingily for his wares—he may not have got his pound of flesh but I reckon he got pints of blood from the scratches these two gathered in their pickings.

It was a perfect, very warm sunny Sunday on Anniversary day. Pretty outfits for me were still a figment of my imagination; meanwhile I must put up with whatever Mother could muster for me to wear, being one of five children. No matter, I had my bit of glory to come; ever ready to show off, and blessed with a good memory, I was always given a 'spot' in the proceedings reciting a poem. We children who sang or recited sat on raised seats facing the congregation.

The chapel was soon packed, but the preacher, a local man,

well knew that two of his flock had not yet arrived, so he hung about in the pulpit. Vernie was hanging about, too, crouched down behind her gate waiting to see Lydie emerge from hers. Lydie had been impatiently waiting for Vernie to go past. She looked at her clock—it was no good, she would have to start out.

Funereally garbed, hobbling painfully up the rain-rutted path ('Like a pig on stilts,' as Vernie gloated afterwards)—Lydie was hot, bothered and perspiring in her black velvet before she was half-way to the chapel. When she was sure Lydie had got as far as the chapel door and the point of no return, Vernie started out.

What eyebrows I had shot up under my fringe when I saw Lydie hobble in and sink into the only vacant space at the back of the chapel. I thought she looked a miserable sight, and serve her right for copying Vernie's idea; for now the penny had dropped as well as the custard.

It was the turn of my big mouth next. It opened wide enough for all the trapped flies beating their wings against the chapel panes to come in for a flight, when Vernie made her entrance.

She was a vision in a cream silk sleeveless dress—a wide-brimmed cream straw hat trimmed with a peachy-pink rose and ribbons, cream dainty shoes and, crowning touch, a cream silk parasol, sprayed with roses to match the one on her hat! No black for her! The male organist had kept his seat right in the front row warm for her; he kept other things warm for her, if local gossip was anything to go by.

Lydie's face went a quite dreadful red that clashed with her ginger hair. The look she gave Vernie's back view ought to have set fire to her rival, and the one she gave me wasn't suitable at all for the chapel either!

Aches and Pains

When I was a child, as they aged, the old people in our village drew up their chairs nearer the fire, accepting their physical deterioration with a fatalistic stoicism, waiting for the Almighty to take them in His own good time. The doctor's pills and potions had not then superseded the powers of the Almighty. God and His angels were still up in the sky watching over them.

Sophisticated technology had not yet sent men soaring to the moon, destroying their comfortable illusions.

They still fought sickness with all the means at their disposal. Pneumonia might be cured with linseed-meal poultices on the chest—raw sheep's kidneys tied round the feet till the kidneys went putrid, drawing the poison out—and boiled onion liquor to ease the throat. Often these 'cures', bolstered by love and encouragement, worked!

When the doctor diagnosed consumption, heads were shaken and the slow heartbreak began. When it was 'galloping consumption' the heartbreak came quicker.

Sonny Banes was only eighteen years old when the horrified whispers began to circulate that "im 'ad got it'.

The scourge could not have hit a less likely victim. Sonny had always been regarded as 'a regular caution', a cheerful extrovert ready for any mischievous fun afoot. He brought rosy blushes to the girls' cheeks with his welcome ribaldry, and he was a very good-looking boy, too.

At fourteen years old he cheerfully plodded to the pit in his heavy boots with the village men and other boys. A bit of 'chestiness' was so common he wasn't especially noticed. When opportunity gave Sonny the chance for a bit of idling underground the older men laughingly observed he was the exception to that old saying, 'One bwoy'll do one bwoy's work—two bwoys together'll do 'alf a bwoy's work—and dree bwoys together be nothin' but a 'indrance.'

His bouts of coughing and obvious exhaustion were put down to 'the bwoy's outgrowin' 'is strength findin' 'is road to monhood'.

When, however, the ebullient Sonny kept lagging behind them on the walk home ('Me bloody boot laces be undone agyun') sympathy turned to alarm. 'Better take thic bwoy to the doctor f'r a tonic and 'av a check-up, missus,' they advised his widowed mother.

'I zid 'em comin' back dru the 'ood on their way wum from the doctor's, and thic 'oman was carryin' twenty more years on 'er shoulders than wot 'er started out wi'.'

The doctor had broken the news to Sonny's mother that he had the symptoms of advanced consumption.

She made him up his bed downstairs by the fire and fed him with the best at her disposal augmented by 'a bit o' this and a drap o' that' from sympathetic neighbours.

Poor Sonny's youthful contours dropped to skeletal proportions, but between his blood-flecked coughing bouts he was as cheerful as ever, flirting outrageously with any female from nine to ninety who popped in to see him.

He was fond of my father, who visited Sonny for a chat and a game of snakes and ladders whenever he could spare the time. One fine mild day Sonny made up his mind that he would come down to our house to visit Father for a change, and he was determined to make it on his own; it was all of 300 yards. When Father heard this he got out our wooden chairs and asked some of the neighbours to place one every few yards for Sonny to have a rest. Then Father resisted the impulse to give the boy his arm— 'Let 'un come on 'is own if 'im can make it,' he begged us.

Eventually Sonny got to the chair in our little courtyard. Mam poked the fire to a blaze under the kettle to give Sonny 'a nice 'ot cup o' tay'—and cut him a cheese sandwich from Dad's pit rations.

When he could get the strength, Sonny accepted the cup of tea placed on another chair near him. He was too weak to hold the cup for long—but he shook his head refusing the sandwich—'It's a waste o' your victuals, missus,' he grinned, 'for 'tis no sooner in one end than 'tis out o' the t'other. There's a pretty wench thee bist gettin'.' (I wasn't, I was as plain as a pikestaff.) 'Thee 'urry up an' get old enuff f'r me to take thee to the pictures.'

Sonny couldn't stay long; Father walked behind him between his chair-rests and let him totter up unaided to his own cottage door.

Sonny never took me to the pictures. We never saw Sonny again. A week later his neighbour called asking if we could spare a couple of coppers towards a collection to help his mother with the funeral expenses.

Jarge

Normally, simple old Jarge was as placid and untemperamental as the sheep lying under the trees in the surrounding forest chewing their cud. After a few days of uncharacteristic grumpiness from the old man, one of his butties asked, 'Wot's the matter, old 'un?' 'Ast thee bin gettin' out o' the wrong side o' the bed lately?'

One worthy who could have been a born medico in more affluent conditions hit the nail on the head with his diagnosis of Jarge's trouble.

''Ow long is it since thee'st went to the mon 'ole, old butty?'

The 'mon 'ole' was a natural hole in the forest, well hidden with surrounding undergrowth, where the men went for nature's calls and left the bucket privies in the gardens for the use of women and children.

Jarge rubbed the stubble on his chin and shook a negative head until enquiries had gone back a week.

'That's the trouble with thee, old 'un; thee bist bunged up—I reckon a lump o' thy old 'oman's bread pudding 'a' got stuck an' caunt't goo up or down—thee'lt vill up wi' gas like the cows do. Thee goo to the docter's tonight an' tell 'im thee bist constipated.'

Like most simple souls, Jarge was apt to do what he was told. That evening he turned his muffler cleanest side out and walked the two miles to the doctor's surgery.

'And what is it that's troubling you, Mr Dobbins?'
'I be constipated, zir.'
'I see, when did you last pass anything?'
'On the road 'ere, zir.'
'And what was it like?'
'A 'oss an' cyart, zir.'

A bottle of senna mixture and a few sprints to the 'mon 'ole' and old Jarge was chewing his twist of baccy again as contented as the sheep. He outlived the doctor, and when he was in his nineties the doctor's successor, by now an elderly man himself, humorously suggested to the old man that the only way he could send him on his way was to shoot him!

A Bargain

When old Jarge had a couple of coppers to spare he toddled down to the pub at the bottom of the village, there to reflect on the vocabular glory of his peers. He loved to pick up what he considered smart sayings to pepper his own limited conversation. When the two Wills cousins were arguing about the selling and buying price of a young pig, Jarge was all ears.

'Dree pound I do want for thic pig, and 'im's wuth every penny on't.'

'Two pound ten I'll gi' thee, an 'im byunt wuth a grunt more.'

'Dree pounds.'

'Two pound ten.'

'Dree pounds!'

'Two pound ten!'

And on and on.

'Tell thee what then, I'll split the difference. Give I two pound fifteen.'

'Done.'

'Two 'alf pints o' zider, missus, and charge 'em to thic Shylock,' demanded the seller.

Split the difference! Split the difference! The saying sounded very grand in old Jarge's ears. One evening some time later, he went into the pub with a dead cockerel he had fattened up in the coop. It was a fine fat bird.

'I'll gi' thee one-and-six for thic 'un,' offered one of the men.

'I'll gi' thee one-and-nine fer'n,' said another.

'I'll make it two bob,' and the offers went on mounting up until the grand sum of half a crown waited for the hammer of Jarge's fist.

Blue eyes a twinkle with his own importance, chewing hard on his cud of tobacco, rubbing the grey stubble on his chin with the effort of getting his punch-line in the right order round his tongue, old Jarge kept the last bidder waiting. Looking round his eager audience and savouring his moments of drama, he brought his fist down hard enough to spill drops of cider from the glasses of the more parsimonious drinkers. Then Jarge got it out. 'Split the difference,' he boomed. 'Give I one-and-drippance.'

'Avin' a Goo

'Thee 'ave a goo, old butty' is the Forester's way of expressing encouragement. Fifty-odd years ago, when I was a child, the lack of necessary skill did not deter a Forester from trying to help another in distress, even a bit of dentistry on one occasion!

One day when there was no work in the pit, Joe, Tim and Albert were squatting on the grassy slope outside Joe's house, when Dan lurched up, moaning and groaning and shaking his head from side to side.

'Wot's the matter, old 'un?'

'The bloody jawache, that's wot's the matter; it be got that bad I'd be willin' for 'ern o' you to chop me yud off wi' a 'atchut.'

'That's a bugger that is, I've 'ad some on't in my time.' sympathized Joe. 'But I'll tell thee wot: if thee bist willin' I'll take thic tooth out for thee.'

''Ow?'

'Wi' me pinchers as I do castrate the animals wi'. Tim and Albert can 'old thee down, an' I'll pull on the bugger till 'im do come out. We wunt take no notice o' thee 'ollerin'; it'll be wuth the agony for to putt thee out o' such misery.'

Desperate, Dan agreed. With four hard knees on the chest, and two pairs of pit-toughened arms holding him down, and a mouthful of castrating pinchers, Dan had little chance to get a holler out, but a cry of triumph came from Joe as he fell over backwards on to the grass.

'Thee'lt be all right now, old butty; I 'a' got the bugger!'

His enthusiasm was not shared by the patient. Dan continued to roll his stricken head, and after poking about in his bloodied mouth, though grateful for the well-meant intentions, he said sadly, 'My jaw do veel wurs than ever; I be afeared thee'st took the wrong bugger out, Joe.'

Big Ambitions

I could see my Aunty was nearly crying when she kissed us all goodbye before going back to her job in domestic service. All my five aunts who lived next door in Granny's cottage cried when their holidays came to an end. From what I heard them saying it was horrible being a servant. True, they came home smelling all scenty and powdered my nose with little pages from a paper powder booklet, and they got three-and-sixpence a week wages to buy pink silk stockings and pretty blouses, but I knew they would much rather be at home.

I was nearly five years old and was well aware that when I left school I, too, would have to go into service.

I hated the thought of leaving my mam and dad, and the family and our village, so I began to lay my own future plans.

I decided I would *not* go into service. I would go to work daily at the village pub, where I knew the landlady paid two shillings a week for doing the scrubbing and cleaning, with a bread-and-cheese dinner thrown in. I would live in Miss Phillips's cottage at the end of our garden. Miss Phillips was already old; she would have to be dead or go in the work-house by the time I left school.

I loved babies, so I planned to have a dozen—six boys and six girls—all bastards, as I had heard the grown-ups say. Bastards were very easy to come by, and I knew you didn't have to bother with a husband for that sort. I was puzzled why the women bothered with husbands, they were often so grumpy about them afterwards. I wouldn't mind one like my dad, but of course he was a very special sort of man: there wasn't another like him in the whole world.

I hated cheese, so I would bring home my cheese for the twelve babies and I could feed them on the forty-eight halfpenny ice-creams my two shillings would buy. I kept my plans all to myself—until the day Miss Gabb called.

Mam was emptying the slops between the cabbages when she spotted Miss Gabb approaching our gate. Mam rushed in all in a tiz, taking off her sack apron, removing the nappies from the fireguard and the newspaper cloth from the table. 'Quick,' she urged me. 'Goo up to Mrs Brown's and ask 'er if 'er can lend me a bit o' sugar— 'tis no good askin' Granny. 'Er'v' let me 'ave 'alf o' wot 'er's got in 'er sugar basin. Tell Mrs Brown 'er shall 'ave it wi'out fail when our grocery do come tomorrow.'

Dear Mam, she loved to put the rare visitor a cup of tea, especially such a grand caller as Miss Gabb.

I put on my pig-headed, unco-operative, bribe-demanding expression.

'If you can borrow me a bit o' sugar you can 'ave a suck o' the babby's sugar teat when 'er's gone.'

It was bribe enough—Mam sometimes kept the baby quiet with a spoonful of dampened sugar tied in a piece of clean rag.

I got the sugar from kind Mrs Brown and I had the gumption to take it into the back kitchen behind my back. I had long sensed that Mam did not like to advertise her poverty in these circumstances.

Miss Gabb was sitting by the fire, and I took up my perch on the corner of the big steel fender to give her one of my thorough optic going-overs.

How prim and neat she was: snow-white blouse collar over her navy-blue costume, hair drawn back into a tight little bun, and black shoes as shiny as brand-new ones—all very suitable for a prudish middle-aged spinster who taught at Sunday School, had a preacher for her father and who was of independent means. She began to wilt a bit under my intense scrutiny and tried to break my concentration by asking me when would I be starting school and what I intended to do when I grew up. So I told her all about my twelve bastard babbys, my job at the pub and my intention not to be bothered with a husband.

She went very red in the face and slopped her tea into the saucer. Mam went red, too; they didn't share my enthusiasm at all. Granny seemed quite pleased—I could see her trying to keep her mouth straight, and her soft child-rearing belly shaking under her pinny.

She cut off a lump of the bread pudding she had brought in as an excuse to be in on the *tête-à-tête* and 'cup o' tay'. Holding it in front of my nose like a carrot to a donkey, she got me outside.

''Ere you be, my wench, thee'st better goo off to play with the t'others afore thee'st put some o' thy ideas in Miss Gabb's yud, and I shouldn't hurry back if I was thee—I don't think thee mam's in a very good 'umour.'

I went down the path well pleased with my bread pudding, but very puzzled about the frequent oddness of grown-ups' reactions to my bright ideas.

The Meeting

Only those too old, too ill or too young did not come to the Meeting. People came from the outlying villages and hamlets to converge at the Hall, a plain oblong building used for the social activities of the community.

This particular evening it was not for pleasure—we wouldn't be laughing at Mr Stott's comic recitations, or, come to that, the rather unappreciated singing of the grand local lady contralto.

We were going for a scolding—at least our dads, brothers, uncles and granddads were, so it amounted to the same thing.

The menfolk were miners—miners who had dared to come out on strike rather than take a cut in their already pitifully inadequate wages.

Now the bosses and their managers were holding this meeting to remind these common, two-a-penny sparrows how grateful they should be for the crumbs thrown to them from the rich man's table. They were not a lot in number. As benefited their superior social and economic status, they sat on the stage looking down at their crowded, standing audience.

How marked was the contrast! Proper suits, starched white shirts, gold watch chains across well-filled bellies. Their ladies, grand in Sunday-type hats, fur-trimmed coats, well-shod feet and plump pink faces.

In the audience it was mufflers and caps, down-trodden boots, the gaunt, grey, underground faces of the men, and mostly pale, under-nourished faces of the women and children. Chesty coughs punctuated the waiting silence.

One of the men on the stage stood up, cleared his throat in an important sort of manner, and advised the men to go back to work—*or else*. Time has dimmed his speech but not his pompous, condescending, down-his-nose attitude; but time has not dimmed the expression on my father's face as he listened to this rhetoric. Though Father was a great man in my eyes, physically he was a slight, pale-faced man, who had of late made extra holes in his leather belt to hold up his shabby trousers where his stomach should have been.

He looked at the speaker—then his eyes travelled round the audience, and the compassion in them came, for want of another word, from what we call the soul.

Father was gifted with the sort of exceptional intelligence that made him a good man—a widely-read man, a thinker, slow in his judgements and willing to see both sides of an argument—and Father had made up his mind now which side he stood on.

The cruel economic systems geared to profit instead of human needs, man's foolish inhumanity to man culminating in wars and poverty—man's capacity for self-destruction, was a burden he carried in his mind that often found him staring sadly into space. He had his blessings, too—a great sense of wonder and appreciation for all the beauty that came his way, from the flora and fauna in the forest around us to the genius of artists, composers and scientists, to the very earth itself.

He waited until the speeches from the stage had finished. The down-trodden audience had sighed and coughed on, seeming visibly to shrink in their hopelessness. Then Father raised his hand to ask questions. Again the words are dimmed by time, but never their effect.

At first this upstart miner got some sarcastic comments—but, quietly, Father continued to demand answer for question.

Soon their pomposity and bluster were pierced by his shafts of truth—it was they who began to look small, to squirm, to fidget, to get angry.

A change came over the audience. They had got a voice—an advocate the bosses had not the means to put down. Dull eyes shone, heads were lifted, shoulders squared to the world—they were men again, and as one man they called 'no' to their oppressors' demands. Belts would be pulled even tighter, for their future's sake women and children must suffer further, their backs were against the wall but now they had a pillow to support it.

During his seven-year victimization from the pits these men did not forget us.

Father was killed in the pit in 1945, aged 57 years. He did not live to see the affluent miner, or the garage, car and bathroom a common-place in workers' homes, but I wonder, if he were still alive, would he smile wryly to read as I did the other day that one per cent of the population still have control of eighty per cent of the nation's wealth!

Entrance and Departure

In our village, life was simple and 'near the knuckle', food for an extra mouth was hard to come by, yet it could not diminish the glory of each new birth.

The stairs to the bedroom might only be of scrubbed wood, but the new father, perhaps too many times over, would tip-toe up them reverently to marvel at the tiny fingers he could curl around one of his pit-calloused ones.

'Well done, my wench, that's a little beauty thee'st got there!' would be thanks enough for the tired face on the pillow.

However long the black angel hovered, the deaths of even the oldest inhabitants got their share of sighs and tears.

'I be afeared 'er time be come,' the bed-watchers whispered out of hearing of old Ginny, when the indomitable old woman could no longer infuse the strength of her spirit into her worn-out body and took to her bed.

Resigned at last, she saved her gasping breath to talk over old times with the old faces still around her. There was no need to dip into the carefully hoarded pittance, saved 'to putt I down dacent', for a doctor's diagnosis.

'We'd better get Edie Paine to come and 'ave a look at 'er; thic 'oman can see death in anybody's eyes as soon as it be knockin' on the door.'

'Ay, an 'er can see by a 'oman's eyes when a babby is on the way, sometimes afore the 'oman be sure of it 'erself.'

Edie Paine, widow, washerwoman, midwife and layerout of the dead, dispenser of goose-grease for the chest, herb-teas for the colic, and a trusted friendly ear for private troubles. When called she went to old Ginny's bedside.

Honest kindly eyes looked into honest eyes.

'I do know wot thee bist come for, Edie, but I ben't quite ready for thee yet.'

The soapy-water-wrinkled hands took the emaciated geriatric ones in hers for a warm goodbye.

'Some time between midnight and six o'clock,' Edie advised the neighbours who accompanied her to the door.

Old Ginny didn't let her down. Just after 4 a.m. she gave up watching the flickering candle on the wash-stand and let the darkness come.

Conscience Stricken

Big-eared, chopsy and tactless, with a penchant for letting cats out of bags and for exposing the skeletons in the family cupboard, I was the sort of child mothers like out of the way when visitors are around. However, this was a special occasion and Mother was determined to show her brood off.

By our terms this visitor was a proper somebody. I had learned that he was elderly, a lay preacher who had settled many years ago in Yorkshire after leaving our impoverished mining village to look for work. He had made himself 'a tidy bit o' money' keeping a grocery shop up there, and, most important to a mercenary little six-year-old, 'There might be summat in it for you if you be a good little wench.'

'Summat' might mean a toffee, two toffees! a halfpenny!! or even a penny!!! My optimism travelled like a kangaroo by leaps and bounds. I decided it was worth co-operating with Mam. It was quite a trial; it meant giving in without a struggle to having my knees washed as well as face and hands, the tangles combed out of my hair, the responsibility of a clean pinny, and, worst of all, sitting still and keeping my mouth shut. Strictly speaking he wasn't really our visitor at all; he was coming to see our aged great-aunt with whom we lived.

Old Auntie who was chair-ridden with arthritis didn't have to have her knees washed—no one could see them under her long black skirts—but we brought her a wet flannel and towel for her face. Mam tied a clean pinny on her and brushed her sparse strands of white hair into a tidier little bun, assuring her that she looked 'quite respectable'.

The freshly-nappied baby lay on the sofa contentedly sucking his sugar teat, Mam kept rubbing over the big, black-leaded grate until it shone. We youngsters tried to be as still and as wooden as the chairs we sat on. It was purgatory, but after one of Mam's quick peeps outside, she dramatically hissed at us that ''im was a comin' down the garden path'.

He took his time, for he was quite old. When he came in I thought he looked like a cross between Methuselah and one of the

Disciples. He had white hair and a long white beard, watery blue eyes below bushy white eyebrows, puffed pinky cheeks and a moist pink mouth I didn't take to at all. It wasn't his physiognomy I was particularly interested in; it was in listening for the crackle of a sweet packet or the chink of coins in his pockets. He looked affluent enough for both; in a black suit grand enough for funerals, starched white shirt and gold watch-chain shining across his chest. Mam pulled up the other best chair with arms on nearer the fire opposite old Auntie's. They took an interminable time reckoning up the dead and gone, and recalling old times, before Mam's polite coughs got a bit apprehensive regarding our forbearance, but at last he turned his attention to us.

The baby got a short nursing on his lap, spent a penny in the form of a big wet patch on the visitor's knee, and made a profit of twopence by getting a silver threepennybit in his hand. The omens were good! My little brother next. He was soon off his perch having tried hard to pull the old man's beard off. I decided he was like a Disciple, for he still gave my brother a penny. I was a bit worried, though, about this sort of financial index—there was still a little sister to come before me. She was a pretty, quiet, fair little creature and sat long enough to absorb most of the damp patch and she, too, got a penny. My evaporating patience returned. At six years he considered me eligible for a sermon, advising me that if I said my prayers every night, attended Sunday School regularly, and never disobeyed my elders, I should go to Heaven when I died. I wasn't struck with this bargain—we had texts and pictures of angels hanging around the walls upstairs and I had come to the conclusion being an angel was very boring; just floating around in the sky all the time. I much preferred it on earth, where I could get broken bits of china and rusty tins off the ash-mix to play shops with, and make houses out of the lush green ferns under the trees, and only get a smack if Mam could catch me when I was naughty instead of going to Hell. However, I didn't aim to risk a possible penny by correcting him, and at last I got one, and I knew just what I was going to spend it on—lucky, lucky me! Oh! what a lovely day it was! I was up our garden path like a rocket.

As far as I was aware there was only one cherry tree in the world, and it was in Prudence the witch's garden, the cottage below ours. Many a dribble had gone down the front of my pinny longing for some of the luscious ripe cherries on it. Now I could buy a whole pennyworth and hide down in our empty pigs-cot for a feast.

We reckoned Prudence was a witch because she never wanted to mix with the rest of the village and had a nasty habit of crouching down behind her gate in the dusk, popping up like a jack-in-the-box making a weird crackling laugh if a child went by. She could perform miracles, too, because all the women said it was a miracle where Prudence's son had come from. She hadn't got a husband, was never seen ever talking to a man, and the village women seemed very annoyed wondering where she had got him. He was quite big and strong but not quite all there in his attic—but he was very good at shinning up the cherry tree to pick the wares. We forgot about her being a witch when her cherries were ripe!

I was stopped in my tracks when I reached our garden gate by a most unusual sight! A beggar woman, *in our village!* I had heard about beggars, and how sometimes they had gold sovereigns hidden under their ragged clothes. Perhaps that was the reason no one came out of our penny-pinched community to give her anything. Apparently it was against the law to actually knock on the doors to beg, so this old woman was supposedly singing for her supper—I thought she sounded worse than a cat on the tiles and anyway it was cherries, not charity, that occupied my mind. I ran down to Prudence's door and soon got a nice lot of cherries in a piece of newspaper. I didn't have to share with my siblings, they had all got their own money, so clutching my precious hoard I made my way back to our gate en route for the pigs-cot.

I wasn't pleased to see Dilys Pugh leaning up against it. She was a few years older than me—a 'stuck up', well-dressed only child with a caste system of her own. She regarded me as one of the head-scratching, droopy-drawered, inferior untouchables.

She had a long nose and plenty of practice looking down it. She was a born scolder, worse than a governess at school, and kept showing off by pulling her proper hemmed handkerchief out of the legs of her drawers even when her nose didn't need wiping.

If you said 'bugger' when a sharp stone went up through the hole in your boot sole she was so shocked she told your mam and probably got you a good hiding. I had no intention of offering *her* any cherries.

'I'll tell your mam if you yut any on 'em,' she warned me.

'I don't care, they be mine anyroads.'

'Pooh, don't tell lies. You've got a pennoth there and the likes o' your mam can't give a penny fir yourself.'

'It bent lies. We got a visitor, and 'im gid the lot on us a penny, and 'im gid the babby drippunce, so there!'

Dilys pulled herself up to a bit above her normal height, pursed her lips to a thinner, narrower line, and took a deep breath through flared nostrils that swelled out her narrow chest. She looked at me with her 'God help them for they know not what they do' expression. Her eyes concentrated into accusing slits. I thought she was going to explode.

'Dost thee mean to tell I that thee'st spent a whole penny on thee own greed guts with thic pore old varmint up there a tryin' to sing 'er 'eart out to get some money fir summat to yut!—'er's likely to drop down dyud afore long from starvation—the trouble with thee, thee'st got no conscience, I'll bet thee'st 'ad some dinner today, not like thic pore old creature.'

I looked at the old woman again with 'seeing' eyes. Oh, how pitiful she was, so skinny, so raggedly dressed. I remembered my dinner; Mam had made a big suety pudding and put a good sprinkling of sugar over it. Oh! what a thoughtless, wicked, greedy girl I was! If only I could get my penny back, but I didn't dare ask Prudence such a thing. Never mind, I would give the old beggar-woman my untouched cherries. I ran up to her and thrust them in her hands. To my intense surprise and disappointment she didn't seem at all pleased. She put them away somewhere in the folds of her ragged skirts without even a thank you or a smile. I staggered back against a garden wall and started to walk down to Dilys who had been watching. Dilys, too, appeared to have lost interest; she turned and went on her way down the village. I stood by our gate; I had no penny, no cherries, not even a thank-you.

I was square with my conscience but it brought little comfort—I decided there and then that me and my conscience didn't get on very well together.

A Loss

There was a proper midwife who wore a navy-blue bonnet tied under her chin, a navy cape, and carried the bag 'she brought the babies in'. Most of the women managed with the village midwife, a skilled, kindly, self-taught woman who took a mere pittance for her services and was the soul of discretion regarding the lack of sheets and other necessities for the confinement. She often added the bonus of bowls of her own gruel and pieces of clean white rag for the new mother to hem napkins whilst she stayed the statutory ten days in bed.

The village midwife, the proper nurse *and* the doctor were called in on one occasion but between them all they could save neither mother nor child.

Letty was a bonny young wife who had carried her first pregnancy right up until the ninth month as easily as she carried her bundles of kindling wood home from the forest. By then her neat slim little figure had such a dimensional preponderance folk laughingly observed it would be bound to be twins there, if not triplets! There were no clinics for the measuring of pelvic bones, urine tests or the other safeguards now in practice. Only the wise village midwife felt alarm for Letty. When the girl's labour started, before it got too protracted she sent the young husband for the proper midwife. The professional midwife had no wish to diminish her own status by calling in the doctor, but after many hours she relented and the fleetest-footed teenager in the village was sent running the two miles for the doctor.

The worried, bewildered young husband was reluctantly made to go to his shift at the pit by the midwife. 'You'll do no good here—just be in the way, and with another mouth on the way to feed you can't afford to miss your work.'

He put his feet towards the pit but his head kept turning back to the cottage window where Letty suffered in the big iron bedstead. Before he reached the pit head she had bent the iron bed head in the mad agony of her turmoil.

The good old doctor was away on an urgent case of pneumonia, but the boy left the message for him to visit. By the time his horse and trap drew up at her cottage gate, Letty's eyes were glazing over and her knuckles were bitten to the bone in her suffering. The doctor knew this child would never be born. Not for the first time he cursed nature and its methods of reproduction. The nearest hospital then was eighteen miles away, and transport a horse and cart. He knew the girl would not survive the journey. He had not the skill, the means, or the trained help to perform the necessary caesarian operation in a primitive cottage bedroom. He had only laudanum and it was getting too late for that, but youth dies hard.

The village midwife, stricken by the turn of events, asked the weeping neighbours to send a couple of men to way-lay the young husband, now on his way home from the pit. 'Tell 'em to kip 'im away from 'ere somehow—'tis better 'er be gone than 'im should see the wench like this.'

Sick in their hearts, two men hurried off through the woods trying to think up a ploy to keep the young man out of earshot of his cottage. He saw through their false cheer and hindrance. Sensing a conspiracy and full of foreboding, he broke from the physical constraint they were forced to use. He rushed indoors and up the stairs and watched his sweetheart wife die.

The women wept and said, 'I shall 'ear thic poor wench's screams till the day I die.' Men hung their heads in sorrow—'Thic pore bwoy, 'im'll be like a young tater that 'a' bin nipped by a black frost—'im'll never be the same agyun.' The young man never was the same: he never married, he relinquished his man-hood. 'I'd never do anything that 'ud putt a 'oman dru that agyun.'

We children knew him as a kindly, eccentric, white-haired old man, who looked at us with tender, rheumy eyes. Perhaps we were all like living ghosts to him, ghosts of the child he never had.

A Good Clane Out

Facts are facts and have to be faced, and in truth when I as a little girl, next to my Dad, I loved my belly. It was a tyrant, always sending messages up for anything I could scrounge for it. I was a good scrounger, from old Great-Auntie's bacon-rinds and crusts, too hard for her toothless gums to chew, to the bits of corn I could peck up before Miss Phillips's fowls gobbled them when she threw a couple of handfuls to them over her garden gate. Best of all, my stomach and I mutually agreed, was suet treacle pud, and Granny was our greatest benefactor in this respect. Granny's bevy of daughters were all away in domestic service or married; only her son remained at home, but Granny never made suet pud for just the three of them. She waited until she could get enough ingredients for her household, our household and any other children within sniffing distance. Pudding cloths were her problem. Clean white rag was hard to come by and there were so many other uses for it. Babies' bums, for instance, and there were plenty of them about!

Granny's problem was solved on one occasion when one of her daughters brought home from service a couple of white cotton tennis stockings given her by her mistress. Just the job, thought Granny!

Granny mixed her puddings in her huge bread-crock, then stuffed them by the yard down the stockings. She filled her copper with water and lit the fire underneath it. When she finished her washing, it was Granny's habit to rinse the copper out with clean water and soap, and dry it. Something must have distracted her on the previous washday, for a residue gel of Hudson's Powder and soap had been left in the bottom. Now, Granny's copper was in the darkest end of her dark little kitchen, at the back of her cottage. Unaware of the soap, when the copper came to the boil the clouds of steam hid the frothy water and Granny couldn't smell it. She had lost her sense of smell from a severe sinus illness years before. The puddings bubbled about like a bunch of anaemic Loch Ness Monsters.

We children and our friends stayed near at hand playing

hopscotch on the piece of hard-trodden earth outside our garden gate—waiting—waiting for Granny's calls.

At last—'Come on in, me butties; bring summat wi' yer to putt yer puddin' on.'

We lined up with our saucers et cetera by her back-kitchen door, taking our turn by her salting slab for our dollop of pudding and ration of warmed treacle. Then we perched in tiers on the stone steps leading from her garden down to her tiny courtyard, just in case a second helping might be forthcoming.

A second helping! We could hardly down the first!!

Something had gone amiss; the pudding tasted bitter and soapy. We were no gourmets, and the anticipation had been so great; besides, we were well mannered enough to hide our disappointment from our beloved Granny. We controlled our grimaces of distaste and swallowed every mouthful.

Granny always left herself till last, but there was some in the toe of one of the stockings for her.

Life hadn't made Granny a gourmet either, but she pulled a very wry face with her first spoonful; then, realizing what she had done, she said, 'Laird o' merssy, this puddin' be awful—Oh my Gawd I 'ope I 'an't pizened the lot of you—oh well, if I 'ave I might as well pizen meself, too'—and she ate hers all up as well.

The stomach spasms didn't hit us all at once—but it was frequently one-in-and-one-to-go doubled up outside the garden bucket-privvy.

However black the clouds gathered on Granny's horizon she always poked in them for a bit of silver lining. She found some then.

'I'll tell thee what,' she observed to Mam, 'thee 'outn't need to give any of 'em doses o' brimstone and treacle f'r a bit—I reckon all their insides 'ave 'ad a good clane out.'

A couple of years later Granny moved to another part of the Forest. We missed her even more than her treacle puddings. Through Granny's eyes the world was an infinitely richer place. When I was a young married woman of twenty-six and visiting my parents, Granny walked through the woods the two-and-a-half-miles to us for 'a squat an' a chat'.

When it was time for her to go I walked most of the way back with her. We stopped for a breather in a little valley with steep wooded sides. It was so peaceful and beautiful there: a sparkling little stream meandered through beds of watercress, birds sweetly twittered in the branches over our heads; the dappled sunshine through the trees gave a perfect mixture of warmth and shade and the moss-covered earth was soft beneath our feet.

Granny stood there for some minutes quietly gazing around, then she sighed, 'Ah, my wench, I mustn't grumble. The Almighty 'a' bin good to me, f'r 'im a let me goo past me dree score years and ten, and the time be comin' soon f'r me to goo—but oh, my wench, I shall miss all this!'

Now I am getting old, dear Granny, I know just how you felt.

Dashed Hopes

'I'll tell you what we'll do, Maggie.' Granny's voice was low, urgent and conspiratorial. 'We'll make up some pizen—we can make it out o' some deadly nightshade—then if thic Kaiser gets 'is armies over 'ere and they come anywhere near us—we'll pizen the little uns fust, then take zum ourzelves—I'll never let them varmints put they dear little young uns on the end o' their bayonets.'

I knew I was one of 'them dear little uns' Granny was talking about. It was 1917. I was three years old—and I knew there was something called a war on—it was all the fault of a wicked man called the Kaiser who lived in a country named Germany and was sending his armies into England to kill us all off and have it for himself. The war—the war—everyone, especially the women, kept on talking about it—but I could see no sign of it anywhere. Old Great-Auntie, sitting in the chair nearest the fire, was fast asleep, her toothless mouth agape—she didn't seem worried. It was a comfort. I had never seen a soldier—the men in our village were all miners and exempt from call-up. Coal, and more coal, was needed, all the coal that could be got to stoke the fires of this man-made hell on earth.

It was lovely when Father was home from the pit and I could take my turn with the others for a sit on his lap. Then I felt safe and secure from the Kaiser, from the war, from the shadows on the wall, even from the thunder and lightning that sent Mam cowering in the coalhole under the stairs. Granny often came into our house from next door. Granny couldn't read herself, but she brought Grancher's paper in for Mam to read. She, old Auntie and Mam would cuddle us round the fire while Mam read all the awful news from the war front, news exacerbated by all the ghoulish rumours about the wicked Germans. Father had no patience with these sessions.

'Them Germans be no different to we lot or any other country—them soldiers over there do as they be told the same as our lot. They be no more responsible for this war than we be—and you women do want your yuds examined if you do swallow all you read in the papers, or what do get about on people's tongues. 'Twas the Boers last time—and when this lot's over, after a bit, another war'll break out somewhere else. We 'uman bein's be supposed to have brains but we be wuss than the animals. The world's a sick place—all us 'ave bin from what I've read, and all us will be till they got enough sense to share things instead o' fightin' over 'em, and they've got more gumption than you dree swallowin' everything you be told.'

Such conversations were beyond my comprehension, but even at that age Father had an aura for me that made me his ally.

The war came into our house with the grocery man. Miners were now earning enough to keep their families' bellies well filled, but rationing kept us short. Old Auntie got a precious ounce of butter—she loved her 'bit o' best butter'. When it went missing off the table one day the house was in a turmoil. Mam and she had definitely seen it when the grocer had delivered it along with Auntie's three-cornered blue paper bag of sugar, a tin of Nestlé's milk, bit of red-rinded cheese, etc. How could it have vanished into thin air? I had been playing with a neighbour's toddler son indoors; my mouth was inspected inside and out, and my small person thoroughly frisked for evidence—despite my denial of the crime.

Only when our neighbour undressed her little boy for bed did she find the bit of greasy paper in his pocket and the oily stain on his trousers. This little tragedy was recounted for weeks.

I knew the war had ended when Granny came in and picked us up one at a time and did a dance in our tiny courtyard. Old Auntie kept thanking the Almighty for his deliverance. I almost stopped worrying about the Kaiser coming to kill me in the night. The need for coal slackened down—gradually the men were put on short time, especially when coal was imported from the Saar as reparation from the beaten enemy. Rationing finished, but our grocery deliveries didn't improve all that much.

At five I started school. On winter evenings, perched on the end of our steel fender, I often listened to Father and his pit butties talking. Their talk ranged on many subjects—war was one of them. I knew that the subject of war particularly saddened and angered Father. I sensed that he might be worried lest my little brother go to war when he grew up.

One evening, when I was about eight years old, Father came in from a meeting. He had a book in his hand, his face was white and taut. Granny, old Auntie and Mam were sitting round the fire.

'Here,' said Father to them. 'Take a look at this book, then you'll see what war is all about.'

I could see the title of the book was *War Against War*, but I was not allowed to look inside. I knew where Father put the books he thought unsuitable for childish eyes—on top of the cupboard by the fireplace. I waited my opportunity to climb up on a chair when no one was about.

I turned over the pages and became a pacifist for life. Here was proof of man's bestiality to man—if his capacity for evil was exploited. No wonder Father worried. I could not comfort him or go to him for comfort. I had disobeyed him getting up on the cupboard. The dread of war, though often forgotten in happy playing, hung over my childish head.

A quarter of an hour before school prayers for the end of lessons one day, our teacher told us to put away our composition books because she had something to tell us. As she spoke the sky grew a more fairy blue through the windows, the flowers in the jam-pots on the window-sills more exquisite, and her pleasant face with its aura of fair hair began to look like an angel's, for she was telling us about something called the League of Nations—about the treaty the leaders of these nations had signed to prevent another war.

No dawdling home from school for me that day—no joyous runs into the ferns from the woodland path. No linking arms with the other girls, whilst singing our favourite school songs—I was the bearer of magic news—weighed down not at all by my black leather studded boots.

'Where's our dad?' I demanded breathlessly of Mam.

'Down in his shed—wot's up?'

I couldn't stop to tell her. Father was in his little shed at the bottom of the garden. He was quite a handyman. Here he mended our boots, did a bit of amateur carpentry, and soldered his and his pit butties' carbide lamps. It was mostly an honorary pastime—there was often no money to pay for his services. He had fashioned his own brazier from a large round tin with a fire-bellows fixed in the side to heat the soldering iron white-hot. I loved to watch Father soldering. The tiny balls of liquid metal needed such a delicate touch to spread it on the cracks in the metal lamps with the soldering iron. It was not a time for distraction—but my wonderful news cast such considerations aside.

'Dad! Dad! There ben't goin' to be any more wars!'

He went on with his soldering. My words could not have sunk in. I tugged at his sleeve. 'Dad! Dad! Did you 'ear wot I said?—there ben't goin' to be any more wars!'

'And wot makes you think that, my wench?'

'Our teacher told us, Dad. A lot of countries 'ave done summat called the League o' Nations. They've signed a treaty so there won't be any more wars.'

Father lifted me up on to his work-bench. He looked through the window with sad, faraway eyes.

'I be afeared, my wench, that this treaty by un't wuth the paper 'tis wrote on.'

My spirits sank down in my heavy boots—but I had grown never to doubt the truth or wisdom of Father's words. As simply as he could, he explained to me about the moving balances of world trade—about the discoveries of natural resources and how, even by going to war, nations sought to obtain the lion's share of these things. He told me about man's ego patriotism, and ego religions, about all the things that made them enemies.

My stricken face must have disturbed him. 'There, there, my wench, Father shouldn't 'a' worried thy young yud wi' such talk. Doosn't thee worry, there may never be a war in thy time. Eh, I'll tell thee what—I 'a' got a nice bit o' rope 'ere, and two pieces o' wood that'll do for handles. Thee goo and ex thee mother to wet I a cup o' tay and I'll make thee a skippin' rope.'

I have lived through a second world war—the powers of East and West threaten each other with atom bombs—somewhere or other a war is always going on on this earth. Unlike Granny, Mam and old Auntie, I never believe all I read in the papers.

Kezzie

Because she was such a bright little scholar, our exasperated teachers often overlooked some of Kezzie Larkin's shortcomings, for Kezzie was a bit of a handful.

The cottage 'over on the Green' where the Larkins lived was looked down on by us villagers. It was overrun with little Larkins; 'nothin' but a bloody rabbut warren', was how one man described it.

Kezzie was the eldest of six children. Despite her ragged clothes, tangled nitty hair and dirt-engrained knees, Kezzie had enough charisma to be accepted by the rest of us. God knows we village children had absolutely no grounds to be toffee-nosed about anyone, but children, of course, form their own hierarchies just as grown-ups do. In our childish eyes, pretty girls were those lucky enough to have be-ribboned curls and tidy clothes; looks and form had nothing to do with it.

Grown-ups were more observant. I remember one man remarking to another as they watched us at play:

'I doubt thee'lt ever clap thee eyes on a purtier wench than thic young Kezzie. I bet the kings o' England 'ould give zummat to 'ave daughters as looked like thic little wench.'

Recalling Kezzie in my mind's eye, I see a thin little face with a pair of long-lashed, expressive eyes, flecked with green and hazel, a neat, small, straight nose and a mouth that rarely turned down at the corners. My eldest sister and Kezzie were the two top scholars in their class. Kezzie was the younger by six months, but they were close chums. Kezzie knew where the rain made puddles for illicit paddling, where the best wild strawberries grew, and the right places to go scrumping apples. She organized us into 'concert parties', performed acrobatics like a monkey from tree branches, and could make up the most exciting fibs to scare us out of our wits. Her skinny, muscle-knotted arms packed a terrific punch in defence of her tribe of small brothers. Carrying no ballast, she could run like the wind, leading us to safety when pursued for our misdemeanours.

The Larkins' fecundity was a sore problem to many of the

village women; they were full of sympathy when rumour had it that Kezzie's mam was 'in the cyart aygun'.

''Tis a cryin' shame, there's more mouths over there already than victuals to put in 'em.'

Mrs Larkin had her baby, a girl this time.

The words, 'Gone to a better place,' seemed only too true when the news got round six weeks later that the baby had died. Mrs Larkin was in a bad way too, hardly able to walk, with swollen, ulcerated legs.

As it neared chapel treat time I stepped up my attendances at Sunday School to get enough marks for this special day of the year. The kindly old man who took Bible class asked Gladys, Dolly, Lil and me if we would be four little Christians and act as pallbearers to carry the baby to church. There would be no mourners and no service inside the church because the baby had not been christened. The mother was too ill to go but the vicar was willing to say a few words before she was buried in some unconsecrated ground at the back of the churchyard. We were eleven years old—too young for any depth of feeling, but we felt very sombre and important as we looked at each other for assent and nodded. 'Yes.'

All our mams picked us a little bunch of flowers to go on the coffin and Lil's mam made us a black armband each to wear.

It was a lovely warm sunny day, a day to shin up trees, scamper in and out of the ferns beneath them, and jump for joy over the huge oak-roots exposed across the woodland paths, but we felt the solemnity of the occasion and walked sedately, remembering all the miserable things we could talk about. It would be cruel to the dead baby to feel cheerful.

I had never been in Kezzie's house before; I was shocked. I thought our house was a palace in comparison. Our Mam made rag-rugs to put in front of the grate; we had a pair of brass candlesticks and a vase on our mantel-piece; our Dad had made some shelves for Mam to show off the cups, saucers and plates she had got with tea coupons. Here there was only an old sack on the floor, the bits of lace curtains had more holes than lace, not an ornament anywhere, and the table and chairs looked very kicked about.

The little home-made coffin was on the table. Mrs Larkin, who looked very ill, hobbled over to it, I could see her swollen ankles all ulcerated and bleeding . . . she lifted the lid of the coffin. I had been privately of the opinion that new babies looked little different to skinned rabbits, but this one looked like a white marble doll, paler than the nightdress she was laid out in. The Larkins had to lug the water much farther than the villagers from the communal well. A little posy of wild flowers had been placed between the baby's hands. Two tears from Mrs Larkin's eyes bedewed them as she kissed the baby goodbye. There was pride as well as grief in her voice as she called on us to witness what a little angel her baby looked.

The lid was fastened down, two ropes were tied round with loops for carrying, and we started out. Mrs Larkin picked a toddler up from the floor, rocking him in her arms for comfort. A couple of her other little boys followed us as far as the well. 'Where's your Kezzie gone?' Lil asked them.

'Nowhere—'er ben't gone nowhere—'er's zittin' round the back o' the 'ouse wi' 'er pinny over 'er yud a cryin'.'

It was a mile to the church. We kept to the grass verge of the main road. Only one timber wagon passed us, cars were still a rare sight in those days.

The vicar stood in the church porch. He met us outside while a man stood by the open grave to let the coffin down. The vicar mumbled a few words and led us out of the churchyard.

'Don't worry,' he said, 'I'm sure the Good Shepherd will take this little lamb into His flock.'

When we were out of earshot Lil observed rather tartly, 'Of course that babby'll goo to 'eaven. All babbies do 'cos they 'an't done nothin' wrong.' We felt quite comforted.

We didn't go back to the Larkins' house; we knew there would be no funeral meats—not even a cup of tea to spare.

By the winter all the village was in similar straits to the Larkins. Our dads—all miners—had come out on strike rather than submit to even worse conditions than they had already endured in the cruel economic climate of the twenties. It was an awful struggle for our mams to get something for us to take to school for our mid-day break. Our Mam had melted some mutton fat down for dripping, spreading it on the bread whilst it was still warm. It had re-congealed into hard white lumps but was going down sweet enough until our young noses sniffed the unfamiliar odour of meat. *Meat!* Who could possibly be eating meat?

We were allowed to sit in the main classroom for our lunch-break. The whispers came back up the row of desks.

'It was they Larkins lot *yuttin' meat.*' No bread, they hadn't got any bread. 'Just girt chunks o' lean *meat.*' It was astounding information. And they kept bringing meat day after day.

Then one day none of the Larkins came to school and the rumour got around that the police had taken Mr Larkin away. He had been sheep stealing. Fifty years before he would probably have been hanged for the crime. Instead he was summonsed—sent to jail—and the bailiffs called in to sell up his household goods towards recompense for the sheep-owners.

'Poor bugger, I'd a done the zame livin' up there out o' sight with me young uns starvin'. They baillies got to leave the beds; it's the law: they mustn't sell the beds.'

We were as a rule ready gawpers at anything outside the common rut—funerals and weddings. A cat stranded up a tree, a harangue between neighbours, the odd drunk—all got our rapt attention.

But with no means to help the Larkins, no one from the village had the heart to go and watch.

'Their veow sticks o' farniture zold over their yuds; I doubt the lot put together'll vetch a couple o' quid.'

'Poor devils. It'll be the work-house for 'em now.'

Children and mothers were segregated in the work-house; her children were all that Mrs Larkin had left.

''Ave you 'eard about the Larkins? They've gone in wi' the gypsies.'

'Never.'

''Tis right enough. Our Tom was walkin' dru the wood by the gypsies' camp and 'im zid the Larkins bwoys a playin' wi' the gypsy young uns and 'im could zee a iron bedstead in one o' the tents.'

The strike was over, the beaten men went back to work, but not our Dad. There was no job for him. He was labelled a radical upstart because he had openly spoken up against the oppressors. He tramped the days away looking for work, but a day's work of any sort was almost impossible to come by. His pit coal allowance was gone, but we drew our chairs up to a good fire that winter. Buckets of coal were tipped inside our garden gate, and there was kindling wood to be gathered in the surrounding forest.

One bitterly cold night, a cruel east wind, full of icy sleet, beat against our window and blew the piece of sacking away put to stop the draught from coming under the door.

'I wonder 'ow they poor little Larkins young uns be standin' this out in them tents in the 'ood,' said Mam sadly. I shivered in sympathy, soon forgotten as I cuddled with my siblings under Mam's heavy home-made patchwork quilts. We survived the winter, spring came to cheer us up, then summer and a day of great anticipation. After a year in service our sister was coming home for her annual holiday. We didn't know what time. Dad was in the back kitchen shaving and Mam was polishing over the black-leaded grate for the umpteenth time when a neighbour came puffing down our garden path to tell us she couldn't be sure, but somebody was comin' up the village that might be her!

Dad wiped the lather off his face and ran through the door— his face naked with love for this treasured home-comer. I saw him take her into his arms through the window. How could this glamorous, beautiful young woman be our sister?

I thought she had been dressed up to the nines when she left home in a new navy serge dress and black shoes off the packman topped with a second-hand straw boater, her long brown hair hanging down her back. Now, taller, plumped out, with shiny, short, marcel-waved hair, dressed in a smart brown suit, a cream silk blouse, with dainty brown shoes and pink silk stockings—no wonder Father looked beside himself with pride as he brought her in through the door. Short-sighted Mam blinked her tears away behind her glasses. The warm, scented hug my sister gave me made me feel I was polluting her.

'Quick, goo upstairs and fetch the best spoons and knives down,' Mam whispered urgently to me. Mam kept our best bits of cutlery well polished with brick dust in a cardboard shoe-box on the wash-stand table. There was a mirror over it. The reflection of my very plain face, straight dull hair, steel-rimmed glasses and old frock was too awful: I burst into tears. The strongest emotion was shame that such a beautiful sister had to own such as me.

We all felt a bit shy at the tea table. After tea, too shy to take her arm, I followed a worshipful distance behind my sister as she walked around the top of the village—marvelling at her magnanimity for talking and laughing with the local young chaps. How I bragged about her to my friends at school the next day! About her beauty, her clothes, and the proper nightdress trimmed with lace she wore to bed.

My little brother and I hurried home from school. Mam told us our sister had walked to town to buy us some fancy cakes for tea; with our adoration increased, we ran through the woodland path to meet her. Her eyes lit up at the sight of us but she looked as though she had been crying.

We walked each side of her in subdued silence for a bit. I couldn't stand it. 'Wot be the matter?' I asked.

She burst into tears. 'Tis Kezzie Larkin. I seen her in town today. She was dressed in long old rags carrying pegs around in a basket wi' a gypsy 'oman. Poor Kezzie, her's nothing but a gypsy now.'

Our Scott

I don't remember when we got him; he was just there, part of the family, a small black and white mongrel, our Scott.

His appetite was very catholic, but the scraps he wheedled from our poor-man's table gave him a prodigious amount of energy. He was a master scrounger. I can still see the swollen veins on the butcher's face when Scott stole a string of sausages from his basket and ran off for safety in the narrow gap between our garden shed and nextdoor's thorny hedge. Poking sticks, well-aimed stones, curses and threats did not deter him from his stolen feast.

The wails from a short-sighted neighbour still ring in my ears. She had put two slices of fish she had fried for tea to keep warm on her steel fender. She found only a well-licked plate and Scott sitting by her open cottage door, contentedly smacking his chops.

He landed me into some scrapes with Mam before she started to shut him up in the back-kitchen at meal-times. Before that, he would sneak under the table, pushing his head persistently against the legs of us children, begging us to pass him down scraps from our plates. Even ever-hungry Scott turned up his nose at the little dollops of cabbage I dropped down to him from my Sunday dinner-plate. There they still were, soiling the scrubbed stone flags under my chair when Mam cleared up.

He constantly dropped me in trouble at school, too. It was difficult for Mam to keep our cottage door shut with my toddler siblings about. I rarely progressed more than half-way through the long wooded walk to school before he was there, trotting behind my heels, tail wagging madly, ready for school.

'Goo on wum, you naughty dog!' I would scold him. Down went his tail between his legs, his body made an about-turn but his head turned to me, his eyes two brown pools of hurt betrayal.

I couldn't bear it. 'No, no, you be a good dog. I do love ya,' and back he would rush at me, all reproach gone.

Keeping this up all the way to the schoolyard gate was a dreadful hindrance and gave me no option but to leave him looking the picture of misery outside, made worse by his put-on bout of the shivers.

Assembly and scripture lesson would be over and sums begun before I poked my head round the classroom door. A terrible duffer at arithmetic, I copped it from my long-suffering teacher.

'Ah! Miss Sloth has arrived at last! Now we must all wait until she gets to her desk; no need for her to arrive at lessons early, because she never gets a sum right. Oh well, she can have a black mark in her book, and stay in during playtime for an extra arithmetic lesson.'

No good telling teacher about Scott. My burdens were heavy, but his suffering, left scolded and abandoned outside, was much worse.

Though he wasn't allowed to attend school, we considered our Scott a genius. How else could he be clever enough to know when the dog-licence man was coming round the village? When this happened, on his own initiative, Scott hid in the coal-hole in the back-kitchen with never a sniff or a whine to betray his presence, so that Mam could look the man straight in the eye and deny we kept a dog. The licence was seven-and-six per annum; we just didn't have that sort of money, and Scott knew it.

Our small living-room and back-kitchen-cum-coal-house were always overcrowded with a crawling baby, toddlers' feet, old Great-Aunty's corn-calloused rheumaticky ones, Mam's busy feet, Dad's heavy boots and the fidgety feet of us bigger ones. But if Scott couldn't find a lap to sit on, he was adept at finding a corner to curl up in out of everybody's way. Ever ready to defend us all, he would growl only when the rare strange footstep—bar the dog-licence man's—approached the door.

Nearly every child's father in our area was a miner, and it was the hungry twenties. Unsurprisingly, when the men went on strike rather than submit to even more inhuman conditions, food scraps became too precious even for well-loved dogs.

Father explained to us why he had found another home for Scott. It was with a kindly old pit-butty of his, whose children had grown up and left home for work, and were now able to help their parents out.

Father walked over three miles to take Scott to his new home, where he was given a bellyful of food as the initial bribe to stay. He had returned, almost to our garden gate, when the dog came panting up behind him, and the tear smudges were still on our faces as we welcomed him back.

Father had to be firm. The next day he walked Scott back to his new home. 'Kip'n shut up f'r a couple o' days to settle 'un in,' he advised his old friend.

Three days later Scott bounded joyously back through our door.

Father sighed. 'All right then, old bwoy, if thee'st rather starve wi' us lot than live wi' a vull belly zomewhere else, thee shal'st stop 'ere.'

Scott was getting on a bit, but still very agile, when I left home at fourteen to go into domestic service. The strike was over, but not for father.

Pit owners and management had black-listed him for his courage in speaking up against their demands. Mine was one less mouth for Mam to feed but, dreadfully homesick, I lived for the day when I could go home for the holidays.

Not knowing what chores my mistress might want done before I started out, I could not let my family know what time to meet me. When I had walked from the railway-halt to the edge of the forest where a woodland path led to our village, I would call, 'Scott, Scott, come on, Scott.'

In a matter of minutes, a small black and white bundle would come bounding through the ferns, impelled like a small rocket by his own enthusiasm, right up into my arms; my herald, to welcome me home. Sensing what his urgent departure meant, my little brother and sisters would come running in his wake, turning my heart over a little as they pulled up shyly in front of the big sister who had become a bit of a stranger after a year from home.

I was seventeen when I went home for my annual summer holiday from my job in London. At the woodland path I called out for Scott. No Scott came, despite repeated callings. Disappointed, I walked home through the forest.

Disappointment turned to heartache when I stepped indoors; matters had turned from bad to worse. Father still had no job; his loyal butties helped out from their own meagre resources, but sad-eyed and grey-faced, he seemed to have shrunk. So had Mam, and the pot-bellies and skinny legs of the little ones told their own story.

After the hugs and kisses, I sat down to a good meal that, by hook or by crook, Mam had mustered for my homecoming. 'Where's our Scott?' I asked.

Father took a time to answer. 'I be afeared, my wench, that we an't'n any more. The poor old bwoy was in bad shape. No doubt 'im could 'a' gone on a bit longer if we could 'a' give 'im the right sort o' victuals, but 'twas cruel to let'n goo on. 'Is poor legs was givin' out, an' 'im was sufferin'.'

Our way of life had not included such luxuries as the services of a vet. I sensed that it had been Dad's job to put Scott out of his misery. I knew that Father, intelligent and utterly humane, would have thought of the most merciful way. Just then I could not harass him further to find out.

Mam pushed my plate of food towards me, but it was not easy to swallow with no warm head pushing my knees under the table.

There are Worse Things than Debt

In 1926 the miners' strike was over. Beaten and dejected the Forest of Dean miners went back to work. But not our Dad. He was black-listed and victimised by the pit owners because of his outspoken attitude in support of the strike. The poverty was bad enough before the strike, but now things were desperate for us.

With one of his butties who was also a Forest free-miner Dad dug a slope to get some surface coal. It was inferior stuff, back-breaking to hack out, and difficult to sell. It earned them a pittance to give their wives. The poverty trap had already driven our Mam into debt with the local shopkeeper for the barest necessities to keep us alive. A younger brother and sister had both spent periods in sanitoriums. Putting some food on the table for us was the urgent priority of Mam's life.

Now she had to go into hospital with a bad leg. I was twelve years old, too young to leave school and follow my older sister into domestic service. Now I had to manage the role of Mother to my younger brother and two little sisters, and look after Dad's meals. I had never heard the words protein, calories, or vitamins in relation to food. Anything edible was consumed with gusto in our house. Well, it had been, until I took over!

My vocabulary may have been limited, but the word 'debt' was burned in red shame on my very spirit. I hated the terrible humiliation of going to the shop and begging for food on tick from the reluctant creditor. Whilst I was in charge I would ask for no credit. Indeed I determined to be so frugal that I might even save something to pay off our bill. So instead of dealing at the local shop I walked the two miles into town to look for food bargains, stale bread, hard cheese, et cetera. But no meat. Not even the cow's heart that Mum usually spent two shillings on for our Sunday and Monday dinners. Instead I spent twopence on a bottle of gravy browning!

We did our cooking on the fire in black iron saucepans which were scoured out with a damp rag dipped in ashes from the fire. I peeled enough potatoes to nearly fill a saucepan, added the two onions left in the pantry, covered it all with water, and balanced the saucepan on the open fire with the poker placed across the hobs. Then I got on with my idea of doing the housework.

Alas, when I went up to make the beds I found by Dad's bed a couple of old copies of a periodical called 'Harmsworth's Encyclopedia'. I loved reading, and attempted anything I could get hold of. I must have found plenty to interest me, because what finally distracted me was an acrid smell of burning. I ran downstairs; the potatoes had boiled dry. I poured water in from the black iron kettle singing on the hob, and stirred and scraped the burnt potatoes into the remainder, now well and truly brown with little black flakes in it. I could save the gravy browning for another day!

My brother looked at the daub of brownish grey mush on his plate. 'That do look like a cow's turd,' he said. 'And it do taste wuss,' he added as he tried a spoonful. Hungry though they were, it was a desperate struggle for the little ones to get theirs down, and there was plenty left to keep warm in the saucepan for Dad. But even he could not quite bring himself to compliment the 'cook'. But he did eat his without a word of complaint.

My next culinary inspiration for a cheap and filling main meal was Yorkshire Pudding. During the long strike people sympathetic to the miners' cause had volunteered to take miners' children into their homes for a holiday, and I had gone to a nice working-class family in Kent. It was here that I had first eaten Yorkshire Pudding. Even without the Sunday joint of beef they had I still thought the Yorkshire Pudding was wonderful. They had kept me for four months and by then I knew that the pudding was made with eggs and flour beaten up with water and baked in the oven. In Kent they cooked in a gas stove. We had an oven at the side of our grate, but I knew nothing about cooking temperatures.

I bought two penny eggs from the old couple in the cottage at the bottom of our garden, and I beat them up with plenty of water and a lot of flour to make it go further. I used our biggest fork but there were still plenty of little lumps when I poured the mixture into Mam's baking tin. I had overlooked the fact that first some fat had to be rendered boiling hot in the oven before the mixture went in. To lighten Dad's burden of carrying home the coal I kept the fire as low as possible. No wonder my pudding didn't rise to the occasion. No puffing up to a golden crispness! Three hours on, and I had produced a pale, flat, brick-hard, tasteless oblong. I was near to tears when a kindly neighbour, Mrs Browning, came to the door with the remains of a large bread pudding for us. I put a piece by for Dad.

'I'm sorry Dad, my Yorkshire Pudding didn't turn out right.'

It's no wonder that forty-five years after our Dad was killed in a pit fall, the thought of him brings on anew the terrible heartache of bereavement. He ate some of my pudding by soaking it in his tea cup. 'Never mind, my wench, we've all got to learn 'ow to do things right.'

At the end of the week there was a bit of silver lining for me, three silver shillings and four pennies. Proudly I handed them over to the shopkeeper to take off our bill. Luckily Mam came home a couple of days afterwards and rescued the family from my woefully incompetent management.

I still squirm with shame at my stupidity, and this is aggravated by the shame I feel as a member of the affluent Western world for letting people in the Third World die of starvation, because they cannot afford to pay for the huge surplus stocks of food that we store at enormous expense, or even destroy.

Back to the Forest

PART I

Now we had come past Gloucester I began to believe it. I really was coming back to the Forest; not quite back to the heart of the Dean, where I had spent my childhood, with its unique landscape and miles of woodland paths to roam at will, but to a good second-best. This was an isolated cottage on a country estate of farmland, woods, and orchards only a few miles from the Forest's edge.

Over the back flap of the huge removal van I watched the landscape pass; cottages, farms and homesteads that had become so familiar in my many journeys home for the holidays when I was a domestic servant in London.

Syd had moved up into the cab now to act as guide, and sat squashed between the driver, his mate and the gear-stick. Our three sons, aged fifteen, eleven, and nine, were perched as comfortably as the driver could arrange us, with Jenny, aged six, on my lap. Between Syd and the children and me were packed all our worldly goods.

Now, one hundred miles from London, I began to think more objectively about our situation. It seemed odd that one human being, a middle-aged, dumpy, homely-looking little woman at that, had driven us to make this momentous decision. I pondered on the power of one human being to affect the lives of others. Two outstanding examples came to mind, Jesus Christ and Hitler. Millions of lives had been changed by their opposing influences. Our experience was microscopic, but all-important to us just the same.

For the umpteenth time I wondered what the cottage would be like. Syd had seen it briefly when he had come for his interview at the sawmill, but all he could tell me was that the surrounding countryside was beautiful, and the interior of the cottage a bit rough and primitive. I hoped we were not again jumping out of the frying-pan into the fire! Never, I thought! No matter what the place was like, it would have the wonderful compensation we needed above all; the freedom to live as a family, not afraid to make a bit of noise, away from the dangers of traffic, and above all, from 'Her downstairs'. Anyway, my curiosity would soon be satisfied.

Then thoughts of our finances took over. After we had paid the driver and his mate we would have only a few pounds left to last us till Syd drew his first wages. I had already decided to double the tip for the driver's mate; coming down the notorious Birdlip Hill must have added five years to his age, and he was already getting on a bit. The driver, who was also the owner, had ignored Syd's warning to take a longer route to avoid Birdlip; he had lived to regret it, but only just.

Nowadays traffic is diverted to a new and gentler slope, but then there was no alternative. Faced with this unexpected challenge, driver and van went at it manfully. The huge pantechnicon, already past retirement age and over-loaded, swayed and groaned its way down, exploding with fury at such treatment. Brakes and steering had a terrible job negotiating the headlong descent. On reaching flat ground at the bottom the driver stopped. You could feel the relief; even the old van, still hissing with indignation, cooled off and put on a brave face again.

The children and I clambered out to stretch our legs. I could see the faces of the three men were putty-coloured, with beads of sweat oozing out of their foreheads. I was feeling a bit sick myself, and I told them that the boys and I had been pressing hard against the flap to slow it down. This brought tiny smiles to their wan faces but it was obvious my fear had not been groundless; it could have been a near thing. We all had a little rest, the driver and his mate shared a few swigs from a brandy flask, Syd assured them there were no more hills like that, and we re-started.

A few more miles, and we turned off at the end of a village and drove down a hedgerowed lane, and then up between two lodge houses, the entrance to the private drive of a manor house. It was like a royal welcome, between banks of glorious multi-hued rhododendrons in their full majesty, for this was the latter end of June. The manor, built in the style of a French chateau, was fronted by spacious well-kept lawns. The wide tarmac drive ended at the stables, but forking sharply off was a narrow cobbled road winding steeply up for about three hundred yards between a wild woodland copse and grazing meadows. After climbing a sharp little crest under a huge old chestnut tree, the road gently flattened and came to a peaceful end in a wide stone-pillared gateless entrance. Inside, surrounded by old stone barns, was an area of tangled nettles, thistles, couch-grass and brambles, with a little footpath trodden through. To my city-saturated eyes, even this weedy undergrowth was not objectionable.

The old barns were beautiful; the weathered tiles were patchily patinaed with yellow-green moss, and the stones had delicately absorbed all the colours of the rainbow. This is not at first obvious to the naked eye, but look long enough and the porous surfaces reveal they are not simply grey but are stained with the blended dyes of nature. Standing forlornly in dusty archways beneath the barns were old farm-carts made redundant by the tractors. They conjured up pictures of the stalwart carthorses that would never again stand harnessed to their cobwebbed shafts. The place had an air of abandoned, beautiful, peaceful sadness.

The pathway led to a little wooden gate under a crumbling rustic arch that was held together with rambler roses. Here I gave a little squeal of delight, 'Look, kids! It's even nicer than Little Grey Rabbit's house!' In London, to keep the children as quiet as the proverbial mice before bedtime, we used to indulge in our favourite daydream, looking through the 'Little Grey Rabbit' books. 'One day maybe we'll have a cottage in the country with woods and fields for you to play in, and you'll all be able to make a noise indoors, and if Mummy nags you, then you can hit me on the head with a hammer.' The way the boys' faces lit up at the thought of bashing me revealed the torture I was putting them through by perpetually hissing to them to *Be Quiet*.

The gate opened on to a small, stone-paved courtyard flanked by a one-storeyed extension to the cottage proper. There was a pump for our water supply with a stone trough in the front; a pink rambler rose climbed up the cottage wall; winter jasmine had sent its hardy roots under the flagstones and almost covered the low extension; a few weeds grew in a narrow flower bed under the rose; the small picturesque windows were latticed. All this far exceeded my anticipatory dreams.

The original door of the cottage had been boarded up and replaced with one in the extension. I was charmed by the small octagonal lattice window let into it. The key had been left under a brick by the door. I had the privilege of turning it in the lock. Then I let out another squeal of surprise, this time of disappointment. I suppose one could say that the 'room' it revealed was full of character. A black miserable character it was too, for black seemed to be the predominant colour in it.

'I warned you it was a bit rough,' said Syd, looking at me warily. I was speechless at this understatement. The entrance wall was of normal height, with a 'ceiling' going up to a peak of about fourteen feet which then sloped down to a back wall about five feet high. This wall was of rough stone covered with patches of mildew, and the floor was a rubble of dirt and loose dry bits of concrete. The other three walls were a mixture of brick, stone, and small rough concrete patches, covered, where it could adhere, with flaking smoke-blackened yellow-ochre distemper.

Cobwebs hung from the flaking ceiling, and the doors, once dark green, were now almost black with age and smoke. This 'room' had one surprisingly agreeable feature, a charming, hand-made brick fireplace. The front of this, too, was blackened and sooty, and there was no basket to light a fire in. A rough stone archway led into the rest of the extension, a small square room. Here the floor was not so bad; there were only a couple of rubbledy holes, and whoever had mixed the concrete had made a better job of it. This room was graced with a ceiling of a sort, plasterboard with the joints pasted over with paper. Here and there the paper had cracked open enough to allow dirt-encrusted cobwebs to hang down like stalactites. The walls were unplastered rough brick, and the room was bare of fitments of any sort.

A false wall ran across it to form a narrow cell at the back, the door to which was at the side of the brick fireplace. 'Oh, no!' I gasped, when I saw what was housed in there. But oh, yes, it was; a bucket toilet, which would have to be carried through the 'living-room' for emptying, because there was no back door. The bucket was empty but the odour lingered still. There was a tiny window, but the earth at the back had encroached up beyond the bottom of it and rampant weeds and brambles let but little light filter through.

Bewildered and depressed, I hastened to see the rest of my new home. The door into it was wide enough to let a milk-float through, but it opened easily enough, and my spirits rose a little. Now there was a small proper room, with a staircase going up from it, there was a good window, there was a boxed-in fireplace, and the walls were smooth and nicely distempered in cream. Big enough for a single bed for our Chris, I thought. On my left a door opened into a large larder. Here, too, the ceiling went up to a fourteen-foot apex, but there was a reasonable window and ample storage shelves of sound wood. It was well hung with cobwebs and flakes of whitewash fell everywhere, but it was a very handy storeroom.

Another door, another room, a good square room, big enough for two single beds for Richard and Nick. This had actually been papered, but the damp from outside had bulged it well away from the walls. The floor was of red tiles thick with mildew, there was a tiny, usable, grate, and the remains of bacon hooks were hammered deep into the ceiling. This was better; I began to feel I could live here after all. I went upstairs; two rooms, one very small, had been recently papered and painted. There were not many damp patches on the walls, and though the ceilings sloped down in each room and were veined with cracks and slight mal-formations, they felt sound enough to the touch. This was an improvement.

But what about that shambles downstairs? I could not help feeling very depressed about it all, so sharp a contrast as it was to the modern streamlined flat we had left behind. However, the cottage was wired for electricity, if only for lighting, and that was a marvel considering its isolation. Thirty years ago, electric cookers, washers, and fridges had not become part of estate workers' lives. In his efforts to enlarge and modernise his living-space the previous tenant had removed the old cooking range and wash-copper. Being a skilled carpenter and earning extra money outside his regular job, he had bought calor-gas appliances to replace them. He had taken them all away when he moved, and also the fire-basket from the brick fireplace. Oh, well! At least we had a kettle, so I went into the fuel shed to see what I could scrounge to light a fire. There was a small pile of sawdust, a few dry twigs, and a pile of rubbish from which I removed a couple of half-perished gas-masks. I also found some pieces of old brick to balance the kettle on. The chimney had a fit of the sulks; for every wisp of smoke it accepted it belched back acrid clouds into my face as I tried to blow some flame under the kettle.

Syd, the children, and the removal men were busy carrying all our things into the yard. I put out a good spread of the sandwiches and home-made cake I had brought with me. 'Sorry, no tea,' I told the men, 'it'll take till Christmas to boil that kettle,' which was still sitting on some desultory puffs of evil-smelling smoke. We slaked our thirsts with cups of pump water that came up icy-cold and very limey from its source eighty feet below the yard. When they had eaten, we paid the removal men and expected them to go on their way. 'No, no,' they insisted, 'we'll help you upstairs with the beds and wardrobes first.'

We had recently become a 'two-wardrobe family', which gave me a sense of real affluence. One was a double, a utility model, paid for by many hours of charring. The other we bought cheap from a friend's employers. The fact that a budding film starlet had hung her clothes in it gave it a glamour, and it was something to swank about. Syd had wheeled it home from the West End on a barrow borrowed from a street trader.

Looking at the narrow staircase with a right turn at the bottom the driver looked a bit dubious, as well he might. There was just no way either wardrobe was going to be winkled round that bend. And they never were. The same applied to the base of our double bed, metal springs on a stout steel frame. No matter how we turned and twisted, screwed and unscrewed, sweated and cursed, it was not going up. It looked easy enough, and you could start it alright, but you were soon balked. The bedroom window would have to come out, frame and all; meanwhile Syd and I would have to manage on the mattress.

Our two frustrated helpers said goodbye. Cockneys born and bred, it had been obvious since our arrival that they pitied us as a lot of lunatics for leaving the Smoke for such uncivilised remoteness. 'A place for everything, and everything in its place,' had been a favourite saying of one of my employers in service. Our new home still looked depressing and chaotic when I had done my best to follow her advice. At last we got the children bedded down, the boys too full of curiosity and excitement to feel upset, Jenny cuddling her doll to comfort it. Very soon they fell asleep.

It was late evening, but still light, when Syd and I flopped down into a chair on either side of the obstinate fireplace. None of us had been able to have a warm wash; the pump water was too hard to lather, and soap just turned into a floating grey scum. How on earth could I cope with bringing up a family under these conditions, I asked myself wretchedly. It was no good nagging Syd; I was the one most responsible for bringing us all here. It was all very well for him to come back from his interview raving about the beautiful countryside and the views from the cottage! He *should* have noticed there was not so much as a hob to put a saucepan on, and no means of heating water for washing.

The sawmill had allowed him a day off from work to help us settle in, so I began to plan what he was going to do with it.

'You'll have to go to Gloucester to-morrow and order me an electric cooker and wash-copper.'

'What with?'

'You'll have to get it on the never-never, from the Electricity Board. Get them for the lowest deposit they'll take, with four years to pay.'

'What about the deposit, and the cost of installation?'

'Well, I've got five pound and threepence-ha'penny. I've brought some groceries with us and enough bread for a couple of days. How much have you got?'

'My bacca money and two and elevenpence. Don't forget this firm keeps a week in hand, so it's a fortnight before I get any money.'

'Can't be helped, you'll have to ask for a sub when we're right broke, and I shall write to the Estate manager. It's their responsibility to pay for the installation.'

We sat on, not speaking, gloomily chewing over our problems. The night gloom gathered, too, outside and inside. Neither of us got up to switch on the light until a scratching scuffling noise started above the kitchen ceiling. Mice! Or, worse still, rats! I had suffered from an irrational fear of these creatures since a mouse had run up my skirt as I sat on the mat in the fireglow of a darkened room.

I jumped up to switch on the light, and at that same moment a mouse (or was it a *rat?*) missed its footing and fell through a papered-over crack in the kitchen ceiling.

'Now don't you start screaming or having hysterics, you'll scare Jenny,' warned Syd as I panicked up on to a chair. The mouse (or *rat?*) panicked too, as Syd poked it out from under the sideboard with the broom. Much as I detested them, I could not have borne for Syd to bash it to death, and Syd has no killer instinct either. At last it ran out through the gap under the front door. Well, it had been a long day, but I did not feel tired any more. How could I go to sleep in a house over-run by rodents?

'Come on, let's go to bed; there won't be any mice up there.' Syd was fed up and tired. He is a good husband, but when he is fed up and tired his temper is likely to erupt and it can be quite a temper. I had little choice: stop down here alone with more benighted creatures likely to fall through the ceiling, or go upstairs and lie on a mattress on the floor, a floor with mice probably running about under it and even over it. Holding my nose, I made Syd come in with me to the bucket privy.

'I shall have to have the light on all night,' I said. Syd was too tired to argue; in five minutes he was fast asleep. I lay with my shoulders against the wall, tense, and getting tenser, with horror at every creak and sigh, endemic in the structure of old cottages.

Now I had plenty of time to review the situation. Who was it, I reminded myself, that had kept on about moving? Who would not care where we lived so long as it had four walls and a roof and no-one living underneath? Could we go back to that flat, if we phoned quickly in the morning? Would I, I asked myself, would I go back to that flat with 'Her downstairs'? I was not sure; deep down in me was a feeling that the boats had been burned, and we were going to stay. No, no, I cried, and I *was* sure that I wished myself back in our tenement house in Lisson Grove, where we had lived before the flat.

Lisson Grove, that unsalubrious corner of London; Lisson Grove and the patched-up corner tenement; Lisson Grove and our friends and neighbours. It is said you can live in London and never know your neighbours, but that certainly did not apply in our case.

Six tenancies occupied three floors. Each had two rooms and a big kitchen. We shared two landing lavatories, the front door, the stairs, and most of the ins and outs and ups and downs of each other's lives. The ground floor, the basement, and the back yard were occupied by a firm of cabinet-makers.

The other flat on our landing on the second floor was occupied by Lally and her three little girls. From a childhood spent among an amoral family she had blossomed into a full-blown nymphomaniac. Unhealthily pale, she had become an expert in make-up; slight and bony of build she atoned for her lack of nubility by the open lust in her eyes at the sight of a pair of trousers. She was married to a regular soldier who regularly left her pregnant on his infrequent leaves, but never physically deprived.

Nevertheless Lally continued to assuage her loneliness with a variety of war-time soldiers, thick on the ground just then. If nature insisted that we had to creep across the landing in the small hours, there was a likely chance of bumping into a soldier stealthily leaving or approaching Lally's door. She did it all for lust, not money; I often knew her send one of her children up the road to cadge half a fag off her sister. 'Tell 'er I'm gaspin' for a puff,' she would say.

She often left me gasping with her uninhibited accounts of the ways of a woman with a man. For convention's sake she attributed these to her life with her husband, but even he could not have been that much of a Don Juan. She certainly showed up my own shortcomings in the nuptial field; I had not even passed my 'Oh!' levels. Lally gave me some shock therapy treatment; poor Syd, I had been a dull bed partner. When we had moved there I was pregnant with our second child. We had been married six years, but I was still basically an inhibited prude, due to the childhood influence of a well-meaning but un-enlightened mother.

I am a one-man woman and Lally's generous distribution of her favours held no appeal for me. But just as most women would like to be a Cordon Bleu cook, recipes for cooking a husband's goose are also very handy. Our marriage improved no end.

Lally's family also provided us with our Saturday night 'viewing', not on a TV screen, which had not then become part of life, but through our kitchen window. Every Saturday evening her seventeen-year-old sister baby-sat for Lally so that she could join her large family for their weekly booze-up in the pub opposite. They gathered at the pub entrance in a mood of great affection and camaraderie. Around closing time they either came out or were thrown out, all their pent-up aggros and grievances now released by alcohol. Soon they were shouting a Kinsey-type report of their sexual behaviour, moral lapses, thieving habits, cross couplings, and who's-whose accounts of paternity. Nudgings and pushings turned into challenges, and then fights, joined by fringe enemies or supporters. Heads crashed against fists, walls, and even pavements. This weekly boil-up of their dirty habits was forgotten and forgiven in time for the next booze-up, even if a couple of heads still sported plasters.

The widening of my sex education, initiated by Lally, was continued, as chance would have it, by Annabelle. Annabelle was a
glamorous woman living in the block of flats opposite, and I did a
bit of charring for her. She too was prone to entertaining soldiers,
mostly from the officer classes, American preferably, but unlike
Lally she charged heavily for her services. In exchange for my
clothes coupons, which I could not afford to use, she gave me
some of her left-off clothing. Tarty tight skirts, high-heeled shoes
and underwear! Phew! Nothing to help me keep warm but enough
to send the steam out of Syd's earholes! I learned, not without the
loss of my romantic idealism, that love is one thing and sex
another. Entwined, they are the nearest we can reach towards the
stars.

Mr and Mrs B. lived upstairs, and the rest of us considered that
they gave a bit of a social status to our tenement. They both
worked in an office, and set off each morning smartly dressed and
carrying rolled umbrellas. She was decidedly snooty, and had a job
to crack her face into a smile if she passed any of us on the stairs.
They did not mix at all, which left the rest of us free to gossip and
conjecture about where she went every week-end. Mr B. was
always left on his own from Friday evening to Monday morning.
He was the nicer of the two. A rather delicate man, he was
allowed a war-time ration of an extra pint of milk a day because of
a stomach ulcer. At week-ends he always left this daily pinta
unobtrusively by Lally's door for her children.

One evening, as I laid the table for Syd's home-coming meal, I
heard the B.'s radiogram playing rather loudly, and I could tell
they were dancing to the music. I joined in and picked up a rather
puzzled Chris into my arms to waltz around the room. We were
happy in the midst of life.

Suddenly I heard footsteps running down the stairs and there
was an urgent banging on our door. Mrs B. stood there, wild-eyed
and trembling, 'Quick, quick! Please come up! Jeremy is having a
dreadful turn. I'm frightened.' I put Chris down and called Lally
to keep an eye on him. Then I ran upstairs, relieved to hear Syd
coming in at the same time.

Upstairs the radiogram was still playing. Mr B. lay on the settee.
I had never seen a dying person before, but my instincts told me
he was breathing his last breaths and every one was an agony.

Gently I put my arm around his shoulders and talked to him soothingly as to a baby, but I did not think he could hear. His thin pale aesthetic face was now swollen and purple, his unseeing eyes bulging almost out of it. I prayed he was not suffering, and almost at once the swollen features subsided and the colour began to go. His breathing stopped, and though he still felt warm in my arms I knew he had died. Mrs B. had turned the radiogram off, and was now having near-hysterics. She too could see he had gone.

'Oh, my God!' she moaned. 'What shall I do? How *could* he die on me like this? We're not married, you see, not married. If my husband ever found out! He's away travelling for his firm all the week. That's why I stay here in London with Jeremy. My God, what can I do now?'

As these revelations tumbled out in her panic I was too surprised to comment. 'Half this furniture is mine,' she went on. At this point I lost sympathy with her; her concern was entirely for herself.

Just then Syd came up and looked at Mr B. He told me to go downstairs with Chris and though he knew little about it, tried to massage life and breath back into the lungs of the dead man.

Meanwhile, Meg from downstairs had got wind that something was amiss. Nosey, but practical and sensible, she sent Syd to ring for the doctor, and took 'Mrs B.' downstairs with her to give her some tea and stop her helpless snivelling. After the doctor had pronounced Mr B. dead, she helped 'Mrs B.' collect and pack her things, called a taxi, saw her into it and watched her disappear from the scene.

A few days later a hearse drew up outside, and some men carried a coffin upstairs. After a while they brought it down. Lally and Meg and I stood by our doors for a moment paying our last respects to our lonely unwanted neighbour who could be such a gentleman. They handed him over the banisters as if he was a piece of furniture. There were no flowers, no mourners, just Mr B.'s last solitary quiet descent down our stairs.

His weekday 'wife' came back just once, to arrange the sale of his furniture to a second-hand dealer. We were not sorry to see the back of her; superior class indeed!

Meg lived in the rooms directly below ours. Many years in London had hardly watered down her Welsh accent, nor diminished her passion, surely shared by the majority of Welsh ladies, for a nice clean doorstep and entrance. With a bunch of young children playing a great deal on the doorsteps, achieving this ambition was a sore trial to Meg. She would chivvy and scold them for the mess they all too frequently made, and then destroy the whole effect by handing out to the miscreants sweets, and toys and crayons, etc., that she got from her charring jobs in the West End.

Some years before, Meg had discarded an erring husband, and now kept herself by being a daily treasure to a variety of people. Many of these were household names at the time, connected with the entertainment world. For the rest of us, Meg was very often a treasure trove as well. By now, war-time rations had been cut to the bone; but the affluent people Meg worked for were able to patronise the black market. Far from feeling the pinch, their cupboards and larders were over-stocked. Whenever she could, Meg relieved them of small amounts of tea, sugar, fats, or anything she could lay her hands on, sharing her pickings with those of us who had children.

She also shared with us her accounts of the unconventional behaviour of the well-known people she worked for. Gulps of juicy scandal went down with our shared pots of tea. Meg had no inhibitions about listening at, or peeping through, keyholes, and anybody's unlocked correspondence was hers for the reading. Once when she was temporarily cleaning the office of a top West End solicitor, we knew about a forthcoming divorce in Royal circles months before the story broke in the papers.

Meg was every bit as generous with her help and advice to these straying sheep, as she was to her neighbours. One famous lady journalist she worked for was a widow who was entertaining high matrimonial hopes from an elderly and wealthy city tycoon. At the time he was tied to an invalid and mentally-handicapped wife, who was incarcerated in a very expensive nursing home.

One night a week he stayed with his unofficial fiancee; most other nights she shared her bed with a handsome TV personality. Meg was no prude about this arrangement, but one morning when she took the two cups of tea in, she found the TV man replaced, on one of his working nights, by a well-known well-married actor. Meg waltzed back out again with the tea, and later gave her employer a good scolding for getting a bit too promiscuous. She did not get the sack, which was just as well.

The city tycoon's unfortunate wife obliged everybody by dying quietly, and he quickly upped and married his young secretary. The betrayed lady journalist, her pride mortally wounded, became hysterically suicidal. A fortune had slipped through her grasp and her reputation as a *femme fatale* had been totally undermined. Now forty years old, almost alone, used and rejected by the men she thought she was using, life seemed to have nothing left for her. There was one final, irreversible way out.

Meg told me everything, and analysing her chatter I felt sure she had saved her employer. Her commonsense lectures, and her ability to make Madame see things in proper perspective, slowly brought her back on to an even keel. During this time Meg neglected her other jobs and stayed all hours to help restore the lady's sanity.

Meg was also the house 'Banker' for us penurious tenants. Not a bank that we ever put money in; we only had overdrafts of odd shillings when the week was longer than the housekeeping money. Meg earned her living by long hours of charring, yet she never refused a borrower, never charged any interest, and often had to be persuaded into accepting repayment. She was just simply good-natured, but she was practical too, and dealt with the things life sent her as they came along.

One of the things that came along was her boy-friend. Meg had a boy-friend of her own, a Canadian soldier some fourteen years younger than herself—Meg was nudging forty. She was no glamour girl; she had a pleasant little face, a short dumpy figure, and she was a natty dresser. But the Canadian bowled us over; he was exceptionally handsome with a height and physique to match.

Aware of Meg's generous nature, we sniffed disapproval behind her back, convinced that she was just being used as a convenient free lodging for his leaves, and as a provider of hot meals and free gin.

As the time approached for the birth of our second child, the war was still a terrible curse hanging over us all. Here we are, I would think, a large ecological mass going in orbit round the sun, a planet with a core of still-molten fire, its thin crust covered with countless thousands of species of life, flora and fauna, liquids and chemicals, subject to earthquake and flood, tempests, and fires, host to continuous death. Yet we added to our burdens of disaster the man-made holocaust of war! We hang the blame handily on such as Hitler, Napoleon, Genghis Khan, and so on, but one evil being could easily be eliminated in the cause of justice. Why did we kill rather than reason? What was in us that made us love to hate?

When I worked as a maid in a London boarding-house, I had met people of many nationalities and colours. They were all just ordinary people, some nice and some not so nice, just the same as everybody else. It was not logical for a whole nation to be the enemy of a whole nation. It could not be, and I did not believe it. I was puzzled and resentful to find myself part of a war, and as helpless to do anything about it as a leaf carried down a turbulent stream.

I was also a coward, with a strong sense of self-preservation, especially for Chris and the coming baby. When the sirens sounded in the small hours, people poured out of buildings like ants whose nests have been poked with a stick. Hearts in our mouths we ran, hoping to reach the comparative safety of the underground station before the bombs fell. Heroic street wardens shouted at people to take cover. The blacked-out streets became caverns of Hell lit up by vipers' tongues of streaking red light as the guns and searchlights sought the dark enemy. The Devil's orchestra of the bass rumblings of explosions put wings on our feet.

Though handicapped by the large bump in front of me I ran like the clappers, easily keeping up with Syd who carried a sleepy, bundle-wrapped Chris. When the buzzbombs started, they would come anywhere at any time. Warnings were of little use, sleep was out of the question. So I persuaded Syd that the three of us, almost four, must sleep on the Underground platform every night.

The platforms were packed with people lying right to the edges. The few late-night trains broke up the sleep of any who had found it, and the passengers picked their way daintily among the blankets. Against the wall at the back were a few bunks occupied by the very old and the very young. Sometimes Chris had a bunk, if it were not too far from us. Often the three of us huddled together on the draughty stairs, snatching at sleep, waking again, talking in whispers to strangers whom adversity had turned into friends.

Then Hitler started his rocket attacks. There were no warnings;

there could be none, because there was nothing to see or hear. Just an earth-shattering ominous explosion somewhere. Some poor soul had had it; not us, yet! These inexplicable explosions were not explained by the authorities for many weeks, but Cockney wit smelled it out, and dubbed them 'flying gas-mains'.

I was now over eight months pregnant, and one particular dread obsessed me. Supposing that all around us was hit by a rocket, and Chris was buried under the rubble, and we could not get at him? After all, it was possible; it was even likely. The thought of it was enough to make me give in to Syd's persuasions, and to the entreaties of my parents, to go back to the Forest to stay with them.

My two younger sisters were living at home. Ironically, the war had saved them from a life of domestic service by bringing plenty of factory work to the locality. My parents were now in their fifties, and it caused a considerable upheaval in their little cottage to fit in a small grandson and a heavily pregnant daughter. My time was coming, and the district nurse arranged for me to have the baby in a municipal nursing home twenty-four miles away. Three weeks later I had a bonny boy almost nine pounds in weight. It was a Nature's miracle, really, for that baby had drawn his sustenance from dry porridge oats, health salts, cider, and surreptitious sniffs of metal polish.

The first four months of my pregnancies have always been a living hell of nausea. My taste buds go mad; all normal food smells and tastes like poison. I cannot tolerate tea, coffee, cocoa, or even plain bread and butter. But after four months I become a real pig for dry porridge oats, dry health salts by the handful, and as much cider as I can get; all items I have no liking for normally. Sniffing the metal polish is a great little luxury. Once they were born, however, I was a failure to all of them as a source of nourishment, and reluctantly had to put them on the bottle.

Meanwhile, the principal cause of these troubles, Syd, stayed in London and went on with his job. His wages were none too grand but he came down to see us pretty often. In our small crowded cottage, the brevity of his visits did not help me to re-adjust our marriage. I was worried, too, about the proximity of his lonely manhood to the lustful Lally.

'Wouldn't touch her with a barge-pole!' he would declare

breezily. But that would not cure my jealousy; it was not a barge-pole I was worrying about.

Impulsively, obstinately resisting advice, I decided to return with Syd from one of his visits. It was a mistake. The dread of the children being buried by bombs or rockets took over in my mind more strongly than ever. What joy we had from being together again was quite overcast, and though we renewed the old routines they brought us no contentment.

Lally's philosophy was calm acceptance. 'If your number's on it you'll get it, so meanwhile, while you're waitin' for it, 'ave a good time. Enjoy a fag an' a drop o' booze, gel, an' a bit o' the other.' This did nothing for my jitters; I did not smoke or drink, anyway, and spent my nights tensed up to the point of hysterics waiting for oblivion from a rocket. Lally never even bothered to run for shelter.

Meg was brave too. She no longer went charring, as most of her employers had left London. She now worked at the headquarters where comforts for the troops sent from America and Canada were sorted. Early evening she took herself off to a newly-opened shelter under the Great Central hotel, where she enjoyed the luxury of a bunk bed.

Syd had never thought he was likely to get any special protection from Above. He was working very long hours and needed his sleep, so after taking me and the children to the Underground station he went back to bed in the tenement. Now that the rockets were coming day and night without warning, and the old bombing raids had stopped, people seemed more resigned, and calm in despair. The Underground platforms were almost empty; the normality was abnormal; the night-time fraternity had disbanded. The war was not being lost, nor was it being won in a hurry. Every day we wondered, should I leave again, take the children, and return to the Forest? At least, till the war was over?

PART II

Providence made up our minds. I had a letter from a second cousin in the village who was going to stay in Margate with her soldier husband's friends. I could have her cottage at the top of our village, furnished, for ten shillings a week. I wrote by return, saying yes, please, and thank you, and I told my Mum and Dad we were coming back again. It would be a struggle to find the ten shillings, but it was better than imposing on them.

It was a small and primitive cottage; downstairs, one room and a back-kitchen which also served as a coalhouse; upstairs, two small bedrooms. The bucket privy was at the bottom of a narrow strip of untended garden. There was a cold-water tap in the back-kitchen, but no sink or drainage. Cooking and water heating had to be done on a big open black-leaded grate with an oven at the side. The downstairs floor was stone-flagged, the furniture strictly utilitarian, and not the sort to worry about. But even without the cheery fire lit by a friendly neighbour for our cold evening arrival my heart was full of gratitude for this comparatively safe haven.

Then at three in the morning I faced a new sort of fear. At this awkward time Richard would wake for a bottle. Soft talk, cuddling, or a drink of Government orange juice were not acceptable substitutes, and his whimpers would develop into furious howls of frustration until he got what he wanted. Coming downstairs by candlelight to re-kindle the fire was an eerie business. The unlatchable back-kitchen door moaned creakily on its old hinges, the shadowy corners seemed full of ghosts. On this same sofa under this window an elderly relative of mine had been laid out. As a child I had seen her corpse there, for at the time, my shoulder augmented the walking stick of our arthritic old great-aunt. Viewing the corpses of her old friends was a social ritual for her. This particular old friend had been a kindly soul, but lying there emaciated by age, with her loose white hair and bony folded hands, she had looked already like a spectre.

I knelt by the fire blowing it into life. The candle flickered in the draughts, this way and that. As the fitful light fell on the sofa I could see it first empty, then in the dark, what shade was lying there? The back-kitchen door moaned open again; the leaky tap was dripping into a zinc bath. Plop, plop. Water, was it? Or maybe blood from the talons of a ghoul? I had to go in there for water to cool the bottle! I felt prickles of fear up the back of my neck, as candle in hand I pushed open the creaking door. Now, save for the firelight, the other room was dark, and the empty sofa waited for the wraith. Oh, come on, I told myself: brave enough by day scoffing at the notion of spirits coming back, yet now expecting an apparition any minute.

My task completed, I hurried back upstairs, courage returning with every step. What a comfort it was to hold the fat red-faced screaming little tyrant and put the teat to his lips! He was comforted immediately, and apart from a few little grunts that might have been scolding or satisfaction, soon fell quiet. Chris had slept through it all in the old iron double bed he shared with me. I knew I would have to face this caper always at this time, for unlike to-day's mothers I had no plug-in gadgets for preparing night feeds. Anyway, I thought, imaginary things that did not really go bump in the night were better than bombs and rockets that did!

Adding to these nocturnal discomforts, we soon found that the roof leaked. When it rained I had to sleep with my knees up so I would not kick over the tin bath I put at the bottom of the bed to catch the regularly plopping drops. In this small room there was no way to place the bed so as to avoid the cascade. The back bedroom was even tinier, and quite unusable.

With two rents to pay out of Syd's modest wages we had to live very frugally. War-time rations were now at their most stringent, and kept the food bills small. Even so, I could not afford to buy coal, and my parents gave me a generous portion, though it was ill-spared. Mam needed a fire almost day and night. Dad was on shifts, and there were winter-wet pit clothes to dry. There was the washing for four grown-ups and the drying and airing of it round the fire. Then there was all the cooking. Domestic life revolved around a grate seldom empty.

Dustmen had not been thought of then, in our area, and village housewives tipped their ashes on to rubbishmixes peppered about on the fringes of the woods. This was lucky for me, and I found it quite delightful going out into the snowy frosty beautiful forest to scrape the cokes from the ashes. Maybe, too, I would pick up some kindling wood, dead twigs sticking up through the snow.

Sometimes when we got home a bucket of lump coal, a cabbage, or a few vegetables had been put by my back door. Knowing my inability to repay these kind gestures, the donors never embarrassed me by giving away their identities.

Worry for Syd's safety, and guilty feelings that I had no right to be luckier than those who still battled on in the bombed city, were my biggest headaches. When we could manage the fare, Syd came down for the week-end. He looked thinner every time, and eventually came out in multiple boils on his arms from poor diet and lack of wife's attentions. Once again I began to have doubts as to where my duty lay.

The dark days lengthened into a glorious Spring and an early Summer. Baby Richard was approaching his first birthday. The Forest was green again underfoot and overhead. It was a glorious place for me to take my two lovely children out walking. Suddenly my problem was solved. The war in Europe was smouldering to a halt; not, alas, because lessons had been drawn from its macabre futility, but because the military power of one side had overwhelmed the other. Just as when a baby is born the relief from pain is too great to comprehend, so it was too wonderful to believe that the war was really over, that we had survived it, and that the tenement house and our neighbours had been spared. The war was over, nothing else mattered, and we went back to London. To be all together again in our ugly little corner made light of my regret at leaving our lovely pastoral surroundings.

Our euphoria soon took a bit of a knock. Syd might have got thin from malnourishment, but he soon proved that he was still in working order. To my great distress, and despite the teachings of Marie Stopes, I was pregnant again and Richard barely a year old! Old wives' remedies, potions magic and absurd, kangaroo jumps, carrying heavy loads, and wishful thinking, all had no effect. It was back to the nausea, back to the cider, the dry oats, the health salts, and the metal polish sniffs again. Never mind, perhaps this time it would be the longed-for girl. I day-dreamed of tying bonnet ribbons instead of popping on round woolly hats, and I tried not to think of our inadequate finances and the escalating laundry problems.

Our rooms had a sink and cold-water tap in the kitchen, and

nowhere at all outside to dry the washing; so twice a week I went to the municipal wash-house half-a-mile away. I had to push two prams, with Chris hanging on to my skirts. The one pram held Richard and all his paraphernalia—orange juice, bottle of feed, biscuits, and rattles to keep him amused—for often there was a queue. In the other pram, big, ancient and hoodless, I put our dirty washing tied up in a sheet like a gargantuan Christmas pudding. Wheeling a pram with each hand, with a protesting little boy hanging on your skirts, takes a bit of doing. Pedestrians had the choice of squeezing up to the shop-fronts or stepping off the pavements to let us through. At the busy crossings I took Richard's pram over first and made sure the brake was on properly, before coming back for the washing. Not once did I ever have to cross over again. Gentlemen abounded in London. Sometimes it was a road sweeper, a road mender, a barrow-boy, or a man in overalls. But gentlemen come in other guises. Once it was a city type, complete with bowler hat, natty striped suit, gold-topped umbrella and all. He made an incongruous picture, wheeling my old pram of dirty washing across the busy road, and raising his hat to me before calling a taxi. The two prams, with Lally's one, were housed under the stairs in the entrance passage.

One afternoon, when I was about seven months pregnant, I was feeling so relieved as I pulled the prams up the front steps, carted the load of clean washing up four flights, and came down again for Richard, to bring him up. Chris clattered up in front ready for his tea. I was just in time to see to Syd's meal. The casserole and rice-pudding had been put in the oven on a low heat, and had cooked to a nicety. I put the kettle on for a longed-for cup of tea. Chris sat to the table, and I put Richard up in his high chair beside him. I stood and looked at them while the kettle sang behind me.

There was a knock on the door, and I stepped happily across to open it. With some surprise, and a little apprehension, I found a telegram boy standing there. He thrust the little envelope into my hand, and hurried away down the stairs. Standing by the open door in a daze I opened it and read it.

PLEASE COME HOME FATHER BADLY HURT CISS

Dad badly hurt? Badly hurt! How? Where? Why had Ciss sent the telegram? She was a close friend to all the family, but why was it not from my brother, Dick, or one of my sisters? Shocked and confused, I stood where I was. Only one thought came again and again through the jumble of dear memories and dreadful speculations; I must go home to him at once. Whatever the difficulties, they must be overcome; I must go. Somehow, I and all the family, and all those around him who loved him, would make him better again, no matter how grievous the wound.

Then Meg came up, nosey helpful Meg, curious to know what the telegram was about. Without a word I held it out to her. She took one look at me and ran downstairs, coming back with a glass of brandy. She led me back indoors, pushed me down into a chair in the corner, and gave me the glass.

'Meg, I must go home. *Now*,' I moaned.

She was getting the boys' tea out, and she said calmly, 'Now, Win, you mustn't upset yourself so much, not in your state. It may not be as bad as you think. Anyway, here's Syd coming up the stairs. Good job the kettle's boiling; I'll wet him a cup of tea.'

Syd came in and his eye met mine immediately. 'Whatever's up?' he said, and Meg handed him the telegram. His face paled, for he too dearly loved my Dad. Unable to speak, he sat down, looking at the telegram again and again. Meg put the cup of tea in his hand, and rummaged through her bag for a handful of change. 'Go and phone the policeman in Win's village,' she said in reassuring tones. 'Find out how things are.' He knew there was no policeman, but he phoned the garage on the main road. They would know. He had hurried to the phone box but he came back slowly, his feet dragging, his mind in turmoil as he sought for words and ways to tell me.

There was no need; his stricken face revealed his thoughts; the dismal truth was etched in his drawn cheeks and his downcast eyes. Though muted by time, the mental anguish of that moment lives with me still. The emotional torture swelled into a pain that threatened to burst my head and heart. Father dead. Merciless logic insisted I accept it, but everything else, mind, soul, body, being, emotions, memories, all shouted it down. I screamed out, 'No, no, no.' Then I was broken, and unable to move. Syd stood there with his cap and coat still on, dull, grey, helpless. 'He didn't suffer, Win. It was instantaneous, a fall in the pit.'

I could not take any comfort from his words; there was no comfort now, nor sense, nor any meaning to life. If Father was dead, why carry on with this cruel joke called existence, where, whatever our merits, our lives and deaths were ruled by a feckless destiny? Where one so good as Dad, so true, so loved, could be destroyed as thoughtlessly as a gnat swatted by a gardener? Yet even the poor gnat has feelings; does it too not suffer pain? The world was full of pain, and by living in it I was contributing to it. Never had I wanted to cause suffering, but it was too late. There at the table sat two little human beings I had brought into the world and another lived inside me. They, too, would suffer, and cause suffering. I was trapped in despair. What was love, where was its power or purpose, if one could not even bid its inspirer the last goodbye?

I picked Richard out of his chair, and sat cuddling him to me, rocking back and forth and moaning, 'I must go home, I must go home.' Syd came to me and said again and again, 'He did not suffer, Win, he did not suffer. How can we go, now, to-night, with you like this? We'll have to go in the morning. What good can you do now?' I took no notice as I sat there in my stunned and helpless dismay.

Meg had fetched Syd's sister, and the two of them were moving about doing what had to be done. To me they were like figures in a dream; everything seemed unreal except the hurt inside me. Syd's sister said, 'All right, dear, all right, Win, you shall go home. Now. Pull yourself together a bit, and we'll get you ready. I'll take Chris and look after him till you come back.' I knew Chris would not mind. Syd got up. 'Oh, come on then,' he said. 'It's no good arguing. Might as well get on with it.'

The two women packed Richard's clothes and nappies and some things for me. We had almost no money, and the shoes I wore, my only pair, were shabby and downtrodden. Meg fetched up a pair of hers, and one of her smart coats, and helped me into them. She pushed some pound notes into Syd's hand. Syd's sister called and paid for a taxi to take us to Paddington Station. We kissed our Chris goodbye for now. He went off with his Auntie, and we got into the cab.

The steam train rushed on its unseeing way through the cold dark. The rhythmic swaying of the carriage, the muffled music of the wheels, the dimness of the light, nothing could make us doze, or even close our eyes. We sat the whole way in miserable silence. One mad ray of hope came again and again to my fevered mind;

the man at the garage could be wrong, he was at the far-end of the village, and everything got exaggerated. No, Dad was not dead; badly hurt, true, but not dead; it could not be. Yet at the same time my mind was trying to adjust to the thought that I would never see him again. I had often heard the stricken and the crippled talk of life 'before I lost my leg', 'before I lost my hearing'. Now the curtain of bereavement was cutting my life into two.

I had lost my begetter and my life-long friend; my heart would never be whole again. Father had travelled the decades with us, cuddler of babies, interested listener to our childish chatter, widener of our grown-up horizons with his rich mind. How he had loved to spend his holidays with us in London, tasting its culture at the museums and exhibitions, thirsty for knowledge never acquired in his brief schooldays. At the age of eleven he had gone into the pit as hod-boy to his stepfather. Torn away from school, he had never stopped learning since.

Science, in particular, fascinated him, and he loved to dwell on man's discoveries and his inventive ingenuity with the earth's resources. He would ponder on what man had achieved, and discuss the pros and cons of the way he used it.

Dad had a scientific ambition of his own, 'when I 'a' got the time an' the money to do't'. He was convinced that a pedal-powered plane could be achieved. One day Syd and I had taken him and Mam to the West End, and on to Selfridge's roof garden. While Mam marvelled at a garden stuck up so high in the air, Dad looking critically around observed that it would be just the place to land his pedal-plane. 'Just think on't, Mother, thee an' I flyin' in over thic Marble Arch, an' all they crowds o' Cockneys a-gawpin' up at us, an' thee wi' thee best 'at on a-wavin' to 'em.' Mam automatically straightened her shoulders, adjusted her hat, and put on her Sunday chapel face, rehearsing for the occasion.

One of his many talents, buried for lack of time, was an ability to draw and paint. We took him to the National Gallery and watched him shaking his head in reverent bewildered homage at the great master-works. This aura of acute appreciation of so many things transmitted itself strongly to us all. He enriched his world, and asked us into it.

In the process of his logic Father had come to share Macbeth's opinion, that life was a tale told by an idiot, full of sound and fury and signifying nothing. It was a bitter philosophy, yet it had not embittered him one jot. Now his untimely death, crushed deep under the earth, seemed to prove it. But it was too strong a truth for me to take, and all through this sad and silent journey I clung to my illusion that our Dad was still alive.

It was well past midnight when my eldest sister let us in through mother's cottage door. Her face was grey with grief.

'Oh, Bess, is it true?' She nodded, and took me in her arms. Mam sat beside the fire, for the first time in her life not jumping up to welcome visitors by putting on the kettle. Syd put Richard in her lap, and a lifetime's instincts took over. She chaffed his cold little hands in hers, began to take his woolly wrappings off, and pulled her chair nearer the fire for him. She seemed to have shrunk.

My two younger sisters raised their tear-swollen faces, their eyes sad dulled question marks. My brother sat with drawn white face staring into space. We could find no words to comfort one another. Bess had already drunk the bitterest dregs of bereavement some years before, when her first-born, a lovely little boy only four years old, had died of cancer. It was she who saw to Richard's bottle and put out some food for Syd. In a couple of hours Syd would have to catch the dawn train back to London.

Bess and her husband and five children lived in the next door cottage, so my brother-in-law took him into their place to get a little rest. Presently my brother rose from his chair and went through to the workshop on the other side of the cottage. Ironically, the war had given better wages and plenty of overtime to the miners. With the extra funds, Dad and Dick had fashioned a rough extension, housing a wood-turning lathe and other tools. On a bench by the lathe were some unfinished wooden toys, fire engines, scooters, destined for the grandchildren's Christmas stockings.

They had built in an old range, and Mam put ready by the fire the tin bath for Father's home-from-pit wash, his change of boots stood on the fender, and his trousers hung from a hook by the mantelpiece to be warm and aired for him. The shape of his knees bulged in the cheap tweed. The poignancy of these reminders was so overwhelming that I felt a scream rising in my throat, but the sound of my brother's indrawn sobs stopped it.

'I wish I'd a' bin a better boy to'n,' he wept as I put my arms around him.

The day of the funeral was bitterly cold with a cruel east wind laced with sleet and snow. My brother had ordered cars for the mourners, but there was an overflow. Numbers of Father's pit butties wanted to carry him to his last rest on their shoulders. In times of great emotional stress Nature provides a safety valve for our sanity by surrounding events with an air of unreality. Ignoring Father's known agnosticism, a little service was held over the coffin outside the cottage, by a local preacher. The little yard, the steps, and the long garden path were crowded with men and women, come to pay their last respects. Bare-headed men with saddened faces, women with tear-filled eyes, huddling together against the bitter wind, singing the beautiful old hymns and finishing with 'Rock of Ages'.

There was no comfort for me in the preacher's words or the sentiment of the hymns; they brought me no visions of a benign Almighty receiving Father's soul. Indeed these man-made notions seemed a betrayal of reality. The sympathy, respect and sense of loss in the singers' faces were beautiful to me, however. I felt grateful and proud that they had held Father in such high esteem. I felt love, too, for the pit-scarred hands holding the coffin, the men's hard shoulders, their brave set faces as they carried their comrade into the teeth of the freezing wind. They carried him in relays, nearly two miles to the church, and every one was glad to take the burden. He was a man.

In spite of all the loving kindness shown me by my neighbours and friends when I came back to London, I could not climb out of my misery. I had not the character to take the first long step out of my slough of despair. I went into labour with my third child a month prematurely. I was taken to Paddington Hospital where I was delivered of a fine boy, and we called him Nicholas. He was perfectly formed, but he lacked the flesh he should have put on had he stayed his full time in the womb. Not for him the cooing joyous baby-talk of a happy fulfilled mother; instead, his round little head was constantly christened with my tears.

I became fearful and anxious about the children, and suffered from an obsession when I took them out that holes would suddenly appear in the pavement and swallow them down. Any form of beauty, from a sunray to a snatch of music, would start me weeping because Father's eyes and ears were closed to it. Selfish in my grief, I failed even to be a wife to Syd. One day his sister called and found me listless and abject as usual. She had been very kind and helpful for a long time, but she now risked my displeasure and our affectionate relationship by giving me a little lecture.

'You can't go on like this, Win,' she upbraided me, 'it isn't fair to the children. What kind of mother are you now with all this misery? And what about Syd? And just think how you're letting your Dad down! Would he have carried on like this? How miserable he would feel to be the cause of all this suffering!'

Letting Father down? She spoke the truth; I was, and it was the very last sin I would wish to commit. It was a cruel little jolt, but I felt deeply ashamed, and I realised that she had given me a straw to grasp. From now on, for Father's sake, I would pull myself together.

And so the healing began, but only just in time. How true were the words of my sister-in-law! I was puzzled and distressed to find that as I combed Chris's hair it began to come out in handfuls, leaving two bald patches. I took him to the doctor. 'Have you had a shock recently?' she asked. Still vulnerable, I burst into tears and told her of my loss. 'Your little boy has been grieving about you; that's the cause of the trouble.' The doctor was a Jewish lady, a humanist if ever there was one. Her surgery was always packed, often with a queue outside as well, but she spared the time to help me with her understanding of bereavement. I came out determined to be a more mature person.

This resolve was soon put to the test, for I had not escaped a physical repercussion either. I began to have spasms of feeling strangely ill, but without any particular pains. I felt I was going to die, my stamina would give out completely, and I got palpitations. I noticed a small lump developing in the front of my neck. Again I went to the doctor, and within three days I was admitted to St Mary's Hospital, Paddington, for the removal of a growth on my thyroid gland. Again I was asked if I had suffered a shock, and the tears welled up within me, but this time I contained them.

Never in my life have I been so cosseted and spoiled as during my week in that hospital. The nurses really seemed like angels, and Syd came to visit me every evening after work. His sister took care of the children, our neighbours sent me fruit and flowers, and all these kind attentions began to heal my pain. Back home again after the operation I felt so much better in every way.

With three children it was a struggle to manage on Syd's wages, and it was difficult for me to get charring work, with a baby and a toddler to see to. But a bit of luck turned up, almost literally on our doorstep. Opposite our tenement was a large block of flats called the 'Mansions', stretching from the pub along the street, round the corner, and on again to end by another big pub. These buildings had three communal stone staircases, three large doorsteps, and of course three sets of stairs down to the basement areas where the dustbins were kept. For sweeping down and scrubbing all these stairs and doorsteps, plus sweeping and sluicing the basement areas, I could earn fifteen shillings. This was done once a week; the old woman who used to do it was now unable. I jumped at the chance; fifteen shillings was a welcome boost to my housekeeping money. The blessing of it was that I could do it and keep half an eye on Richard and the baby at the same time, by putting one in each pram, tied for safety to the iron railings surrounding the mansions.

The sweeping was the worst part of the job, especially the areas, for besides the thick coating of dust all sorts of debris blew down and got trapped. Scrubbing down with bucket after bucket of hot soapy water was quite a pleasure by comparison. Resolutely I coughed my way through the dust, for sometimes there were perks to be had. After I had enjoyed myself sluicing down with water laced with Jeyes' fluid, I felt quite justified in beating the dustmen to the first pickings. The more thoughtful tenants would leave little parcels in clean carrier bags round the bins; odd crockery, a rug with plenty of wear left in it, occasionally clothing, and once, a white Grecian-style vase. Certainly this had a crack down one side, but that could be turned to the wall. I put a jam jar inside the vase for water, and filled it with sprays of the greenery growing among the rubble on the bombsites.

When I had finished sluicing down the areas, I usually had another little area to mop up. Richard, sitting up in his pram, endeared himself to the women passers-by with his beautiful big eyes and ready smile, his mouth open ready for anything they could contribute. I used to check on him every time I fetched water and he always seemed to be eating something. The offerings were varied; a few chips, a chocolate biscuit, a piece of peeled orange, a cold sausage. He must have had a digestion like an ostrich. It all went quite easily down one way, and by gum it came out with no difficulty at the other. 'Tut-tut', some mothers may be saying as they read this. 'Why on earth didn't she have a notice on his pram asking people not to feed him?' In that part of London such snubs to kind intentions would not have gone down very well. Richard's gannet appetite did him no harm; he was never sick, and because of these attentions he never objected to his sessions of waiting by the railings.

Meantime, Chris had started at the school across the road, and was telling the teachers how to go about their business. 'That ain't like a beetle,' he informed the infant teacher when she drew one on the blackboard. Then he marched out of his desk, picked up a piece of chalk, rubbed hers out and drew one himself. His talents did not match his precociousness, and the class laughed loudly at his inferior effort. Justly punished, thought the astonished teacher, but Chris was not at all pleased. When they lined up at playtime for their daily spoonful of malt he dodged out of the queue and ran home to me. There were many occasions when I had to take him back.

A natural extrovert anyway, Chris suffered from the frustrations of a child bright beyond his years. At four and a half years old, without tuition from anyone, he could read fluently with a vocabulary astonishing for his age. I was too busy to notice the phenomenon; it was Mother who pointed it out to me when she was staying with us.

'D'you know, that boy's reading the paper!' she observed with astonishment as Chris sat with the newspaper in front of him. I thought he was just soliloquising. The paper was the *Daily Telegraph*, no less, brought up by Meg wrapped round some soap that she had nicked for me from one of her jobs.

So I pointed to a paragraph and asked Chris to read it, which he did with very little hesitation or difficulty in pronouncing even the longest words. He had no idea himself how he had learned to read. Syd's theory was that his manual had been advertising posters—for example a picture of a packet of tea identifying the word by the product—and he must have gone on from there.

It is more widely recognised now that children of high intelligence have special problems often channelled through lack of understanding into naughtiness. Poor Chris, as the first-born he suffered most as I struggled for my own maternal education.

I do not suppose I was unique in suffering from the illusion during my first pregnancy that this much-wanted baby would grow into a perfect example of humanity. Would it not have love and care lavished upon it, and all the comfort we could provide? If a girl, then she would be as beautiful as my sisters; if a boy, as wise as my father, and at least as handsome as his. I quite overlooked the fact that Syd and I had at least the average amount of flaws in our characters, and that an obstinate streak can be handed down as easily as a fine complexion. I meant well in expecting my children to be infinitely nicer than myself, but what a bad, even cruel, philosophy it was. As the years passed, I realised my mistake and paid for it.

About this time I also got a 'posh' job. Although I was beginning again to count my blessings, sleep still did not come easily. I needed to be absolutely exhausted to fight the melancholia that came with time to think. Through one of her employers, Meg recommended me for an evening job as a general help in the Wimpole Street household of a famous surgeon. It meant that Syd would have to mind the children, a task he did quite well and without too much complaint. His hand was firmer than mine but they seemed none the worse for that.

Because of the way that 'resident' staff came and went so capriciously, my work at Wimpole Street was varied. Perhaps one evening I would just have to sit and clean a tableful of silver-ware, and have a good supper brought in by the cook. Another time I assumed the duties of an absconding housemaid. So I became temporary charlady, surrogate butler, deputy cook, and general dogsbody.

One evening I was met at the door by an absolutely distraught mistress. She had no staff at all; the cook and housemaid had taken umbrage and taken themselves off with it. Two guests were coming to dinner; an elderly and famous Belgian actress and her friend. They could not be put off; it was seven o'clock. The mistress had prepared the dinner for cooking herself, and made the sweets, strawberry angel-cake and apricot compote with cream.

This still left the vegetables to be cooked, and a dish of partridge to be roasted with all the trimmings.

Could I, would I, do it? And also act as parlourmaid? This would mean putting on a black dress left behind by an ex-maid, covering it with a voluminous white overall for doing the cooking, then removing the same to don a maid's apron and cap, taking the food up in the lift to the dining room, and serving it as well.

This was a challenge. I said I would do my best, and hurried into the big kitchen in the basement. I do not know what the guests thought of their hostess's frequent disappearances. She was checking me. Had I laid the table properly? Oh, the beautiful cut glass, the solid silver cutlery, the hand-made lace tablecloth, and the bowls of roses! The exquisite bone-china coffee-cups! The gold-embossed dinner-service! It made me a bundle of nerves just to handle it, but I had a lot more than that to do. Luckily there was no time to think.

With enough pushing I can be very competent. The vegetables were easy enough, and with a dash of luck and a sprinkling of judgement the partridges came out just right. On my own initiative I garnished them with sprays of watercress, then took it all up just on time. Straight-faced despite my inward amusement, I remembered to serve from the left and clear from the right (or was it the other way round?). 'Thank you, *thank* you,' said my mistress's eyes as they caught mine during my parlourmaid role. Then I served coffee in the drawing-room, and politely accepted a complimentary message to the cook from the actress guest.

Back down in the kitchen, surrounded by what seemed acres of washing-up, I complimented myself all round, and then started as kitchen-maid at the sink. No slap-dash clatter washing-up with this lot; everything had to be handled with gingerly reverence. By the time all was in order it was well past midnight. My mistress had boosted my energy with a ten-shilling tip for my efforts, but there were no buses and I had to walk a good mile home. I was too tired even to walk straight. Like one drunk I staggered up the tenement stairs, into the bedroom, and without the energy to undress fell across the bottom of the bed and slept like a log.

The war was receding into memory, food was becoming more plentiful, and our funds were being boosted by my part-time work.

The three little boys were thriving, and we were surrounded by friendly neighbours. Syd was tall and handsome and had put on a bit of weight. In exchange for clothing coupons, the surgeon's wife gave me one of her husband's overcoats and a suit. They fitted Syd well, and he looked a proper toff on Sunday when we all went out together. Now I began to really count my blessings, and little did I know then that another blessing was on the way.

One morning the familiar unmistakable nausea hit me again. It could not be, it just must not be, that I was pregnant again. Nicky, the youngest, was three, our quiver was full, and our tenement rooms stretched to capacity. Dr Marie Stopes could not have let me down again? Thank goodness abortions were almost impossible for the poor in those days, although this pregnancy was the worst, the most nauseous and difficult of them all. This time I did not indulge myself dreaming of bonnet ribbons; it was sure to be a boy. So I just ate my dry oats, and health salts drank all the cider I could lay hands on, and prayed for the months to go by. I knew the women shook their heads and said 'Ah, she's a boy-breeder, that one,' as if it was somehow all my fault.

I had become friendly with a young woman in the Mansions, a sweet Yorkshire girl married to a nice Welsh fellow. She often gave me coffee and biscuits when I was cleaning the stairs by her door. Once she had shyly asked me if I would mind accepting some clothes that her only child, a boy, had grown out of. I had accepted with gratitude, and we had become firm friends. Our windows were opposite each other across the narrow street. I promised her that if the baby arrived in the night I would get Syd to put out something blue or pink on the windowsill to let her know at once. 'But it's sure to be blue,' I told her, defying Fate beforehand.

This time I had decided to have the baby at home, and I warned the friendly tenants I should probably wake them all up with my howls if it happened at night. Meg would not mind; she was all agog, and anxious to be in at the birth. My labour pains started about midnight but it was one o'clock before I felt sure enough to poke Syd awake. He got up and dressed at once as he had to go to the nurses' centre two miles away. Hanging on to the back of the big chair doubled up with pain, I gasped to him, 'Go on, go on, get that gas and air. Hurry up.' I had been through three births without any form of pain-killer; this time I was demanding something, anything. Giving me a quick peck on the cheek he hurried downstairs.

Marylebone Road was almost empty; what buses were still running were not in sight. A taxi came along heading east and Syd jumped out into the road to stop it. 'Come orf it, mate,' said the driver. 'I've turned it in, ain' I, goi'n 'ome.' Hanging on to the door, Syd quickly explained his errand. 'Oh well,' said the cabbie, 'that's different, ennit? Jump in,' and he swung round in the empty road.

Syd asked him to wait outside the nurses' centre while he ran in. The two nurses on duty seemed very calm, gave him the gas-and-air machine in its heavy case, and said they would follow on their bikes in a few minutes. The taxi hurried back and dropped Syd off at the tenement.

'How much do I owe you?' asked Syd.

'Go on, nuffin', mate, nuffin. Wet the baby's 'ead wiv' it. Good luck mate, 'ope it all goes alright fer yer missus,' and he swung away to his doubly-earned rest.

I suppose all was going all right for me, but it was a distressing and very painful sort of all right. As soon as Syd had gone I went into the kitchen. The three boys were sound asleep in their room. The pains were now doubling me up. It was March the eighteenth and bitterly cold; I would make a cup of cocoa for the nurses. Immobilised every other minute by the contractions, I could not seem to get from cupboard to table. Then Syd hurried up the stairs carrying the gas-and-air. He rekindled the fire and sat beside it, cleaning his boots for the morning of all things.

The nurses tip-toed up to our open door, took one look at me, and helped me on to the bed. 'Just in time,' said the elder one. On separate occasions both these nurses had visited me to check up and advise how to prepare the bedroom for the birth. They were friendly nice girls and they knew we had three little boys.

The last stages of labour had begun, but I was too engrossed in the painful procedure to remember the gas-and-air. 'It's a girl, a beautiful girl!' they chorused ecstatically under their breath, as soon as our daughter emerged. Their kind faces were full of pleasure and congratulation. Warm from the womb, and I think still attached to the womb, and to the umbilical cord, they put her straight into my arms; a precious moment, and I loved them for the gesture. The new-born in the animal kingdom gets its immediate welcome from the tongue or nudging of the mother. In hospitals at that time the babies were all too often washed, wrapped up, and taken away without being put in the mother's arms, and not brought to her for hours, a bad breach of primitive instinct when the birth has gone without complications.

When all was done, the baby tucked up and comfy against the pillows, they got their cocoa and cake. Syd had managed that as well as all the hot water, and his boots! Then they left, going down the stairs very quietly. Syd came in to look at his daughter and knelt by the cradle as if afraid to breathe on her. As he got up and turned to me, the look of thanks he gave me was never to be forgotten. 'My two ladies,' he said, kneeling down with one arm round me and one round the cradle. Not a soul could be heard stirring in the rest of the tenement.

Meg left for work in the mornings just before six, to do a little office-cleaning before going on to her regulars. As usual at lunch-time she popped up to me to dish out her daily dollop of news.

'Isn't Win well then?' she asked when Syd opened the door.

'She's fine,' smirked Syd. 'Pop in and have a look at her.'

'Poor Meg, her eyes nearly popped out of her head at the sight of the *two* of us. 'It's a girl,' I bragged, 'it really is.'

'But when did you have her?'

'Half-past two this morning.'

'But I never heard a sound, nothing. I can't hardly believe it,' and she looked again into the cradle for verification. She was at a loss. Her expression said it all. How could I do it to her? She had been robbed. All that going on, and she had missed it, slept through it all!

By the evening I was forgiven; up she came with a plate of daintily cooked supper for me.

In our tiny corner the coming of our daughter was treated like a royal birth. Syd had put a pink cloth on the windowsill, and this must have sent my friend in the mansions post-haste to a toyshop for a doll. She must have spent the rest of the day sewing its glamorous outfit of silk, lace, and ribbons.

By the following evening our baby had acquired eight silk dresses trimmed with pink, bootees and bonnets, and a pink frilled pram-cover. Syd kept answering our door to a conveyor belt of food offerings, and for the first time since I had known him he dashed out and bought me a bunch of flowers. It was almost overwhelming.

The three boys, however, were not unduly impressed. After Syd gave them their breakfast, they were rather taken aback by his lining them up, brushing their hair, making sure their hands and faces were spotless, socks pulled up, shoes shined, before leading them into the royal presence. Standing them round the cradle at a respectful distance he announced proudly, 'This is your new sister.'

'Pooh, she don't look much, ain't got no 'air,' said Richard in a stage whisper after the inspection. Syd, of course, adored his sons, and he had never hinted at the slightest disappointment about my single-sex reproduction system. But fathering a daughter seemed to soften his character at once, and put me a couple of notches up on the wifely pedestal. For me, the choice of her name was no problem. I had read the 'Forsyte Saga', and I felt a profound joy for Soames when his second wife gave birth to his daughter and murmured 'my petite fleur'. There and then I made up my mind that if ever I had a daughter Fleur should be her name. Syd agreed, but he feared that odd names could be a handicap to his children and he liked Jennifer. So she became Jennifer Fleur; 'our Jen' for short.

The problem now was our cramped accommodation and lack of amenities. We put our name down on the Council housing list. Two years later a letter arrived inviting us to the housing department at the Town Hall. Here I was handed the keys of a second floor flat in a post-war block three streets away. If the accommodation suited us, it was ours.

Suited us? I could not believe our luck! It was palatial, it was luxurious, far better than many flats I had gone charring in! There was a communal courtyard for the children, each tenant had a brick-built shed, and there was a large modern laundry with the latest facilities for the tenants' use at a token price. The flat had piped hot water, and consisted of a hall, bathroom, separate toilet, good-sized kitchen with plenty of cupboards, a stove and a fridge and a hatchway service to a spacious lounge-diner. Three good bedrooms opened up from a passage fitted with a built-in wardrobe and broom cupboards. There were two small balconies, a roomy airing cupboard always hot, as were the chromium towel rails in bathroom and kitchen. Coal was delivered from the landing through an aperture in the wall into a coal-cupboard just inside the front door. All our rubbish went into a similar aperture on the landing, and slid down a chute. I would bet that Aladdin felt no more gratified when the Genie opened the door to his treasure cave than I did. The rent would be double what we were paying, but now the three boys all went to school and there were plenty of charring jobs about.

Unable to contain my delight, I returned to the Housing Department, deliriously grateful to accept the flat. The lady at the desk was very nice, 'but I must warn you,' she began. Then she told me we would be living over one of the most difficult of tenants whose behaviour had already affected the three previous occupants of the flat above her so badly that they had asked for transfer. Investigating her complaints, the Council had found most of them either quite unjustified or grossly exaggerated. She advised me to ignore this tenant's behaviour, as they now intended to take no notice of her complaints. Feeling full of magnanimity towards the world in general, complainers included, I said I was sure we could manage. To get such accommodation we would bend over backwards to be the quietest and most considerate tenants possible.

After moving into our grand new flat I gradually began to understand why slum-dwellers, uprooted and taken to bright new towns, confound well-meaning sociologists by longing to go back. After the first flush of excitement had faded, as I moved about in my streamlined warm kitchen and polished the smooth composition floors of our big new flat, I became aware that something was missing. We had left the tenement behind us, and we had left a community. Nobody was bringing a cup of tea to my door, nobody was having a chat on the landing, there was no smiling face in the opposite window. There was no nosey vital Meg clattering upstairs full of scandal and good humour, no dozy sexy Lally with her pale face and eternal fag. Syd's sister, too, had moved away now.

On these new big clean stairways there was no fellow-feeling. Everybody seemed in a hurry, exchanging perhaps a tiny smile or a little nod and sometimes no greeting at all. These fine new glossy doors were always shut. They opened only partly for the inmates to slip through, and then not very often. The old tenement was only half a mile away round a couple of corners, and sometimes Meg came to us and sometimes I saw Lally in the market, but the old feeling never came back. Something had been destroyed and would not revive. Never mind, I thought, this place is so much better for the children.

But I wish I could blot out the memories of my own guilt about the children for what I did to them in the next few months. For a start, I became that most unsuitable creature, an over-house-proud mother. That flat had gone to my head and partly covered my heart. After living in the tenement I never really felt at home in the flat, but more like a daily cleaner. Not a speck or spot of dirt or dust, not any sort of muddle would I tolerate. Our old furniture and secondhand rugs and mats were simply not good enough for our new grandeur, and I was determined to replace them. These resolves and the constant necessity of keeping quiet for the sake of 'Her downstairs', caused me to make more demands of my children than I should, sometimes more than they could bear. And I was blind to it! Our Nicky, born premature after his grandfather's sudden death, was especially affected. My behaviour made him a highly-strung nervous little boy, and he responded with what we took to be wilful naughtiness. Excessive nagging was the last thing he needed, but Heaven forgive me, that was what he and his siblings got!

As soon as the boys went to school and I had fixed up toddler Jenny in her pram, I was off with her, putting in an hour or two's charring wherever I could get it. On Saturdays Syd had to take them all out whatever the weather so that I could go washing-up in a fish-and-chip shop. One objective filled my thoughts, the purple patterned carpet in Jordan's window. This large store did not oblige its customers with credit but would allow payment for goods in advance. The going rate for charring was half-a-crown an hour. I earned this mostly on my kness, scrubbing and polishing floors, or washing paintwork down. Be it half-a-crown, three and nine-pence, or five shillings a stint, I did not keep it in my hand long enough to get warm. I hurried back to Jordan's to knock a bit more off the nine-guinea price of the carpet.

One day when I was eagerly handing in three shillings to the man at the cash desk, I saw him give a very meaningful glance to a male shopwalker looking on. I read the message, and felt a flush of anger and embarrassment come over my face. So that's what they thought! That I was 'on the game', and for such paltry sums as that! I did not know which implication annoyed me the more. After that I saved up my earnings and paid weekly.

Pretty soon, between our new carpet and our rugs and mats, every part of the flat except the tiled kitchen floor was covered, hopefully to reduce still further what noise our shoe-less feet made. Apart from meals, baths, and bedtime, we made every effort to take the children out. On winter Sundays we had the frozen parks almost to ourselves, and I took sandwiches and flasks of soup to warm us up when our aching legs forced a rest. We were banishing ourselves from our new-found comfort for the sake of an anonymous nuisance whom we did not know and had hardly even seen. When we were indoors because we had to be, the monastic atmosphere was almost comical.

Meanwhile the object of all this consideration, 'Her downstairs', never even took her turn at cleaning her part of the stairs. No matter, I scrubbed her flight as well as ours. Not surprisingly, my supine attitude and conciliatory efforts did not appease, but rather made matters worse. She took the offensive and opened her campaign to drive us out.

I was flabbergasted one day, as I passed her door, to see her open it, give me one vicious look of concentrated hatred and then slam it with all her might. She must have sat behind her curtains watching who was coming in, because she treated my women friends from the old tenement to the same door-slamming performance. It was puzzling and hurtful for them and humiliating for me. I was further disheartened when I was doing the washing in the communal laundry and a woman from across the courtyard said, 'What a shame you gotta live over that old cow; she says you're an awful woman. Mind, she said just the same about the people before you. The last one had to go to the hospital with her nerves before the Council give her a transfer. Hateful old cow! If I was you I'd ask to be moved. Put the poison in.' I felt sick and near to tears. To be the object of a well-founded dislike is an uncomfortable experience. To be held in contempt without any reason, especially if prepared and anxious to please, is like being locked in a room with no window or door. If we were giving cause for complaint, why did she not approach me and explain what it was? I realised later, that that was the last thing she wanted.

One day the two youngest boys came in from school and asked me, 'What's that woman shaking her fist at us for when we come up the stairs, Mum?'

'Were you making a noise?'

'No, Mum, honest. Just walking up quiet.'

So they, too, were being puzzled and hurt by her. Chris came in with the same tale. 'That woman downstairs is a nutter,' he said boldly. 'Shook her fist at me as I came by her door. I made a face at her as though I was mad as well.' He was quite unabashed and a better psychologist than I, but I reprimanded him severely for his reaction. I expect he continued his little vendetta on the quiet. Left alone long enough, he would have driven her out.

Another time I saw our little Jenny coming across the courtyard. I began to think she was a long time coming up, so I went down to investigate. I found her cowering, literally cowering, in a corner of the stairway. Her large brown eyes were filled with fear and she was trembling.

'What's the matter, darling?' I cried. 'Why didn't you come on up?' I took her in my arms, and with a lot of cuddling and coaxing I got it out of her. She was scared to come by that woman's door because she made a face at her like a witch. Oddly enough, just recently, Jenny had worried us two or three times by waking up in the night with nightmares. These had made her delirious for a short while so we had to take her into our bed till morning and by then she had forgotten. Now I put two and two together, and realised that I was dealing with a villainess, a real witch. Looking back, I cannot understand why I did not go down straightaway, and in the local idiom, 'sort' er aht'. Instead I felt hopeless, and inadequate.

'Her downstairs' wisely ignored Syd's comings and goings, so her behaviour had not perturbed him unduly. After all, the Council had warned us and said she should not be taken notice of, and that was his opinion. 'Take no notice at all of the miserable old faggot.' He often became irritable with me because of my perpetual insistence on silence, and did not think she was worth a confrontation. As for her husband, poor little bloke, an inoffensive wraith who came and went and never turned his head to speak or acknowledge anyone, he and his personality had parted long ago.

Syd expected his boys to be tough enough to withstand the eccentric behaviour of a miserable middle-aged woman. So they were, but I knew he would feel differently about his small vulnerable daughter. When the boys escorted Jenny home from school they stayed outside playing until teatime. When Syd came home they were sitting quietly indoors, and while he was eating I told him about Jenny's reaction on the stairs. I regretted it instantly. His face went pale, his eyes darkened with anger, and he put down his knife and fork. Getting up he said quietly, 'I'm going down to sort this out.' It was the way he said it, and the look of him, that reminded me of what sort of temper he had when thoroughly roused. Just then I really feared for the safety of 'Her downstairs'.

'Oh, no, no!' I begged, hanging on to his coat-tails. 'Finish your tea and calm down a bit.' This only added to his exasperation, and the boys too sensed his dangerous mood. I began to cry and the children joined in. His hand was on the doorknob, but the sight of our distress made him pause. 'Syd, Syd,' I cried, 'think how bad it would look if you go assaulting her, you a big strong man. People would not understand. I'll just have to write to the Council and complain about her.'

'Look,' he said, 'look, I'm not goin' to hurt her, just frighten her a bit, get this bloody silly stunt stopped for good. She won't slam the door in *my* face.'

I pleaded with him again and eventually he sat back down to his meal. 'Right,' he said. '*You* see to it then. Better not happen again. That's all.' It was lucky for her Syd did not catch sight of her that evening, and from then on I fetched Jenny up the stairs.

The time had come for Syd's annual holiday, two whole weeks off, fourteen days when we could all be together to do just what we liked, go where we wanted! Rather gloomily he ripped open his pay-packet. Taking his tobacco money and few shillings, he handed me the rest. 'There,' he said, 'a decent week's pay!' Three weeks' money at one go seemed quite a lot to me. Cautiously, providently, I paid three weeks' rent in advance, and three weeks' milk money. Then such affluence went to my head and I bought the four children a pair of winter shoes and wellington boots each. I counted what I had left of the money; I had made a tidy hole in it. Somewhat dismayed, I still felt sure I could manage the three weeks until the next pay with careful budgeting, but it would have to be careful indeed.

Never mind! It was August, and the weather had turned warm and dry. After breakfast Syd took all the children out until lunchtime. This gave me the chance to get the housework and shopping done, prepare a meal, and pack food and drink for our afternoon and evening out in one of the parks. The first day they came in from their morning walk in high good humour. Chris and Richard smirked at each other across the lunch table; obviously they were enjoying some little secret, but did not intend to tell me.

As soon as I had washed up we set off on our usual free excursion, taking our books, some balls, and a doll for Jenny. We decided to go to Regent's Park, the far end of it near the Zoo and the Canal. Here we had one of our special 'places', quiet and lonely, with a little hill to roly-poly down, well away from traffic, and sometimes a barge to look at, its prow barely wrinkling the limpid waters of the tree-lined canal. The children could play in safety, and we could sit on the lush uncut grass and read, and sometimes do nothing at all but stare at the trees that leaned over the water, or watch the slow progress of a chestnut leaf sailing down to a watery grave. The sun shone on us, but its full glare and heat were tempered by the maze of limbs and twigs above. Traffic rumbled in the distance, and sometimes we saw a squirrel. So greedy were we for the sylvan peace we often went the long way round, just to enjoy the tree-lined quiet roads and the mock rusticity of St John's Wood.

This day Chris led us on an unfamiliar detour, and we came across a block of large war-wrecked Victorian houses. In front, alongside their mosaic paths and porticoes, were small gardens strewn with rubble through which were struggling all manner of half-hearted weeds, seeding before their time, desperate for reproduction. Tall wooden gates mysteriously surviving, led through an enclosed passage to tradesmen's entrances at the back. The boys ran forward and unlatched the first of these gates.

'Come on, Mummy, come and have a look!'

'It was only because Richard couldn't wait to get to the park to have a pee that we found it!'

We followed them through the gate and shut it behind us. I could hardly believe my eyes. There in front of us was an oasis of green stretching the full length behind the ten bombed residences, an acre of long grass, unpruned shrubs, tumbledown walls, a magnificent mulberry tree, and not a single soul in sight! We had found ourselves a country holiday estate, rent-free, right in the heart of London! No park-keepers, no keep-off-the-grass signs, no scouting around for a spare seat! We moved in. I was as ecstatic about their discovery as the children. The boys had trees to climb, walls to crouch behind to shoot the Indians, a jungle to creep through stalking the enemy. Syd and I spread ourselves out on a patch of long grass, and Jenny played mother to her doll in a make-believe house between shrubs. We had books, drinks, and food, and the glorious sun overhead. Jenny had her afternoon nap, and so did Syd, and I had a struggle to keep awake. Syd reached up into the mulberry tree and gathered enough to make a big pot of jam, the boys began to flag, and we made for home. I was thrilled to pluck some sprays of foliage from the shrubs to arrange around our sitting-room.

Had we been the sort of family to say our goodnight prayers we should have prayed that no-one else would discover our paradise. No one did. Right through till the Sunday before Syd went back to work the weather remained gloriously sunny. That holiday in our private Elysium acted like a balm on all our nerves. We woke up on the Sunday morning to rain-drenched streets and a sky full of scurrying clouds threatening more rain. At last the weather had broken, and I was broke, too. Apart from Syd's fares to work I had three shillings and ninepence left, very little food in the house, and six days to go before Syd got his next wages. It was my fault; I should not have bought those shoes and wellingtons for all of them in one go. Luckily I had paid the rent and milk in advance.

Well, I would have to borrow off Meg, much as I hated the idea. Now we had moved it did not seem right to go on asking her, and it would have to be a big borrow, thirty shillings or so, however carefully I budgeted. We had no money for bus fares, but this did not worry us. It had stopped raining now, so we decided to go for a walk; up Edgeware Road looking in the shop windows, through Hyde Park to the Serpentine, and if we felt like it and could dodge the showers, we could go to the museums. I left it till the last minute to tell Syd of our bankruptcy; not that he would be surprised.

Londoners do not patronise Hyde Park much in wet weather. It was almost empty; anyway I was glad the children had their new wellingtons on in that long wet grass. Hands behind his back, head disconsolately down, Syd walked by my side. Suddenly he bent down and picked something up from the grass; it was a soaking wet, neatly folded ten shilling note. Honest moralists might think he should have taken it to a police station; I must confess it never crossed my mind. A good deal of cuddling and kissing goes on in Hyde Park, amateur and professional, but few men get a warmer hug and kiss than I gave Syd there and then when he handed it to me. We were solvent again, at least for a couple of days. Now I felt like a spring lamb again and raced the boys across the grass.

By Tuesday I was broke again. Oh well! After Syd had had his tea I would go round to the tenement and ask Meg for the loan of a pound.

Coming home from work Syd used to get off the trolley-bus at Paddington Green and walk through the market. Apart from the sawdust in his hair and down his shirt, the only perk of his job was a daily sack of wood blocks, which we stored to eke out the coal in the winter. We had many a merry fire, a silent comfort that even 'Her downstairs' could not complain about. With a sack on his back a man must perforce bow his head. This day, as he made his way along the market, among the debris in the gutter Syd's eagle eye noticed a piece of paper of a distinctive reddish hue. Putting his sack down he picked up the little piece of paper. Yes, it was, another neatly-folded ten-shilling note. The road sweepers were coming down that side, and no doubt this would have been a little bonus for one of them. 'Sorry, mate,' thought Syd. 'To each according to his needs,' and he brought it home to me. For a moment we both felt a bit awestruck by the coincidence, but I was elated; with care I could manage another couple of days.

However, by Thrusday, our cupboard was again nearly as bare as Old Mother Hubbard's. Chris decided to go round knocking on doors asking for old papers and magazines; he could get a few coppers at the rag-shop for a huge bundle of papers, and he would buy us some buns. It was a lovely day and I would have liked to take them out, but I had accumulated a huge pile of washing. Richard was pressing me to let him take Nicky to the park on their own. I gave in eventually, but he had to solemnly promise to ask a lady, and it had to be a lady, to see them across the two busy roads on the way, and that they would only go in the childrens' playground, and were to ask the lady in charge to tell them when it was half-past three. Then they would be home by four o'clock without fail. Richard promised faithfully to abide by these conditions, nodding eagerly at every one, his brown eyes fixed sincerely on mine. I rustled up a little food for them, then I took Jenny and my huge bundle of washing over to the laundry. Our entrepreneur paper merchant, Chris, could look after himself. Cockney boys of his age, especially one who had passed for Marylebone Grammar at eleven years old, had their wits about them.

We were not going to have a very rich stew that evening. A shilling's worth of scrag end (for the dog!), a few pennies worth of potherbs, and two eggs for pancakes, had emptied my purse again. But worrying about our dinner took second place when by half-past four none of the boys had come home. The stew was simmering and so was I, and I kept going with Jenny to the street corner to see if they were coming. I had forgotten to tell them which route to come home, and if I went the wrong way they might come home tired and hungry to an empty flat.

By the time Syd was due in I was frantic. Chris and he arrived at the same time, Chris proudly carrying a bag of penny iced buns. I was too distraught to thank him at the time as I quickly explained to Syd about Richard and Nicky.

'Seven hours they've been gone, seven hours,' I wailed.

'Keep calm,' said Syd. 'I'll go and find them.' He swallowed a cup of tea. 'I've got my fare for the morning, but I'll use it now for a bus to the park and keep an eye out for 'em on the way. It'll be quicker. Now don't worry, you know how kids forget the time when they're playing.' Don't worry? I could see that under his calm front he was worried.

'I'll go and look for 'em the other way,' said Chris.

It was just gone eight when I saw them all plodding their way homewards. If Chris and Syd had not been with the younger boys I would hardly have recognised them. They were both covered from top to bottom with soot. I did not care; my four men were all there safe and sound and the relief was indescribable. 'Little perishers!' said Syd. 'I found them in the park, down that bank near the canal. They'd found a heap of soot dumped there by the barges.' Syd looked tired and unusually pale, but neither of us had the heart to scold them just then.

When the boys had sat down to eat Syd drew me by the hand into the kitchen. Sitting down, he rubbed his brow and said 'Well, I don't know what to say. You'll never believe this, Win, it's making me feel quite queer. Look what I found again!' He opened his hand and in it was yet another neatly-folded ten-shilling note.

'Where on earth did you find that?'

'Well, I got on top of the bus, you see, to watch each side of the pavement in case I spotted the boys. I was the only one up there. A penny slipped out of my hand down the back of the seat. I had to get it back before the conductor came up, so I squeezed my fingers down there and up came the penny and this little bit of paper, another ten-bob note folded up just like the others. It's weird.'

I began to feel a bit spooky myself. My agnostic convictions were getting a shaking. Was this money manna? Pennies from heaven? A hundred and twenty at a time, sent for convenience in the form of neat little notes?

I did not dwell too long on the matter. After all, it was pay-day to-morrow so there was no need to stint too harshly. While the family sat eating their anaemic stew I popped out for the second course, six fourpennies of fried fish and six-penn'orth of chips.

For weeks after that Syd walked on the kerbs with his eyes on the gutter, but all he ever found was a broken biro and a comb full of dandruff. Eventually I stopped him, but I sometimes wonder what we have missed.

With a young family, winter inevitably brings its quota of ills and chills. Nicky had come home from school on the Friday with the sniffles, and by Sunday he was feverish. After an early lunch Syd went out with the other three. I tucked Nicky up in an armchair by the fire in the sitting-room. Then I went into the kitchen to do some ironing and kept an eye on him through the open serving-hatch. We were both very quiet, and at least we were not doing anything to offend 'Her downstairs', I thought. The ironing finished I made a glass of orange juice to take into my feverish little boy.

As I got to his chair I froze with horror. Suddenly a strange unseeing flash came into his eyes, his body contorted, he went purple and then pale, and his breathing laboured. I had never seen a fit or convulsion before. Panic-stricken, I held the writhing convulsing little body tightly in my arms until the spasm passed. Ignorant, terrified, heartbroken by his distress, holding him tight in the blanket, I ran out across the landing and knocked on the door of the elderly couple at the other end. They were a gentle nice old pair who always had a kind word and a smile for us and the children.

'Oh, please, please help me,' I sobbed. 'My little boy has had a fit. Can you get the doctor for me? I mustn't leave him, I mustn't!'

'All right, my dear,' she answered kindly and calmly. 'Yes, of course, right away,' and she turned to call her husband.

I ran back to the fire, and almost at once she followed me in, carrying a glass. Nicky appeared to be asleep now, so I sat down by the fire with him on my lap. 'Drink this drop of brandy, dear,' she said. 'My husband's gone down to the phone box. Doctor'll be here soon. I'll make you a nice cup of tea; I can see you've had a nasty shock. Where's your hubby?' I told her he had taken the other children out. She sat there with me till the doctor came, and then till Syd returned.

Usually, once a doctor is on the scene nothing seems quite as bad as it did. This time, despite her calmness and efficiency, the tumult inside me was hardly stilled. Yes, Nicky had had a convulsion, she said almost casually, as she examined him. But this sometimes happened to children with high temperatures. Yet Nicky's temperature was not all that high. The doctor confessed herself a bit puzzled and asked if the child had been under any sort of stress lately. She left medicine, and would call again on the morrow.

How incredibly precious we realise our children are when danger threatens them. Nicky, vulnerable and ill and dependent on my care; how bitterly I regretted every reprimand and unjust scolding I had given him. Stress? Of course, of course. The realisation of my guilt was almost more than I could bear; my melancholia at the time of his birth and my selfish indulgence in it afterwards; keeping him quiet because of 'Her downstairs'; this bloody posh flat. How cruelly selfish I had been with my priorities! Nag, nag, nag, that's all I did.

That night I spent at Nicky's bedside, watching his every breath, terrified of another convulsion.

The next day the doctor decided further tests should be done in case Nicky was suffering from a form of epilepsy. I kept him home

from school for three months and gave up all my charring jobs.
Syd slept in the boys' room so that I could have Nicky in my
bed. An appointment was made for an E.E.G. test at St Mary's
Hospital, and for regular visits to a neurological specialist at the
Childrens' Hospital. Nothing definite emerged from the inves-
tigations, but during these three months Nicky distressed us all
with another though milder convulsion. As far as we know that
was the last, and he has grown into a strong well-balanced man, a
good husband, and father to three children. During this time of
trial I was amazed to discover how many families had a similar
problem to face. I only hope that in the long run they were as
lucky as we.

The strain of bringing up four children in a flat surrounded by
busy dangerous roads; the perpetual worry of 'Her downstairs';
the lack of sleep in case Nicky had a turn; at the same time
struggling to be, for everyone's sake, a calm and kind mum; all this
left me exhausted, with my nerve-ends in tatters. Gradually the
worry of Nicky subsided and I began to think about going out to
work again. Also our rent had risen little by little till we were now
paying twice as much, so I was glad to accept the chance of a
Saturday job washing-up in a fish-and-chip shop.

This meant that Syd would have to cope with the children most
of the day. Quite apart from 'Her downstairs', we had always taken
them out for all the fresh air they could get. So between breakfast
and an early Saturday lunch Syd took them out, and then again
for the afternoon and evening while I was at work. They always
had a fish-and-chip supper to look forward to, bought out of my
earnings.

The fish-and-chip shop was in the crowded street-market that
ran along the front of our flats. It was owned by Sam, a very
untypical member of the Jewish fraternity; he did not believe in
pleading or wooing or wheedling for custom, not Sam. Sam stood
his ground and defied the world, customers included. His fish and
chips were superb, and his temper appalling. He sold over the
counter, and also to the dozen or so tables for dinners at the back
of the shop.

Sam had been there as long as anyone could remember, and the
years of self-incarceration in that atmosphere had taken their toll.
He was beginning to look like a fish, a fish out of water, a

lugubrious cod on a slab, a fish with a chip on his shoulder. His pale formless face, the watery blue eyes, the receding close-cut grey hair, the large rubbery toothless mouth, the piscine lack of humour—he bore more than a passing resemblance to the poor creatures that earned him his living. Sam knew that he did the best fried fish in the world, and the world had just better come and buy it or else. When they came too quickly for him, that did not suit and they got a cussing, and when trade was slow the blaspheming was even worse.

His opening hours were elastic. Each Saturday he cooked the same enormous quota of fish; in winter he effed and blinded the queueing customers who were making life hard for him and his assistant fryer; in summer he would still be sitting in his empty shop effing and blinding the occasional passer-by for not coming in to buy the last lone piece displayed in glory in the window. He *would not* leave until everything was sold, but if all his stock went too early he cursed his customers for leaving him hours of idleness to spend at home with a wife he detested.

His fryer had been with him for years; tall and thin, his hair, body, and overall saturated with frying-oil vapour, he was like a piece of greasy string. The flat-footed Cockney waitress must have been nudging seventy. Sam gave her the sack every half-hour or so, insulting her with such epithets as 'an effin' dehydrated ruptured old duck', all of which she was expected to ignore, and did. New customers had been known to run out, and some brave souls ticked him off for his language and behaviour, but never the Cockney women who queued for his succulent wares.

'Christ, Sam, s'cold enough ter freeze them things orf a brass monkey today.'

'Garn, eff off.'

'Wosser matter, Sam? D'yer 'ave ter use a winkle-pin ter get it out s'mornin?'

'Eff off.'

Like his waitress, they ignored his rudeness. His fish was worth it, and they knew that he often shoved half the price back with the fish-and-chips if the customer was old and doddery.

My job was to stand at the sink in front of the window and cope with the piles of washing-up. Right beside me was a boiling urn from which I made pots of tea for the diners and jugfuls for the stallholders to take away. In between, and when I could manage it,

I dashed to help old Flossie clear the tables. Nearby, Sam was in charge of the till, the clink of the coins as he flung them in, his heavenly orchestra.

For him, Sam was reasonably polite to me, except when I asked him for soda or washing-up liquid, or dish-cloths. Nothing would persuade him to lay out a farthing on these necessities, and I had to take my own. He paid me half-a-crown an hour, gratefully telling me to bugger-off when nearly all his stock was sold. He knocked nothing at all off the price of the fish-and-chips I bought, but I still got a bargain.

That job, the infinite variety of Sam's insults, matched by the repartee of his Cockney customers, glimpsing the polyglot crowds passing the window, hurrying eagerly home with the warm newspaper-wrapped bundle for our supper, my few shillings' earnings swelling out my lean purse, looking forward to the hot bath that I really needed, my lovely kiddies enjoying the fish; yes, Saturday was quite a day.

Some months later old Sam's frustrations and blasphemies came to an end. Everyone around was shocked and truly sorry to hear that he had suddenly dropped dead. His widow and the fryer carried on the business, but it was never the same without Sam.

One memory of old Sam lives with me still like a photograph. Meg and I, returning from the music-hall at nearly midnight, passed his shop. In the window was the last lone piece of cod, and leaning on the counter above it was old Sam, gazing lugubriously at the dark cold street. I could see his lips moving as he cursed the world for not buying that fish. I knew he could not leave it; I had to put him out of his misery. 'Hold on, Meg,' I said, and I went back and bought it. He could not manage to smile, but he gave me quite a warm grunt.

After Sam's sudden death the job lost its flavour and became just another tiresome job, and a smelly one. Word came through on the charwomen's grapevine of a job that might suit me near Regent's Park. This one, too, turned out to have a rather fishy flavour. It was in a flat in one of the houses in a Nash Terrace. The facade of the tall narrow house was indeed architecturally lovely, but the interior was falling into a state of decay. It had recently been bought by a charming lady civil servant. She was a spinster in her forties and planned to live on the rents during her retirement. She shared the basement and ground floor with her recently-widowed Welsh mother.

Two single gentlemen each had a room on the next floor. Above them a small flat was rented by a couple; she a masseuse with the business name of Miss La Monte, and he with no business at all but to live on her earnings. At that time my knowledge of sexual deviations, despite Lally, could have been written on the back of the proverbial stamp, mostly owing to my lack of interest in the subject. I knew hazily about 'queers', but a massage parlour was still an unknown quantity. I accepted them, and the adverts for colonic irrigation, as a private medical service.

Certainly, on the morning Miss La Monte opened her door to me she wore a starched overall as virginal as any hospital nurse's. Other than that, with a few exotic fruits pinned into her high contorted jet-black coiffure, she would have made a stand-in for Carmen Miranda. Her French accent was as thick as the make-up on her rather coarse lascivious little face. She wore very high-heeled shoes and sheer black stockings. No wonder she had to practise privately, I thought, no self-respecting hospital matron would employ such a common-looking person. Her husband was on the point of going out. Had he stood still, I could have mistaken him for a wax model in a West End store window. He looked too immaculately handsome to be flesh and blood. His dark hair and moustache were flecked with just the right amount of grey to set off his flawless features and his after-shave-lotioned pink and white complexion. He topped six feet, and she just over five feet in her spindly heels. She looked up at him as though he were a god, and by God she was welcome to him, I thought, as he took a long caressing glance at himself in the landing mirror.

The flat had a bedroom, sitting-room, bathroom, toilet, and tiny kitchen. It would be my job to clean these rooms, and the landing and two flights of carpeted stairs, and answer the front door to her clients during my two hours. An elderly, very respectable-looking widow named Mrs Murphy also came. All she had to do was sit by the phone in the sitting-room. The clients came by appointment about every half-hour. I was surprised that they were all men, and even more surprised that so many were young. They bounded up the stairs so eager, so agile, whatever did the likes of these need a massage for? I wondered. I did become quite concerned, however, for one of her customers, a really old man, in his eighties I thought. He could hardly climb the stairs; I could have carried him up quicker. I thought a vigorous massage would just about finish him off for good, and sometimes I wondered if he would even make it up the stairs. Still, he kept coming, so I presumed she was doing him good.

The walls were rather thin between the rooms, and after a client went into the bedroom I could hear the sound of smacking on bare flesh for a minute or two. It was odd the way Mrs Murphy would suddenly burst into snatches of song when a client began to moan a bit. I found out that she only came in the mornings; Miss La Monte had a young woman assistant in the afternoons and she was a 'foreigner' as well. During (funny) business hours the husband kept out of the way, and just in case a client was still there he used a special ringing code on the doorbell.

My first half-hour was spent cleaning the bedroom before the first client was due. One day I was in there conscientiously hoovering and I opened a cupboard to clean its base. I was immensely surprised to find in there a number of riding-crops and whips and boots. Somehow I could not picture Miss La Monte on a horse!

I began to have my suspicions; this was a very queer set-up. But hypocritically I was reluctant to admit it to my conscience. The work was easy and she often gave me a couple of shillings over the odds. However, one day, the elderly Welsh mother of the landlady approached me as I emptied the rubbish basket into the dustbin. She was nearly as green as I was, poor old dear, but as a dedicated chapel-goer she was perturbed about the constant stream of men going upstairs.

'I shall have to speak to my daughter about it. It looks so bad, and I don't like the look of that woman either. Indeed she pays a terrible high rent, but I think we'd be better off with someone more respectable for a cheaper rent.'

I was now inclined to agree with her. It did seem rather sad and sordid that men should find relief in such a fashion, especially when I thought of all the lonely girls and women there were about. That this was indeed the set-up here was proven to me the very next morning. Mrs Murphy did not turn up to answer the phone and enliven the morning with her strategic bursts of song, and

Miss La Monte herself had to go out somewhere urgently. I was alone in the flat, and the phone rang. I answered it.

The caller was a man, and I told him Miss La Monte was out, I was only the daily cleaner and would he ring later. To my astonishment he immediately suggested that I would do. Could I meet him in his car by Regent's Park and do a special service for him and he would pay me fifteen pounds? Special service? All my special services of that nature were devoted exclusively to Syd! I slammed the phone down.

An unknown voice, coming from someone I had never seen, asking such an intimate a thing from someone he had never seen, it was like a mental and emotional rape. My puritanical impulses came to the boil. I got my coat, overlooked the two mornings' wages I had earned, and hurried away out of Miss La Monte's life. I was only a char, and my job was to make things clean, but she was too unclean for me.

My observations had given me a clue to the war of the sexes; a cold war, cold because of woman's attitudes as judged by man. But a true woman likes the path to sex strewn with compliments and flowers, a path that twists and turns and meanders, taking its time to reach its goal while she practises her femininity. The urgent need in the loins of man makes him want to tread rough-shod and unhindered to his ultimate desire. Bridging the gap between these extremes, the Miss La Montes extract their greedy toll-gate fees.

It is no wonder that the rich have town houses and country houses. When I was fourteen and had to leave my beloved Forest of Dean and my cottage home, for a life of service in London, it had seemed my heart was breaking. However, like a baby at the mother's breast, I was gradually weaned to the mixed feeding of our wonderful capital.

At about the half-way point on my journeys home on the long-distance coach during holidays, a certain black-and-white Elizabethan cottage became the frontier of my opposing tastes. 'Dear London', I mentally promised as I passed this landmark, 'I'll be back'; and 'Dear Forest, I'll be back', I promised on my return to the city.

After twenty-six years in London, married to a Londoner, with four Cockney offspring, I had begun to consider myself a

Londoner. Only occasionally had I felt a pang for my country origins. Now the tables began to turn, and more and more often I felt like an exiled Forester. The strain of living over such a difficult neighbour, the problem of Nicky's nerves, the traffic dangers for the children, the doubts about their future, the claustrophobia of the streets compared with the wild sweet country freedom I had enjoyed, all this brought on a recurring dream. In this dream I ran and ran all the way from a London which had turned into dust. At last I reached the green, grassy, dew-wet bank near the chestnut tree where we used to play houses. In an ecstasy of relief I threw myself down on to the wet grass and buried my face in it, running my hands over its damp clean freshness, adding my tears of thanks to those of Nature. But when I woke it was only my pillow and my cheeks that were damp. There was no green through my window, just the tall grey blocks of flats blotting out the sky. It was time to tip-toe to the bathroom and wash the tell-tale tears away, and square up to another urban day.

Until 'Her downstairs' made me so sensitive to noise the sounds of London had never disturbed my senses. They were the pulse, the heartbeats, the pains and the joys of this wonderful old capital. One Saturday morning I was alone in our flat rushing through the washing-up. The porridge saucepan slipped from my hand and fell, not on the mat by the sink but with a clatter on the bare tiles. Oh, my God! 'Her downstairs' would think I had done it on purpose! By then the sound of a dropped saucepan had assumed the importance of the crack of doom. I started to tremble. I felt trapped; trapped in a purgatory of noise: the automatic dust-cart clanging in the yard; the yelling and shouting of the children playing round it; the bawling of the street traders exhorting customers to buy; the rumbling hum of the customers' voices; a pneumatic drill just down the street repairing the drains of the public lavatories; and, trying to fight the din with a loudspeaker-van, the voice of Sir Wavell Wakefield asking us to vote him in as our next MP.

Hands to my head I cowered against the wall of the passage that ran through the flat. Was I going mad? I wanted to scream my own neuroses into the din. I heard the letter-box open and went to see if it was the postman. On the carpet was a postcard of a picture taken in the Forest of Dean. Sunlight filtered through the branches of the oaks on green ferns and foxgloves, and a woodland path led peacefully through this pastoral beauty. The pent-up tears broke; I sobbed and sobbed for the green peaceful aura of my childhood years. Oh, if only I could summon a magic carpet to take us all there! I pictured our children running as I did, arms outstretched to the wind and the sun, with no one to say them nay.

I took paper, envelope, and stamp, and there and then wrote to my mother, asking her to let us know if any place turned up at home that we could rent cheaply. So long as it had four walls and a roof, and was in the country, that would do. That evening, after we had got the children to bed, Syd and I sat and had a long talk about it. It seemed a momentous decision, but the more we pondered it the easier and more attractive it became. Anyway, no harm could be done by posting the letter, so we did, and with our minds full of pictures of sunlit fields and floral glades we went happily to bed.

After that, everything happened with surprising speed, as if it had been meant. I checked with the Childrens' Hospital whether such a move would be better for Nicky and they approved. Within a few days my mother wrote back and enclosed a cutting from her local paper; an advert offering a job as a sawyer in an estate sawmill eight miles from Gloucester, cottage available. Syd applied, they seemed keen on him, and he went down on his own to have a look at it. So, in less than a month, the question had been mooted, the decision taken, the move made, and a new life opened up for the family. And here I was, none too pleased yet at the return of the native, lying awake on the creaking bedroom floor, in fear of the mice, casting my mind back over my life in London, marriage and children, joys and sorrows.

The summer dawn came early, greeted by a rapturous chorus of birdsong. As its grey light struggled through the dusty lattice I snuggled down by Syd's back and fell into the sleep that I had so justly earned.

'Wake up, wake up Win! Just come and have a look through this window.'

I struggled back from my oblivion and on to my feet to join Syd who was standing at the open window. Puffing out his chest, stretching his arms wide, breathing deeply, he looked like an emperor surveying his domain. On this summer morning the outlook was rich indeed; golden sunshine on a field of golden corn sloping up behind the barns; the berries of the rowan branches that almost touched the back roof beginning to turn a brilliant red. And who would long for caskets of emeralds when there are such trees to behold? The cherry orchard. The copse of oak and ash and chestnut and pine complementing each other with their differing shades and shapes. The mellowed old barns, and the pale pink rambler rose that covered the rustic arch at the yard entrance. All set against the perfect backdrop of a cloudless blue sky.

'That's what I call a heavenly outlook!' enthused Syd.

'Yes, so it is,' I said. 'But what about that hell-hole of a living-room and kitchen downstairs? The Crumbles, that's what this place ought to be called.' Of course he could look on the bright side, he had had a good sleep. He hadn't lain awake all night for fear of a mouse running over his face.

The children slept on, so we tip-toed downstairs into the living-room. Putting her house in order is a satisfying job for most women, but I felt defeated about achieving it here. The two wardrobes looked incongruous and overpowering against the wall, and added to the claustrophobia brought on by the sloping ceiling and the small dirty window. Above all, I needed a cup of tea to lift my downcast spirits. I had not been born a child in the Forest for nothing. Telling Syd to scrounge up our newspaper packaging I hurried round the house to the copse at the back and returned with an apronful of twigs. It took a lot of paper, a lot of blowing, and a lot of patience, but when eventually the kettle began to sing, so did I.

The children woke up in high good humour, but Syd lost some of his when I pointed out that he would have to go at once to the Electricity Board in Gloucester. After a cup of tea and very little else he dashed off to trot the mile to the bus-stop, his ears still ringing with my exhortations. 'Mind and emphasise how urgently we need a cooker and a boiler, and mind and buy some bread, because till I get a cooker that's all you're having, bread and eggs.' Boiled eggs was all I could hope to achieve on that fire, at least until the chimney was swept.

Jenny pottered about with me, putting our clothes, crocks and oddments into some sort of order. The boys, being boys, disappeared to investigate the surroundings. They came home somewhat chastened, having had a lecture on estate disciplines from the bailiff. Boys did not go into the orchards. They did not go into fenced woods because they might disturb the pheasants. They kept to the footpaths through fields with sheep, cows and horses in them. They left gates as they found them and in general behaved like civilised human beings. It was asking a lot, but it was his duty. They recovered from their little depression probably quicker than he did. Meanwhile there was plenty of scope for their surplus energies right here, and for a start they could go into 'our' copse and gather twigs and fallen dead wood for the fire.

Syd came home with some welcome news. For a two-pound deposit with four years to pay he had been able to order an electric cooker and a boiler, and they would be delivered within four days. Heartened no end, I thought we could struggle through till then. At the end of the four days nothing had been delivered. Never mind, they would be sure to come any minute. At the end of a week, with the washing piling up, and no hot meals, I wrote a polite but urgent reminder to the Electricity Board. A week later, another one, more urgent and less polite. By the end of a month, my sore-tried temper was reaching boiling point much quicker than the old black kettle on its heap of twigs. Camping-out is fun, but not in your own home.

Well, I had given them long enough. Taking the four children I walked the mile to the phone box in the village. In those pre-automated days one could put twopence in the box and natter on ad infinitum. Just as well, I thought, as I got through to the electricity showrooms, because I was choked up with anger, frustration and self-pity. I demanded to speak to the manager. Yes, I could hang on, it was an urgent matter; only the manager would do. Eventually I told the male voice at the other end that if the promised cooker and boiler had not arrived on the morrow, four hungry unwashed kids and their hungry unwashed mother would come and squat in his showroom until they did.

There was no need for us to hurry home. The weather was lovely, and we took the footpath across the meadows to the tiny stream in the dipple where the children had a paddle. Up the other side into Sawpit meadow and we stopped again to see how the blackberries were coming on in the hedges. A friendly cottager's wife was by her door, so we paused for a chat and were rewarded with an armful of juicy rhubarb. Eventually we emerged one at a time through a little swing-gate right opposite the drive.

Now we had to climb, but the step was in the chestnut's shade and we were nearly home. We had just got past the big old chestnut and in sight of our entrance, when the electricity van passed us. The sight of it gave me the energy to run up the last bit, rancour now forgotten. I could have hugged the driver and his mate. I was already visualising golden-crusted rhubarb pies. But I felt like walloping the pair of them when they told me they had not got the gear with them to install the cooker and the boiler.

'Right,' I warned them. 'If you're not here first thing in the morning to get the job done, I shall carry out my threat, and you can see what a lot of gypsies we look like already, thanks to you lot.' Suitably chastened, they left full of promises, and returned the next morning and fixed it all up. I spent the whole afternoon up to my elbows in flour and fat. We were making progress.

We had a lot of relatives and friends in the Forest, and they began to call on us, many of them on our very first day. So did some of our Londoners; it was amazing how some who were too busy to walk round the block to see us in town, were now ready to drive over a hundred miles for the same dubious pleasure. 'Such a lovely day!' they would announce blandly as they got out of their cars dressed in their Sunday best, the women with their hair done. 'Such a lovely day, we thought we'd come and see you. What a place, aren't you lucky?' Standing there being nice, in my dirty old trousers, my uncombed hair full of soot and smuts, I sometimes had doubts. Never mind, throw some more twigs on the hearth, and bang on the poor old kettle again. We had no warning from those on foot, but the sound of a car coming up the hill raised cries of 'Bucket, bucket!' Chris, or Syd if available, or if not it had to be me, had to run into the cubby-hole and grab the privy bucket. In 'our' copse round the back Syd and the boys had dug holes for emptying it, but more often than not we met the visitors head on as we were hurrying round with it. They made no comment on this quaint old country custom, and the hardier souls even managed a rather brief handshake. Everybody meant well, bless them, but they did add a few complications to an already complicated existence.

The beauty of this place has always drawn people to it, and as we gradually got it civilised we enjoyed their company properly. They may have got some entertainment from our antics in those early days, but they provided some for us. All the men fell into the wardrobe trap. All the women said at once, 'But what about the wardrobes? You can't leave 'em here, surely?' I shrugged. 'Can't get 'em upstairs, not yet. Doing something about it later.' The men, who had probably not even noticed them, perked up their ears. 'Why not? Let's have a look.' Away they went, looking up the stairs, measuring with arms outspread. 'Reckon we can, you know. Give us a hand.'

We got quite blasé watching them heaving and sweating, to me, to you, whoa, back a bit, up a bit, down a bit, sideways a bit, try him the other way round. We knew there was just no way. Eventually the bedroom window had to be removed, and it was still an awkward feat getting them in. We got them in at last, but how we shall ever get them out I do not know. Perhaps we shall have a lot of visitors.

Jenny was more entertained by the kitten Mother got us to keep the mice out of the house. It quickly grew into her beloved fat pet cat, and sure enough it kept the mice out of our rooms but not out of the cottage structures. Those mice had been there for generations but they did not mind our moving into their house. In fact they were quite curious about us and used to come to the hole in the wall by the beam and look down at us as we ate. They were healthy sturdy mice, and once battle was joined they went down with flags flying.

Between getting up in the morning and going to bed at night Syd is far the more patient of us two. But night disturbances, be they from crying offspring, wailing tom-cats, or mice scrabbling behind the skirting board near his head, bring out the black side of his character. He had no aversion to quiet mice; if they napped peacefully on the bottom of our bed it would not worry him. But after many nights of their persistent scrabbling behind the skirting board Syd's temper reached explosion point. He came to the irrational conclusion that the mice were deliberately picking that spot for their nocturnal skirmishing in order to drive him nuts. One night, after banging the skirting board and revealing an unsuspected streak of sadism in his threats to the so-and-so perishers, he was reduced to banging his own head on the wall in his frenzy. I could not help it; I started to giggle.

'That bloody useless cat,' he moaned. 'What's *he* doing all day?'

'It's not the cat's fault. He can't get inside the walls any more than you can.'

'It's your fault. You overfeed the lazy sod.'

I humped myself over to the extreme edge of our bed. 'You're a bigger nuisance than the perishing mice, keeping me awake all night with your temper.'

It was a relief to get up in the morning. 'I've got the answer,' said Syd through his toast. 'I'll put the cat up in the loft over the kitchen before I go to work. That's where their run is, straight in from the barn where it meets the kitchen roof. Mind you leave him up there; I'll get him down when I come home from work.'

I called the cat, and under Syd's eagle eye I gave him a stingy bit of breakfast. We dragged the table out, put a chair on top, and Syd lifted the protesting cat up through the trap-door. We turned a deaf ear to his disgusted miaowings.

I was glad that evening the boys had been invited to the Scout party; after his tea Syd could indulge in a nap and make up his loss of sleep. He looked tired when he came in from his eight-hour day of manual work and the uphill mile-long walk home. He had just swallowed his first cup of tea and started on his cooked meal, when he suddenly remembered the cat. We dragged the table with a chair on top under the ceiling hatch. Syd clambered up out of sight, but no cat came down.

'Hand me up the torch. I can't see or hear him.' It was quite dark up there. Jenny climbed up with the torch, and I lit a candle in a jam jar. There was no cat to be seen, but the dim light did reveal a broken disused chimney in the far wall that had once served as a fireplace for farmworkers.

'Oh dear, oh dear!' cried a contrite Syd, 'I think I know what's happened. That poor cat must have fallen down this hole in the old chimney. He could never have got up, it's too tall and straight. He must have gone down. Poor little devil, he's probably lying injured down at the bottom. But I can't see him down there.'

Jenny had been scolding us for putting the cat up there in the first place, and now she burst into tears.

I had more faith in feline agility than they. 'Don't worry, darling, I'm sure that cat climbed out. You go out and call him. I expect he's asleep in the hay-barn.'

Her call got no response. Syd poked about in the attic, and his dinner congealed on the plate. 'Tell you what we'll do,' he shouted from the gloom above. 'Tie some meat off my plate on a long string, and I'll lower it down the chimney. He must be hungry by now. If he takes it, we'll know he's alive.'

Jenny climbed up with it herself, and they took turns hanging it down the chimney, peering down into the murky cobwebbed depths, calling 'puss, puss.' All in vain, the bait was ignored. Finally they pulled the dusty meat back and got down in despair.

'Well,' said Syd, 'I'm going to knock a hole in the wall. He must be down there somewhere. Now where do I start?' All he had for the task was a small hammer and a cold chisel, and the centuries-old cottage has stone walls about two feet thick. The sweat was dropping off him before he managed to prise out the first stone. By the time he had made a hole a couple of feet square we seemed to have half-a-ton of rubble and stone piled up on the kitchen floor. It was just unbelievable that all that had come from that small hole. At ten o'clock I put a tired and reluctant Jenny to bed, bolstering up her hopes as best I could. When the boys came home it was nearly eleven, and they reckoned pragmatically that the cat must have snuffed it anyway, if it was under all that rubble. I gave them a milky drink and biscuits and hustled them off to bed.

At one a.m. Syd was still pulling out stones and rubble. 'Well, I must have knocked the hole in the wrong place. There's no chimney shaft there, but it looks right. Just have to knock a hole further along.' He put the hammer down and filled his pipe. All the evening I had been falling in love with this overtired worried man so concerned for the cat and his little daughter's feelings.

'Go and sit down,' I ordered him, and as he did I kissed the top of his balding head, and banked my love for a later date. 'I'm going to warm up your food, and while you're eating it I'll go round the barns calling the cat. You're *not* going to make another hole in that wall tonight. You're beaten, and you've got to be up at half-past six to go to work.' He ate his food, while I went around calling in vain; now I too was convinced that the cat was a corpse in that wall. It took all my persuasion to stop Syd making a fresh start. By two a.m. he was washed ready for bed, and then made a last abortive stroll round the cottage calling, 'puss, puss'.

'Win, Win, listen! I can hear the cat miaowing!'

I struggled awake to Syd's excited voice as he jumped out of bed and ran downstairs. The alarm clock said four o'clock. In a few minutes Syd came back beaming like a lighthouse, with the cat in his arms. Before I could stop him he went into Jenny's room.

'Darling, wake up, look, look what Daddy's got, the puss! There now, he can stop on your bed with you till the morning; he's not hurt at all; he was outside all the time.'

'Why on earth did you wake her up this time of night?'

'Well, I thought she might have a nightmare over him.'

'He'd have had my toe up his behind and gone for another mystery trip if I'd got hold of him,' was my grumpy retort. I did my bit, though. My maiden name was not Mason for nothing. I got hold of some cement, and during the day I reconstructed the wall. I must have done it with remarkable economy, because when I had finished it took me ages to carry away the left-over stones and rubble.

The cat went up a few more times and earned his keep. The mice decided upon a tactical retreat into the barns after they had lost a few bold scouts, and we never heard them behind the skirting boards again.

Now the problem was—was I a timid mouse or a woman? I decided I was a woman, and no woman could be expected to put up with that living-room floor, and not having a back door to take the privy bucket out. I wrote to the Estate Manager asking him to call at his earliest convenience, an apt word, and he kindly came within a couple of days.

Old cottages can be a headache to their owners; they are always needing repairs which are in no way covered by the token rent. However, he agreed for us to have a back door installed, and a floor laid in the living-room. The work would be done at week-ends by Fritz, with Syd offering his own labour free. Fritz came up by the same evening. He was a German, an ex-prisoner who had chosen to become a British subject, and worked in the same sawmill as Syd. He put me in mind of a human pneumatic drill, there was so much energy exuding from his wiry frame. His blue eyes were like a pair of laser beams, and they cut a way through the most difficult problems at once. For a few minutes he sized the job up, looking at the back wall, and then at the living-room floor.

'Ve manage,' he said, and somehow I knew he would. 'Ve manage. I tell zem get the stuff 'ere by Sunday. I come seven o'clock.'

'I suppose the floor will just be concrete?' I said with a little sigh. 'Wouldn't it be lovely if the estate would let you do it in red quarry tiles to match the grate?' I thought I might as well push my luck; nothing ventured nothing gained.

He bit at once. 'O.K. Ve manage,' he said with reassuring conviction, and he was gone.

Sunday morning he reappeared sharp on seven, looking as keen as a razor blade, while we were still rubbing the sleep from our eyes. Immoveable objects meant little to this irresistible force. Bash, bang, wallop, the huge stones fell out of the back wall, and he soon had a door-hole. This alone was a wonderful start: no more carrying the privy bucket through the living-room! By the end of the third Sunday the new door was hung, a perfect fit. The lowness of the back roof meant that the door was only five feet high, and for weeks afterwards Syd, Chris and I sported a variety of lumps on our heads! By the time he had laid our new red-tiled floor, I had put Fritz on a pedestal. He went up a few more notches when he decided to build on some more courses of bricks atop our chimney to stop the down-draught—and it worked! It was hard to say whether all this was from innate generosity or for the pure joy of doing the job. Fritz tactfully shrugged off our thanks, and marched away to destroy the next problem. Once or twice Syd quietly made it known to me that he, too, had helped; Fritz could not have quite all the credit!

Our living-room now had a nice brick grate that worked properly, and a tiled floor that gave me joy to scrub, but the rough and grubby walls still made it depressing to live in. Syd, as usual, willing to put up with almost anything for a bit of peace, wanted to put the matter off till we could do 'a proper job'. Privately I told myself something was going to be done before that, an improper job if necessary, as soon as I could earn a few pounds of my own.

Towards the end of August, Chris and Richard started at their new grammar school, a five-mile bus ride away. Nicky and Jenny I took to be registered at the tiny school next to the church, a half-mile walk. An inconvenient distance in wet or icy weather, but a beautiful walk at all seasons: down the hill to the back of the Manor; then up a wandering pathway through a kissing gate; along the top of the 'seed-beds,' where a dozen or so men and women were busy hoeing and weeding seedling trees; on to the Park, a wide stretch of grass dotted with a few magnificent oaks and grazing sheep. The Park was overlooked by dense woodlands that climbed over the foothills, and pushed back into their lee stood the gamekeeper's black-and-white Elizabethan cottage. Its terraced garden paced down the slope and tumbled over with vivid scarlet and gold nasturtiums, a sight that stopped us in our tracks. If Snow White and the Seven Dwarfs had come trooping out of the door we would not have been surprised. Nicky and Jenny soon discovered that the gamekeeper's wife had magic pockets which produced sweets for any child that crossed her path.

At the end of the Park a stile led into the Nursery where an enormous variety of shrubs, roses and decorative trees was raised for sale. Many were in bloom, and some were heavy with perfume on the still summer air. Our earthly Eden. But Eden's end came suddenly at the churchyard gate. The flower-decked little monuments of the common folk were dotted at random down the grassy slope, while up at the top wall under the mourning yews stood the damp grey tombs of their masters. Distant and distinct in death as they were in life; the worms mocked their folly. How many laid beneath this turf had once run chattering over it to school? One day—how soon—but I closed my mind.

The infant children were gathering at the old school door. The ancient church and the little school, built in the same Norman style, snuggled together under the wooded hillocks, and delighted the eye. The school had only one classroom, shared by all the pupils and the two teachers. They were suitably named: Miss Bird and Miss Sparrow. Miss Bird, the Headmistress, was a middle-aged lady from the North of England, who had come to the school as a 'temporary' and was still there thirty years on. A shrewd and kindly woman, she summed me up: four children, coming to live in a tied cottage, well, well. So during our conversation she tactfully let me know that there was often casual work to be got on the estate. Quite probably, she said, they still needed pickers in the plum orchards.

I left Jenny and Nicky in her capable charge. I could only guess at what scholastic standard they might achieve in that tiny one-room school, but just the abiding memory of its heavenly environs would be an asset beyond price.

One of my primeval ancestors must have fallen out of a tree; at any rate I have no head for heights. Nevertheless, on the way home from the school I made enquiries about the plum job and was relieved to hear that there was some work left picking up off the ground. Most of the orchards had already been picked and marketed; the two as yet unpicked were for the jam factory and would be shaken down. The pay was half-a-crown for each half-hundred weight box you could fill, and I could start the very next day! Not only would the extra money be a godsend, but what a relief to get away from the rough-hewn living-room!

It was half-a-mile to the orchard and I had to be there by nine o'clock. I do not know how Dr Spock would have coped with getting my brood out of bed in the mornings. It reduced me to bad temper, frayed nerves, and threatenings, and it brought home to me how my mother had suffered from my own slug-a-bed nature. I was sure that growing children needed a good breakfast, and I often ran after one or another screaming like a banshee for them to stop for the sandwich of congealed egg in toast that I was carrying. With work to go to myself, I too had to hurry. Once, in desperation, I threatened them with the ultimate: I would leave home and go back to the comparative luxury of domestic service! This left them apparently unmoved, and seemed even to encourage their tardiness. What a blow to my mother-ego! What would Dr Spock have made of that?

'Right,' I screamed. 'Any of you not up, washed, and at the table in four minutes flat, gets no breakfast *nor* anything to drink.'

'That doesn't apply to me,' called out a grumpy Nicky, ''cos I'm still asleep and can't hear you.'

Somehow I got them all out of the door by quarter to nine. I threw their leavings into a paper bag, put it in my pocket, and made a dash for it across the fields to the plum orchard. The other four women pickers were already there. Two elderly farm men had just started shaking the branches with long hooked wooden poles. A pair of dear old codgers they were, and well past retirement age, but work was an ingrained habit necessary to these men who had started odd-jobbing on the estate as children. Wizened old apples they were, still ruddy of cheek, and their talk full of the flavour of the fields.

Before they moved to the next tree they left a purple circle of juicy plums for us to start on. Piles of wooden boxes were placed strategically between the rows of trees, and we pickers were each supplied with a basket and told to work from the outside towards the tree-trunk. The weather was perfect, and the company of the other women a welcome change. Between them, my four companions seemed to have most of the traits commonly associated with our sex.

I was surprised to see a type like Moira doing this job. A woman of middle age she still had the remains of what must have been ravishing good looks. She clung to her fading glamour with lipstick, powder, and eyebrow pencil. She wore rubber gloves to protect her hands and her varnished nails were the colour of plums. I soon found that whatever sweetness had illumined her nature had faded with her youth. Red in tooth and claw, with a conspiratorial drawling hiss of a voice, she was a real cat. As I picked at her side she gave me a running commentary on the other three, their indiscretions, failings, and faults. While she criticised them icily behind their backs, she spoke with the oiliest of tongues to their faces.

I had enough sense to be tactful and kept my tongue still and my hands busy. Gradually I sidled away from her and worked my way nearer to Rona. It was difficult to tell Rona's age, but not difficult to see that she was a true child of the earth. Plenty of it clung to her ragged old jacket, to her shabby wellington boots, and to her person. The undermost layer looked as though it had been clinging for some time. She was as thin as a bean pole and round-shouldered, and what you could see of her face was quite plain. It was lit up now and again with a companionable grin from ear to ear, a lopsided grin enabling her to keep the everlasting fag going in the corner of her mouth. Her bony fingers picked up the plums with the speed of a chameleon's tongue after a fly. She looked like a downtrodden waif. Probably, I conjectured, she had an out-of-work lazy husband and a brood of offspring at home. I thought that it was greatly to her credit that she grinned so much and occasionally hummed the latest songs. Moira had told me how Rona and her husband lived like pigs in a hovel. By the end of the day I had learned that Rona was only twenty-four, and that she lived in happy squalor with a husband as hard-working as herself. They both worked on the land, planting, weeding, and garnering the fruits of the earth without a grumble for the parsimonious pay it brought them.

On Saturdays they washed off the top layers of the week's

accumulation of sweat and earth, and took themselves and the best part of their wages off to the pub. When they had got their skinfuls they entertained the customers with Rona's version of the conga and their own interpretation of the latest songs. They brought in a good deal of custom for the landlord. Years of practice had taught them to hold their drink with proper dignity as they walked the dark mile-and-a-half home. But once even Rona was temporarily overcome by the strong local 'stun-'em' cider. They held each other up till the top of the steep-sloping lane which led to their cottage. Then Rona fell down, still singing. Her husband could not get her up so he did the next best thing. Gathering up her long hair in his strong right hand he dragged her in true caveman style the rest of the way home to their cottage by the stream.

They had no children; they were never known to quarrel; they contributed greatly to society, and demanded very little in return. As the day progressed and the boxes filled and the tidal wave of plums receded, I warmed more and more to Rona.

Minnie reminded me irresistibly of Mole in *The Wind in the Willows*. In her little woolly hat gathered into a point at the top, with her nose to the ground—and it did not have far to go for she was very short of stature—and with her completely domesticated outlook on life, she gave off an aura of cosiness. Her talk was all of domestic bliss:

'So I thought to meself I'll turn round an' make Sam a nice dumplin' stew for 'is tea'; 'That back-kitchen could do with a bit o' whitewash, I thought, so I turned round an' done it'; 'It's no good, I shall 'ave to sort that muddle in the cupboard drawers out, so I turned round an' done 'em'; 'It blowed up that nice an' windy I might as well do me bit o' washin' so I turned round an' done it *and* got it all dry by teatime'; 'I shall put some o' these plums in the bottom of me bag; then I shall turn round after tea an' make a bit o' jam.'

I tried to picture this miniature whirling dervish at home. When later I called at her tiny cosy overcrowded cottage I wondered how she managed to get all that turning round done!

Dolly had brought her four-year-old son with her, a handsome sturdy little boy who ran ahead with the two old men. She too was handsome, tall and Junoesque, but though, as they say, well-preserved, obviously in her forties. She must have read my thoughts.

'Yeah, I'm a bit long in the tooth to have a kid that age,' she laughed. 'I'd already got five, two of 'em married, and me a grannie, my poor chap was still alive then, hale and hearty, too bloody hale and hearty. We had a nice piece of rented land of our own them days, but we had to work dawn till dark to make a livin' off it. 'Twas gone eleven one night when we just finished bringin' our hay in before a spell of rain broke that might a' ruined it. I was that tired I hardly had the strength to wash meself and climb into bed. But *him*; he was that pleased we'd got it all under cover, he came up to bed like a young colt. "'Ow about a bit, then?" he said when he got into bed. I can tell you I wasn't interested, but anything for a quiet life, so I opened me legs and said help your bloody self and he did. And that's the result, and me fourty-four year old!' She looked fondly at the fruit of her generosity. 'Poor Bill,' she went on, 'he never lived to see that 'un. Had a stroke in the cowshed and was gone before the doctor could get to us, and 'im only fifty-two. 'Course I couldn't keep up with the rent o' the land, but d'you know, I don't seem to work so hard these days as I did when us worked for ourselves.'

Maybe her work-load had lessened, but I thought this fine full-blooded woman must find her nights lonely. Meanwhile I pressed on; my ears were open but my hands were full. The novelty of the job, the sunshine, and the beautiful pastoral surroundings more than made up for the ache in my back. The thought of that half-a-crown for each filled box made me a very nifty picker indeed.

'Just look at the galloping manger!' cried Minnie as they noted I had filled the most boxes. Unaware of it herself, Minnie mispronounced something in every sentence; she had hyder-angles in her garden, and summed it up by often singing 'I'm just a little peculiar in an onion bed'. Her feathers got very ruffled if any iggerant listener dared to correct her, and she was always ready to turn round and give them a good lecture.

The two old men whistled to let us know it was one o'clock. I had popped a fair few of the juicy plums in my mouth but by now I had a raging thirst. We all sat down on the grass near a hedge. I jumped up very quickly when Moira languidly observed she thought I had sat on a grass-snake. 'Won't hurt you, silly,' she said tartly in response to my ignorant panic. My scraps of toast were going down very dry indeed; if there had been any moisture left in my mouth I would have drooled at the sight of the tea they poured from their flasks.

I tried to look indifferent. 'Didn't you bring nothing to drink?' asked Rona. I shook my head in what I hoped was an offhand manner. The stained, dirt-encrusted cup on the top of her flask was as black as the brew she poured out of it. A bit of ash dropped into it from her fag-end, but she drank it with gusto, poured out a second cup, and handed it to me. In my hurry to get off to work I had not even had a cup of tea and by now my thirst was unendurable. I am not a very fastidious person, but still I was daunted. There were hours more to go, for Rona worked till six whereas I was leaving to get home for the children, so it was a most generous gesture. There was concern and kindness in her face. Eventually I took the cup, shut my eyes, and gulped down half the contents. 'That's plenty; thank you *very* much.' She had no qualms about drinking after me.

The other three had all brought their 'bait' in generous-sized bags, and before they started picking again they carefully filled the bottoms of these bags with the firmest plums they could find. I was learning. Tomorrow I would bring my food in a shopping-bag with plenty to drink. I was learning too that a stomach needed time to get used to a sudden excess of plums! Sharp at four o'clock I bade them a hasty cheerio, and had to do a galloping manger sprint across the fields for a dash into our privy, and just in time.

At the end of three weeks' plum picking I had earned quite a few pounds. The biggest percentage of it went into the housekeeping but I kept some back for an idea that had been fermenting in my mind. I was going to have a go at papering our living-room. The new Polycell paste had just come on to the market, and unlike the old flour and water, this stuff stuck the paper to bulges and dips. I had a good testing-ground for it. To help camouflage the uneven walls I decided it would have to be a patterned paper, a quiet pattern in pastel shades of grey or mushroom. I had it all worked out and could practically see it, but I kept the idea to myself to give the family a lovely surprise by doing the job all in one day.

That day came. I could hardly wait to get the children off to school. It was late September and a sunny balmy morning. I had the choice of walking down the tarmacked lane to the village, or taking the short cut across the fields. Though time was precious I had a good look across the fields first to make sure there were no cattle or horses there. I have an irrational fear of animals great and small since a childhood experience of being in a field with a charging bull. They seemed to be all clear. Happy as a lark I hurried on past the small tenant farmstead and down the sloping field to the plank bridge across the tiny stream, and then up the grassy slopes on the other side.

Now I could see the police station, the first house in the village, and something else! I got a nasty shock when I saw the corner of the last field was enclosed in barbed wire, and in it a bovine animal raging at his confinement. It had no udders so I knew it was not a cow; I did not bother to inspect whatever else it had! I found the energy to run like the clappers over the stile that led to the snicket path into the village. The bus passed me about a hundred yards before the stop, but in the manner of country buses it waited for my breathless arrival.

A seven-mile ride through the country is very pleasant with so many individual types of cottages and gardens peppered along the way. At the next stop the driver waited again for two familiar travellers, a pair of jolly red-faced women. They settled down in the seat behind me.

'No need for me to come in the mornin', but the old man give me such a treat last night,' one said with a roguish giggle, 'I thought I'd give *'im* a treat wi' 'is tea—'e do love the individual fruit pies from Lyons's.'

'No wonder thy old man a' got to 'ave a nap in 'is bait time! I be getting some wellington boots for meself; 'twill be tater pickin' soon an' my old 'uns a got a great split in one on 'em.' Mentally I took note that potato picking would be in the offing soon.

Right opposite the bus stop at the entrance to the city was a wallpaper shop, and I planned to nip over to it, make my purchases, and catch the same bus on its way back. In the shop doorway there were some bargain sale offers stuck up in large cardboard boxes. Among them were eight rolls of excellent quality Regency-stripe paper, one side ready trimmed, at a real knock-down price. As far as I could see, there was nothing wrong with it, and it had a pattern of close red, gold, and white stripes. My ideas on decor took an instant about turn. Of course, Regency stripes, very posh, just what the room was crying out for, and good thick quality too! I should have enough money left to get a tin of gold paint for our knick-knacks and picture frames to set it off. With two parcels of four rolls each, a tin of gold paint, and a large packet of paste, I still had enough change for some chocolate to treat the kids. I felt full of the milk of human kindness. A two-minute wait and I was on the bus again, wishing it would not dawdle so much on the homeward journey. Time was of the essence to get it all done in a matter of hours.

When I got off at the village I was in a dilemma. I could save at least ten invaluable minutes by going across the fields, but this would mean passing the enclosure with the bull again. Impatiently throwing caution to the winds I decided to risk it. After all, how could it get out? If it could, why had it not? And why should it choose this moment? Full of Dutch courage I marched boldly through the snicket, and though hampered by my purchases I began to run across the field. I could see the animal, and it was now in a proper frenzy, stampeding up and down inside its barbed enclosure. Running must have been my mistake, for just as I got opposite him and he could see me, he charged his way out.

I know what the expression 'rooted to the spot' means. He came running right in my direction. Frozen with horror, I could just imagine headlines in the local paper: 'Woman gored to death by bull only yards from police station.' There was no sense in running, he had a bull's strength and four legs: I only had two. I threw my parcels headlong and waited for a horrible death. When I could almost feel his breath I stood aside in a manner that would have brought the house down at a Spanish bull-ring. The animal rushed past me apparently indifferent to my presence; no wonder, in a distant field separated by two hedges were a herd of similar bovines. I did not wait for him to do a U-turn when he met the next hedge.

Picking up my parcels I ran somehow on legs turned to rubber and scrambled over the hedge bordering the lane, throwing the long-suffering wallpaper on to the road. A four-foot thick hawthorn hedge takes some scrambling over, but it is amazing how athletic sharing a field with a bull makes one.

Scratched, torn, and breathless I still had enough inspiration left to hurry along the lane and up the hill to home. It was a bit of an anti-climax to find out later that it was only a bullock isolated from the herd with an eye infection.

With one hand I mixed a bowl of paste, and with the other made a pot of tea. There was no time to eat. Then I realised that I had not got the pasting-bursh. No matter, Syd had a large and splendid shaving-bursh given him for last Christmas; that would have to do.

Papering by oneself a fourteen-foot wall that reaches up to a peak is quite a feat. I measured, cut, and pasted. I had to stand on a chair atop a table with extra height provided by Syd's precious thick volumes of Shakespeare. He was going to kill me when he came in and found out, but I had already escaped death by inches, and as soon as he saw the new-papered room he would forgive me. I had achieved two walls before I stood back to admire the result. Well actually, I reeled back; the effect was psychedelic. Over the peaks and into the valleys of the uneven walls the stripes had run into each other, and away, and back again in the most alarming clashes. I began to feel a bit giddy, and a headache started up like a first cousin to a migraine. I was in no mood to believe the evidence of my own eyes, and pig-headedly put my symptoms down to the encounter with the bull. Anyway, I was forty-one years old; perhaps this was a sudden start to the 'change of life'. I hoped it would not be as drastic as the change that was coming over our living-room!

Never mind, when the other two walls were done and the room more unified, there would be a better effect. So I hurried on, earning a medal for speed if not for skill. Finishing, I felt a bit cross-eyed, and my head was worse, so I was glad to escape into the kitchen. I still had fifteen minutes before my hungry brood came charging in. As a child in the twenties I had once seen a miner's wife making some hurried 'workhouse gallop' for her husband's dinner. Into a saucepan of salted water she put some thinly sliced onions and potatoes. They cooked in minutes, and then she added a knob of dripping and thickened it all with well-peppered flour. I could do better than that; I could throw in a tin of corned beef and a tin of peas, and for dessert the old standby, the remains of a plum pie. This would fill them up, and perhaps take their minds off the wallpaper.

Long-legged Chris arrived first. Fifth-form grammar-school boys consider themselves a rather shockproof lot. However, as he came in he did not quite hide his stagger before quietly commenting, 'Mum, it's time you were certified.' Richard followed closely on his heels, and let out quite an oath before saying, 'Sorry, Mum, it was the shock.' Nicky—well, for the first time in his life he was struck speechless. Six-year-old Jenny, whose vocabulary had been somewhat coarsened by her three brothers, put her hands on her hips, her budding feminine instincts outraged by my taste. 'Mummy,' she scolded, 'Mummy! It looks bloody awfuller than it did before!'

Poor Syd, after a long day in the sawmill and a tiring walk home, had to come in at the best of times to four lively extroverts and an unpredictable spouse. Now this! As he opened the door he reeled back, shading his eyes with his hands. 'God help me,' he cried and it was a prayer from the heart. We all shaded our eyes, eating our meal with hanging heads.

While I was washing up, one of Syd's mates called to offer him the chance of a week-end fencing job. I asked him in and proffered a chair. He sat for a while looking out of the window rather pointedly and acting very fidgety, and then said 'D'you mind 'avin the door open till I go, Missus? I've got a bit of 'eadache comin' on.'

Well, they would all just have to get used to it, I thought, but when my brother-in-law called and sat through his visit with his sunglasses on I knew I was defeated.

That night I went to bed knowing that I had murdered good taste; it ran in blood-red wavy stripes down our bumpy walls. It took me two days and several coats of cream emulsion to bury my mistake.

Luckily there was now plenty to lure me out of the house. For a start there were the ripening blackberries. Down through the woods at the back of the cottage the gamekeeper had cut rough paths ready for the pheasant-shooting season. Brambles heavy with ripening fruit grew profusely on each side and spread under the trees fighting for survival in the wild undergrowth that made such excellent cover for the beautiful doomed birds. Each year the gamekeeper's busy sickle pruned the vigorous plants and they responded with strong young shoots and fine big fruit.

A lovely mixture of flora and fauna; teeming insect life that would bring joy to the heart of the entomologist; sinuous grey squirrels making lightning forays among the branches. What a feast for the eye in the myriad shapes and hues of the foliage, the graceful languid tendrils of delicate parasite plants drooped gently from those sturdier growths whom they caressed and climbed for their share of the sun. Summer's bold colours still blazed, although the margins of the woods were touched with Autumn's soberer hues. Hardly a soul went into these woods. Instead of the human voice there was the busy hum of the insects, the sudden secret rustlings in the bracken, the singing, whistling and twittering of the birds. What a strange and beautiful world to walk through all alone! In the gloaming this was the haunt of the ghostly barn owl that swooped and glided through the trees as white and silent as a spectre, while his lesser brethren called him names from wood to wood as the sun sank over the hill and the gardeners cleaned their spades and thought about their suppers.

I picked my colander full of berries in a very short time, spotting as I did so plenty of tinder-dry wood felled by wintry gales. I gathered a load under my arm and made my way out. Emerging from the wood I could see in the field above it a patch of whitish round things of varied size, showing brightly in the grass. Mushrooms? Could it be? I put down my wood and blackberries and climbed over the wire fence to find out. Yes, the fine-pleated pale pink undersides confirmed my hopes. What treasure, more than a couple of pounds to tie up in my pinny! Awkwardly, but richly laden with wood, blackberries and mushrooms, and glowing with some primitive satisfaction I went indoors. I would give the family a meal fit for a king to come home to! Blackberry tart, and mushrooms, figured largely on the menu for the next three weeks, and in the larder, next to the jewel-red jars of plum jam I soon added a store of dark purply-red blackberry jam.

Too soon the days grew short, the Autumn sun gave way to rain and damp cold mists. Now it was time for potato picking, and I got myself a job. Potato picking is one of the hardest and most unpleasant jobs I have done on the land. A potato field is usually a cold and muddy place, squelchy mud and reddish clay, mud that clings. It clings to your boots so that every step is a slippery misery, and every time you pick your foot up you are lifting several pounds' weight of mother earth. It clings to the bottom of the boxes which are cumbersome enough when clean and empty. It clings thickly to your hands, caking and shaping the gloves you wear to protect your freezing fingers.

Perhaps the method is more mechanised these days. Twenty years ago, a contraption on the back of a tractor lifted the hoed-up rows of potatoes into the large wooden boxes. These boxes were heavy in themselves but they had to be dragged along until they were filled. By that time the outsides were caked in wet mud, and with their insides filled to the brim with big muddy potatoes, they nearly dragged my arms out of their sockets. The perpetual bending was back-breaking, and how we all longed for our one o'clock bait-time.

We made sure we took a perch on a box with potatoes in it, and a few went into the bottom of our dinner-bags. We could not afford to have scruples about these perks, not at the two shillings an hour we were being paid for our non-stop labour. We had to work at the double to keep up with the tractor. Even so, we were getting paid something, which was a change-about from what had been the Squire's perks a few decades beforehand. There were still some old hands about who could remember the times. The farm bailiff would go into the village school and pick out the strongest boys who were sons of his tenants. Out they had to go, into the clammy fields, to pick the Squire's potatoes for nothing. They had no dinner bags to take some home to their mums. Some of the old men said it did them good, but it seemed no bad thing for the Squire either.

By knocking-off time on the first day I felt I would never be able to stand up straight again, and I nearly went up the last steep bit of hill to home on all fours.

When the picking-up was finished, a few of the regular farmhands bagged the potatoes for market, delivered plenty to the tenants at a special price of ten shillings a hundredweight, and stored the surplus in huge clamps. Potatoes, potatoes, mashed, chipped, boiled or roasted, we seemed to eat little else.

Meanwhile other farmhands had been in the apple orchards hand-picking the best of the fine crop of Bramley cookers. The rest of the apples were shaken from the trees and fell among the windfalls to be picked up for the cider makers. Now accepted as a member of 'the casuals', I was glad of this extra job, especially with Christmas not so far away.

This was much nicer work, with no noisy beast of a tractor breathing down our necks. There were just eight pickers-up, all women. We divided into two groups, each taking a row of trees at a time. We put the apples into large round wicker baskets, and then took turns holding the sacks open, tipping in the apples till there was barely room to tie the tops with baling string. Then we left the sacks holding each other up in rings round the tree trunks.

Some mornings the apples were frozen to the grass until the sun was out long enough to melt the ice. We were kept warm enough meanwhile, not only by the work but by the patches of tall nettles under the trees. They stung our faces and hands liberally before we could tread them down. Everything went into the baskets, even the bad apples, even those that had dropped in the cow manure. 'Help it ferment,' they said, 'do it good; give it some flavour.'

Woolly gloves were soon soaked by the frost and had to be discarded; the experienced pickers wore rubber ones over theirs. Putting these on warmed up the tongue of one our number, a conversational sex maniac, who did her best to keep our blood on the boil. Any initial disgust at her professionally rampant sexual appetites was soon dispelled by her comical ability to find a carnal innuendo in every innocent remark. Scolding her for shame's sake only acted as an inspiration, and even the prim among us were often reduced to helpless laughter by her genuinely funny crudities. For her, sex had to be sublimated by ribaldry, for she was married to a limp-handed soft-voiced effeminate sort of man, who was as good as gold to her everywhere but in bed.

For our half-hour bait-time we sheltered between bags of apples. Chilled through and through we were glad to start again and shiver away the short and shady afternoon. It was uphill walking all the way home, and I got as warm as toast. My pockets, and the bottom of my capacious 'dinner-bag', filled with the firmest of the windfall apples, weighed me down, but it was a welcome burden. We pickers pooled our culinary methods of using them. We saved on tooth-paste by eating them raw. They went into tarts, pies, and fritters. We had them plainly stewed. We added them to jams, grated them into fruit-cake mixture, pushed them into chutney, used them liberally in the Christmas pudding and mincemeat. That first year the apple picking-up lasted into early December.

After the apple picking came the winter proper and our long evenings were confined to the fireside, at least those of us who could get round it. Our thick stone walls had tempered the summer's heat and now kept out a good deal of the cold. Nevertheless, our living-room had four doors and an open archway into an unheated kitchen, and there was no porch. Sometimes with luck we might roast our knees, but there was always plenty of icy draught to cool our backs. The fire became a god, our smoke-stained grate his altar, and we his worshippers sat in a sacred semi-circle round him.

During the Christmas holidays we were joined by our fourteen-year old nephew from London. Accustomed to central heating he was an ardent devotee of our 'real' fire, watching it so intently that he never remembered to make it up. He and our three boys manoeuvred and competed for the warmest place right in the front. Let one vacate his chair, perhaps for a quick trip to the frozen privy that he could no longer postpone, or to fetch a book from a satchel, and there would be a scuffle among the other three to fill his seat. Jenny was assured of her own perch on a stool by the hearth. Syd and I, well, we had to finish the odd jobs and the chores, and then we took a back seat till the younger two were prised out to get ready for bed.

We had no television but we all had long tongues and individual opinions on matters great and small. Discussions flared into arguments, and arguments subsided into discussions. I learned quite a lot in the process. Supper was usually toast and cocoa. I would put a pile of sliced bread on a plate on the mantelpiece and the butter-dish and some plates among the assorted feet on the hearth. Starting with Jenny, each took his turn with the long-handled toasting fork, getting his own supper.

There were quiet lulls for games of chess and 'I spy', for reading and for anagrams, but there was plenty of noisy grumbling when I made bedtime preparations. We had acquired an anti-quated oil-stove to warm up the little space next to the privy that we graced with the name of bathroom. In here we washed for bed; the water was heated in the copper and carried in through the living-room. Each shivering victim returned quickly to the fire for the last few minutes warm-up before the arctic trip to bed. Jenny was no problem, but I suspect that my stern admonitions to the boys 'mind and wash all over', were largely ignored.

In the winter holidays when there was no need for them to get up early for school, it was often quite late before Syd and I had the dying fire to ourselves. With our chairs pulled close to the hearth we soon dozed off, to be awakened by the cramping cold as the untended fire turned to the dead powder of ashes.

That winter followed an old-fashioned summer, and was itself of the same vintage. By the end of February our winter's store of coal was down to the last few knobs, and Syd's wages would not stretch to buying any more. Being the depth of winter, there was no casual work for me. Every day Syd carried home a small bag of firewood on his back, but this gave us a blaze for only an hour or so. Doing my housework during the day I kept warm, or almost, with Syd's old woolly socks over my own, a woolly hat pulled over my ears, and an old dressing-gown tied on round my peculiar assortment of clothes. I looked like the proverbial sack of manure. A re-filled hot water bottle tied round my waist kept my hands thawed. Thus I could endure the day without a fire and only lit it just before the children came from school.

March did not come in like a lion, more like a polar bear. Freezing winds as vicious as a snarling vixen's bared teeth heralded a blanket of snow as soft as her tail. A flawlessly pure covering and ornament to the lifeless scenery of winter, it turned coats, scarves, caps and boots to soggy suffering dampness, and melted into little puddles all over the kitchen floor. There was no adequate means of drying the damp clothes, let alone the forlorn washing, dripping from the clothes-horse on to sheets of news-paper. When we went to bed I arranged it hopefully in front of the lukewarm grate. I had no spin-drier, and not even an airing cupboard. The fire had become more and more the very hub of our existence and we were running into a crisis.

Then Syd came home with some good news. Behind the Manor was a tree-clad hill, and at the bottom the woodsmen were thin-ning out. After the usable timber was trimmed, and pulled out by the patient old horse, they burned the brushwood. There were plenty of small limbs and pieces still lying around, and we should do no harm if we helped ourselves to them. Besides, we would get warmed three times—carying it home, sawing it up, and burning it. After a hurried tea we parcelled ourselves up in old scarves and woollies and set out. The robin on our pump gave us an asthmatic wheeze as we passed. No blithe spirit he, but he had had his few crumbs.

The hushed world seemed even quieter. A thin cold mist had come from nowhere and divided the landscape into sections. One landmark disappeared before we caught sight of the next. Crossing the clumsy humps of the ploughed field we entered the secretive wood. We had never really set foot here before, for these were the real coverts, keeper's country, and the powers-that-be frowned upon entry. Now the shooting was over. Away on the edge of the mist we could see two hen pheasants busily doing nothing, and one lucky surviving cock bird croaked dismally from afar. Gingerly we negotiated our way down the steep narrow icy path cut by the gamekeeper between the trees. Sometimes we slid on our feet, sometimes on our behinds. From time to time we clutched at a tree to get our balance back. Masses of brambles under the trees impeded progress and caused more tumbles. All of us except Syd came some sort of a cropper.

'Not much good taking you lot for a skiing holiday,' he observed loftily as we approached the bottom, and promptly lost his own footing and made an undignified sprawling descent right the way down. As he went, his pipe flew out of his mouth. 'My pipe, my pipe,' he wailed piteously. He got no pity from us; we were all doubled up in laughter, although we knew that without his pipe we would be living with a bear with a sore head. Nobody had a clue where it had flown to, but more by luck than judgement Chris found it for him. Putting it safely in his pocket, and ramming his cap squarely back on, Syd resumed his role of captain. 'Right,' he said, 'let's get on then.'

We found plenty of small branches and pieces of brush, and each carrying as much as we could, we laughed ourselves silly, slipping falling and struggling with them to the top of the hill. By this time we were all as warm as toast, not exactly sweating but definitely glowing, and the evening light held out long enough for a second foray. On our return our fire had gone out. While I tried to start it Syd and the boys worked in the yard by the lighted window, breaking, sawing and chopping. All I could get for my puffing and coaxing were spitty froths of melting snow, and sap boiling out of the twig ends from the heat of the paper I had lit under them. We did not indulge in a daily paper, and the little store I had was almost gone, and still there was no spark. Jenny and I were beginning to shiver.

'Tell you what,' shouted Syd from the yard, 'tell you what. We're going to have us a real fire tonight! One bloody great blaze! I'll make you lot sit back, I'll roast your legs!' He sounded desperately cheerful; a good job he could not see the dismal failure in the hearth.

In the middle of the kitchen floor I had a small square of lino. It was in a bad way, dying of old age and cracked in several places. It would have to go! I tore it up into pieces small enough to push between the twigs. After a moment's hesitation it caught and a glorious blaze filled the grate, and the chimney. 'Look at that!' I yelled jubilantly.

'Look at that!' echoed Syd as showers of soot and black-caked lumps came down everywhere, especially on to my new-born fire.

'The roof's on fire,' shouted Richard. From under and between the tiles, smoke was billowing out into the yard. While I ran in and out like a hen in a panic Syd brought in shovels of snow and mud to put out the fire in the grate. Chris and Richard pumped buckets of water to throw over the low roof. Climbing on a chair Syd got up through the hatch in the ramshackle home-made kitchen ceiling to have a look round. The timbers were not alight and the smoke was pouring from a crack in the chimney. Nevertheless, the fire would have to remain out for the evening so we could check up again to-morrow. The relief gave me strength to face mopping up the puddles of sooty muddy water overflowing from the hearth and all over the floor. Syd shovelled up the soot. The chimney, at least, had had a good clean. 'Oh well,' I thought hopefully, 'lighting that lino has cleaned our chimney, and there's enough left for me to start the fire tomorrow.'

We simply had to look for some little consolation. What a fiasco! All that work, all those high hopes and expectations! Syd had had his bloody great blaze all right, but not quite as he had expected. When we stopped running about, the arctic cold hit us again as we looked at our dismal empty grate. We huddled round the paraffin heater with our cocoa mugs between our palms, then we made somewhat reluctantly for the warmest places, our beds.

Underneath the ice and snow the dormant roots began to stir and make ready for the Spring. In their burrows and their warrens the little hibernators rolled over in their sleep and opened one eye to the light of promise. As the sun broke through in short but glorious bursts, transient samples of what was soon to come, my own inherited gardening senses began to itch.

'A garden is a lovesome thing, God wot', and God, what a lot of work goes into making one from scratch. In our case we would have to start well behind scratch, for ours was a large piece of rough overgrown earth at the back of the cottage, heavily populated with tree saplings, brambles, nettles, thistles and docks. Country-born, I knew the value of a garden, and with six mouths to fill on a small income I began to wish my husband was more of a man of the soil. Syd had grown up in a London back-street slum without as much as a bulb in a flower-pot. His only interest in vegetables had been where to get the best pennyworth of pot-herbs for his mother's stews. He and Chris had become quite handy with a spade, however, because they regularly dug deep holes in the copse at the back for emptying the privy bucket.

One autumn Saturday afternoon when we were shopping in the old Woolworth's in Gloucester, Syd's eye had been caught by the display of roses on sale. The truncated, leafless, barren bundles of thorn were packed in cartons that gaily illustrated the glory that was to come the following summer. Uncharacteristically, Syd sorted them over in his deliberate manner, then counting up his pocket-money took out half-a-crown and actually bought one. Next morning he had dug and weeded a tiny square of earth by the yard gate and pushed the root somehow between the stones beneath. Stamping the ground down with his heel, he turned away, and apparently forgot it. During its long dormant winter he never mentioned it, and I felt he was convinced he had wasted half-a-crown. No light matter.

In the Spring, when it began to sprout its tiny leaves, if he could have crowed he would have cock-a-doodle-dooed his achievement to the whole world. In early June the first bud began to open.

Through our kitchen window I saw him coming in through what would one day be our front garden. He looked tired from his uphill walk home. Coming to the rose, he dropped his bag of firewood and straightened his back. He removed his shabby cap, as a gentleman should in front of a beautiful lady, and stood there in admiration. It was no wonder; her flawless creamy pink complexion, her perfect form and subtle perfume had turned his head. He bent down as if to touch her, changed his mind, picked up his bag and came in.

In deference to my country upbringing he damped down his pride and allowed himself only, 'That rose I planted seems to be doing well enough, so far.'

'Yes, it's smashing,' I enthused, 'and there's quite a few more buds on it.'

I could see that, with luck, Nature had sent me an ally, a seductive guide to lure Syd up the garden path. My plans for that jungly patch at the back of the house took more definite shape. If only we could get started! Until now, my horticulturally ignorant husband had snorted at the idea, and put me off as usual with his 'Later on, later on, one day we'll make a proper job of it.' Now Rose, it seemed, had hooked him. With considerably fewer charms, it was my task to lure him out into the wilderness round the back.

It worked. There was no sudden conversion, but he did agree to come with me and try just a tiny piece for a sample. Tiny it was, just one square yard the first day, but weakening resolution was reinforced by pride. The weeds were not going to have it back now! So we went on. What we did not know was that the roots had insinuated themselves between the hardcore and the big flat stones of what had once been a rickyard. No spade or garden fork would pierce that ground, but we had a secret weapon, a heavy old pickaxe; out came the stones, in went the spade, over went the earth, and out came the weeds. The whole thing was an ecologist's paradise, sheltering every weed, insect and pest in the book.

It brought out in us a streak of mad obstinacy as we laboured on, and it also brought our antics to the notice of some of the local old codgers, whose evening jars of cider were enlivened by talking of our predicament.

'What's thee think o' they nogmens o' Londoners? They be tryin' to make a gyarden where thic old stone rickyard used to be!' Ignoring advice, and despite obstacles and good-humoured ridicule, we battled on—I was going to say in our spare time. We just fitted it in with everything else. We had no wheelbarrow, but the boys helped to carry the stones away in old buckets and tipped them helpfully into the tractor ruts in the path to the cherry orchard.

In my childhood our Mam had spent plenty of her energy nagging me to do some weeding, or to carry a spare bucket when she followed the horse tracks for their precious droppings. Grancher lived next door at the time; he was a good old gardener, and there was a good-natured, sharp but unspoken rivalry between them. Oh, the smirk on her face when she bestowed on him one of her monster cabbages, or a couple of gargantuan parsnips! He was a man of the strong silent sort, and made little comment except a mumbled thanks. But he knew what she meant, and got his own back. One thing I learned from it, that manure is excellent for the garden. If horses and cows and sheep had been sent to us just to convert grass into dung, that alone would justify them. Manure contains the very elixir of life. It drives plants mad with joy. Sucking up the lovely, lively stuff, they reach up for the sun like oak trees. Determined to colonise the world, they throw out their blooms and seed with profligate vigour. Stuffed full of beneficent bacteria, they defy disease and pests. And we had an absolute treasure trove of it handy! A mine of muck!

On the cobbled floor of the biggest barn was a two-feet deep coating of well-rotted straw and manure; residue of the days of horses and carts. It was so old it did not smell, and so dry I could pick it up without soiling my fingers. We could cut it into little blocks like peat, and we did, and carried it round the back to smother our new-born garden. I was not content till all was gone, and I could sweep up the last crumbs off the cobbles. By then, hundreds of bucket-shaped mounds of it peppered our ground. When we got that ground finally dug, manured and planted, it still looked as humpy as a battlefield, but there, we had put up a fight!

The results of our efforts gradually brought us enrolment into one of the finest organisations in the world—the gardeners' club. 'Could you do wi' a feow cabbage plants, missus?' ' 'Ere's a couple o' rows o' early taters, me own grown, I a' got these over an' you be welcome to 'em.' 'Try these kidney bean seed. My brother give me a yup on 'em, a new sart 'im sent away for.'—and so on ad infinitum. Gardeners are interested in anybody's garden, even ours, and more than once we had expert spectators leaning on our rickety fence. Some who had come at first to jeer remained, not to cheer perhaps, but to give faint praise, then non-committal encouragement, and eventually even compliments. We also got advice, enough to fill a gardening encyclopaedia, and often contradictory. We learned the valuable lore, unwritten, handed down the generations from cottage gardeners who had never heard of ICI or aerosols or artificial fertilisers. They knew the value of compost and manure, bonfire ash, soot, leafmould, and the planting and digging-in of green humus crops like mustard, turnips, and lupin. To them a spade was a spade and dung was dung; phosphates, iron, potassium, and trace elements were things for they new fangled breed of gardeners to worry about and mess with.

At first we could hardly tell the weed seedlings from our

germinating seeds, but oh, the never-diminishing thrill of re-
cognising embryo lettuce, the tiny carrot, the pushful pea! No
wonder our Mam had used to nag us for help; the prolific weeds
got a head start on everything. Raw students though we were in
Nature's university, before the year was out we gave ourselves
several honours degrees for our achievements.

Who would envy the lady of the Manor who goes into the
kitchen to plan the menu with the cook, who then instructs the
gardener what fruit and vegetables she requires for the day? How
sad in comparison to walking up the garden yourself, gathering the
crops of your own labour, and planning the menu accordingly.
Then to sit outside in our sunny courtyard shelling our own peas,
hulling our own strawberries, top-and-tailing our own gooseberries, and getting a suntan and a rest at the same time! My
sweet little forays into Summer's paradise.

All the seasons have their magic. The excitements of Spring,
the spade going into the thawed earth, and the first rows of early
seeds lovingly patted down; body and mind in tune with Nature's
timely start. Smug Autumn feelings, admiring the strings of
fat brown onions and the straw-covered boxes of home-grown
potatoes, tipping the carrots into dry earth to store in the shed,
snatching the odd half-hours to gather sacks of chestnut leaves for
the compost heap. Time to stand awhile and pay homage to the
last tints of Autumn as the first winds of Winter blow them
victoriously away. Now we must wrap every apple and pear, each
in its separate paper, ready for the Winter pies, jams and pickles,
gold and red and yellow, far better than useless jewels, they gleam
on the pantry shelves. At last the Winter darkness comes and
forces rest upon us, as we hibernate cosily round the roaring fire.
Now for a short spell only, we can wag our tongues and work our
brains and give our muscles ease.

That first year the stones made our carrots stump-rooted, and
we had corkscrew parsnips, but we also had potatoes almost as big
as our heads. On one root I counted thirty! Not all big ones of
course; but thirty! The blackfly sneaked up on our broad beans,
and they went into mourning overnight. We also gathered a little
crop of advice.

'Allus plant yer broad beans in the Autumn, Missus; that road
they be ready to pick afore them dattlin' peskies be about.'

We were shown how to grow hydrangeas and other plants from

cuttings and how to economise by saving our own seeds, and which of them to save, and how to encourage fertility, for which purpose apparently 'a sheep's fart were better than a 'osse's turd.' These old gardeners never tempered the seriousness of their advice with squeamish misgivings about their candour of expression.

Our four long rows of peas began to drip with pods. I had not bought the expensive packets of seeds, but just planted the cheap dried cooking peas. I reckoned that the mass producers of this vegetable would use the hardiest and most prolific strain.

Just when the tiny green pearls were beginning to form the green-finches and the blue-tits had moved in, stripping one side of each pod for the tiny succulent immature peas. The birds, the birds! What friends, what foes! In Spring these little gluttons, sprucely uniformed in greens and blues and yellows, had made an enchanting living picture as they played hide-and-seek in the sunlit pink blossoms of the American currant thriving in the shelter of the barn. Thrush and blackbird sang their pastoral symphony to accompany the ballet of the tits. Now these blithe spirits that had sung and danced with joy turned into brigands and pirates who sought their booty with ruthless determination and fiendish ingenuity. The labourer was worthy of his hire; any blackbird that scratched a slug from our garden was welcome to it, and a crust for his whistling. But not our peas, they were not going to have our peas!

I made a scarecrow, and the birds used him for a staging post. I festooned the peas with strings of milk-bottle tops, and they swung on them in the wind. I threaded cotton over and around like a web until it was almost impossible to get between the rows; the birds coped better, they found a way in, and a quick way out. They did not leave us so much as one picking of peas! I suppose those little blighters did not count their chicks before they were hatched. I was learning that a gardener does not count his crops until they are gathered, and then he must protect them from the mice!

Fortunately birds and pests are capricious in their onslaughts; some years they will leave the peas alone but help themselves to most of the soft fruit!

Men of the land have a dignity in their mien and their gait, in their steady eye and their horny hands. It is no wonder; they work for the Earth, man's greatest and all-important benefactor. They deal with high-ranking aides and enemies, the sun, the rain, the winds, the snows and frosts. Urban sophisticates may patronise, but their sneers run off the country labourers like water off a duck's back. They know they work hard with poor pay for a 'simple' life, but to them the environment of bricks and mortar and tube trains and rush hours and traffic jams—that is where the true simpletons live. Technology or turnips; it is all a matter of taste.

PART III

After Christmas the two spiteful months January and February had to be endured. A handful of scraps scattered on the snowy yard produced a good cross-section of native English birds. Bundles of nerves they were; for each other and for any cats that might be lurking about. The robins were the exception. Conscious of their special status in the bird world, they perched on the frozen pump handle in front of the kitchen window, demanding of me, beady-eyed, that I open the window of our chilly unheated kitchen for them to dine in style on the sill inside.

The pheasants were not so lucky; occasional ones strayed in from the woods to eat our Brussels sprouts in the back garden. Poor victims, I did not shoo them off. Their fate hung close about them; come Saturday the beaters and guns would arrive, scaring them out of their ground shelters to shoot them on the wing and bring them thudding forlornly down to earth. A primitive exercise for the rich, 'our betters'. When Saturdays were wet, cold and stormy and they had to plod among the trees in the mud, I thought 'serve 'em right'.

Soon afterwards the golden trumpeters arrived; battalions of them on grassy banks, in woodland clearings, and dotting the sides of the Forest paths; brave soldiers against the biting winds, to announce that Summer was once again on the way. Many thousands of them fell to the estate workers' children; a golden treasure trove to bring them pocket money for Easter eggs, and a treat or two. Basketfuls and bucketfuls were gathered and taken down to the main road where the children offered them in bunches to the passing drivers.

Our tight budget left only the occasional copper to give our children their spasmodic bits of pocket-money. When they announced their intention of going into the daffodil business I offered to help them pick and bunch. Nicky had been told by a school chum where the best pickings were, nearest to us. Nicky led the way along the bridle path bordered by copses to the wide wooden gates at the bottom of the cherry orchard, gates that were only kept closed in the picking season. These led into thick woods going steeply down into a valley with a small stream in the bottom. We walked in the rutted path made by the timber tractor.

'Oh look, Mummy, here's some primroses,' called Jenny, rushing ahead of me. I love primroses; they look up at you with such sweet and guileless faces from the decayed vegetation around them. When a clump peeps up at the base of a tree, the accidental artistry of their delicate cream-and-yellow flowers against the rough grey bark forms a picture to be carried always in the mind's gallery. We came across so many that I decided to gather some on the way back for bunching, impressing on the children as we went never to disturb the roots of wild flowers or pick too many of their leaves, because as they died back the plant gathered nutriment from them.

The wood we were stumbling down was called Castle Wood. It was said that in medieval times, a castle had dominated the hill opposite it, and the stream had once been the moat that kept enemies at bay. You could well believe it. In that lonely thickly-wooded area it only needed a few wild boars and a couple of peasants with bows and arrows to step back into the Middle Ages. Nothing much had changed.

The stream was now narrow enough for us to jump across, and there they were, the daffodils. In the bottom of the valley was a large clearing, and it was absolutely crammed with them. 'Must be millions here!' enthused Nicky, and he could have been right, though nobody stopped to count. We started at the edges, and by the time we had packed our odd assortment of containers you could hardly notice the difference. I removed my pinafore to put the primroses in, and we started back.

When we got indoors, cups of hot cocoa went cold, and sandwiches were half-heartedly bitten, as we turned the living-room into a 'Covent Garden'.

'Being that we got them free,' said Richard, 'let's give the customers real big bunches, and charge 'em tuppence a time.'

'Can't do that. It wouldn't be fair on the other kids. They charge fourpence a bunch, an' they don't make 'em very big; we should be undercutting them.'

Oh dear, the problems of the business world! We compromised at threepence a bunch, and no stint with numbers, and the same for the primroses which Jenny should carry in her basket. ''Course, if nobody wants 'em at threepence, we'll let 'em go for a penny, Mum.' Pennies were riches for our children in those days.

Warning them that it would be much colder standing by the road than scrambling about picking I insisted on what extra scarves and wrappings I could muster. I arranged the few broken-stemmed flowers left behind in a vase on the table, and I set about doing my housework and making a hot tea-time meal for Syd and our flower-sellers.

They had left home just before noon. Poor kids! They could not be having any luck, and they must be freezing by now, I worried, as five o'clock came, and they were not back. Then they all came bursting in, cherry-nosed, cheeks mottled purple with the cold, eyes shining, like a lot of pools' winners. Pockets rattled with their earnings.

'We sold the lot.'

'We nearly gave up.'

'We're famished.'

'We're freezin'.'

'We'll go again tomorrow.'

After hours of standing in the bitter cold, and with almost all their stock left, they had decided to wait until six more vehicles had passed and then come home. The fifth vehicle had been a crowded coach-load of Welsh day-trippers, mostly elderly ladies. Whether from patriotism aroused by their country's emblem, or from the sight of four red-nosed children all looking alike and stamping their feet to keep warm, they had bought every bunch. 'They would have had more primroses off Jenny if she'd had them.'

Every day of the Easter school holidays we picked and bunched, and they went to the roadside with their wares. Trade was unpredictable. Sometimes every container I could muster, including jam jars, was filled with unsold stock, for unlike most of the children, Jenny could not bear to throw the unsold daffodils over the hedges to die. Not until she pronounced the death sentence was I allowed to put the withered blooms on the compost heap. By the time the Easter holidays finished, my appreciation of Wordsworth's famous poem was considerably diminished.

The day before they started back to school they made an important announcement; they were going to take me to the pictures.

'Don't worry Mum, it won't cost you anything. We'll pay your bus fare and the money to go in, and treat you to an ice-cream. You can leave Daddy's food in the oven, and we can go to the first house in the evening. It's a smashing picture, Mum; all the kids are talking about it; it's called *The King and I*.'

Apart from my delight at their suggestion, I felt it would be a real treat to go the pictures. In their chattering company, the mile walk to the bus was no problem, and a seven mile bus-ride through the countryside is a treat in itself. The bus terminus was quite near the picture palace, and as we alighted we could see the beginning of a queue. It was quite a walk to get to the end of it, and I felt dismayed as we tagged on to it. 'Must be a smashing picture to have a queue this long,' enthused Chris, 'I'll go and see what time this house comes out.' We had a twenty-minute wait.

More people came and added to the queue. Shifting my weight from one foot to the other, and listening to the cheerful magpie chatter of the children, the twenty minutes went by quite quickly. We could not see the cinema entrance, but word came down the line, 'They're coming out,' and a lot of people streamed past us, all enthusing about the programme. Our queue began to move forward, and I happily envisaged lowering myself into a comfortable seat for the three hours of escapism.

We were still about three yards from the pay-box when the 'House Full' notice was put up by a commissionaire who informed us we would have to queue another three hours for the last house, unless enough stragglers came out to let us in.

Three more hours of standing, and my ankles already beginning to puff up! 'Let's buy some fish and chips and go back home,' I suggested.

'Oh, Mummy, no,' they groaned. We played 'I spy'. We had guesses how many people would pass the queue whilst I counted a hundred. We thought of all the girls' names from A to Z, and then the boys'. Two long hours went by.

By choice, I would not have stayed another five minutes if the stars of the film had been coming to greet us in person, but the children were in a mood of patient anticipation. My feet were killing me. 'Shan't be a couple of minutes,' said Chris, and he came back with twopence worth of chips for each of us. Warm, salted, and vinegared, they tasted like manna from heaven. His example was soon followed by more people from the ever-growing queue. Still fifty minutes to go. Daffodils! It was all very well for

Wordsworth lying in pensive mood on his couch! I could have done with a couch, or anything to put my swollen burning feet up. Some treat this was!

At last, at last, the cinema doors were opened. The crowds streamed out and we streamed in. It was heaven to relax in the warmth and comfort. Even the trailers, the adverts and the cartoons seemed wonderfully entertaining, but they were only the appetizer for the strutting dominating King figure of Yul Brynner, the charming Deborah Kerr, the enchanting Siamese children, the music and the colour; all sent over our heads and on to the screen by the man in the magic box at the back. As well as our chips Chris had bought an ounce of tobacco for his Dad, and Jenny, Richard and Nicky paid for our ice-creams and something towards the tobacco.

After three hours of euphoria, the chill and the dark hit us as we hurried to the comfort of the bus-ride. As we stepped it out sharply on our mile walk at the other end through the lanes the children drowned the hooting of the owls with their rendering of the show's songs. 'Shall we dance?' they carolled and skipped, but I could not, not even for Yul Brynner. My legs were getting heavier with every step up the hill. I felt like the pious little boy who fell behind in the school races, and looking skywards he beseeched, 'Oh Lord, if you pick me feet up, I'll put 'em down.'

Syd had a lovely blazing fire and our cocoa cups ready, and a ready ear for our praises of the film, and a proud Dad's beam when he was presented with his extra baccy.

Young seedlings rarely wilt for long when transplanted. Even fifteen-year-old Chris appeared to find more distractions than regrets in our new environment. It is older plants that find difficulty re-establishing; some of my roots had become pot-bound in the cracks of London's pavements. Much of my insignificant identity had been moulded by the sights, sounds, colour and culture of city life, and the friends I had left behind. I missed them all. I had got used to the strident extrovert bustle of packed humanity. Nevertheless it is true that when life has battered us about a bit we dream of the solace and balm to be found in the quiet countryside, a peace for the spirit.

Such a mood came over me one day in early summer. After a night and morning of much-needed gentle rain the sky cleared and the sun came out warm enough for it visibly to coax back some moisture from the soaked earth. The birds began to sing and whistle about their business again. In narrow flower beds round the courtyard we had planted scented stocks, sweet williams and pansies. Having drunk deep, they perked up and seemed to turn their beautiful faces upward to say thank you to the heavens, and sent out their perfume for added measure. Back from their enforced break, the impatient bees resumed their nectar-gathering; a fat bumble-bee kept a precarious hold on the blossoms that bent under his weight.

As I stood leaning against our open doorway the cat brushed by my legs, rubbing his head good-naturedly against them, before relaxing on a sun-warmed flagstone in the courtyard. From the cottage down the field I heard the proud cackle of one of Mrs Saunders' Rhode Island Reds, and I pictured the big warm brown egg lying in the straw of the nest-box. I knew now that the faint mewing sounds I could hear from above did not come from some distressed cat in one of the barns but from a pair of buzzards way up there in the sky, two circling airborne acrobats giving their graceful display and looking like dots against the boundless back-cloth of blue.

There was water to be pumped, salad from the garden to be washed for tea, and gardening and housework to get on with, but I could not break this idyllic spell. Like the flowers I was about to raise my face to the sun, when a sudden pouncing movement of the cat showed he had scooped up a mouse between his paws. I knew we kept the cat to keep the mice away, but I was also aware of the sadistic ritual with which this warm-blooded little creature would be worried to its death. The mouse appeared to be still unharmed as I picked up the disgusted cat and shut him indoors.

That taloned paw had pierced my mood of self-delusion. In my heart I knew those buzzards were up there as birds of prey waiting to swoop down and take some living creature for their dinner. I remembered the writhing worm I had accidentally cut in half with my spade only yesterday, and how many more of them were casually consumed alive by moles and birds and other enemies. What was it the poet had written, great fleas have little fleas upon their backs to bite 'em, and little fleas have lesser fleas and so ad infinitum. That was Nature's pattern right enough, but not just to bite, but to kill and devour, red in tooth and claw. From microbe to mammoth we are all links in the chain of prey. My train of thought almost put me off washing the lettuce in salt water in case I tortured the little predators it harboured. Not your fault, I comforted myself, let Nature carry her own cans.

It was quite a relief to hang the bucket under the pump and give the iron pump-handle a good bashing up and down. A few heave-hos and the pure ice-cold water gushed up from its source eighty feet below the yard. As I pumped water I was often reminded of a song my Granny used to hum to herself, 'Ah, you never miss the water till the stream runs dry'. It was water from a tap I was missing. Despite all the family taking turns at the pump, the large white enamel bucket on the kitchen table needed perpetual re-plenishing, and oh, the slop-overs, as kettle and saucepans were filled with a jug that stood on the tray next the bucket. Damn it! I groaned as I caught the bottom rim of the bucket on the table as I heaved it up, spilling most of its contents.

'Mrs Mopp,' that about summed up my role in life, I thought angrily. For some time my patience, never Job-like at its best, had been running dry from every little aggravation. I put it down to the dyspeptic symptoms that had been plaguing me lately. In moments of truth I put my dyspepsia down to my lack of patience. Either way it gave me continual burps and sessions of sharp pain in the stomach. My tendency to hypochondria and secret morbid diagnosis of my own or anyone else's symptoms, had been sub-limated in the past by worrying over the children's illnesses. They had now all been through the usual childhood infections, Nicky's nerve trouble was almost a thing of the past, the family were hale and hearty. So I had begun to concentrate on my own aches and pains.

I had one genuine grumble, a slipped disc, and here fellow-sufferers will surely sympathise. The agony when the offending discs press on the spinal nerve can be fairly equated with the last stages of childbirth, and can keep one immobilised from a few days to a couple of weeks. I was free of trouble for long periods but once experienced, a little cloud of dread hangs permanently in the back of the mind.

What with this and my indigestion, I was not the most cheerful of hostesses to my young nephew from London who always joined us for the school summer holidays.

Five children in a household always attract more, even though at such times Chris used to find a temporary job on the estate. By mid-morning, Jenny's special school-friend Julie had arrived with a carrier-bag of her toys for them to play with. The two set up house in one of the smaller barns. Provided with dustpan and broom and odds and ends from the house they were little trouble. Boys, however, will be boys. By the time friends Roy and Graham had joined the four already on my hands I was as jumpy as a cat on a hot tin roof. With so much of the estate out of bounds to boys I tried to keep them within eye-and-ear shot. Boys thrive on challenge and they are full of curiosity; these traits got man to the moon. If there was nothing else about, they would challenge each other, going into three-a-side rugby scrums at the drop of a hat. It was too much of a challenge for one of our two fireside chairs; when they went into attack upon it, it collapsed.

'Get out, you perishers! Can't turn my back on you two minutes before you behave like a pack of wild animals. Take that broken chair with you; put it in the woodshed until your Dad can have a look at it, and you'd better have a good look for that hammer you took out yesterday, which you were supposed to be making a rabbit-hutch with. Your Dad'll do his nut if he can't find it! And one of you pump me a bucket of water.'

'Get down off that barn roof, Leslie, you'll break your neck. Don't be silly; of course the hammer's not up there.'

'I said pump me a bucket of water, not break the handle swinging on it like that.'

'Stop swiping that ball in the courtyard; you'll break a window next.'

'Give the girls that sweeping-brush back. I can't help it if you are trying to balance it on your finger; they asked for it to play houses with.'

On average they drove me to hysterics twice a week, when I would go and sit in the woodshed and have an hour's nervous breakdown. My performances fascinated them. They watched my oncoming bouts of madness with the detached interest of playgoers watching Ophelia going crazy.

'Hungry already? It won't be dinner time for more than an hour yet. Oh well, if you're famished, just you all come inside and sit dead quiet and I'll make you all some toast and cocoa. Ask Jenny and Julie to come in for some too.'

Better do twelve slices at least. Oh, Lord, here's young Micky turned up now; better make it the loaf, and put it on this meat dish. Before I could put the dish of toast down on the table their outstretched hands had cleared the lot. Our income was stretched to feed our own brood, let alone their friends, but remembrance of my own often hungry childhood, and the bliss of getting the unexpected piece of bread and jam, made me love to give food to children. Especially ever-hungry growing boys, even well-fed ones.

Keeping them out of mischief was not so much to my taste. Then I thought of a way to kill two birds with one stone. While they drank their cocoa I got them all enthused with the idea of setting up a camp on the rough ground at the top of the back garden. If they would gather some of the old bricks lying about I would help them build a barbecue. A couple could go down to the rubbish hole by the chestnut tree to find some old iron for a grid to put the frying-pan and saucepan on. Nicky and Graham could gather some kindling wood for their fire. I would contribute a few knobs of coal, a frying-pan, a saucepan, enamel plates, a tin of baked beans, potatoes, an onion or two, two cold sausages to cut up in the fried onions, and some cornish pasties I had made the day before. They would have to pump and carry their own water. I would supply them with soda and bowl to do their own washing-up afterwards. After all, real cowboys did not cart their mothers round with them.

The gypsy in me got quite carried away with the idea, and the boys were enthusiastic too. The two little girls were happy to keep out of the arrangement. I turned them outside for their argu-mentative pow-wow about the delegation of chores, and I insisted on the role of safety officer regarding the construction of the barbecue. I would have liked to have mucked in with them really, but I was glad of my ploy to keep them busy. By the time I had handed over all the supplies my cowboys demanded, my kitchen utensil cupboard was looking quite bare. They promised me a plate of chips to share with the girls, and how about a bottle of sauce, and what had I got for their pudding? They made enough fuss, bustle and noise to mount an assault on Everest, but event-ually the barbecue was lit. They had fashioned seats from bricks and scraps of wood.

Thankful to be able to get on with my own jobs, I left them to it. After a few arguments about who should be the cooks, the rest settled down to make themselves some pipes of peace from the hollow-stemmed old man's beard fixed into sort of pieces of wild cherry wood burned out with a hot poker to hold their 'bacca, coltsfoot leaves dried by their fire. I peeped through the back door now and again; it was comical to see them all aping the way Syd sat, held his pipe, and puffed away. But coltsfoot 'bacca soon separates men from the boys. When I called for one of them to fetch a jug of squash and some cups, only Richard was able to stand up straight and make a wobbly green-faced totter to the back door. Just in time, I thought, as I saw Leslie make a quick dash into the trees. None of them was willing to lose face by putting his pipe out first.

Their nausea must have been short-lived, for soon afterwards I was presented with a thumb-blackened plate of greasy chips. My faulty digestion baulked at the prospect, but I fried them to a crisp brown, and Julie and Jenny accepted them enthusiastically to boost their picnic lunch. My own stomach felt sort of sore inside and could only manage some bread and butter and cups of tea.

After giving the bedrooms a clean and a tidy-up I opened the back door to check on the cowboys. The camp was deserted, and piled up on the back doorstep was all their unwashed cooking paraphernalia, fire-blackened, burnt, and covered with grass, dirt and congealed grease. I caught a glimpse of the last back sneaking off round the barn. 'Come back, you rotters,' I yelled, but I knew my screams fell on deaf ears. I stopped worrying about where the young blighters had got to, as I tackled the mess from my bright idea. I could not leave it for them to do because I needed the utensils to cook our evening meal. As I suspected, they kept out of my sight until hunger drove them home, all carrying bundles of firewood for peace-offerings. Washing-up dodgers, embryo chauvinists, hobbledehoys all, yet I still loved them and my love was not misplaced.

By evening the sore feeling in my stomach had become a sharp residual pain, brought on, I supposed, by my all-day mood of irritability. I got them all off to bed a bit sharpish and earlier than usual. Chris was no trouble; he had done a hard day's work hoeing a tree plantation, and he sat out the evening reading, chuckling at the antics of Bertie Wooster and Jeeves. Syd was glad to escape from my general air of the miseries by doing some weeding. At bedtime I took a good dose of stomach powder and hoped that sleep would provide the cure, as it so often had. This was a case of putting a calm mind over a hysterical stomach, I thought, but by two in the morning my stomach had not given in. I crept downstairs for another dose of stomach powder, then sat on the edge of the bed rubbing my fist between my ribs, trying to soothe the pain.

'What on earth are you doing?' grumbled a sleepy Syd.

'Dying!'

'Not again! Well, go downstairs and do it quietly. You're keeping me awake.' I am still giving him the benefit of the doubt when he said he must have been dreaming.

I felt even worse in the morning; Syd and Chris had to get themselves off to work. When I heard the others stirring I tried to get up, but I doubled up with pain. I told Richard they would have to get their own breakfast, and to please behave until I felt well enough to come down. Meanwhile I tossed and turned trying to find a position to make the pain more bearable. This was by far my worst bout of indigestion.

Later in the morning I heard them answering the door to Julie, Roy, and Graham. Oh God, I thought, what sort of mess should I get up to? It was gone eleven before I felt fit enough to crawl downstairs, and I opened the living-room door on to an army of little Mrs Mopps, and kindly persuasions to 'Go back to bed, Mum; we can manage.' I felt like hugging the lot of them, bless their hearts. It showed they really did care for me, even if none of them had thought to bring me up a cup of tea.

'What's the matter with Mummy?' asked worried Jenny.

'Nothing much, darling; just the stomach ache.' I did not know then that my gall bladder had been packing itself with stones, and one had decided to emigrate down through the tiny tube leading to the liver.

By the next moring I was free from pain, and so grateful for that and for the children's helpful behaviour that I determined to be very patient and tolerant for the rest of the school holidays until I could go back to work.

Countless books have been written by people who have attempted to opt out of the rat-race and live in primitive isolated cottages far from the madding crowd. They usually reckon to have spent all their capital on some tumbledown dwelling, but in no time at all they manage to install an Aga cooker, and a Heath Robinson contraption to provide some sort of electric power. Good luck to them for their efforts, I say.

It is all very well to live in primitive conditions if one is not expected to maintain modern standards of hygiene. After nine years of pumping water, and the difficulties of drying and airing clothes round the one fire we could afford fuel for, I had begun to reckon that prehistoric women did not have it so bad. No weekly shampoos or baths, no constant changes of underwear for their families! What got me down the most was drying our washing in wet, frosty or snowy weather. Urgently required things had to be put one at a time on the guard in front of the fire. All our underwear and the children's school sports vests and shorts had brown singe marks, often in embarrassing places. How I envied the women with airing cupboards!

Over the years I had become friendly with Helen, the game-keeper's wife. Like me, she suffers from a complexity of aches and pains. On a couple of occasions she had called and found me lying on the hard floor with my back 'out', and hoping and sometimes praying that promptly stretching out flat would bring a quick cure. She called on me between jobs, and over cups of tea we oozed sympathy for each other's long lists of symptoms. She still has a lovely soft Scots accent, a dry wit, and is much more conversant with Estate matters than I. So I can always enjoy her reminiscences of the local characters.

We usually greet each other with long self-pitying expressions, but during the afternoon we get more and more cosy and com-fortable. It was her kidneys and blood pressure in particular that had been playing her up on one occasion. Tea and sympathy and free-ranging chat helped us to forget all about them, and about my suspected peptic ulcer, as she enlivened the time with interesting and amusing anecdotes garnered during thirty years on the Estate. Laughter is infectious, especially Helen's; smiles became grins, grins chuckles, and soon we were giggling out loud.

As she took her leave across the courtyard I reminded her she *must* go to the doctor about her troubles. Her sweet bonny face, still smiling broke again into laughter.

'I feel a lot better now,' she said. 'I feel fine after our little chat!'

'So do I,' I giggled. 'That's funny!' which set her off again. But I added, 'Do be careful; they say you can die o' laughing!' We both fairly doubled up now, the tensions from our 'ailments' released till her next call, and as she walked through the old yard I could see her shoulders still shaking.

She always brought a little gift with her; a few new-laid eggs, a bunch of flowers, some of her gooseberry tartlets, or a plastic bag of specially luscious blackberries picked on her way up. One day she brought some wonderful news, so wonderful that I kept expressing doubt of its truth just to hear her repeating it. *Our cottage was going to be put on the mains water*!

Was she sure? Yes, she was quite sure. The digger was already in operation, a good way further up the hill, making trenches to other out-lying cottages.

'But it's such a long way down to here! The expense! Surely the Estate would never bother?'

'Ah, but it will be for the animals as well; there are going to be cattle troughs installed at intervals on the way down.'

A tap in the kitchen! A tap that one had only to turn with thumb and forefinger to get all the clean running water one wanted! The very thought made me feel better than a visit to the finest health spa. My aches and pains, real and imaginary, took a back seat. The only celebration I could manage just then was to make a dish of toffee for the children, and that was part ploy—'Three lumps each, if you'll go up the hill after tea to see if you can see a digger!'

With toffee-bulging cheeks, Nicky and Jen hurried up the fields, and came back with the wonderful news. Yes, there *was* a digger up there, though it was still a long way off.

Chris by now had left home. Lucky Chris, he was going steady with a delightful girl, now one of our treasured daughters-in-law. Family circumstances had made it necessary for Carole's mother to move to Dorset, and she was not well at the time. Torn between love and loyalty to mother and boyfriend, Carole unselfishly put her mother first. Chris could not bear the separation, and left his job as reporter on the local paper to follow her. With his talents he had been a round peg in a round hole there. Now, with his impulsive move to Dorset he was working as a baker's roundsman in the mornings, and as a café counter-hand in the evenings; temporarily the only work he could get. It was obvious from his letters that he felt enriched by the sheer beauty of the Dorsetshire coast, and by the charm of the cottages where he delivered bread. 'In places it's more beautiful than round home'—and for Chris that was praise indeed.

As it was vacation time Richard was at home. He had got a County Major award and was taking economic geography at Sussex University. He was working as a builder's labourer, partly as a principle that he ought to put some hard work into society, and partly to earn some money to boost his grant. Not only did he cover the cost of his keep whilst at home but he also delighted Syd and me with presents, gardening tools and much-needed crockery.

I was all agog waiting for our well-spring of riches to arrive. At last, one day when I got home from work, I could see the digger against the skyline only one-and-a half fields away. I ran in and made a jug of hot sweet tea, put a piece of home-made cake on a saucer on top, and hurried up the hill to proffer it to the driver. It was warm weather and I had never known a manual worker who could not down a jug of tea. No handsome film star had ever received a more idolatrous smile than the one I gave that driver as I offered him the tea. He was not a bit handsome; in fact he was downright ugly, a bit long in the tooth, rusty of physique and dusty of boots and trousers and jacket. A good match for the great dirty unwieldy contraption he was driving, but handsomer to me than St George on his charger. I stroked the rusty side of the giant digger, and I felt like stroking the driver as well, for between them they were making a dream come true.

Some dozen jugs of tea later the driver drank one at last in the old farmyard that had now become our front garden. His part of the project was finished, and the pipe-layers and ditch-fillers were coming behind him. Then builder's workmen would put a stand-pipe in the barns and lay a pipe across the courtyard into our kitchen. As he drank his tea and ate his cake he revealed that he was a keen gardener who now had only a pocket-handkerchief piece in town. He walked around admiring Syd's giant pansies that edged our colourful flower beds. He left with some pansy roots and a bulging bag of vegetables, herbs and soft fruit from the back garden.

If patience is not one of my virtues, at least anticipation is one of my joys. My spirit soared and slumped in turn, waiting first for the pipes to be laid down the fields, and then for the builder's workmen to arrive. It actually took less than a month, although it did seem like a year, before we could turn our tap on.

A year later the ingrate in me had grown quite blasé about water on tap. Now it seemed such a pity that we still had to empty the privy bucket and could never indulge in a proper bath.

Except for a few weeks in the depth of winter, I was now a regular worker on the seedbeds, and a good speedy one at that. Syd worked conscientiously in the sawmill. Nicky and Jenny did holiday work on the Estate lands, for they too were now at the grammar school. Adding it all up, I reckoned we were worth some mod cons, and once again I wrote to the Estate office for this request to be considered.

Our benign elderly squire had died the previous year. He was almost eighty, and on his feet to the last. His son and heir from his first marriage had been tragically killed in an air accident during service in the Second World War. Handsome, affable, and capable, he had been struck down by fate just after his twenty-first birthday. We can only imagine what his parents suffered, but there was worse to come. Three months later the Squire was a widower; maybe the heartbreak had accelerated his wife's death.

Politically and morally it seems to me very wrong that large areas of our beautiful country should be owned by wealthy private families. No man or woman, however hard they work in a whole lifetime, or whatever their skills, can ever earn such a reward. Therefore there is a parasitical element in the situation, and some stealing of other human birthrights. Yet I understand the unquestioning acceptance of it. In my present circumstances, here in our tied cottage, with its large productive garden and a pantry full of food, with power and light, I do not often compare my lot with that of half-starved natives in other lands, living in tin shacks, watching their children die of malnutrition and disease.

Another thing, although our Squire lived in a manor house, he lived in it simply, and even when he was in his seventies he would go out spade in hand to dig out overgrown ditches.

At sixty-two years old, left quite alone without a wife or heir, administering a large estate and lands elsewhere, a lesser man would have broken. But the Squire shouldered his burden and earned the respect and often the affection of his tenants by the way he carried on his duties. Behind his back, the old hands always called him 'father', and I did not think the nickname would have offended him. It was considered a blessing when he married a young war widow, herself with two young daughters, who soon produced for him not a son and heir but two beautiful girls. Soon she too had died, the one girl only a toddler and the other a baby in a pram. Now he was indeed a father, to a brood of four.

One day I was working with another estate wife, weeding seedling trees near the manor gardens. His youngest girl was about nine years old and she came out to talk to us.

'And how are you and your sister getting on?' asked my workmate.

'Oh, my sister is in the study with Daddy now. He's been looking at our school reports.'

'Did you have a good one?'

'Well, I had good marks for ballet and swimming and riding, but not very good for the other subjects. Daddy's just given me a wigging and says I must do better next term. But he gave me some chocolate afterwards. Would you like a piece?'

A few short years later, in awed whispers, the word went round the Estate that the Squire was dead. He had suffered a seizure late one evening as he prepared himself a bedtime cup of cocoa. A couple of days before, when I was gathering wood, I had seen him getting out of his Land-Rover. He was in his eightieth year. I saw him get down from the driver's seat a little bent, but he had stood erect, squared his shoulders, and strode on as though defying Time to take him from his land.

I thought of his two younger daughters. There was no Mummy, and now there was no Daddy. No Daddy to call them into his study for a wigging about their school reports. I wept for them, and so I am sure did many other mothers on the Estate. Yet the warm arms of sympathy could not break through the cool barrier of social class. The two children were materially wealthy, and endowed with outstanding good looks, but we all sighed deeply and often on their behalf.

The administration of the Estate was left in the hands of excellent trustees and a close friend of the Squire's. It was this gentleman who came up to our cottage to discuss my request. Scrupulously conscientious for his charges's interests, he still had to admit that our cottage left much to be desired. He promised us a bathroom, a flush toilet, and that the kitchen walls and ceiling should be plastered. The work would be started without delay.

A couple of weeks later a bath and toilet fittings were delivered and stored ready in one of the barns. I almost trod a path to the barn door to keep peeping through the crack to make sure I was not dreaming. When the three workmen arrived the next week I was beside myself with excitement. To live in such pastoral splendour, *and* have all mod cons: my cup runneth over! I kept those men's energy levels at top pitch by running to them at intervals with hot cups of tea and coffee, and samples of my best baking.

When all was done I let the rest of the family have first bath. Then at last I had a wallow, a long wallow, in a bath, a bath I could lie down in, a bath where I could turn on hot water with the push of a toe.

'You all right, dear?' called Syd anxiously, when he noticed how long I'd been missing.

'Mm—m—m—mm.'

'You old soak! Come on, it's time for bed.'

It was wonderful! No more digging holes in the copse to empy the privy bucket! A streamlined kitchen that was a pleasure to cook in! Warm baths on tap! A real airing cupboard built around an immersion tank! But there was a snag: the size of the electricity bill at the end of each quarter.

However, there was plenty of work for me on the land. At apple-picking time, one other woman and myself were put to bag up cider apples in a small orchard on the side of a bank. She was a pleasant companion and we worked well and happily together. The setting was Elysian, and the autumn weather, as often, the best of the year. She was holding the sack open for me to tip my basket in; it was a bit awkward on the slope; as I picked up the heavy basket, tilting backwards a little as I did so, the now familiar agonising pain shot through my back. It had come out yet again. It was impossible to lift anything now. Even trying to bend brought the sweat to my forehead. I could not walk straight, but shambled with undignified gait, legs apart like a little boy who has messed his pants. I had to go home.

Home was three-quarters of a mile away, and every dragging reluctant step hurt more and more and exacerbated the trouble, as I forced myself over the stony paths and bumpy meadows. I begged my companion not to leave her work to come with me. Her own way home was a mile uphill in the opposite direction, and having a young family she needed to put in the working hours. My own family came home to find me lying on the floor in front of the fireplace and hardly able to bear the discomfort of lifting my head for their quickly-brewed cup of tea.

By early evening I had to try to get to the toilet, and luckily for me it was downstairs. When I came out, Nicky had decided to run the mile to the nearest phone box to call in the doctor. He came and gave me a pain-killing injection. He advised Syd to make me up a bed on boards, and said that this time he would arrange for an X-ray. It was a miserable eight days before I was able to get on my feet again—an eight days made even more uncomfortable by bouts of severe indigestion.

By the time that my X-ray appointment was due I was feeling fine again. I hurried to the bus stop feeling slightly guilty that I was wasting the hospital's time. After the X-rays I waited my turn to see the consultant.

He sat back in his chair, and asked, 'How is your general health, Mrs Foley?'

'Very good, doctor, apart from this back trouble, and bouts of indigestion.'

'Indigestion! My goodness! D'you know, you need a plumber's job doing on you. Just look at your X-rays. Your gall-bladder is packed with stones! I'm afraid you have some back trouble too, but Nature has been trying to help you. See here how you have grown two extra bits of bone that are helping your vertebrae to adjust. We can fix you up with a surgical corset for your back, and you will have to have your gall-bladder out. I'll write to your doctor.'

So I must face another operation! Despite the wonderful kindness I had received in St Mary's Hospital, Paddington, when I had my throat operation, and despite my rapid recovery, I am still a morbid coward where sugery is concerned. And I have a morbid egotistical imagination to go with it. I, of course, would be the rare one who dies under the anaesthetic. The unimportance of my life in the scheme of things bears no relation to my fears. I cannot help it; I only have one life, and I am besottedly fond of it.

This life, I really believe, is my only one. Logic will not allow me to indulge in the notion that I am worth reincarnation, or that I am any more worthy of it than the humblest living creature on the Earth. Nor can I believe that a just and omnipotent Presence is keeping an eye on me. I would love to enjoy that comfort. Myriads find it by calling themselves Christians, Muslims, Catholics, Jews, etc., yet these labels depend on circumstance or place or the people surrounding one at birth.

Man's scientific quest in search of his origins has revealed beyond doubt some incredible facts of evolution. But in so doing he has destroyed many of the myths that comforted humanity. Most religions are based on Man's desire to improve himself, to seek some spiritual comfort to reassure him there is a meaning to his existence. But it seems that it is from his own mind's resources, rather than from facts that he has tried to solve the mystery of the Universe and create his gods. Religion is like a soap bubble; it has some beautiful facets but it dissolves as soon as it touches hard reality. For this opiate to work Man must have faith in it. Religions other than his own are a dangerous threat to his beliefs, and he will oppose them and all too often kill the 'enemies' who practice them.

Yet biologists reveal that the shape colour and perfume of beautiful flowers were created to attract insects necessary to their survival, and only incidentally to delight the eye of Man. On the television screen we can see the embryo of Man's beginnings in the lowest forms of life. We cannot comprehend Time in millions of years, but we can begin to comprehend the incredible limitless ingenuity of that life force we call Nature; its adaptability, its magic, its all-powerful creative drive, and its total indifference to the individual and to the suffering wreaked by one species on another.

We all bear the cross of our mortality, and we live on an Earth rich with material pickings for the greedy and unscrupulous. So, in general, we back ourselves both ways. I am cursed with the sort of ego that cries out against my knowing why I exist, and I cling to the idea that perhaps in the act of dying the answer will come. It is only a faint hope, but meanwhile I am grateful for every day I remain among those I love and who love me.

In my bewilderment I could not commit my fate into the hands of any particular god, but into the skilled hands of fellow human beings, the surgeons and staff of Gloucester Infirmary. Even as I did so I still threw out a tiny plea for mercy to the Unknown.

That year it looked as though Syd and I were going to have a quiet Christmas to ourselves, a great change for us. His sister was adamant that this time Richard and Nicky must spend Christmas in London with her family. They accepted with alacrity. She and her husband were lavish hosts and there would be visits to shows and pantomimes. Chris was going to stay down in Dorset for

Christmas with his fiancee's family. Jenny was now fifteen and had got a Christmas holiday job some twelve miles away looking after two young children from boarding school, while their mother pursued her riding activities with the local Hunt.

Then only ten days before Christmas, I had my admittance card from the Infirmary. With only twenty-four hours notice it was a mad rush for me to pack the childrens' things and prepare what food I could for Syd. Jenny offered to forgo her job, but I would not hear of it. It was too late now, and like any teenager she was longing to buy some new clothes with her wages.

My own wardrobe at the time was very sparse. That was no deprivation for me; I am a slummuck by nature, and can manage to look untidy in anything. However, I did have a posh winter cover-up, an ankle-length Jaeger woollen topcoat, a throw-out from one of Meg's charring jobs. I rummaged around for the tidiest things I could wear under it, and packed my hospital case. Richard came in with me for company. In the ward I undressed behind the screens, re-packed my case, and told him to put it under the bed, where it would be (hopefully) ready for Syd to bring in when he fetched me home. Poor old Syd! He would have to get his own meals, walk the mile to work and back again, and then run to the bus-stop to visit me most evenings.

The almost forgotten luxury of lying for most of the day in bed, the novelty of being an object for the skilled attentions of the doctors, of having kindly nurses fussing around me, of talking and listening to the other patients, a bunch of women varied in age and character; all this was marred and saddened for me by the plight of an old lady in the bed opposite. At the age of seventy-eight her left leg had been amputated at the top of her thigh! In mind and spirit she was tired out, and all she wanted was to die. Her still-beating heart was her enemy. She would turn her mouth away from the nourishing drinks and messes. The young nurses would persist, 'Come on now, Gran, we shall stay here till you get it down.' Helpless against their cajoling she would at length give in and swallow, and then weep hopelessly in protest at their ministrations.

Mind you, the sister in charge of the ward would have taken it as a personal affront if anyone had dared to die on her. A highly skilled martinet, she was one hundred percent devoted to the mending of the human body. But God help you if you showed her the slightest sign of enjoying life while she was in charge of it. Patients, nurses and staff were as nervous as jumping beans as soon as she breezed in like a shaft of icy east wind through the ward doors. Knees straightened out, locker tops were hastily tidied, and teeth were gritted ready not to sigh or tremble as her hypodermic jabs went in. She still managed to find a fault at every bedside, with every nurse, and with the cleaners.

But she met her match, a dark-haired, dark-browed Spanish girl who could not speak a word of English. Oh that crowded minute of glorious life when Sister came on duty and the girl was polishing the ward. She had not noticed the water spilled nearby a patient's locker, but Sister had, of course. Her icy reprimands were no match for boiling-over of fiery temperament. 'Whoof' went the polisher, spinning across the ward bumping into the bed of a newly-removed appendix. A torrent of screaming Spanish, accompanied by a frenzy of gesticulating arms and threatening fists, left little need for an interpreter to tell us the wardmaid's opinion of the sister. But the starched Presence kept her cool, while a lava of angry tears ran down the cheeks of the erupting volcano. Though her muttered rumblings continued, she resumed her polishing. There was no relief for us until Sister's lunch hour; then all of us, nurses and patients, turned into a ward of helpless gigglers.

My operation went well; there were no complications. I had two small glass jars of gallstones for a memento. I had been on a non-fat diet for some months, and did not need to have a tube inserted in my side. I was a very slim eight-and-a-half stone. When the doctors and the elderly surgeon came on their rounds he told me playfully that I was a good girl to be so slim. It had been a pleasure to operate on me. I was fifty at the time and felt quite flattered, though I hoped never to give him the pleasure again. Sister, standing by him, gave me a look as lethal as a laser beam; I was now properly in her bad books, especially as earlier she had observed a young doctor tweaking my foot as he passed.

Twelve days was the normal stay in hospital for the removal of a gall-bladder. On my eighth day, two days before Christmas, Sister told me acidly that there was no hope of my being sent home for Christmas. Some others were to be discharged early to clear the ward for the expected holiday casualties. I was not dismayed; it had never crossed my mind that I might be sent home so early. 'I don't mind at all,' I told her. 'I'm quite happy to stay, thank you.' I was, too. I had of course endured quite a lot of post-operational pain, and I still had eleven painful constraining clips in my flesh, but the last few days of comparative comfort in the hospital bed was something I could appreciate.

Besides, Syd and I had got it all worked out. On Christmas Day all patients well enough could have a visitor to high tea. Syd was quite looking forward to it, although there would be no buses. 'Might get a lift in or out,' he said cheerfully. 'Anyway, I'd enjoy the walk. Give me an appetite.'

Christmas Eve, the surgeon and doctor came round with Sister to decide which patients could be allowed home early.

'Mrs Foley could go. She's making an excellent recovery,' said that turncoat.

'But she still has her clips in.'

'Yes, but it's all healing nicely. I could arrange for her district nurse to take them out. We're very pushed for beds.'

Obviously the surgeon felt the force of her character, and anyway I smiled cheerfully up at him about the idea just to show her. I fibbed that I could have a lazy convalescent three weeks when I got home.

At lunch time, Sister briskly informed me that my husband had been contacted at work and would be fetching me home that day. Then she hurried on and gave me no chance to ask her anything. I ate my spartan diet lunch of boiled fish, dry potato, and an apple; then I stripped my locker and sat down to wait in a visitor's chair. At heart I was grateful it was all over, and happy and excited to be going home.

We simply could not afford to buy all the nurses a present; I could only say thank you. But I had one for Sister. Syd had got me some expensive soap, which I had hidden unused, and I asked one of the patients to give it to Sister when I had gone. That cantankerous but conscientious healer; she was the one who had the most need of appreciation.

I knew Syd was working that morning; perhaps he would be let off early. Mentally I timed his actions. He could be at the hospital by three o'clock. The other two patients, a young girl appendix and a middle-aged varicose vein, had been fetched within an hour. At three o'clock there was no Syd. Oh well, he must surely catch

the next bus. Confidently, I kept looking through the glass door
and along the mosaic-floored corridor. Four o'clock came and
went. I began to feel like a sore thumb, and imposing on their
'hospitality' when I had to be given my tea. I was still there, feeling
utterly mortified, when the supper trolley was wheeled in. The
other patients did not have to say, 'Your husband isn't in much of
a hurry to fetch you.' I could feel them thinking it.

I had no idea how I was to get home. Sister had made no
mention of ambulance transport, and it was too late to request it
now even if I had had the nerve. Perhaps she assumed we had a
car, and she was not to know we lived a mile from a bus stop.

Then I spotted him, that tardy rotten husband of mine, hurrying
up the corridor to the ward door. 'Took your time, didn't you?' I
said tartly. 'And where's the case?' He handed me one of our old
well-worn shopping bags, with my down-at-heel winter boots and
on top the smart little red felt hat that Meg had retrieved for me
from a West End dustbin. Over his arm he had my topcoat. He
looked a bit harassed.

'What case?' he said absently.

'The one under the bed, with the clothes I wore in here.'

'Haven't looked under the bed. I just put in what I could find of
yours in the chest of drawers.' Camouflaging the old shopping bag
with my topcoat I hurried through the ward to the bathroom.

By the time I had unpacked the shopping bag my cheeks were
burning red with embarrassment, but my feelings towards Syd
were more bitterly cold than the frigid weather outside. He had
packed me a tatty vest, a petticoat with a broken strap (that was
my fault), a tatty blouse, two tatty cardigans, and a pair of odd
stockings. There were no knickers, no skirt, and no suspender belt
to keep my odd stockings up! Draped along the side of the bed the
lot might have fetched twopence in a rag-and-bone shop. I put
them all on, twisted the top of each stocking and tucked in the
resulting knot in the hope that they would not fall down on the
way to the bus stop. Thanks to good old Meg for that long button-
up topcoat! But I knew my nether end was going to feel the cold
outside. That would be nothing to the cold venom gathering on
the end of my tongue to spit at Syd.

I got out of that ward as quickly as I could, giving a general
wave of good wishes to the remaining occupants. I shook Syd's
arm off and turned my cheek away from his kiss. The draught hit

my bum as soon as we went down the hospital steps and across the
car park, and then luck stepped in in the shape of my eldest
brother-in-law. He had come with some Christmas goodies for me
on his rounds with the presents for their friends and the family.
He was delighted to hear of my early discharge, and I was more
than delighted to accept his lift home.

He would not come in, not even for a cup of tea as he still had
quite a few calls to make. My teeth were gritted as Syd opened
our door, but when he did my mouth fell open and my temper
evaporated. I was walking into surely the most cosy and delightful
room in the world! A banked-up fire was just breaking into
glorious flame, the brick fireplace and tiled hearth glowed with
polish, the big hearthrug had been given the beating of its life, the
red tiles surrounding it gleamed in the firelight, and so did the bits
of furniture that could be seen between the bowls of flowers and
dozens of Christmas cards. Glorious chrysanthemums, a jug of
hot-house jonquils, pots of primulas on the windowsill, all sent by
family or well-wishing friends. In the immaculately tidy kitchen
there was not so much as a dirty cup. I understood why Syd had
been late. I flung my arms round his neck.

'Oh, it's beautiful, it's just beautiful here! It's just like heaven to
be home!'

'I had to do it all in a bit of a rush,' Syd admitted. 'Well, I
hadn't done a stroke indoors since you went. I just couldn't; there
wasn't time. The grate was piled up with ashes, dust everywhere,
not a clean crock in the house, the bed just pulled up every night.
I was going to do it all tomorrow morning and Boxing Day. Sorry
about the case. Richard must have forgotten to tell me.'

I stood in front of the fire, lifted up my coat, and showed him
my bare-cheeked effrontery. 'They say red hat, no drawers,' I said,
then I had to sit down and hold the clips as the laughter shook me
in the stomach.

'Sorry, darling,' said Syd. 'I'll make you a lovely hot cup of tea.
That's another thing, I had to get a bit of shopping today. I've not
had the chance to get much in the way of food in, but there's a big
parcel come. It's in the pantry. I'll bring it out to you and open it.'
It *was* a big parcel, delivered by rail, a box containing a chicken,
tinned ham, Christmas pudding, cake, mince pies, dates and biscuits. It had come from Syd's sister. I was so happy I began to cry.

'I don't care now if it snows,' said Syd, and it did. Next morning was awoke to a world under several inches of it. It was still there on Boxing Day when the kindly district nurse called. She had to leave her car at the bottom, and trudge up to us through the snow, to take my clips out. Well, that was her intention, but it appeared that the surgeon had used some new-fangled clips that left a minimal scar, and the pincers she had with her could not deal with them. By the time she had got hold of the right sort, and the weather enabled her to get up, the clips were becoming embedded. She removed them with great skill and gentleness to ease the discomfort. Once again I could stand up straight.

The snow thawed, the sun came out, the children came home, and I proudly showed off my two jars of gallstones.

Mother's health had been failing for some time. To relieve the burden on my younger sister who lived near her, I sometimes took a 'day off' to help out. This meant I had a seven-mile bus ride and a mile walk each end.

As soon as I started up the woodland path that led to Mother's gate, in that familiar habitat of childhood my middle-aged identity slipped away. The child me took over, and the path became peopled with characters from the past. Here, in imagination, was elderly Mrs Box, stepping out briskly for such a short little dumpling of a woman. A fresh white apron was tied over her ankle-length black skirt, and on her head was balanced a large square basket. This, I knew, contained a choice selection of home-grown vegetables and eggs fresh from her hens. She had her shopkeeping customers, and would come back with tea, sugar, flour and rice in return for her wares. My mind ran ahead to her garden path, walled at the bottom to accommodate the slope of the garden.

There her equally plump dumpling of a husband would be tending his neat rows of vegetables, fruit, and flowers. To save her treasured garden space he grew his flowers in long wooden boxes atop the path walls. Oh! The nose-level beauty and perfumes in their season; old-fashioned pinks, sweet williams, narcissi, ranunculus, tulips, leading to the bushes of lavender, peonies, and roses round the cottage door. What pleasure to peep inside and ask please for a penny egg for father's home-from-pit tea. The tiny interior was always spotless and tidy. By day the scrubbed-top table was bare; at dusk the red plush cloth went on, and the shiny brass paraffin lamp in the middle vied with the firelight to sparkle on the steel fender and on the pretty china on the shelves. She never asked us in lest we soil her scrubbed flagstones or her well-shaken rag mats, but just to look on such cosy domesticity was a privilege.

'Mind you fasten the latch on the gate properly, or them dattlin' sheep'll get in the garden.' In its tiny sty and run at the bottom of the garden a fat pig snorted friendly greetings. They always had a pig, and there was perpetually a flitch hanging on the white-washed wall of the back-kitchen, and everlasting manure for their garden.

These two lived comfortably enough on their joint old-age pension of ten shillings a week. Their daughter had married well from her domestic job in London. Twice a year she came down from somewhere called Wimbledon, and always left them enough gold sovereigns to keep any wolf from their door.

Growing near the house they had a laurel known locally as a box-laurel. One day Mr Box was standing on a box to trim this laurel. Overcome by ego and puerile childish wit, I piped up at him 'Mr Box stood on a box to cut his box.'

'An' you mind I don't get down an' box your ears, you cheeky little wench,' he answered. He was grinning, though. He was just as pleased with his wit as I was with mine.

Perhaps the excitement of the biggest marrow even he had grown on his manure-rich mound killed Mr Box. He was found dead with his head close to this prize-winner. Despite his age, eighty-four, the sudden break-up of this seemingly imperishable old pair shocked the village. Mrs Box still appeared hale and hearty. With loving intentions her daughter persuaded her to sell up the cottage and go to live with them in Wimbledon. In a matter of weeks the old lady was dead. 'T'would 'a bin better to 'a let 'er bide at wum,' was the villagers' verdict.

Primitive tribes are often credited with better manners than their superiors. In our backwater little village we children were brought up strictly to be polite and to respect our elders.

All the same, I did not have to say 'hello' to Ferretty as he came into view with his lurcher dog and his pocket bulging with a ferret. He was not walking on the path. True to his character, he was taking a devious route between the tall thick ferns. If he got near enough I would practise my monkey-face on him, and serve him right! I took my attitude from the grown-ups. Ferretty was a thief; we all knew that.

Since his major crime, stealing Mrs P.'s Christmas puddings, he had been mentally hung, drawn and quartered and sent to Coventry by his neighbours. Now he became the guilty peg on which to hang the blame for stolen cabbages, missing hens, and sometimes even their eggs. Had he not trained his lean lurcher dog to sneak into hen-runs and bring the eggs out unbroken in his mouth? He was as sly as mustard, and too fly to be caught in the act, but two and two could be put together. He would not work, but his wife and two children could eat meat most days, and it was not always rabbit that a curious nose might sniff roasting in their oven. He grew no onions himself, but plenty went into their stewpots. Suspicion became confirmation when from his own wife's mouth he was shown to be the pudding pincher.

Mrs P. was perhaps the most respected woman in the village; a hard-working widow of impeccable character, who by her hard-earned shillings and frugal ways had brought up her family and never asked a crust from anyone. A few weeks before Christmas she made her puddings from ingredients scraped from savings throughout the year. Top-notch puddings they were; six of them, to last as special treats until the next Christmas. So rich were they in fruit and spices, they went almost black in the boiling. For their cooking she used the wash-copper in the back-kitchen built on the end of her cottage. She boiled them for eight or ten hours, gathering and chopping the fuel from the surrounding forest.

Late in the evening she flour-sprinkled six snow-fresh pudding cloths to re-cover the basins for their long storing. Then, lantern in hand, be-shawled against the cold, she went out to the copper to fish out her gourmet treasures. The long copper-stick poked nothing solider than the sides of the copper. Shocked, dismayed, and shaking with disappointment, she realised her puddings had been stolen. There was no policeman in our village; short of murder it would not have occurred to anyone to call on the services of one so high in rank. No-one had a touch of the Conan Doyle talents, either. The news brought suspicion, fury and disgust, and the vexed question of who could bring such disgrace to our village. Few other women made this festive luxury; now none would, in case when put on the table it would arouse suspicion.

Even the guiltless could not rest easy in their minds, for all knew the power of gossiping tongues.

Suddenly, months later, the mystery was solved. It came out during one of the heated rows that Ferretty and his wife indulged in. He must have driven her beyond the realms of caution, for she was heard to scream at him, 'I'll go an' tell Mrs P. who stole 'er Christmas puddens!'

'An' doosn't thee ferget to tell 'er thous't 'elp to yut 'em.'

From now on the pair of them were ostracised, and the pity hitherto felt for the wife was dissipated. ''Adn't thic good Mrs P. brought up 'er own tin o' linseed meal an' clean rags to make poultices when Ferretty's little boy got the pneumonia? And 'adn't 'er sat up day an' night 'elpin' wi' the nursin' of 'im? Saved thic boy's life, that's what 'er done, an' that was the thanks 'er got for it!'

There was not much I could say to poor old Liza Baa. I could hear her cackling moans before I saw her, holding up her sack apron to gather kindling wood. Why ever did God let people be born deaf and dumb? It was so difficult to know what they were trying to say. All one could do was to try and put on the right expression and pretend to understand. Sometimes she seemed angry about something; then I could shake my head and mutter 'tut-tut', as the grown-ups did when talking about things that we children were not supposed to listen to. It was lovely when Liza Baa smiled; she was not really like a witch at all, although her grey hair hung in straggles down her face, and she was so thin, and her hands looked like claws.

It was an advantage having her living at the top of the village. When some of the school bullies from the Hill chased us home threatening us with sticks, they all stopped in their tracks if we beat them to Liza's gate. It was handy to tell them she was a witch, and would put spells on them if she saw them. I knew she was quite kind, really. When Mam sent me up with some coal in a bucket for her she cut me off a thick piece of bread and dripping, although I kept shaking my head to say 'no thank you'. She showed me what she had in her chest of drawers by the fire; nice clean ironed pillowcases, and a proper tablecloth with a green border round it. I could tell by the noises she was making, like a cat purring, that she was very proud of these nice things. Mam

and all the other women were just the same when they'd got
something to show off, but because Liza couldn't talk none of the
women ever went into her house.

Now, I had to stand and listen to her; she put the wood down
out of her apron so she could 'talk' with her hands. What a job it
was trying to make head or tail of it. She seemed to be pointing at
our house. Now she held her arms together and rocked them as if
it was a baby. How could *she* know if the nurse was coming to
bring somebody a new baby? We didn't want any more; the nurses
ought to have had more sense. Instead of taking some to Mrs
Harper who'd got none, they kept bringing 'em to people who've
already got a lot! Wonder why Liza hadn't got any babies? Perhaps
it was because she'd married old George who was a bit simple and
didn't know how to write a letter to order one!

It was no good, I couldn't stop; I could see our Dad coming
down the dip in the path on his way to work. There, I've put your
sticks back into your apron and somehow I've told you that I'm in
a hurry. She'd spotted him, too; I thought she loved him nearly as
much as I did. How different she looked when she saw our Dad;
her face lit up. It was because he knew how to 'talk' to her with a
lot of funny signs he learned from a book on deaf-and-dumb
language. Fancy, when she was young, Liza was sent to a home a
long way off to learn it. But there were no other deaf-and-dumb
people in our village for her to talk to.

How odd it always seemed to see Dad's clean face and hands
when he started off for the pit in his clothes all stiff with dried pit
dust. He'd got the nicest most handsome face in the world; if he
had had a beard he'd have looked just like the sailor on the Navy
Cut packets. I ran to meet him before he got up the other side of
the dip.

Now everything has gone misty. Dad is not here; no-one is here;
just the path, the ferns, the birds, the sky and the trees. The little
girl that took me over is gone too. She has probably run down
under the one huge chestnut tree to play with Gladys, Lill, and
Dolly, those other creatures of memory. Wipe your eyes, woman,
for goodness' sake. There, I can see Mam's gate already. Don't
forget you have come to give her a surprise and cheer her up;
don't let her see you have been crying.

It was hard not to cry as I approached the gate. The roof of the little stone pigsty beside it had fallen in, and the door had rotted off, forlorn reminders of our 'Sukey', 'Squealer', 'Tig-tag', and 'Rush-at-the-bucket', grunting great softies that Mam had miraculously reared from the runt piglets given her by other villagers. The flat piece of trod-down earth by the gate was no longer marked with hopscotch scratchings. A growth of tall nettles filled the ash-mix hole now the village had been upgraded for the services of a dustman. Fecundity was out of fashion; there were no children scrambling among the ashes and the rusty tins for the wares for their 'shops' and 'houses'. No little girls were playing five-stones on the grassy bank we called the tump, or pulling each other down it on old sacks for helter-skelters. It was all so quiet.

As I passed her window I was glad to see Mam busy with some sewing. With her physical strength so weakened by age and ill-health, she was hard put to find ways of making herself useful to her family. Sewing had never been one of her skills, but now despite her bad sight which had got much worse, and holding the material almost to her nose, she would turn every bit of material old or new that she could lay her hands on into pinafores for us daughters, pillow-cases for the children's beds, or teacloths from the best pieces of worn-out tablecloths. On the table by her side she had her treasure-tin open. In this once gaily-painted toffee tin were kept the garnered baubles of her life-time. Stripped of association, their worth could be measured in shillings, but among the pretty buttons, and the cross and chain given her by her first mistress in service, and the bracelet with a broken safety chain, and the cameo brooch with no fastenings, among all these were two things of priceless value to Mam.

One was a brooch of pretty coloured stones with the word Mother in imitation mother-of-pearl across it. This was a present from my brother, all the way from a day's outing in Blackpool when he was a young man. The other was the first Mother's Day card she had ever received, bought for her by my younger sister, Gwen. It was quite small and dainty, with roses and violets surrounding a verse of tribute to a beloved mother. We had been brought up in a childhood devoid of greeting cards of any sort, too poor for such mementoes to be indulged in. This graceful gesture of Gwen's from her first few shillings earned in a factory had thrilled and pleased Mam beyond words.

Our mother was not a demonstrative one. Once we were able to get off her lap, I cannot remember her kissing any of us, yet she would work her fingers to the bone on our behalf. That brooch and that card must have seemed to Mam like the words 'I love you', words her heart ached for. I am sure that none of the gifts any of us brought her in later years, or the large fancy Mother's Day cards we sent when the custom had become commonplace, ever competed with those two little pledges of love.

It took her a second or two to blink me into recognition through her thick-lensed glasses. 'Hello, my wench, oh I *be* pleased to see you. I'll get the kettle on.' With belated wisdom I kissed her, told her not to get up, and bustled about with the teacups, preparing the meal I had brought to cook for her.

'Them broad beans I planted be showin' up!' and as she said this a rare look of pleasure lit her face.

'Never!'

'They be! I scrawled up the garden somehow wi' me walkin' stick, an' they be all up through the ground.'

Mam had inherited a passionate love of gardening from her humble Welsh forebears. When even her tough spirit could no longer conjure up enough strength in her frail body to dig the ground, she had given almost all the garden to my sister to cultivate. Almost all. Unwilling to accept complete defeat she had kept a tiny portion for herself, and to humour her my brother dug it over. A couple of months previously, Mam had filled her apron pockets with broad bean seeds, hobbled up to her garden on her walking stick, and then used the tip of it to make the holes and drop the beans in, and then worrit the earth over them with it. Had she lived till those beans had podded, her ulcer-ruined digestion would not have tolerated her eating them, but they enabled her to give and to keep a contact with the earth.

What a bustler-about Mam had once been, banging the day-lights out of her rag mats, dolly-tubbing the washing, polishing the grate till you could see your face in it, scrubbing a grain into everything! Now unable to indulge in energetic domesticity herself, how she enjoyed watching me play out my role as her surrogate. 'What job would you like me to do to-day?' I asked her.

'Well, I expect the bedrooms could do with a bit of a turnout by now.'

Mam had long since given up sleeping upstairs. A very cold

winter had made it expedient to have a little bed downstairs beside the fireplace. To the old, the ill, and the lonely a fire is like a friend and companion. Mam kept hers going summer and winter, although her cottage now had an electric cooker and kettle. Her life was narrowing to the confines of the two downstairs rooms of her tiny cottage, but just the same it worried her to think of the dust settling upstairs. No doubt as well, the empty half of the double bed up there discouraged her from climbing the stairs at night.

That small domain, the bed. That six feet by four feet private island, where love, travail, illness, and death had waited their turn between the sheets. Now it stood shrouded in its old-fashioned best white coverlet, and mourned top and bottom by the black iron of the bedstead. A layer of dust filmed the wash-stand, the chest of drawers, and the bedside stool. A few dead leaves blown in by a capricious breeze through the narrowly opened window added to the melancholy unused atmosphere. Hanging on the wall above the bed was a framed text. Gold letters on plywood spelled out the words, 'Put thy trust in God for I am with thee.' But there was no-one there.

From the wall over the tiny fireplace a large photograph of Mam as a young woman looked down at me. Not a conventionally pretty woman, but the smooth, plump, youthful contours of her face, topped with a mass of dark hair dressed in the fat rolls fashionable at the time, the shapely bust set off by a white lace blouse, and the sweet round neck, made a charming picture. I remembered Mam telling me, 'It wasn't all my hair, see, we used to put pads of paper inside to puff it up more.'

And Dad often mused, 'A reg'lar pockut Venus your Mother was when I met her first,' and he had first met her through the good offices of one of her four brothers. It came about through Dad going down to Wales to work. With six younger stepsisters and a baby stepbrother crowding his mother's cottage, and with a slump in the Forest coalmines, Dad had taken himself off looking for work in a Welsh coalfield, near Abertillery. He walked most of the forty miles, found a job in the Six Bells colliery, and obtained a mean, cheap lodging in the town.

Dad's pit butty was a young Welshman, the son of a farm labourer. He came down daily from the mountain to earn a bit more than the pittance he could get on the farm. He was quick to notice the inadequate rations that Father's landlady gave him for bait, and every day he supplemented it with a lump of his mother's home-made cake. Eventually he suggested that Father might be better off lodging at his home. The young man's mother was willing to look Father over. He passed her scrutiny, and went there to lodge. Now he had his own bit of home-made cake in his bait bag.

Dad used to tell us of our Welsh grandmother, 'A fine-lookin' 'oman, your granny was. Must 'a bin a 'andsome wench when 'er was young. Er was good wi' the vittles too; 'twas plain but plenty on't. And 'er give us plenty o' sharp tongue to goo wi' it. Er 'ad a temper like the weather, never two days alike, 'specially if 'er runned out o' baccy for the little clay pipe 'er smoked. I s'pose that's why your grancher left 'er when the young 'uns was growed up an' able to stand on their own vit. Im didn't goo far, just a bit further along the mountain, to the littlest house you ever saw. But 'twas bit enough for'n, cos 'im only reached about 'alf way up your granny. Like a ugly gnome, 'im was, but I never met a man I liked better. I reckon 'im could a' charmed a rabbit out o' 'is bolt-hole. And talk about an artist! Give thic mon a bit o' paper an' pencil an' 'im could draw a bunch o' flowers lookin' real enough to pick off the page. Im an' your granny was still sort o' friends; 'er done 'is washin' every week an' baked 'im bread an' cakes an' such. It was just they couldn't stand each other's company any more. Twas a civilised arrangement when you come to think on't.'

At the time Mam was working as a servant on a farm nearly four miles away. Every Sunday on her afternoon off she walked home. Her first impression of my father, confided to her brother, was 'Indeed, he's nothing but a white-faced Gloucester tup.' Father thought her a bit of a 'hoitytoity'. It took a long time for him to pluck up the courage to offer to replace her brother as escort for her long lonely walk back to her job.

Summer came, and sometimes they sat down for rests on the way. Mother was twenty-three years old and all woman, for time was to show that babies, housework, cooking and gardening was all she needed to fulfil her life. Father was just twenty-one and into full manhood. One balmy evening they sat too long in a mountain dell with only the sun, the birds and the wild flowers for company; and as the old song says, 'they found the way.' Two months later they were married, and seven months afterwards Mother gave birth to a beautiful baby girl. By then they had come back to our village to live with Father's old great-aunt who had always loved him like a son.

It was a relief to roll up the mats, take them downstairs, and make sure Mam could hear me beating them against the garden wall. I made plenty of noise sweeping into the corners and down the stairs, before asking her for the duster, cloths, and polish. By the time I had put the upstairs to rights, my efforts had inspired Mam to action. She cooked the lamb chop I had taken over, laid the table, and made a real effort to eat her dinner. I changed her bed, and gathered her washing together ready for my sister to collect. I knew well enough what to do next. In the narrow back-kitchen behind her living-room Mam liked to keep a handy indoor supply of fuel. I re-filled a row of baskets from the coal-shed, and carried down a good portion of the sticks my brother-in-law had chopped for her. Then it was time for me to go. As usual, I had cut it fine, and would have to run the mile to catch the bus to take me home; and run I did. I was running from the problems of the unhappy, frail, lonely, old and ill woman that was my mother now, running back home for the relief that the life-force of my vital and demanding young family would bring.

Mam did not live to see the broad beans come to pod. One summer morning she collapsed in a coma in her tiny courtyard; she had been potting a geranium cutting someone had given her, and the broken pot with the cutting and the little bit of soil lay scattered beside her. My brother fetched me to her, and with my sister I kept a thirty-six-hour vigil at her bedside. She slept like an unconscious child while we wiped the sweat from her face. Just in case she could hear us we whispered words of love to her; it was as though she were our child now. At last her laboured breathing ended in a sigh, and the downstairs of her cottage became empty too.

Meanwhile the stealthy years had taken our children and turned them into adults. The parent-teenage battles were over, with honours even.

'Aw, Mum, all our mates stay out till two in the morning sometimes, and their mothers don't nag them.'

'If I save up enough, I *shall* buy that motor-bike off Jimmy. It's *not* a load of old junk, and of *course* I shan't break my neck speeding.'

And oh, the lecture I gave those three boys, often enough for them to know it off by heart. 'Now mind what you get up to; I've heard about those parties you lot have in your friends' houses when the parents are away. Just remember the consequences if you do anything silly. Look what happened to young Rowena, had to leave school in the fifth form because she was having a baby. That was the result of a party and letting the lads loose on her parents' drinks cabinet. Just think how Daddy and I would feel if it was Jenny. And as for these one-night stands I've heard about, it won't be a 'bus you'll catch hanging around for them. I hope none of you will ever make me an illegitimate granny, but if ever you are daft enough to, I'd want to know. I don't want any grandchild of mine growing up not knowing who its father was, whoever the mother is. It's the greatest insult to a human being to beget it and forget it, and it means a chap has a very low opinion of himself, no higher than a tomcat.'

Then seeing their crestfallen faces, 'Yes, of course I trust you. It's old Mother Nature I can't rely on. Don't forget I had to struggle with her when I was young.'

With so many lectures preceding her, and with her own innate morality, we never had a minute's worry over Jenny in these matters.

How often in those turbulent years, when I became convinced of young offsprings' thoughtlessness and chauvinism, did I long for them to be married and off our hands. But there were also times when I was puffed up with pride at their achievements. To see our Chris's name on his featured articles and sports reports in the local paper; the joy and excitement of his wedding to his lovely Carole; the news of Richard obtaining a second-class honours degree at Sussex University.

Joyful though these events were, they presented me with a problem. Over the years I had developed a fairly severe type of agoraphobia. I expect the isolated position of the cottage, the fact that we had no car, and that I had been kept too busy for social life, had contributed to the aberration. Going to Gloucester for shopping had become such a terrible trauma for me that Syd had almost given up his kindly persuasions and mostly went on his own. I was quite willing to go down to the milk-box and help him carry the bags up. But beyond the milk-box was a no-man's land for me, except the familiar tracks to work, and contemplating unknown territory sweat would ooze from my palms and I would get palpitations. How I was going to face the journey to Dorset for the wedding was a constant dread, and I did not even contemplate going to see Richard receive his degree.

At least not until Jenny took the matter in hand. She was now a seventeen-year-old sixth former, and she had developed a live-and-let-live attitude to my eccentricities, but this was stretching her tolerance too far.

'Mummy, now listen, of course you're going, as well as Daddy. You *must* see Richard get his degree. He's worked so hard for it. What kind of mother are you?'

'Agoraphobic.' 'Nothing to wear.' 'No transport.'

She admitted these were impediments, but not impossibilities. It began to look as though I was going. The idea of spending money on new clothes for myself had not occurred to me for years. Meg, and Syd's sister, and jumble sales, had kept me adequately covered for next to nothing. Besides, I just was not worth the effort. I have my vanities, but they do not include dress sense; I am just naturally untidy. For once at least, Jenny was determined to defeat this failing. With every penny we could muster she took me, palpitations and all, to Gloucester. Luckily the sales were on, and she 'allowed' me to choose a cream crimplene suit reduced to eight pounds. I was not permitted to point out that, for me, cream was the maddest and most impracticable colour. Cutting me out of it altogether she then decided on a black straw hat, sale price a mere ten shillings, and cheap black nylon gloves. There followed a ruthless round of the shoe shops for a pair of black court shoes going cheap. The nylon stockings she treated me to herself, from the pocket-money she earned by working in Woolworth's on Saturdays. She would cut, shampoo, and set my hair for the great day, but she insisted that I bought some setting lotion to keep it tidy.

Transport was now the problem. How was Cinderella in her crimplene and nylon to be got to the ball? Richard had learned to drive, but we had no vehicle, and hiring one would stretch our pockets badly. My brother came to the rescue. He had a Lanchester of ancient vintage, a grand old upright dowager of a

car, but full of the coughs and wheezes of old age and liable to
stop altogether if too much mileage were demanded of her. A self-
taught mechanic of considerable talent, he gave her a Harley
Street examination. He oiled and greased her, put in false joints to
boost her rheumaticky ones, covered her cracked old visage with a
cosmetic coating of black enamel, polished her to Rolls-Royce
standards, and drove her over. She looked a real old aristocrat.

'She's a bit heavy on her drinking, and only likes stuff from the
best pumps, but she'll get you there and back all right, don't
worry.'

If my eyes popped out at her grandeur, Syd's nearly popped out
at the sight of me when I was ready to step into her. Jenny had
transformed the old scruff into someone approaching an elegant
woman. I was still slim, five-foot-five tall, and had retained quite
a good figure. Jenny's choices, the plain cream suit and black
accessories, my work swollen hands hidden in gloves, made up in
taste what they lacked in quality. I hardly knew myself!

Richard had been given two guest tickets for lunch at the
University. Jenny was quite willing to stay at home, so we left her
in charge, and set off. On the way back we were going to have a
night at Syd's sister's in Pinner. Once I was settled in the car the
long drive that I had feared became an exciting novelty. I was all
ready to be impressed by the architecture of the University, for I
knew it had been designed by Sir Basil Spence of Coventry
Cathedral fame.

Well, we got there, and I did not think much of it. It seemed to
me more austere than many a factory on the Great West Road
approaching London, but I did approve of the oblong pool of
water just inside the entrance, its tranquil depths encouraging the
philosophies of the studious mind. We sat in one of the study
rooms; to me it had a hard distracting influence, with its plain
brick walls and its modernistic, brightly-covered but comfortable
chairs. The cold lunch, served in the students' dining-hall, was
excellent and we were ready for it. We caught a glimpse of some
of the selected guests going into a more luxuriously appointed
dining-room. Among them were a Cabinet Minister, Douglas
Jay, and his wife, and she was wearing a cream suit with black
accessories. I began to feel that stuck-up I remembered the old
rhyme, 'The Colonel's Lady, and Judy O'Grady are sisters under
their skins.'

The degree ceremony was held in the Brighton Pavilion; a confection of overstated architectural curves and trimmings, enough to give Sir Basil a nightmare, but I could not stop gawping at it. We squeezed into a great crowded room, and the stage itself was crowded with dignitaries, among them Harold Wilson and Yehudi Menuhin. We found seats right at the back, and in front of us was a gangway along which the students filed their way to the steps to mount the stage as their names were called. Among them were the pretty twin daughters of Mr Jay. When Richard's moment of glory came I had to bite my lip and swallow hard to choke back the tears of love and of pride in him. I noted that he had got a better degree than the Jay twins.

Syd's sister and one of her sons had driven down from London; movie-camera in hand, they filmed us proudly walking on the campus with our capped and gowned BA son.

It was a wonderful day. The old Lanchester felt quite proud of us, and purred her way back to Pinner. We did not let her hear us say she would not look out of place on the London-to-Brighton vintage car rally. Nor did we tell her straight to her old-fashioned black bonnet that she looked impoverished and outdated among the expensive streamlined models peppering the drives of that select area of Pinner.

Before my agoraphobia had the chance to settle on me again I was taken on another long drive. Richard took us in a smart modern hire-car—the old Lanchester had gracefully retired. We went to Bridport for our Chris's wedding. The Brighton journey had helped me break the ice on the social scene, and I had gained enough courage to play my part at the reception and carry it off smoothly. We all chalked up another wonderful day. After the long journey home through the cold evening, we sat round a lovely fire and talked, and much of the talk was of Chris and his bride. It was a happy time, but when the chatting stopped there was a little chill somewhere in the back of my mind. The first fledgling had flown the nest for good.

Soon enough our Richard followed. He had got his degree, and he took it up to Birmingham and obtained a teaching post. At a vacation party he looked into the eyes of one of the prettiest guests. They both liked what they saw so much that they were soon holding hands for the romantic trip to the altar and domestic bliss in Perry Barr.

While Richard was studying sociology and economics from the tomes of learned professors, our Nicky was not so definite about his going, and chose to take several short dangerous flights rather than one clean break. Unable to tolerate the disciplines of the sixth form he sought the harsher regimes of the outside world. Farm labouring, dustman, bottle washer, battery-hen cleaner, lorry driver, gate-maker, he learned a lot about life. He was an astute observer of character and incident, and enlivened our evenings with his amusing mimicry and stories. It is true to say that we often laughed till we cried, and so did he in the telling.

Eventually he settled down to train properly, as a carpenter, getting his qualifications at the Technical College, and embracing a useful career that stretched his brains as well as his muscles.

Home from his day as farm labourer we greeted Nicky with the stock question, 'Did she?' This referred to the peculiar habit of an enormous sow. Every morning when Nicky filled her drinking trough with fresh water, she would rush to foul it. It had become a battle of wits and strength between them to get her snout in before her bum.

'Talk about pig-headed!' Nicky would laugh ruefully, looking down at his mucky trousers. 'You should see the mischief in those old piggy-eyes as soon as she spots me with the water bucket. No matter how I heave and push and grunt trying to turn her round, she *will* put her arse in that trough of clean water and do her business.' For her hygienic nether-end habits he gave her the Moslem nickname Fatima.

'You did not ask me what happened today, Mum,' he said one evening as I put his food in front of him. There was an expression on his face I had never seen before.

'Well, what did happen, then?'

'I helped the farmer to born a calf. It was so wonderful, Mum, seeing that dear little calf, all legs and head but all there, and in no time at all struggling to his feet to find his Mum's udder. And the way she nuzzled him, and the look in her eyes. That poor old cow, what she went through to have him, and how pleased she was with herself. I could shoot those farmers that take the calves off 'em for veal.'

However, Nicky soon discovered that being sentimental about animals was not part of a farmer's life, or a farm labourer's. So he left.

Meanwhile Richard was at University, and to manage on his

grant, had digs in a run-down boarding-house in Brighton. Nicky joined him there, and looked for employment open to the non-skilled. He started off in a beer-bottling works, washing the bottles, noisy, dangerous and monotonous work. Most of the employees were coloured, and accepted the conditions and the poor pay with a remarkable lack of complaint. Everyone had to wear goggles to protect their eyes from splintering glass. One Monday a flying piece cut Nicky's top lip open. Only the day before, in the business supplement of Richard's quality Sunday paper, he had read the profit figures of the company. 'Bloody brewers,' thought Nicky, and collected his cards.

The landlady gave no credit, so he had no choice but to start work the next day cleaning out the cages in a battery-hen establishment. The smell was abominable, but even worse was the plight of the incarcerated hens, egg-laying machines without room to turn or even stretch their legs properly. It was an economic way of producing eggs, and fertile manure, and tasteless packaged chickens for the supermarkets. It was also a foul, inhumane commercial practice. After a few weeks Nicky could not look those poor hens in the eye.

He came back home and got a job as a council dustman. Now, I doubt that if a hostess needed to make up a number for a dinner-party, she would plump for a dustman. Not even a sedate, church-going hostess; though, if cleanliness is next to godliness, dustmen should be well-seated in the celestial dining-halls. It was Nick's best job to date as regards wages and shortish hours, but it was early start and hard dirty work. The older hands did much better. They sent the newcomers home and then sorted out their perks from the rubbish. One dustman was on the way to becoming a minor property tycoon. He rented empty houses in the less salubrious areas of town, furnished them with cleaned-up discards from the rubbish, and let the rooms out to immigrants at a handsome profit. Eventually he was able to buy up some of the properties. He ran a pricey Rover car and lived in his own lavishly-furnished house.

One might think that Nicky's succession of dead-end jobs was due to his being less intellectually bright than his siblings. This indeed was not the case. Soon enough the novelty wore off, and he decided to train as a carpenter. One day a well-meaning ecclesiastic, undeterred by the stony ground of our acquaintance, made one of his calls to persuade us back into the fold. Knowing that Nicky had been a bright pupil at the grammar school, he was commiserating with us, in Nicky's hearing, about the way this son had thrown away his chances, and was now ambitious enough only to become a carpenter.

'I dunno,' Nicky said to him. 'It was a good enough job for your Master's Son to follow when He was on earth.'

When our Jenny was eighteen she had seven O-levels and three good A-levels, and was awarded a County Major. To our surprise and chagrin she was determined not to go to University. Some of her friends had done so the previous year, and their acquired accents, flashy college scarves, and new conceits, quite put her off. 'If that's what it does to you, I'm *not* going.'

Parents are often a poor match for a sensible strong-willed eighteen-year-old. We said our piece, and left her to make up her own mind. She had already done so, and went on to get a good secretarial job, and a fiancé. When she was twenty she became enamoured of a handsome young engineering student, and now wedding number three was looming ahead. This time, as the bride's parents, we would be the most involved.

Knowing how I would probably get the jitters, Meg, and Syd's sister, and our Yorkshire friend from London, came to stay and to help. Often in the past I had regarded white weddings and their paraphernalia and pomp as an absurd ritual and expensive nuisance. Now I could see something in it. It was an absolutely beautiful day; the little village church, cleaned and decked with flowers, was filled with the two families and beloved friends. The organ, already murmuring something sweet, burst suddenly into triumphant song, and every head was turned. Our Jenny, lightly resting on her proud father's arm, walked stately down the aisle.

Such a blissful compound of profound emotions hit me that like all mothers I could not hold back my tears.

The reception was held at a nearby hotel, and after the wedding repast and the speeches, the stars of the show, the reason for the gathering, swiftly disappeared and left the assembly rudderless. Many of the sixty guests came to us for the evening, and my three wonderful helpers roasted chickens, boiled hams, made trifles and dainties, and lent their best cutlery and glassware. I was not allowed to wash even a glass. Chris, Richard, and Nicky co-hosted with Syd, and an entertaining well-fed evening was enjoyed by all. Little thanks to me, but my own heart was full of gratitude.

Our children were spreading their wings. In a few short years all
four of them had gone and now we were only two; just Syd and
me. For the first week or so, with only undemanding Syd to cater
for, I felt as if I was on holiday. Then the loneliness began to
trouble me. My back had got worse, so there were now very few
jobs on the land that I could manage, and I missed the company. I
kept as busy as I could at home, weeding and hoeing the garden,
gathering kindling wood, and making pickles and jams, augmented
by anything I could gather from the hedgerows. One lovely sunny
September morning I went blackberry picking; plenty were
growing near at hand in the hedges of the adjoining fields. Hating
to see this free bounty going to waste I took a large basket for my
gatherings. It was almost full before I had gone half-way round the
field and the thought hit me, what did I want all these daily
pickings for? To give them away locally was carrying coals to
Newcastle. There was no need now to rush home to get the pastry
bowl out, and make a pile of pies and tarts. Who was going to eat
them?

I looked down the hill, and oh! the emptiness of the landscape!
No school children hurrying up with their satchels swinging, their
faces rosy, their caps on the back of their heads.

'Hiya, Mum. How long to tea? We're famished.' No longer
would I hear it; nor 'Ooh, that was scrumptious. Can I have
some more?' No praises to give, no reprimands to administer, no
schoolday chatter to listen to. The child days were over; they had
gone like Peter Pan to Never-Never land. The blow hit me full
force right below the belt. Like many a newly-retired man, the
relief of being free from the daily grind brought with it a feeling
of uselessness. The loss of old mates and of the stimulus of
discipline; no wonder so many men just dropped dead when their
working days were over. A tear of self-pity dropped on the blackberries. Oh, well, Syd liked blackberries and I could make pots
and pots of jam to give the children when they visited us. And
Syd's sister, and Meg, when they came. There was still plenty to
pick and plenty to do. Comforted, I sniffed my way home.

Going to grammar school had made the children late earners, but
from their very first wage packets they all contributed their keep.
By this I mean they paid for their food; services and accommodation were thrown in with our love. We had managed tolerably well.

Despite the fact that I was no longer fit enough to go out to work on the land, with only the frugal pair of us left I was surprised to find I had some housekeeping money left at the end of the week. Our life had not been complicated by bank accounts, so I started to put my savings in a jam jar, and postponed the decision on which of the multiplicity of uses I might put it to later. All my life I had lived on my daydreams from time to time, but they had never been ambitious enough to imagine that we would ever own a car. I was a bit taken aback when practical phlegmatic Syd broached this possibility as we sat cosily each side of the winter's fire.

'And pigs might fly,' I thought, especially as he based the idea on the hope of one of our premium bonds coming up with a big prize. He knew nothing of my jam jar savings. Nearly a year had passed and I had amassed almost eighty pounds, and was toying with the idea of wall-to-wall carpet in our living-room.

One winter evening when he came from work, Syd sat wearily down by the fire. 'Gosh, it's good to be home. That bloody hill gets steeper every day. Wish Ernie would come up for us. Peter, the carpenter at work, is selling his car. It's an A.35, and an old 'un, but it's in smashing nick. Pete looks after it like a baby.'

'What's he asking for it?'

'Eighty pound. A bit above the average for a car that small and old, but it's a real bargain because he's looked after it. No rust, good tyres, sound little engine. He's a genuine chap; wouldn't sell anyone a pup.'

I fetched out my jam jar of hidden treasure, gave it a magic rub with the corner of my pinny, and began to count out the notes and silver on to Syd's knee. Talk about Aladdin and the Genie's magic lamp! Syd's mouth fell open, and his eyes lit up like a pair of lamps.

'There you are. Seventy-nine pounds four and eightpence; tell Peter we'll have it!'

After all, a magic carpet to get about in was better than a static one on the floor.

Syd was in his fifties. Apart from the small tractor in the sawmill yard, he had never driven anything. Driving lessons were a pound an hour. Our euphoric anticipation of becoming car-owners was tempered by this snag. We had reckoned without our children.

They contacted the young, ex-police, driving instructor, and between them paid for a number of Syd's lessons. At last, during a bitterly cold February, the great day of the test came.

Through the kitchen window I watched Syd coming across the yard (as he knew I would). His face blue with the cold, and his expression impassive (as I knew it would be).

'Kettle's just coming to the boil.'

'Good. I could do with a nice hot cup of tea.'

The blighter! Why didn't he put me out of my misery? Had he or hadn't he? I handed him his cup of tea.

'Well?' I said.

He drank half the tea, put the cup and saucer carefully on the mantelpiece, and said casually, 'Yes, I passed.'

How could he be so calm? Such an achievement, at his age, a first-time pass. I made up for it; I literally danced around the kitchen, and heaped unstinted praise on him all the evening. We had a car, and I had a driver.

But I still had my agoraphobia, and even now I invented excuses to avoid going into Gloucester for a few more weeks. Eventually shame gave me the courage, and I found that getting in at home and getting out at home made all the difference. Years later I still get a feeling of relief when we get back past the milk-box, but the agoraphobia is as good as cured.

There was an exciting unreality about getting into our own car with Syd at the wheel. I could not help it, it made me feel like the Queen Mother; I had a job not to wave graciously at the people we passed.

By the time Syd's holiday came round in August, Chris and Carole had persuaded me to let Syd drive us up to Staffordshire to stay for a few days with them. All the way from Gloucester to Staffordshire, and on the motorway at that! Proudly snug in our little A.35, I was indifferent to the sleek modern cars streaking past us. However, when a tiny dumpy little car went by with a middle-aged couple in it, I could not help observing how comical they looked, like some Enid Blyton characters in a Noddy car.

'Look at them, Syd.'

Syd almost smiled. 'Have a good look, then,' he said dryly, ''cos that's just how we look from the back. That car is exactly the same as ours.'

We took rather more than twice the time that Chris did for the same journey, but we got there, and tried hard to look nonchalant about the achievement. Nevertheless I could see an extra shine in Chris and Carole's eyes as they welcomed us in.

The car was also a blessing to one of our most favourite visitors, Meg, who over the years had become one of the family. Her childhood in Swansea's dockland, and the rest of her life in London, had made Meg a townswoman by choice. She regarded us as amiable lunatics for making a move to such primitive isolation, and this opinion was strengthened every time she walked the mile from the bus stop on her occasional visits. When an unforeseen tragedy struck her, the visits became much more frequent.

Meg's handsome Canadian husband was seventeen years her junior, and she had sometimes pondered what would happen to him when she died. It never occurred to any of us that the boot might be on the other foot. His fine frame gave no clue then of the ravages going on inside it. When the symptoms of his trouble appeared, Meg hustled him to the doctor. A few weeks later he underwent heart surgery and the discovery of other troubles. The remarkable skill of the surgeons gave him a few more years' lease of life. Then he was hospitalised again. Meg, bewildered and heartbroken by the turn of events, but never able to believe that he would die, watched him do just that. Over the years she had made their rooms in the tenement house luxuriously cosy, but now they held too many memories for her to endure living there.

So she was glad to accept an offer to make her home with an elderly sister and brother-in-law on the outskirts of Swansea. The area might be drab and run down, and her sister's house one of a small terrace on a main road. But its front door opened on to an interior that could be fairly described as a little palace; carpeted, polished, perpetually painted and papered, it was a superb example of the best that working-class women can achieve. Meg was now an old-age pensioner, a fact that she ignored, and indeed she was soon at work again, this time in a bake-house, despite the fact that it meant long hours on aching feet, plenty of minor burns, and arms almost too tired to carry home bread and cakes for her sister's family.

Meg loved cooking and had become quite an expert. Throughout the years on her visits to us she always gave me marching orders out of my own kitchen. This arrangement met with high approval from the boys. Meg took infinite time and trouble with her superb cooking, and the boys gave her a chorus of praise. Like a surrogate mother she would stand, arms folded across her pretty frilled pinafore, shining-eyed, lapping up the compliments.

'Wish Mumy could cook like you, Aunt Meg.'

'Don't you go running down your mother, or I'll box your ears.'

Utterly tactless, but without a scrap of spite, she would sort us all out.

'For goodness sake, Win, go and get yourself changed and smartened up a bit before Syd comes in from work.' And from her capacious handbag would come yet another lipstick and partly-used compact for me.

'Nicky, I saw you put that other spoonful of sugar in your tea. You'll end up with diabetes if you don't look out.'

'Now, Jenny, you eat up those Brussels sprouts. Never mind not liking them, eat 'em and you'll have skin like me, not a blemish, even at my age.'

And God help me if I had not a stock of saucepan scourers, vim, and soda and polish in the house. My pots and pans got a birthday inside and out till they shone like new, in a kitchen that she kept as tidy and clean as a hospital. Her scoldings ran off us like gentle rain off a duck's back. In between her visits we lapsed into our old ways, but we loved to have her bustling, cheerful, organising presence around us as often as she cared to come.

Meg was always in the forefront at the weddings and the sub-sequent christenings; dressed up to the nines in honour of the occasion, and looking far more like the groom's mother or the proud granny than I did. Her presents to mark these occasions were always too generous. We got truly cross with her but all our protests were as ineffective as catching Niagara Falls in a bucket. My home is full of mementoes of her visits: a really sharp carving knife; a sensible unbreakable cruet set; a wall tin-opener; a kitchen clock; and all sorts of gleanings from her various jobs. I could never catch up with her generosity, so I bided my time. She was a good deal older than I, and the time would come when she would be unable to work. Then our door would be wide open for her to spend long periods with us 'on the house'.

Alas, she only did this once.

Chris had grown dissatisfied with his situation in Staffordshire, and felt that he was not realising his potential. Seeking more job-satisfaction, though with less money, he obtained a post on the outskirts of Swansea. By a pleasing coincidence this job was within walking distance of where Meg lived with her sister and brother-in-law. Chris and Carole and their little daughter Lorna were soon settled down in a nice bungalow on the Gower coast side of Swansea, but still only a few miles from Meg.

'Auntie' Meg was soon a welcome and frequent visitor of theirs; she adored Lorna as if she were her own grandchild. Whenever they drove up for a Sunday, or a week-end visit, Meg came with them.

Meg had at least one thing in common with me; she suffered from a chronic indigestion. She was a sucker for every tablet, powder, or medicine that came on the market, giving me her unused stocks as she tried a fresh cure. At last it drove her to the doctor, who diagnosed a hiatus hernia but advised against an operation at her age. After that, Meg stopped worrying about it. She enjoyed eating food as much as cooking it, and put up cheerfully with the burps and discomfort that followed.

She would not allow advancing years to interfere with her vitality. She would not tolerate a grey hair, the tiniest flaw in her nylons, or any difference in standards or colours for her appearance. In spite of evidence to the contrary she believed that Endocil cream kept the wrinkles away. It was a pricey cream, but it solved for us the problem of Christmas and birthday presents for her. The rest of us grew older, but, as our boys would say, 'Auntie Meg doesn't alter at all.'

And so it seemed for a long time, until one pre-Christmas visit from her. During the couple of months since we had seen her, Meg had suddenly aged. Though Chris and Carole saw her about twice a week, they too had noticed how tired she looked. Despite my pleas she insisted on doing the cooking for all of us.

The following Easter she spent with one of her nieces near London, and did not come to us again until a week-end in June. This was most unusual, and how glad we were to see her, but her appearance alarmed me. It seemed that the shadow of death was already smudging her sunken eyes. Nevertheless, she would cook us all a perfect roast chicken dinner with all the trimmings, and then for herself only a piece of bread and butter.

Now it was my turn to sort her out. 'Meg, you aren't well. Don't you dare come up to us again until you've seen the doctor. If you don't go, I'll come down to Wales and take you myself!'

'It's all right, Win,' she said, with calm resignation. 'My sister has been nagging me to go. I've been feeling bad in the night; terrible sickness and stomach pains. I sneak downstairs quiet as a mouse not to disturb her, but she's caught me twice, and she's made an appointment with the doctor for me next week. It's that old hernia playing up, I expect.'

I could not help thinking it was something worse than that. Apart from my gall-bladder operation, I had been in hospital twice for minor operations. After each one, Meg had wangled time off from her job to make sure I enjoyed a week's rest. After the children were married, Syd had been suddenly rushed to hospital for a week. Again Meg had come up at once to keep me company. Meg, our true friend. I wanted desperately to help her now.

'Meg, you must give up going to work; remember you're seventy-two now, not seventeen.'

'Well, I like to earn a bit. I don't want to be a burden on my sister. She and Dai are only on the old-age pension themselves.'

'Well, you can come and stay with us a lot. Our kids are off our hands now, and there's plenty in our pantry for one more mouth, and you'll be doing me a big favour, giving me your company.'

The doctor made her an appointment at the hospital for an X-ray; almost immediately after that she was admitted for an urgent operation. Two days later, Richard, who had moved from Birmingham back to Gloucestershire, had a day off and took me down to see her. Chris was already at her bedside.

Morriston Hospital had a drab, run-down look, but the atmosphere inside was permeated with the aura of kind friendliness so evident in Wales. Meg looked very weak, and was obviously in great discomfort. Round her bed was a miniature Covent Garden of flowers. Apart from her many relatives and friends, her local Jones the Meat, Evans the Shop, Lewis the Fish, and Owen the Coal, had all sent a summer memento to gladden her eye.

'I keep telling the nurses to share them around. Now look, you've brought me some more.'

'And you deserve them. How are you, love?'

'Mustn't grumble,' she said, wincing. 'Some of the poor women in here are in a bad state; it's pitiful to see them suffering. I'm not too comfortable myself; whatever they've done, it's knocked the stuffing out of me just now. I can't even raise myself on to my pillows. I don't like to keep worrying the nurses: they're lovely girls, they are, but they're run off their feet.'

'Shall we try and sit you up?'

'Yes, please.'

I watched my two six-foot, rugby-playing sons gently ease her up in the bed. I saw the stricken look they exchanged over her head.

'Ta, that's better.'

'Have they given you any idea how long you'll be kept here?'

'No indeed, they haven't told me anything much. I know they've cut me right across my stomach but they didn't say what they'd found wrong. I asked the doctor that came round this morning, but he just said he wasn't the one who did it. Still, it's over now, thank God; now it's just to get my strength back.'

Richard and I stayed as long as we could, and as we left we found Meg's sister and Carole in the corridor waiting to go in. Their sad faces prepared me for the answer I now dreaded from her sister's lips.

'It's hopeless, Win, they found a malignant growth, and it's spread too far for them to do anything. They say she could last up to six months. She doesn't know, God help her. They think it's best to keep it from her.'

Six months! When the truth is unpalatable, a belief in miracles can creep in. Had I not read more than once of sudden inexplicable cures happening to people stricken like Meg? Of course it's possible, said my heart. On the evidence of your eyes, it's not, argued my mind. By the time Richard and I got home we were both feeling years older.

As soon as her stitches could be removed Meg was discharged from hospital. Syd and I went down to stay overnight with Chris and Carole so that we could visit Meg at her sister's. She looked so frail it hurt me to ask the conventional inadequate question.

'How are you feeling now, love?'

'Oh, I mustn't grumble. I think I'm improving. I wish I could get my strength back a bit quicker. Our Jean here grumbles at me if I try to help her with the housework, but some days I do get up to the shops for her.'

For a moment or two, Meg dredged up a little of her old

brightness, and I felt a bitter helpless anger with the fates, so indiscriminately dealing out their suffering.

Although Carole was a lavish hostess, we had no option but to sit down again to a laden table. Meg proudly brought in Syd's favourite fancy sponge she had made specially for him.

'I have to go to the doctor's Tuesday for a check-up. I'd like to ask him if I could come and stay with you for a couple of weeks, if you'll have me Win?'

Would I have her! 'Have you, dear? I'd love to.' My heart was aching to do something for her. 'Tell you what,' I enthused, 'Syd and I will bring your bed downstairs into the sitting-room.'

I had made the room downstairs, which had been the boy's bedroom, into a cosy sitting-room with armchairs and a television for viewers to watch in peace, away from the chatter of the living-room.

'Indeed,' said Meg, 'you'll do nothing of the sort; a bed in there would spoil it. I can sleep upstairs. You're not to get spoiling me or treating me like an invalid.'

Why, oh why, had I not kept my big mouth shut, and given her no option?

The following Sunday Chris drove her up with Carole and Lorna. I had a dinner up to Meg's standards all ready to put before them. I could see that it was only to please me that Meg struggled through some of hers. Her rouge, lipstick and powder mocked the wasted pallor of her face, but she made no complaint and her talk was full of lively concern for all of us. Nothing would stop her helping with the washing-up.

Meg was obviously still grateful for her life, such as it was, and had no knowledge of her illness. All we could do was to hide the truth from her. To forward this ploy, Carole, who was an excellent sewer, had bought some very nice material and measured Meg up for a new dress. 'I'll take you out to dinner somewhere posh at Christmas, and show you off,' Chris promised her. And so began the bitter charade, in which our children were willing accomplices, paying back a little of the debt of love they owed her. They brought her fruit and flowers, make-up and her special Endocil cream, and plenty of her favourite reading, romantic paperbacks by Denise Robins and Barbara Cartland.

For years Meg and I had had a sisterly relationship, and I took a well-meaning advantage of it. When I took up her early morning

tea, I told her to stay put with a book until I had got all spruce and
tidy downstairs and the fire lit. And what could I bring up for her
breakfast? Poor dear, her appetite and pleasure in food had gone.
For her, I stopped my slap-happy, plonk-it-on-the-table habits,
and put a dainty cloth on her tray and a posy of flowers; grapefruit
carefully segmented, egg boiled just right; or a crisp rasher of
bacon and fried bread as she used to love it. I took the crusts off
her toast, put home-made marmalade on a pretty china dish, tried
to be a credit to her past example, and she tried to eat some of it.

It was late summer, but I knew she loved the comfort of a fire.
When I had one blazing well, I called up that she could now get
up when she liked, and I would help her have a strip-wash in the
comforting warmth. About eleven o'clock she would totter down.
Despite her pain-killing tablets, I had heard the pages of her book
rustling in the small hours, but she rarely complained. Just sometimes the pain would wring from her a little apologetic grumble.

'Ooh-ooh! Sorry, Win. This old pain in my side is playing me
up a bit; I wonder what it is? It can't be anything *very* bad, can it
Winnie, or I'd be having some sort of treatment?'

I knew what she meant, though she never uttered the dread
word, cancer. If a Harley Street consultant could have eaves-
dropped on me, he would have given me the Baron Munchausen
badge for medical fibbing. From my small gleanings of medical
knowledge I had a comforting diagnosis ready for any pain or
discomfort that might, or might not, follow a major stomach
operation. Sometimes I was right, and that made it all the more
convincing. 'The only thing, Meg, is that it may cause you to get
anaemic but they'll give you injections for that if it gets bad.' I
knew the time was coming when morphine would be inevitable.

She became too weak even to help with the lightest housework,
but still I had to discourage her. 'Now look here, Meg, it's a fat lot
of good me having you up here if you don't rest. Besides, you're
doing me a favour keeping me a bit busier. I *need* more exercise;
just look at my behind, half-an-acre round, I reckon.' Sometimes I
could sense she was too weak for my mouthy chatter; then I would
take myself out to do some gardening or gather kindling wood.
She still enjoyed watching television. I would light a fire in
the other room, and after tea she would watch Crossroads and
Coronation Street. When the sun came out and it was warm she
would totter out into the courtyard, and feel very pleased with

herself for walking up and down the length of it, but each day she grew weaker. At the end of a month Chris came and took her back to Wales for her check-up. With some difficulty, we got her fairly comfortable in the car, and she turned and said, 'If he says it's OK, Win, can I come back for a while?'

'Yes, oh yes, of course, love.' I am not an over-tolerant or kindly-disposed woman. My patience was often stretched to its limits when I looked after my elderly mother and my mother-in-law, but somehow I felt it a privilege to be in the company of my brave dying friend. Her lack of self-pity, her genuine interest in other people's burdens, and her ability still to extract some pleasure from her restricted miserable existence, still finding touches of humour, filled me with admiration, and love for her. I had little hope of her coming to us again, but a week later there she was, holding on to Chris's arm and struggling back across our courtyard to our welcome.

This time we had brought her bed downstairs, and we bought a very comfortable high-backed armchair for her to watch the television. Jenny had got her a bed-ring for she was now little more than bones, except for her swollen stomach. Still her spirit was unbroken. 'Oh, I don't know,' she would say, 'there's plenty worse than me.' We played a little game. When I took her morning tea in, I told her I was the night nurse just going off duty, but first I would help her to the toilet and tidy her bed. Then I assumed the role of wardmaid, cleaning the grate, lighting the fire, dusting and carpet-sweeping. Next I would be the day nurse, giving her a wash and taking in her breakfast. Her appetite was pitiful. I put a supply of her novelettes, fruit, and a drink just in case, and let her rest, popping in frequently and racking my brains for any ploy that could bring her any pleasure.

At first she would struggle out for an hour or two by the living-room fire, and we would talk of our days in the tenement house, the amusing things that happened there, her West End jobs, the children's antics. At first, once up, she would want to get dressed and made up. 'I must look respectable, Win, in case you get any visitors.' At last she took to her bed and only got up to go across to the toilet. It distressed her when I told her I could borrow a commode to put by her bed.

'Your consultant will be in to watch the telly with you this evening.' She could still grin at this. After tea Syd would wash and shave, and change into his Sunday suit especially to keep her company. Meg, all woman to the end, would insist I hold a mirror for her to make up, and change into her prettiest bed-jacket.

After another month she was too weak to stand up on her own. Syd went to the phone box and called Chris to tell Meg's sister that we had to bring her home. We would come on Saturday, stay with him and Carole, and return the next day.

'We're taking you home this week-end, dear,' I told her. 'It's high time your doctor started giving you some injections to build you up a bit. Then we'll fetch you up to us again.'

This time she looked at me with eyes full of undisguised sadness. 'I'm beginning to wonder if I shall ever be able to come again, Win.' I wanted to go down on my knees, put my arms around her, and tell her whilst she could still hear me how much we admired and loved her. But in so doing I would have destroyed the flicker of hope that her expression showed she still wanted to cling to.

'Of course you will,' I lied.

'I don't want to go home in my nightie and dressing-gown; it will upset my sister. Help me to dress, Win, and to put my make-up on.'

During the eighty-mile drive there were times when I wondered if she would survive the journey, but with our arms each side of her she made it from the car to her sister's door and into the cosy loving atmosphere inside.

On our way home we called in to see her. She was in bed, propped up on pretty pillows in a comfortable bedroom. She was dressed in a dainty lacy bedjacket and was waiting patiently for the doctor. I kissed the ghastly remnants of her wasted face, and she gave me a long steady look. 'Goodbye Win,' she said with dignity, and I knew she knew.

She got her injections. Tears of relief as well as sorrow welled up in us when, two weeks later, we heard that Meg had died.

Meg was gone, never to return. Syd's sister and her family, now well off, had moved into deepest Sussex among the millionaires, too far for a day trip either way. Our old friends from the tenement house had all dispersed. Of our children, Richard had come closer to us, but Jenny and Nick were in the Cotswolds and Chris in Swansea. People say that routine is good for you; sometimes

I wondered if that were true. With my life now almost totally governed by Syd's going and coming and by petty household duties, any little distraction from my loneliness assumed heroic proportions.

One morning, hearing a lot of early clatter round the back of the cottage, I rightly assumed that the workmen had arrived to repair the roof. When I went up the back garden I could see a young man throwing down the perished tiles. Young man? These days it was difficult to distinguish the sexes; the fashion for masculine long hair had spread even to this rustic backwater. He turned his head and gave me the cursory glance which is all a plain, middle-aged frumpy woman could expect. I took a good eyeful of him; scruffy shoulder-length hair, lurid stencilled T-shirt, skin-tight drainpipe jeans on skinny beanpole legs. What was modern manhood coming to? No wonder, all youth thought of today was cheap popular music, cheap sex, discotheques, and even drugs. They seemed cynical and world-weary before they had cut their wisdom teeth. Still, I had to admit he was tackling our roof with gusto.

By mid-morning the day was turning into a scorcher, and I was more than ready to brew myself a cup of tea. Better give that lad some, I supposed, and a wedge of cake for the skinny ribs. I put it with a jug of tea on a tray. 'Drink here,' I called to him, putting it down.

'Ta!' He climbed down, took the tray, and disappeared, no doubt, I assumed, to eat it in the battered old van he had parked on the piece of waste ground.

At one o'clock I put him out a jug of lemonade and a sandwich; I had heard him working well all the morning.

This went on for several days until he had worked his way round to the front of the cottage. I was busy doing my weekly baking and suggested he should knock for his one o'clock tray. Promptly at one o'clock he did so, and said, 'Would you mind if I brought my friend in to see you, Missus?'

Friend? My mind uncharitably conjured up a girl; no doubt one of the tousle-headed, dirty-footed, long-skirted, hippy types that were much in evidence then, battening on to any male rather than going to work. I am often a coward at speaking my mind, so I gave a very reluctant consent, and put another cup on his tray.

Presently he came back across the yard, but I could see no-one with him. Then I noticed a tiny fledgling bird of unidentifiable species perched on his shoulder. It was a wild variety and I was amazed that it did not fly away.

"Ere 'e is, then. This is my friend Joey.'

You could have knocked me down with one of its immature feathers. 'Where'd you get him?'

'Found 'im in some grass under a tree. Must 'ave fell out o' the nest, or been pushed out by 'is mother. The poor little bugger was bald when I found 'im.'

In the larder I had a bit of liver cooked for the cat. I scraped a bit off finely, and put it in my palm under the bird's beak.

"E ain't ready to take it like that yet, Missus.'

He held a finger out for the bird to perch on, then taking a morsel of the liver, gently held its head back and put it down the open beak. As a mother of four grown-up children, I felt rather mortified at my lack of maternal instinct.

He said, 'I've got 'is lunch box, anyroads,' and from his pocket he took a matchbox filled with tiny worms and bird seed.

'What does your mother think of you bringing up a bird?' I asked.

'She ain't in a position to think anything about it, Missus. My Mam died when I was a little 'un, probably to get away from the old man.'

I looked at his gangly thinness, his ill-washed T-shirt, the cobbled-up stitching that nearly held together a large tear in the knee of his jeans.

'D'you live with your Dad, and what does he think of your bird?'

'The only thing 'e thinks of, Missus, is what goes into a glass, wi' a froth on the top. 'E's all right when 'e's just got a skinful, but me an' Joey keeps out o' 'is way other times. We go up in my bedroom. He threatened to smash Joey's cage and wring 'is neck. I told 'im, 'urt that bird an' I'll smash your face in. I ain't scared of 'im any more since I got Joey. I do think 'o goin' into lodgin's but a landlady mightn't take to me 'avin a bird in my room.' He laughed at his pun. 'Besides, there'd likely be a cat around. Can I bring his cage round in your yard this afternoon, Missus?'

'Of course you can.'

'Usually I leave 'im in 'is cage while I'm workin', but I've made a nice little nest in the dashboard for 'im to sit in when I'm drivin'. But I'd like to give 'im a bit more exercise.'

He came back with Joey in a large home-made cage, and he was also carrying a piece of cloth. 'I put this on one side of the cage so he can 'ave some shade.'

He put the cage down in our yard, and got back up his ladder to the roof. Some time later I went into the front garden to pick some flowers, and the lad called down asking me to open the door of the cage.

'Oh, I'd better not; he'll fly away and you'll lose him.'

'Don't worry, Missus. He'll be all right, you'll see.'

Reluctantly I opened the cage door and waited to see. The lad made a few whistling sounds, and Joey hopped out and flew straight up to perch on his shoulder.

'Now off you go, and have a bit of a fly around.'

Off went Joey, up into the leafy branches of the rowan tree behind the cottage and out of sight. Nearby there were other trees and hedges and meadows to tempt him. 'Oh dear,' I wailed. 'You'll never get him back now.'

'You stop frettin', Missus.'

It seemed a long ten minutes before the lad made his special whistling call again. Almost at once back flew the little bird to his shoulder. They gave each other a couple of kissing pecks, and then the finger of authority was extended, and pointed towards the yard. Joey hopped on to it.

'Now be a good boy, and go back in your cage.' Fascinated, I watched the bird do just that.

'Shut the cage door, please, Missus, in case your cat comes round.'

For the next week or so until the repairs were finished, Joey took up his residence in the yard, making his social calls at his master's break times, taking his afternoon airings in the branches of the rowan tree.

I was sorry to see them go, Joey perching proudly on his saviour's shoulder. I never saw them again. I hope that young man has found a wife to be as tender to, and one who will mother him a bit. If he is now a Dad himself, I am sure he is a good one, long hair and all.

Every decade of our lives brings its sorrows and its joys: the bewilderment of babyhood, the struggles of schooldays, the trauma of the teens, the problems of parenthood, the miseries of middle-age, and then the lingering sadness of senility. Shakespeare summed it all up in the seven ages of man, and then sought his own oblivion from the trials of advancing years in the bottle. When young we look on time as something to be spent without thought, but old age makes us look back on what we have purchased with it and realise how little we have left of the precious hoard. By then our appetites for living have changed, most of our emotional needs have been spent, and physical deterioration too often limits activities. Looking forward into a rapidly shrinking future daunts the boldest spirit; far better to indulge in the comfort of re-living the past. Now I was approaching sixty, and with long hours of my own company, I fell easy victim to this temptation.

Faces from the past loomed up with an importance magnified by time. Granny, for instance. Granny, next door, had been one of the soft cushions that protected me from the harder knocks of childhood. I recalled with guilty pangs how little I had shown my appreciation while she lived. In a fit of contrition I took pen and paper and wrote down my thought about her. I wanted to share my admiration of Granny with others. With only a stamp to lose, I sent it to a quarterly country magazine. It seemed quite an achievement when it was accepted and published, with the added bonus of a six pound cheque!

A little encouragement of that sort goes a long way with me! Now I had an incentive for something to do in those lonely hours. I began to write down some of my early memories. A request in a Sunday paper by a professor of Social History for pieces by working people about their lives soon got one of mine on the way to him. Again I had an encouraging response, and eventually a piece in his book, 'Useful Toil'.

Most days, by means of the radio, I enjoyed an hour's vicarious company with some charming people in 'Woman's Hour'. The pleasant style of the presenters and producers made them feel like friends. One in particular who appealed to me was named Pamela Howe; I sent her a pile of my writings. Excitement mounted when she wrote that she was interested, and even more when eventually she said she would bring them to the notice of 'Woman's Hour'. They decided to have them read out in serial form on the pro-gramme. So far, so good.

So far, so *incredibly* good, it seemed, and then came the bomb-shell; a letter from Miss Howe to say she would like to come and visit me, and bring with her her secretary, and the actress June

Barrie who was to do the reading. June wanted to hear and study my accent in order to imitate it on the radio. They were coming mid-day, and would take me to lunch at the Speech House.

My life as domestic servant, waitress, charwoman, and land-worker, had convinced me that I was a second-class citizen in the eyes of those who were blessed with the social graces. I was ashamed of my rough, swollen and work-toughened hands, and of my inferior clothes. How wrong I was on this matter; a fool with a fool's sense of values. Yet there was some justification for unease. I knew these ladies to be clever talented people who had earned their fame. Had I been meeting the Queen, I do not think my apprehension would have been greater: after all, I knew nothing about her except the inherited trappings of her birthright.

The Speech House is a famous old inn at the heart of the Forest of Dean. Queen Elizabeth the First really had slept there! As a young woman I had once called at the back door to apply for a job as maid, and had been too intimidated by its antique grandeur to accept the post. Now I simply had not the nerve to go there for lunch. So I wrote suggesting that I would like to cook a lunch for my three guests if that would suit, and I got a charming letter of acceptance.

I cleaned our cottage from corner to corner. I told Syd he must have a day off; his ability to take events in his stride would be a help. I planned the meal. I sorted out our mixed bag of crocks and cutlery to see if I could match up four settings without chips or cracks. I actually bought some serviettes, and some new serving-dishes, and even a bottle of sherry. Knowing that my stomach would have too many knots in it for me to sit at table, I intended to be a waitress hostess.

They arranged to come at one o'clock, and promptly at one we heard the car draw up. I had timed my cooking exactly right for once, but my heart seemed to be thumping in my throat. Within a couple of minutes of opening the door to our guests my nervousness had almost evaporated. They were not just charming; they were downright friendly. By the time they had eaten their lunch, with obvious enjoyment, and got down to discussing the scripts, it was not like being in the company of strangers at all. After a drive into the Forest to show them the village where I was born, they came back and had tea with us.

We waved goodbye to them about half-past six. It had been a wonderful afternoon, but there was a feeling of relief that it was over and had gone well. I made another pot of tea, and just sat gloating about how well we had managed, and how easy they had made it for us. Then I remembered with considerable embarrassment that the celebratory bottle of champagne that Pamela had brought with her for our lunch was still keeping cool in the pantry. We had no refrigerator at the time. We treasured the three warm thank-you letters we received.

From a standing start, I felt I had taken quite a plunge into the social whirlpool. I was more than satisfied with this one exhilarating dip, to last me the rest of my life, but I was in for a few surprises. Sweeping the chimney, for instance.

In the good old days our living-room, the one with the peculiar ceiling and so full of character and inconveniences, had been part of a series of one-storey buildings. It had had a copper in it, and as a result the flue was short, narrow and contorted. The chimney was regularly swept by a local man, a friend of ours, who was familiar with its peculiarities. He was in poor health, and sometimes unable to work. At such times it hurt his feelings if anyone else was employed to do the job, and messages were sent that we were not to worry, he would soon be up and about with his brushes. Now he was incapacitated again and our chimney was belching terribly. Syd would not blackleg on his mate, so I decided to do it myself. I poked about in the woodshed and found some long pieces of thin, pliable but strong wood. I tied them tightly together and fastened a bunch of holly on to the end.

I covered myself up in an old dirt-ingrained, land-working coat fastened at the neck with a safety-pin, a tatty head-scarf, and wellington boots. I got the holly right up through the chimney pot, wangling it somehow round the convoluted corners, and then down came the soot. Buckets-full of it, and a good percentage on my person, especially my face and hands. I had just started to shovel it up out of the hearth when an elegant young man knocked at the open door. In an accent to match his appearance he said he had called to take some photographs of 'Winifred Foley, the writer', to illustrate a feature to be published in one of the quality newspapers! He only batted his eyelids a couple of times when I told him it was me. I suggested hopefully that the idea could be scratched. That did not suit; he needed to take the photographs that morning.

I had to think quickly; I had to stall. What was I going to do next? Get the milk—that was it. I got a shopping bag, held it out to him, and suggested he might like to fetch our milk and paper from the box down the hill. If he took his time admiring the view, I would try to make myself presentable while he was gone. It was a case of *noblesse oblige*, and he obliged, tactfully finding the view much to his taste.

I made a rush job of the hearth, and dusted and polished a chair for him. I washed my face—never mind my neck, I had a clean high-necked blouse. A quick comb through my greying, soot-dyed hair and my toilet was complete. Two cups and saucers quickly rinsed of the soot that had wafted through the archway all over the kitchen dresser, and I was ready to make him a cup of coffee and have my photograph taken. He was awfully polite and took quite a number of shots. I realised why, when he kindly sent me some copies! He has quite a name in his profession, his equipment is high-grade stuff, and it did not hide the soot still embedded in my wrinkles!

By now I should have begun to realise what to expect, but I was quite unprepared for my next caller, a few days later. It was mid-morning, and I was in my muddy gardening gear. Anyone who knows me will testify to my flair for spreading mud about me, or soot, or paint. My hair was still in curlers, pipe-cleaners pinched off Syd, and I was smelling like a gypsy from the garden fire I had been making up.

This time it was a gentleman who obviously recognised me from a photo in the local newspaper. To his credit he did not flinch, nor make some excuse to conceal his intentions in calling. He asked me if I would open the annual summer Fete of Dean. What a ludicrous idea, I thought, and I could not help laughing outright. I gave what I thought were good reasons for refusing, but he would not agree. 'You're famous in the locality now, you know.' Famous! I did not feel very famous. Fame must be, like beauty, in the eye of the beholder, then. He continued to be persuasive, so I half-heartedly gave him a semi-promise to consider it by the time he called a week hence.

I had never even attended the opening of a fete, but I had seen photographs in newspapers. If it were a lady, it was always one of repute, smartly dressed and wearing a posh hat. I had not even got a hat. My ten-bob bargain buy had done duty for four weddings and now had our scarecrow's head pushing through it after two years in the garden. Anyway I felt sure that Syd and the children would back me up on the absurdity of the idea.

'Don't see why you shouldn't,' said Syd, the traitor.

Jenny backed him up. 'Good idea, Mum. It might make you start to smarten yourself up a bit.'

I gave in, and promised to go with Jenny to buy a hat, some gloves, shoes, and a blouse to suit my crimplene costume. This was still almost as good as new.

Gilding the lily is a superfluous exercise, and spending a lot of money trying to tart up an old dandelion was equally silly, I thought. So I mentally compromised. I could augment the funds of the 'Help the Aged' shop in Gloucester by getting my things there cheaply. I dodged into the shop before Jenny realised the ploy. Patiently she followed me in. Taking care not to catch her eye I spent about a pound and got it all except the shoes, which I would have new. Jenny waited until we left the shop well behind us, then she exploded.

'You're *not* wearing that lot, Mummy.'

'Why not? It's all in good condition, and the hat's OK.'

'It's ghastly! I reckon every other old-age pensioner was wearing one like it about ten years ago. If you're too stingy to buy things yourself, I'll buy them for you.'

I could not let her get away with that. 'Oh well. All right. I'll give these things to Nanna.' (Syd's mother.)

'Don't you dare! Nanna would be offended. She *does* care how she looks. She probably gave them that hat in the first place!'

I got home with a smart new hat, matching gloves, a new blouse, a pair of smart shoes, and the awakening of some dormant feminine instinct that made me feel that a new hat *is* a tonic!

On the day of the Fete I felt that I looked the part at least, although the high heels on the new shoes made me feel a bit tottery after my habitual slippers and wellingtons. The weather was dry and sunny so I had no worry about my posh hat; the big worry was getting the few words out to open the Fete. For this I had to climb on to a decorated farm wagon, its body camouflaged with a sheet of plastic grass. On it sat the pretty Beauty Queen, whom I had to crown, and her six small attendants.

Feeling every inch the lady, I graciously accepted the helping hands guiding me on to a box that was strategically placed for me to get on the wagon. The curious upturned faces were all friendly and reassuring. I said my piece, crowned the Queen, introduced her and her attendants to her subjects, posed with 'her majesty' for photographs, and then, very relieved and distinctly swollen-headed, I made to get off the wagon. Someone had removed the box; no matter; in my euphoria I felt light-footed and agile enough to jump down.

I took off, but the heel of one of my shoes did not. It caught in the edge of the tailboard concealed by the cover. I landed on my posh hat with my feet in the air, and it was not just the rush of blood that the angle brought to my face that made it rosy-scarlet. There were a good many displays and exhibitions put on for that Fete. Oh well, I thought, they have had an extra one now for their money!

My little interlude in the limelight would soon have died a natural death, for I am sure the amount of demand on a person is nicely geared to publicity. However, the radio scripts were published as a book, and it sold surprisingly well from such modest beginnings. Now more invitations began to arrive, some of a perplexing nature. As a child, the fact that I had nothing to show off about had never stopped me doing so when the chance occurred. Over the years this trait had taken enough diminishing knocks to make me now refuse politely the grander invitations.

I did not even want to accept those from Women's Institutes. I had meanly subscribed to the notion that their members were a toffee-nosed lot, and I had never had the courage to join them or any other women's group. On the whole, I was not fond of my own sex. How wrong I was! How friendly, tolerant, and sympathetic were those rows of faces to the nervous old chatterbox on the platform! The aims of these groups are all based on kindness, help for others, and friendly competitions among each other. There is an atmosphere of sisterhood that I found uplifting. I have a new respect and affection now for my own sex; their claws are shown only on occasions.

I did once accept a request to speak at a W.I. that accidentally gave me a peep into grandeur. We were now on the phone, and one day a very worried female voice rang through to ask could I possibly act as a stand-in for their booked speaker who had been rushed to hospital. The call came from a place some thirty miles away with which I was totally unfamiliar. The lady sounded distressfully urgent, so after warning her that I was not a 'proper' speaker I accepted. She gave me the address, which I wrote down, and rang off.

'Underberry' Court,
Underberry.

A funny address, 'Underberry' Court? Still the name was nothing to go by; it could turn out to be a little wooden meeting hut, or more likely an old house turned into a community centre. Our own local Westbury Court had become an old people's home taking over from the old workhouse. Anyway I had no time to dwell on it as I had to be there the following evening. Also I had not much time to consider what to talk about. My habit was to think about a subject and then just get up and open my mouth. I never knew myself what might come out. Once I had tried making notes, but my glasses kept falling off. I lost my thread and had to ask the audience what I had been on about! Some of them knew! I made a mental note to have the National Health frames changed one of these days.

This time I decided to talk about my days in domestic service, its amusing side, with a few digs about the humiliations of being a servant thrown in.

With his meal still undigested Syd had to have a quick wash and change to drive me there by quarter past seven. En route, after we had left familiar ground, we had to ask directions more often than once, because the place was definitely not sign-posted. Other villages, even hamlets, in the area were sign-posted, but not our mysterious destination. Syd began to get rather annoyed; I could see his jaw working. Assured again and again that he was on the right road he drove on, puzzled and angry.

We were now in the middle of a very rural area indeed. The tiny settlements, each a handful of cottages, became smaller and smaller and even farther apart. The road dwindled into a lane neatly ditched and hedged. Here and there where the roadside was a little sloping embankment some loving souls had cut out patches and literally filled them with flowers, and trimmed the weedy grasses all around. I do not remember ever seeing that before. While we were almost lost in admiration of these and the far-flung pastoral beauty that surrounded us on every side, we passed a little church, old and almost hidden in yew. A narrow gravel road, unmarked, led towards it. 'That's it,' I cried. 'Stop Syd, that must be it.'

He stopped, reversed to the gravel road and looked gloomily down it. "S' pose it must be, but why isn't it marked? We could drive round here for hours!' Advancing stealthily up that road as if we were trespassers, we passed the church, and stopped by a really imposing wrought-iron gateway of what must be one of the most stately homes in England. Old, sound, and beautiful, with a large square courtyard and strips of close-cut lawns, not a weed to be seen. Everything about it seemed to be so well looked after, as if the owners wanted it to last for ever. The gateway bore a coat of arms, but no name, and there was absolutely nobody about. Not daring to enter we drove up a pathway that we thought might lead round the back, but it led into a woodland with grass paths running here and there and even these were mown and edged. We retreated again, back to the front of the house.

Nearby was a row of four old-world cottages, absolutely immaculate and with neat clean gardens laid out in the same patterns and flowers. The weedless paved road beside them ended in a field. There was no sound, and not a soul about. Desperate, I knocked at the door of the first cottage. Almost immediately, a pleasant old lady came to the door and confirmed that this was indeed the place written down on my piece of paper. Apparently we were in the middle of an estate covering several thousands of acres, she was one of the retired tenants, and the big house was the residence of the Lord of the Manor.

It was obviously not the meeting place of the W.I.! Then an idea struck me. Perhaps the lady of the manor let the estate W.I. members hold their meetings in one of the outbuildings around the house. In a lesser courtyard we could see a few cars parked, and they were not all Rolls-Royces! So we entered the majestic gateway to inspect the fine stone outbuildings; an estate office, stables, sundry others, all in the grand manner, but not a sign of life, apart from the horses. Everything so immaculate; more wide sweeping paths unsullied by a migrant blade of grass; more great lawns, well-mown, brushed and combed and edged, not a blade missing or even out of place. Then a view of a beautiful land-scaped garden with a huge ornamental lake. We were definitely in the wrong place!

We were creeping back out through the courtyard and trying not to crunch the gravel, when a gentleman appeared, a very natty specimen in a dark suit, white shirt, and bow tie. Gosh, we had bumped into the Lord of the Manor himself. Syd politely raised his hat, apologised if we were trespassing and explained our errand.

'Oh yes, yes. You are expected, Mrs Foley. Please come this way.'

'See you later,' said Syd with relief, and disappeared.

I was ushered into a palatial hall with arched ceilings, hung with the sort of paintings one sees in the National Gallery. My gentle-man escort excused himself and knocked and entered some grand double doors. 'Could you tell me where Madame is?' I heard him ask.

Good lord, I thought, this must be the butler. Wherever had I landed myself? Just then a lady entered the hall from another door. I had seen her type before, in the pages of the *Tatler*; elegant, charming, with an aristocratic accent. I knew this must be the mistress of the place, and she introduced herself as such.

'I do hope we haven't kept you waiting, Mrs. Foley.'

I was Winnie in Wonderland as I followed her through the doorway from which she had emerged. I was in another nobly-proportioned room, wood-panelled, with an enormous window overlooking the garden. Here at last was my audience, sitting on rows of chairs, some of them looking more like house guests. I took my seat behind a priceless desk with a bowl of flowers and a carafe of water on it. How I wished I had hopped it with Syd!

All the way on the journey my talk had been churning over and over in my mind. It now seemed terribly tactless, in view of my hostess and her friends. They had obviously been used to ordering servants about for generations, taking them for granted, a part of life. I would have difficulty in changing the subject. What was I to do? A picture flashed into my mind; my father's drawn and under-nourished face covered in pit dirt. 'This above all: to thine own self be true', and I was.

I had been ushered in in style through the front door by the butler. Maybe I would be ignominiously chucked out through the back one by the same major-domo. Nevertheless I rattled on, editing a little, as I went, some of the past hurts and indignities. In fairness, I did not entirely overlook the problems of the mistress class.

My hostess was the president of the estate W.I., and graciously invited them to have their meeting in her home once a year. Their choice of speaker must have surprised her. There was no sign of it in the charming vote of thanks she gave me. She warmly invited me to bring Syd in and stay for coffee and refreshments. I politely declined. On the way out she introduced me to her husband and her daughter, which I thought was lovely of her. Then she handed me a long wrapped box and an envelope.

I had explained on the phone that I did not charge a fee, but would accept the petrol expenses. Our little car could have done the journey three times on the generous amount in the envelope. Inside the box were some punnets of the biggest juiciest raspberries I had ever seen, and some cartons of clotted cream, doubtless produce of the estate farms and garden. We shared some of these out, but kept plenty for our dinner the following day, and what a dinner Syd came home from work to! For once, I had mixed with the aristocracy, and for once we were going to eat like lords. I did soup for starters, rump steak with all the trimmings, and raspberries and cream for pudding. All we were short of was the butler!

Indecent exposure is a crime in law, and self-exposure can feel like a crime committed on one's own spirit. The transition from agoraphobic home-body to extrovert public chatterbox, stretched me to a vulnerable thinness in the middle. It was disturbing trying to maintain the two identities, each impoverishing the other, and I had brought it entirely on myself. Having had the sauce to write an autobiography for public scrutiny, I could hardly grumble if the public were interested in me. Not fair now to want to hide away in a corner. I could not have my cake and eat it, and we were certainly getting some cake.

So long as it covers the bare essentials and a little over to save for replacements, living hand to mouth does have its advantages. There are no problems wondering how to spend the money, no income-tax forms to fill in, and no feelings of guilt about robbing the rest of society. No conscience about not giving to charity, for charity must begin at home. In fact, one is in the honourable position of owing the world nothing.

Getting used to having more money is as easy as falling off a log, and the assertive voice of self-indulgence can overcome the still small voice of conscience with little effort. When the cheques began to roll in I gave vent to some of my generous impulses, but the habits of a life-time of thrift soon intervened. Generous impulses became curtailed or postponed, or were very strictly examined. We were none too generous to ourselves either, but we bought a few things. A new, good-quality, firm mattress for my back—the price made us reel. A new, electric, very easy mower for our lawns. A new suit for Syd, and his first dressing-gown! Persuading him to buy these brought me out in more of a sweat than the old lawn-mower did.

For some time we had been fighting our children's notion that they should pay for us to have the phone. 'You've no excuse, now, Mummy. Look how awful it was for you when Daddy was taken ill at two in the morning and you a mile away from the nearest phone! Just think what it would mean to us if we could phone you anytime. Think how you could check up every time you heard one of the grandchildren had sneezed twice!'

There was sense in it; we had the phone installed. After that I had to recuperate from such a glut of spending.

The book went into paperback, and an edited version for schools. An excerpt from it was made into a film for television. For the first time in our lives we opened a bank account. By the time our old car was ready for the scrapyard we were affluent enough to buy a modest brand-new one (to last us out). Surely now our lucky streak would go away and find another home? It did not. I wrote a little sequel which went well, too.

If I wished, I could now replace much of our shabby home, but the novelty of spending lump sums on things that were not strictly necessary was wearing thin. Or was it that I was daring to harbour a germ of a dream, and this was reinforcing my frugality? I honestly do not know.

We tried to share our savings with our children. All such suggestions were met with adamant refusals. 'For God's sake, haven't you two done enough for us? D'you realise you've never been away on a proper holiday in your lives?'

'That bit of money that's worrying you so, why you could blow the lot on a cruise in Daddy's holidays!' And so on. We kept on saving.

After four years my little dream had grown enough to come out into the open, and to challenge a problem that grew more menacing for us all the time. What was going to happen to us when Syd retired and our tenancy of the cottage came to an end? That would not be long now. We would have loved to end our days where we were, but there were several factors against it. The huge garden we had cultivated with blood, sweat and tears, with joy and temper, was now too much for us. We had empty rooms that could be better used by a young family. Also there was no doubt that the Estate would be under no obligation to let us stay on, and if their legal rights were waived, or if we were offered something smaller and humbler, it would be an act of charity. We did not want that. We might get a Council old people's bungalow, but waiting for death in one of these I would feel a fish out of water. No fire to poke, almost no garden to potter on, the convenience-packaged soullessness of their architecture! Why, it would be like putting a free-roaming mongrel into a pampered Peke's silk-lined basket!

If only we could save up enough money to buy a tiny cottage of our own. A very humble sort would do, with enough garden to keep us busy. Something a bit old, not an ancient monument, but not a box either. Something with a fireplace and just a little character. It was not impossible; one such might turn up!

Syd was willing to share this dream, but he shared little of my hope of ever realising it, the old pessimist. The children, however, encouraged me and thoroughly approved the idea.

Many years ago when I was girl, our Dad was doing a patched-up repair to our cottage. He had no means to get the proper materials. Ruefully scratching his head, he observed, 'Well, my wench, I do reckon that if a mon do want to get 'is own back on a enemy, 'im could do wuss than leave'n a old cottage in 'is will.'

Father was no fool, but there must be plenty of fools about now, for any old cottage that comes on the market attracts a queue of customers in no time. We joined the ranks when Chris took us to see one for sale a few miles away. The price was so low that we did not expect much, and we certainly did not expect to get a feeling of affection for it as soon as we saw it. Yet we did. Like a little sister standing for protection by an older one, this cottage leaned against a larger one of identical design. It was a typical home-built shelter of the humble labourer some two hundred years ago. Like the smattering of cottages nearby, it was built of stone from an abandoned quarry some fifty yeards away.

It had two small windows up, and two down, and a good door surmounted by a porch. Though this cottage was very small, it was set in a sizeable L-shaped garden which swept right round the back. Even for early April the garden looked outstandingly clean and well-cultivated. Looking down from the garden gate the walls and the roof seemed sound. Feeling like trespassers, we tripped down the garden path to have a peep through the windows. Though the place was empty, it was still fully-furnished, and you needed no degree in psychology to conclude that the occupant had been elderly, and that death had come unwanted and unexpected. But it had not caught the unwary napping; the crowded interior was in neat order and spotlessly clean. There was even a bundle of kindling wood beside the hearth ready to light the sitting-room fire.

This room was about twelve feet square. It had a low undulating ceiling propped up by an extra beam, tidily boxed-in. This must have raised a few bumps on the unwary heads of tallish visitors. All the same, I mused, with a nice fire glowing, this would make a cosy room for Syd to come in to from work. The other window revealed a six-foot sliver of space contorted into a kitchen. There was a sink-unit, a cupboard, some shelves, and a string line across, with a precisely-hung towel, tea-cloth, and dish-cloth. Everything looked scoured and monastically tidy.

All this tidiness left us unprepared for the jumble of decrepit out-buildings round the back. There was a pervasive inescapable odour that revealed the identity of the smallest one before I unlatched the door. It was a primitive flushless privy with a wooden seat in which were carved a big hole and a little one covered with lids. All was scrubbed to whiteness. There was a carton of powdered disinfectant, a toilet roll, and an aerosol can of air-freshener to prove that the occupant had not turned his nose up at modern inventions.

We had a proper Twenty Questions session about object number two! A nine-foot high, six-foot square, extension abutting on to the back wall and the side of the chimney piece. It was as sturdily stone-built as the cottage itself, and about the same age. There was no way of getting into it from outside, and a quick glance through the window showed it was not accessible from inside. What was it? Our imaginations ran riot. An underground passage to buried treasure? A secret grave for murdered bodies? A buttress to help hold the cottage up? Perhaps an obsolete bake-oven? A bake-oven, that size? This was my inspired guess, and that is what it turned out to be.

Tucked in against the other side of the chimney-piece was a tiny back-kitchen with a rusting corrugated-iron roof. The rotting wood was held together by layers of paint, and inside was a wash-copper with a tall chimney, one brick wide, held together merely by its own weight. There were two rickety rotting sheds, for fuel, tools, oddments, and a worm-eaten ladder. We were glad to look the other way, over the thick hedge that bordered the garden, across a panorama of farmlands, and into the misty distance of the Malvern Hills. Never mind the old sheds; this view was priceless, and the garden too was worth looking at. Just the right size for us, and its clean black soil looked invitingly fertile. A few yards down the sloping garden was a valuable acquisition, a fine upstanding plum tree in its prime of age and health, and around it the pink tips of a clump of rhubarb were forcing themselves up for a share of spring sunshine through a bottomless old bucket.

Next to it two gooseberry bushes carried a bumper crop of green flowerets hanging between their new leaves, and a huge blackcurrant showed plenty of healthy tips. Like cupped green hands the outer leaves of three rows of May broccoli protected the forming curds from the late frosts. There would not be much summer shade under the gnarled old apple tree; most of its branches were dead, and the hollow trunk had a hole big enough for birds to nest in, and enjoy a perpetual larder of insects in the soft rotting interior. The path from the front gate to the cottage door was bordered with the most prolific show of giant-headed daffodils and narcissi I had ever seen.

I looked all round once more. Now I had seen enough to make up my mind.

'If we can get it, I'm willing. How about you?' I asked Syd.

As a rule, Syd does not exactly chew the cud before he answers; he just chomps on his old pipe stem and thinks of all the cons to dash the pros of most of my ideas. With his eyes still roaming the garden, he answered without hesitation, 'Do me.' From him, this was the seal of approval.

'Could be a smashing little place. Just right for you two,' said Chris.

Twenty-three years previously we had turned the clock back by leaving our modern flat and returning to cottage life. Back to emptying the privy bucket, back to no bathroom, back to pumping the water, back to mysterious bulgy ceilings and inexplicably bulgy walls. Well, we could do it again, and maybe have the mod cons installed later. Syd could leave the sawmill; that would please the children. The snag was that we had not saved up enough for the price of the cottage.

'Leave it to me,' said Chris. 'We might be able to knock the price down. Estate agents always try their luck. Anyway, I'll see my bank manager and persuade him to give you a loan; I'll be the guarantor; and don't bloody argue, Mum, because I've made up my mind. You and Dad must think it over well, and I'll come up later for your decision. That place will have to be snapped up quickly, it's a real knock-down bargain!' Knock-down was a prophetic description.

As we left, the next door neighbour 'happened' to be by her garden gate. A pleasant 'good afternoon' from her was enough excuse for my probing tongue to winkle out all the information about the cottage. She was charming and informative. And old widower of eighty had recently died there. An independent sort who had never taken to his bed, he had been digging his garden that very day. He complained of not feeling well, and a few hours later the neighbour from the cottage below called and found him dead in the chair. A merciful end? Who can tell, but if it was he deserved it. His only child, a son, lived up north with his family. He had put the cottage up for sale, and was supposed to be coming down soon to clear it out. This nice homely woman was obviously of a similar background to myself, and if we did get the cottage, she would help me feel at home.

Soon we were looking over the property with an agent, and there were other customers waiting for him, too. With everything still as the old gentleman had left it, it seemed an intrusion to enter. This had been *his* private little world, the photographs on the sideboard were of *his* grandchildren and relations, the diplomas proudly hung on the wall had been obtained by *his* son. The clean-sheeted bed had been waiting for *him* to get into. The very furniture and walls seemed embarrassed by the curious eyes of a bunch of interlopers. Traitor to my agnostic beliefs, under my breath I said 'sorry' to the spirit of the old man, and I told him he could teach me a thing or two about the housework. However, I was diplomatic about the state of his ceilings; there were some enormous bulges showing signs of cracking, and over the landing, plaster was actually falling off. In the bedrooms, the furniture and the layers of mats and nailed-down lino, made it impossible to inspect the floor. All the same, we made our offer; it was all we had and not enough. Chris saw his bank manager, who came out, looked at the cottage from the garden wall, and granted the loan. That fine solid heavy stone garden wall was worth the money by itself. There was a little money over, to pay the solicitor, and to do, as we thought, some ceiling repairs. Six weeks later the cottage was ours. We owned a fruitful little piece of England, we owned that panoramic prospect of Malvern's miniature mountains, and that plum tree, and that rhubarb.

We also owned that smelly cesspit and those ugly derelict sheds, and God alone knew what else in those ancient partitions and crumbling ceilings.

Syd was all for moving in at once. We had not had the money for a survey, and I was surprised at my cautious husband's reaction.

'Look,' he said, 'if that old fellow could live in it, we can live in it. Let's get in there and bodge it about later.'

I could not agree, I felt I had done my share of bodging, and what about that lavatory, and did he expect me to walk all round the house to get into my back-kitchen every time? He took some persuading, but eventually agreed to some repairs.

We already knew of an obliging jobbing builder, and we asked him for a quote to see to the ceiling bulges, and lent him a key. A couple of days later, he called on us, and his pallor was not entirely due to plaster dust. He was gingerly carrying some pieces of ancient wood. He let them drop on the yard and they practically disintegrated.

'These were so-called helping to hold up your so-called bed-room ceilings. I know, because I've just fell through it. You've got dry rot over there, Missus.' He sounded slightly aggrieved. We had got dry rot, and woodworm, and rising damp, and floor joists rotting at the ends that had been reinforced by the boxed-in beam, actually a steel girder in disguise. It became clear, and we reluctantly accepted it, that the interior would have to be gutted. Chris had remarked that we had bought a knock-down bargain; well, the three of us now began to knock it down.

We started with the bake-oven. The summer, what we had of it that year, had come at last. We heaved and hammered, we pulled and prised. The veins came up in knots on Syd's forehead, and the purple flush spread behind his ears. I was wearing my surgical corset, but even so my back felt it had been jumped on in a rugby scrum. We carried the stones to the bottom of the garden. Exhausted, we looked at our work; we had made practically no impression. We knocked off for a cup of tea. 'Well,' I kept on saying for comfort, 'it *is* a lovely view, and it *is* our very own ground we're standing on.' If the way to Hell is paved with expletives and bad tempers, by the time we had got that ancient monument of a bake-oven down, and destroyed the old sheds, and ripped that old back-kitchen off the wall, we had widened that way a fair bit.

I doubt if we shall last long enough to cough up the dust we inhaled knocking down the ceilings and partitions. A couple of hundred years of accumulated debris sent us running and gasping for air while it settled down enough for us to see what we were doing. The mouldering nests of long dead rats and mice and birds came down with it, and we got an occasional bonk on the head from rotted timber, broken bricks, and stones. When all the rotten stuff had come away, there was enough left of the internal structure, like a noble skeleton, to gladden an artist's eye. Luckily the roof beams were of oak; the defeated worms had given up after their initial penetration, and all they needed was a good spray of Rentokil. Of cleft natural limbs roughly adzed, they were put together with haphazard beauty and formed a beautiful arch to support the roof. Had we been affluent enough, I would have left them exposed. Many of the limbs that had formed the partitions were sound inside, though as bent and twisted as an arthritic old man. We marvelled how they had stood the test of time. Their contours were so much better than the sawn timber that would replace them. Of the shell that we had left, thankfully the tiled roof was sound, and the thick stone walls would only need a damp course to cure their gout. It is a fact that a quart cannot be put into a pint pot. We began to doubt this as the piles of stone and rubbish mounted up in the garden. And that was only the start!

Well, there we were then. Four walls and a roof, nothing else of any use, piles of rubbish and almost no money. We had some top-level conferences about the next step. At this point Lady Luck stepped in. Sorry, I mean Person Luck. I had co-written a play which got accepted by the BBC, and I had an advance fee from the publishers. That was still nothing like enough for our new plans. We wanted a kitchen extension built on the back, and the inside of the cottage renewed and a flush toilet and shower included. We saw an architect who did us some drawings which were very good but pricey and knocked a sizeable hole in our diminishing nest-egg. We applied for a council grant; after all, this would really be a loan, for the rateable value would go up and gradually pay it all back. The council promised us a grant, and we went on through the bureaucratic maze of permissions. The all-clear came and we could make a start, but now it was winter and we were short of light and time as well as money.

Summing up all our resources, and some of these were merely hopes, we thought we might manage if we did all the labouring and digging ourselves. Chris and Syd studied the puzzling drawings and the metric measurements.

'Let's start with the hole for the plastic septic tank,' said Chris.

'Right,' said Syd. 'Let's go out and measure up.'

After a few minutes I heard a cry of anguish from Syd. 'Oh, no, it can't be!'

'Yes, it is,' said Chris, 'right under the plum tree!'

'No, no! We can't! We just can't lose that tree!'

'Well,' said Chris, 'you will. Think about it; the architect's right. That's the best place. In fact, you look, it's the only place!'

And it was. Soon afterwards the sacrilege was committed, with a borrowed chain saw, and the root was heaved out. Where that beautiful fruitful tree had stood soon became a miniature waste-land. We had had just one crop off our tree, a good crop of large clean tasty plums.

There was no means of getting a digger into there; the job had to be done with pick and shovel. Eighteen inches below the surface, the soft black top soil ended and the picks hit the stone. It was stone all the way then, and it was a gargantuan task to cut out a hole eight feet deep and seven feet square.

'It's too big,' moaned Syd, 'it's too bloody big.'

Chris was so patient. 'No, Dad, they must know what they're talking about.'

Sometimes I would leave what I was doing to see how they were getting on. As they leaned back sweating against the stone, their muddied faces grey with fatigue, Syd looked up at me. 'Dunno about one foot in the grave, Win, I've got two. Reckon I'm digging my own here. Do the sexton a favour, old butty, chuck the bloody stuff back over me.'

I promised him that when the system was finished he should have the very first flush! Reinforced by this honour, and some tea and cake and a smoke, he soon changed his tune. They became quite fond and proud of their hole. The helpful young builder whom we had contracted to do the skilled work came and looked at it and tended rather to pick holes in it. It did not quite suit.

'And when you've done that,' he said cheerfully, 'I'll show you where to dig your soakaway!'

During the week I cadged lifts over to the cottage and began to wield a pick-axe for the base of the extension and to wheel away barrow-loads of spoil to make a new path under the hedge. Surprisingly, my dodgy, sixty-four-year-old back, that could come out so often with a simple movement, stood up to this for weeks; and I stood up to the nagging I got from Chris for doing it.

We were reaping some of the rewards of parenthood. Our elegant dainty daughter came when she could, and showed a surprising ability to shift large stones, and push heavy-laden wheelbarrows, and even drive the pick-axe well into the stony subsoil. Our carpenter son Nick left his wife and family thirty miles away for several week-ends to do the woodwork inside the cottage, charging nothing for his labour, time and trouble, and losing what he could have earned at home. Eventually, he reluctantly agreed to accept something later, if and when we could afford it. Our daughters-in-law never complained. Even Richard, so far away, came to do what he could and fretted when he could not. Rome was not built in a day, and now we know why. Even in a tiny humble place like ours there was a great deal of dirty, hard and painful labour. Love will not hold stones together as well as mortar, but if old houses can be said to have a spirit, then ours will have a good one.

As soon as a plastered wall dried out enough, I got cracking on the decor. It was a crack-crack here and a crack-crack there from my arthritic joints as I knelt for the skirting boards, stretched for the ceilings, and contorted into the corners. I am sure that Picasso did not get any more happily absorbed with his brushwork. Unlike him, I stifled any original ideas, mostly from fear of possible reactions from the family, and simply laid on many coats of conventional pastels on the walls, and glossy white on all the woodwork. When the weather was dry and sunny, which was not very often, I tackled the piece of garden that was not covered in rubble. Barring the ravages of slugs, birds and blights we shall have peas and beans, and raspberries, gooseberries, and strawberries to pick.

Now our cottage is nearly ready. I should be, and am, grateful, yet each remaining day in our old home becomes in part a requiem. Rooted deeper than us are the clematis scrambling up its trellis for the sun, the climbing roses splashing the grey stone with their scarlet miracles, the honeysuckle by the saddle-stone caressing the old oak pillar, the lilac trees, and the flowering shrubs, vivid reminders of Father's Day and Mother's Day gifts from Jenny. The flower beds abound with shrubs presented by friends. I stand outside where every prospect pleases. I tread the familiar and beloved paths. To leave the old stone barns, our protectors from the icy east winds, seems like leaving old friends. I shall not see the seasons changing the leaves of the rowan tree. My own spring, summer and autumn behind me, now comes perhaps the winter of my discontent. After its icy finger has spent its grip we shall not come into fresh bud again. We must warm ourselves selecting and rekindling memories.

Start at the beginning; turn the pages; but one page will not turn. I see a seventeen-year-old girl running up the basement steps of a house. Upstairs in an attic room a servant's cap, apron, and print dress are folded over the end of an iron bedstead. For the next eight hours she can enjoy her own identity, free from the incarceration of servitude. Her legs are lithe and long; London spreads out before her. She too can now walk miles of the pavements hallowed by its history—she knows some from her schooldays—down the cobbled streets of the old city, where the carts once trundled to collect the plague-stricken dead, where ragged urchins once played in sewered gutters, muffin men rang their bells, and lavender, 'three bunches a penny,' was proffered to the passers-by.

Standing on Westminster Bridge she can share her most daring thoughts with Old Father Thames. Oh Yes! The Houses of Parliament are noble buildings, but what devious schemes are hatched under its roof by the politicians inside them. Serve them right if Guy Fawkes came back and put a squib under some of them.

A cat may look at a king, and princes have been known to marry beggar-maids; so she can stand at the gates of Buckingham Palace and imagine she were Queen. And if she were, what knuckles she would rap, what bonfires she would order of servants' caps and aprons. God gave ten commandments; if she were Queen she could think of many more to whisper insistently in the King's ear! She turns up her snub nose at such wasted opportunities. Not that she feels poor herself; the wind has whispered hints of magic feasts in store for her. She has only pennies in her pocket, but her head is full of dreams.